Socio-Political Risk Management

Developments in Managing and Exploiting Risk

——

Volume I: Safety Risk Management
Volume II: Project Risk Management
Volume III: Organizational Risk Management
Volume IV: Socio-Political Risk Management

Editor-in-Chief
Kurt J. Engemann

Volume 4

Socio-Political Risk Management

Assessing and Managing Global Insecurity

Edited by
Kurt J. Engemann, Cathryn F. Lavery
and Jeanne M. Sheehan

DE GRUYTER

Free access to the e-book version of this publication was made possible by the 21 institutions that supported the open access transformation *Purchase to Open Pilot* in collaboration with Jisc.

ISBN 978-3-11-162042-8
e-ISBN (PDF) 978-3-11-073121-7
e-ISBN (EPUB) 978-3-11-073142-2
DOI https://doi.org/10.1515/9783110731217

Library of Congress Control Number: 2022946459

Bibliographic information published by the Deutsche Nationalbibliothek
The Deutsche Nationalbibliothek lists this publication in the Deutsche Nationalbibliografie; detailed bibliographic data are available on the Internet at http://dnb.dnb.de.

Coverimage: william87/iStock/Getty Images Plus
Typesetting: Integra Software Services Pvt. Ltd.

www.degruyter.com

Kurt J. Engemann, Cathryn F. Lavery and Jeanne M. Sheehan

Advances in socio-political risk management

1 Introduction

A balanced view of risk requires an understanding how to holistically manage risk
in order to mitigate negative outcomes and to reap beneficial results. In this spirit,
Socio-Political Risk Management: Assessing and Managing Global Insecurity covers a
wide range of viewpoints and issues which can be applied to various organizational
agency structures. These perspectives examine how social and political risk can impact an agency, and what recommendations can be made to adapt, improvise, and
strengthen the organization against political risk. Existing establishments in public,
private and nonprofit sectors have seen radical changes and approaches in recent
years. Accessibility to personnel and agencies via social media, the internet and
public exposure compounded with shifting political and social paradigms have led
many agencies to assuage and sustain public viability and relevance.

Socio-Political Risk Management: Assessing and Managing Global Insecurity
serves the readers by raising awareness and the necessity to manage social and political risks in their organizations. It highlights the challenges and ambiguity of
these conditions and how failure to control these situations can result in critical
events and potential irreversible damage to an agency or corporation. This volume
explores pathways for those in different organizational structures to find common
themes pertaining to social and political risks. An important goal of research is to
develop a framework for managing and exploiting risk that can be applied at the
organizational level.

Case studies, simulations, and theoretical constructs help provide clarity of
risks to senior management, personnel, and the agencies themselves. With contributions from scholars and practitioners, this volume situates concepts and theories
alongside their tangible applications. In this overview, we preview the book and its
two main components: chapters covering fundamental concepts and approaches;
and chapters illustrating applications of these fundamental principles.

2 Fundamentals

Risk is conceptualized in terms of uncertainty, and it is recursive and needs to be peri-
odically evaluated. Whereas the concept of risk is rooted in the process of strategic
decision making, the systematic treatment of risks, within the strategic management
and policy-decisions, has not been developed to an acceptable level for implementation. Hence, the need for a broader view of strategic risk, addressing emerging global

risks such as global terrorism, economic instability, climate change, cyber-attacks, environmental degradation, and international trade agreement changes (Strang, 2018).

In his chapter, "The dynamics of global risks: Social-political risks in strategic management and policy decisions," Cesar Marolla presents the research question: "How can world leaders integrate the social and political risks into strategic management and policy decisions?" Addressing socio-political factors affecting organizations requires a deeper understanding of social and political contexts and conditions, leading to awareness of the threats and opportunities in the socio-political arena that could affect outcomes. Moreover, strategic, and realistic time frames and development indicators for addressing risk factors and determinants of the globalization of insecurities must be embedded to assess and manage socio-political risks, putting greater attention to risk analysis and risk management.

Psychological factors play a key role in influencing perceptions and decision making. These play a part in determining different constructions of experience and include heuristics, risk intelligence, cognitive styles, and emotional factors arising from the identity of the social group. Such differences in constructions may result in deviations from thorough analyses of problems that others consider rational. Heuristics or short cuts in cognitive processing may work but their effectiveness may depend on context in unknown ways. Risk intelligence is defined in terms of how accurate individuals are at estimating their judgments being correct. Cognitive styles may be considered as heuristics determining the process that individuals use showing variations in thinking that are linked to personality (Messick, 1982).

Cognitive styles considered here are: (1) complexity simplicity, (2) use of previous memories (levelers vs sharpeners), (3) impulsivity-reflectivity, and (4) field dependence/independence, a measure of the influence of context. Lastly, individuals as well as groups need consistency and so some decisions and behaviors may be influenced by deep personal needs and also by the views of the individual's social group. Gambling provides some examples stemming from personal needs, and perception of social influences are linked to political movements. In his chapter, "Socio-political risk management: Psychological aspects," Hugh Gash examines psychological factors that influence individual decisions in ways that deviate from what might be expected from a thorough or "objective" analysis of problems. These include heuristics, risk intelligence, cognitive styles, and emotional issues associated with identity.

One of the fundamental realities of political and social risk is that while it has been addressed in the broader management literature for over two decades, it has not necessarily been featured as prominently as other types of risk. In his chapter, "Human Resources: Endogenous Political Risk," Saquib Hyat-Khan provides an important example of this as it pertains to Human Resource Management (HRM). Evaluating the importance of efficient HRM practices has been a focus in the literature for decades, however, the case for identifying political risks presented by inappropriate or absent HRM practices has yet to be made. In terms of being a discipline, HRM has a key role to play in addressing and raising awareness of human resource issues as political risks for the organization (Nickson 2001; Hinton 2003).

A first of its kind in-depth review of papers published since 2000 in high-quality management journals shows just how limited research has been thus far as it pertains to political risk management in human resources. Although the HRM and political risk management disciplines stand to benefit from viewing endogenous political risk through the HRM lens, this critical examination shows that further research and development of the phenomenon of HRM is needed; moreover, it provides recommendations that leverage state-of-the-art platforms for managing such risk.

The absence of attention paid to political and social risk in the management literature is made up for by the wide-spread attention high profile cases have gotten in the media. In the spring of 2021, for instance, ransomware-attacks launched against two large corporations in the United States – Colonial Pipeline and JBS Foods – generated an enormous amount of public and media attention on the risks posed by cyber-criminals (Uren 2021). Experts hoped these attacks would also serve as a 'wake-up call' to the critical infrastructure industries and ensure that they are not just paying 'lip service' to these types of risks (Miller 2021).

In her chapter, "Beyond Lip-Service: Content Clouds,10-K Filings, Cyber Risk and the Electric Grid," Jeanne M. Sheehan examines just how seriously these types of risks are being taken in one segment of the energy sector. Using an unobtrusive observation measure – visualization via the creation of content clouds – the chapter examines if and how these risks were addressed in the 10-K filings of a sample of electrical companies (Cidell 2010). This segment of the energy sector was chosen because it has long been defined as a 'uniquely critical' sector to the extent that it enables most of the other critical sectors. The findings of the study are startling because they suggest that for all the media attention, far from paying lip service, the electrical companies sampled rarely mentioned, let alone addressed, the risks posed by cyber-attacks. To this extent, the findings serve as a wake-up call and underscore the need for both further research and regulatory action.

Governments worldwide define the energy sector as 'uniquely critical' because of the potential for widespread disruption. As perilous as that can be, most people consider the impact of human activity on the climate to be the ultimate risk (Perils 2021). Although the full effects and reach of this damage may not be felt for decades, climate change has the potential to fundamentally alter the livability of the planet. In just the last few years, people across the globe have already begun to experience rare and extreme weather events, which have revealed a serious lack of preparedness and responsiveness.

In his chapter, "The Risk of Climate Change and Extreme Weather," Steven Michels lays out the scope of the problem and why it has been such a difficult risk to understand and manage (Oldenborgh, et al., 2021). He then focuses on the specific policies and practices that can be put in place by elected officials and business and community leaders to increase absorptive, anticipatory, and adaptive capacity. The chapter concludes with a summary of the principles that should drive risk-reduction measures related to climate change and extreme weather. In accordance with the conclusion in the previous chapter, Michels argues that mitigation of these types of risk will require an unprecedented level of coordination and resource allocation from both public and private sectors.

Another area of enormous and worldwide public concern is the treatment of women and girls. In 2017, the concern found expression vis-à-vis the *#MeToo* Movement as women became increasingly more open to discussing their experience of sexual harassment and assault, particularly on social media (Feloni 2019; Harris 2018). In her chapter, "Socio-political Risks associated with Sexual Harassment, Assault and Gender Discrimination Among Institutions of Higher Education," Cathryn Lavery examines how one sector which bridges the public and private – institutions of higher education – have attempted to address these concerns. Lavery finds that while colleges have incorporated traditional sexual harassment policies and prevention programs, harassment and assault on campuses remains prevalent (Cantor, et al., 2020).

Moreover, she argues that universities and colleges have not taken into consideration the profound sociopolitical risks associated with the management of complaints, incidents, and legal issues of associated with this topic on their campuses. As a result, sexual harassment, assault, and discrimination remain not only a global social and public health problem, but a critical risk for institutions of higher learning. What is now realized with the United States' 50th Anniversary of Title IX and American colleges and university campuses, is that protections and regulations need to be tighten, institutions of higher education held accountable for handling cases correctly. A global standard on how to deal with such cases need to be created on all campuses, so that students can have basic protections and procedures anywhere.

Arguably no single event has put people around the world at more risk in the last century than COVID-19. Many scientists contend that the pandemic should be understood as part of a trend of increasingly damaging and devastating global disease outbreaks that are the result of humanity's assault on nature. In the final chapter in this section entitled, "Biophilia, One Health, and Human Education" Kimberly Spanjol and Paolo Zucca argue make the case that the exploitation of non-human animals and the environment associated with the inception of this disease and its subsequent spread remain unchanged. Moreover, politicians, other policymakers, and business leaders primarily focus on anthropocentric short-term solutions rather than viewing the COVID-19 pandemic as a symptom of humanity's harms and crimes perpetrated against the natural world (Zucca 2020; Zucca 2021). This approach, they find, obstructs meaningful opportunities to address and transform root causes of the current pandemic, as well increasingly deadly future pandemics, which are inevitable.

With this in mind, the authors explore a Biophilic approach of the One Health Model and Humane Education practices that promote an individual and systemic transformative relationship with the natural world that acknowledges and emphasizes humanity's deep interconnection with the well-being of other species and the environment we share (Wilson 1984). This approach is explored as a step toward so-lution-based interventions that address root causes and mitigates risk in all social and political spheres.

3 Applications

Pandemic risk models are traditionally based on operational factors, referring to preparedness, mitigation, and response. Due to the rapidly fluctuating condition of a pandemic, pandemic risk management pertains to the field of operational risk management (Beroggi and Wallace, 1994). The validity of these models is difficult to assess due to the limited quantifiability of the operational factors. In his chapter, "A Latent Factor Risk Model for COVID-19," Giampiero E.G. Beroggi presents an al-ternative risk model to predict the reported number of deaths. The model is based on nine latent factors, which are grouped into three meta latent factors, referring to business, political, and population characteristics. The model's validity is con-firmed with empirical data from 50 nations. Although the validation of the model is based on data from an early stage of the pandemic, autocorrelation effects make the model also useful for later stages. The strongest predictive meta latent factor is business, while the strongest predictive latent factors are corporate social responsi-bility, employment, and life expectancy. While higher standards of corporate social responsibility and higher rates of employment result in lower number of reported deaths, higher life expectancy values have the opposite effect.

Organizations have frequently dealt with the decision of buying or outsourcing ("make versus buy") a product or service. While organizations have realized numer-ous benefits from outsourcing, both academics and practitioners have identified several risks, including low quality, loss of control, sharing proprietary informa-tion, and sometimes a compromise in the firm's core values and mission. Outsourc-ing is even more complicated if it involves not a single supplier but two suppliers whose service deliveries depend on each other (Tsay et al., 2018). In their chapter, "A triadic perspective on the risks of IS outsourcing in a software as a service (SaaS) context," Markus Biehl and Nisha Kulangara investigate the risks associated with outsourcing in a triadic setup. After a contextual introduction, they focus on the case of triads involved in implementing Software as a Service (SaaS), involving the client, the software provider, and a system integrator. They investigate risk fac-tors that are external to the partnership as well as those that arise from the internal management of the partnership. Finally, pointers for managing such triadic rela-tionships from the point of view of the client are discussed.

In addition to outsourcing, a critical challenge for organizations today – both profit and not for profit – is centered around the requirement for external disclosures of Global, Criminal Justice, Social and Political Risks in the context of ESG disclosures (Herz, et al., 2017). Disclosures of any type of risk to an organization present the danger that organizational secrets and strategies are revealed to the public and competitors. Disclosures of assessed risk may also be used in later litigation against an organization. As a result of the potential downside to external disclosure of risk, organizations have been generally reluctant to provide information on internal risk assessments unless they were required to disclose information in specific required financial and other legal compliance disclosures. In "Environmental, Social and Governance Objectives and Disclosures (ESG) and Enterprise Risk," Katherine Kinkela examines the need to balance ESG disclosure requirements and the need for public transparency with the need to keep strategic risk assessments of an organization private.

The pandemic is a throughline in the work of many of the authors as they address various aspects of political and social risk around the world today. Stephen A. Morreale, for instance, connects the outbreak of COVID with the political upheaval and accusations of police brutality and systemic racism that followed. As he notes, from the United States to Canada, the United Kingdom to Ireland and beyond, the criminal justice system has been under intense scrutiny by human rights and civil rights activists, while also under attack from radical and extremist groups. (Ellison, 2020; Nieuwenhuis.2015) In his chapter entitled, "Socio-Political Risks and their Impact on Criminal Justice Organizations," he explores the efforts in criminal justice agencies in the United States to address risk and react to changing social and political climate.As Morreale notes, while policing and other institutions have a natural reluctance and resistance for change, they can turn on a dime when new laws or directives are issued. This was evidenced, for instance, in the immediate reaction for public safety agencies to issues of Covid-19.

The following two chapters also address various aspects of risk mitigation as it pertains to law enforcement around the world. In his chapter, "The Use of Task forces Internationally: Mitigating Socio-Political Risks for Law Enforcement Agencies." David Mulcahy examines the use to task forces. As Mulcahy notes, task forces in the law enforcement community were created to provide information sharing protocols and develop "fusion centers" for local, state, and federal agencies (Lambert 2010). This process and protocols have been utilized on a national and global scale to address various types of crime. This "one stop shopping" allows each task force partner to share and utilize their unique skill sets, areas of expertise, and available resources specific to individuals/agencies. The "sum of its parts" creates working groups that can address areas of operation and responsibility related to the targeted criminal populations (i.e., terrorism, narcotic trafficking, human trafficking, and transnational organized crime) These partnerships develop comprehensive crime control strategies that address the multitude of competing interests related to geographical, political, and social risks. Task Forces provide a strong foundation of trust and credibility that often eludes these agencies when they operate independently. Many of the problematic issues related to joint investigations, competing agendas and scarcity/limited resources can be mitigated by developing robust working relationships across agency lines. With this knowledge and understanding, participating groups can develop individualized, goal-oriented mission statements related to the joint ventures.

As Mulcahy argues, task force participation alone cannot solve all the inherent problems outlined above. Competing ideologies/philosophies, structural differences, compensatory issues, and social justice modalities are just a few of the difficulties faced creating inter-agency collaborations. With this in mind, the chapter examine the keys to successful implementation and leadership that can facilitate a collaborative mindset that understands the importance of the mission and goals of the respective task force above individual achievement, territorial control, and political posturing.

How do law enforcement agencies and practitioners mitigate the sociopolitical risks that arise as a result of the use of social media? This is the question Michael Sheehy and Cathryn Lavery examine in their chapter, "Freedom to Express, Professionalism, and Public Safety." With the onset of social media outlets, their variations and the unique ability for information sharing and fostering communities of communication has been a learning curve for multiple generations and poised new ones for systematic understanding of news, politics, and forums of opinions (Hudson 2020). While much of the information shared on these outlets can bring people closer and help create new forms of relationships and communication (as seen with the global pandemic and with issues of threats and disasters), it has also been a harbor for hate speech, fake news, misinformation, and unvetted facts. For law enforcement, social media sites have assisted with criminal investigations and helping victims as expediting searches for missing people, etc. Law enforcement personnel, although having personal social media accounts with an intention to be used similarly to citizens, have been under tremendous scrutiny and commentary by the media (Hansen 2011).

From social protests stemming from Black Lives Matter, #MeToo to the January 6th incident at the United States Capital, law enforcement officers are being scrutinized and under watch regarding their comments, opinions, and social groups they are associated on these outlets. Using these and other incidents as a backdrop, this chapter examines general social media policies for law enforcement, how law enforcement officers need to be accountable for their own material posted, and how senior management officials must reduce the risks not only for officers, but for their agency and community but also be cognizant on the impact on personal and public safety.

The final chapter in this section, by Heath Grant, focuses on risk as it pertains to Non-Governmental Organizations and not for profits in particular. In "Social Risk While Doing Social Good–Risk Management Considerations in the not-for-profit world," Grant highlights the advantages of having a strong risk management program where there is open discussion and identification of risks. This is a critical and essential part of a non-governmental organizational culture. It is well known that there are several general risks faced by NGOs which need to be carefully addressed regularly (Stowe 2017). Selected examples included the complexities with fund raising, tax liabilities, monitoring misuse of funds, program development, and incidents of fraud, However, it is essential to examine a multitude of social and political risks for non-profit agencies, and for the organization be aware of risks which can impact their agency in numerous ways.

4 Conclusion

By applying real world examples and current theories and perspectives, *Socio-Political Risk Management: Assessing and Managing Global Insecurity* gives the readers practical guidance and dynamic, proactive solutions that are applicable to agencies and institutions of business, nonprofit and public domains. Contributions from scholars and practitioners establish relevant discussion and talking points that readers can bring back to their organizations. By addressing social and political risks, it is possible to shed new light and direction on an increasingly important issue that is cross cutting all organizations. The chapters examine issues of social and political risks which have critical implications on all agencies and institutions. The chapters focus on different organizational types and gives readers essential takeaways that can be applied to all fields. Socio-political risks are a reality which unfortunately tends to be overlooked in the aftermath of a critical event. This volume gives readers multi-disciplined approach that can be applied to any agency so that the necessary awareness and protections of these risks can be mitigated and prevented.

References

Beroggi G.E.G. and Wallace W.A. (1994). Operational Risk Management: A New Paradigm for Risk Analysis. IEEE Transactions on Systems, Man, and Cybernetics, 24/10, 1450–1457.
David Cantor, Bonnie Fisher, Susan Chibnall, Reanna Townsend, et. al. Association of American Universities (AAU), Report on the AAU Campus Climate Survey on Sexual Assault and Sexual Misconduct (January 17, 2020).
Cidell, Julie. (2010). Content clouds as exploratory qualitative data analysis. The Royal Geographical Society. Vol. 42, No. 4. December 2010, pp. 514–523.
Ellison, K. (2021). The Death of George Floyd, the Trial of Derek Chauvin, and Deadly-Force Encounters with Police: Have We Finally Reached an Inflection Point? Or Will the Cycle of Inaction Continue? Ann. Rev. Crim. Proc., 50.
Feloni, R. (April 2009). The founder of #MeToo explains why her movement isn't about 'naming and shaming,' and shows how she is fighting to reclaim its narrative. Business Insider. Retrieved: Me Too Movement Founder Tarana Burke Says It Needs a Narrative Shift (businessinsider.com).
Hansen, W. (2011). How social media is changing law enforcement: social media raises positive and negative issues for police. Government Technology. Retrieved from: http://govtech.com/public-safety/How-Social-Media-Is-Changing-Law-Enforcement.html.

Harris, A. (October 2018). She founded me too. Now she wants to move past the trauma. The New York Times. Retrieved: She Founded Me Too. Now She Wants to Move Past the Trauma. The New York Times (nytimes.com).

Herz, R., Monterio, B.J, & Thomson, J.C. (2017). Leveraging the COSO Internal Control – Integrated Framework to Improve Confidence in Sustainability Performance Data. https://www.imanet.org/-/media/73ec8a64f1b64b7f9460c1e24958cf7d.ashx.

Hinton, M. (2003) Managing the Human Resource Risk. Franchising World, 2, 58–60.

Hudson, M. (June 2020). What is social media? Definitions and examples. Small Business. URL retrieved: socialmedia: What Is It? (thebalancesmb.com).IA.

Lambert, D. (December 1, 2010). Intelligence-led policing in a fusion center. FBI: Law Enforcement Bulletin. URL retrieved: Intelligence-Led Policing in a Fusion Center – LEB(fbi.gov).

Messick, S. (1982). Cognitive styles in educational practice. Paper presented at the American Educational Research Association, New York 1982. ETS Report Series. doi.org/10.1002/j.2333-8504.1982.tb01299.x.

Miller, Maggie. (2021). Colonial Pipeline attack underscores US energy's vulnerability. The Hill. May 10, 2021.

Nickson S. (2001). The human resources balancing act. Risk Management, 48(2), 25–29.

Nieuwenhuis, M. (2015). The Netherlands' disgrace: racism and police brutality.

Oldenborgh, G.J. et al. (2021). Attribution of the Australian bushfire risk to anthropogenic climate change. Natural Hazards and Earth Systems Science. 21: 941–960.

Perils of Perception: Environmental Perils. (2021). Ipsos. April.

Stowe, E (2017). "Managing Risk to Scale Impact." Navigating Risk in Impact Focused Philanthropy, Summer 2017.

Strang, K. (2018). Socio-Political Risk-Contingency-Management Framework for Practitioners and Researchers. DOI: 10.4018/978-1-5225-4754-9.ch007.

Tsay, A.A., Gray, J. V., Noh, I.J., Mahoney, J.T. (2018). A Review of Production and Operations Management Research on Outsourcing in Supply Chains: Implications for the Theory of the Firm. Production and Operations Management 27 (7), 1177–1220. https://doi.org/10.1111/poms.12855.

Uren, Tom. (2021). Colonial Pipeline Cyberattack Exposes Serious Vulnerabilities. The Maritime Executive. May 27, 2021.https://www.maritime-executive.com/editorials/colonial-pipeline-cyberattack-exposes-serious-vulnerabilities.

Wilson, E.O. (1984). Biophilia. Cambridge: Harvard University Press.

Zucca P. (2020) The Zoonosecene: the new geological epoch of intensive breeding, of wildlife trade, of antibiotic resistance and of pandemic diseases, following the Anthropocene. Platinum, Sole 24 Ore English edition,11, 114.

Zucca P. (2021) Illegal animal trade across Europe as an organised crime: the time is up. Communication at the Intergroup on the welfare and conservation of animals of the European Parliament, 21 April 2021, DOI: 10.13140/RG.2.2.26063.41121.

Contents

Part I: **Fundamentals**

Cesar Marolla

1 The dynamics of global risks: Socio-political risks in strategic management and policy decisions

1.1 Introduction

The development of the risk landscape has shifted significantly in recent years. The magnitude and consequence of more varied risks than ever previously experienced create new hazards, and exacerbate existing ones. Global risks such as climate change, environmental pollution, globalised economies that are increasing the polarization of wealth and income, public health hazards disrupting socio-economic and political stability, and cyber-terrorism are just some examples of the sources of uncertainty in deterministic dynamics of shocks in risk. The aforementioned risks that arise from political (governmental and other) behavior and events, and adverse social conditions associated with poor health, such as food insecurity and housing instability are rooted into the challenges of the 21st century, and they create social, political and economic shocks that shape a particular environment and how these affect organizations, nations, and the lives of its inhabitants. This chapter addresses the research question: *"How can world leaders integrate the social and political risks into strategic management and policy decisions?"*

Due to the uncertainty of these events in the near and long-term future, a proactive approach is necessary to minimize detrimental impacts affecting the socio-political spectrum. Recognizing all of these factors, and the risk to the public and private sector as well as the stability of society's balance, a risk management strategy for effecting change, and measurement of social and political risks for improving organizational performance serves to identify potential opportunities, and then manage and take action to prevent adverse effects. The risk strategic approach also emphasizes the probability of events and their consequences, which are measurable both qualitatively and quantitatively (Jones and Preston, 2010; Marolla, C., 2018). A risk management framework addresses the full spectrum of challenges in areas such as planning, strategy, operations, finance, and governance. It also recognizes the specific needs of the entity's different departments and functions as well as the potential impacts of parallel threats and events. The systematic analysis and management of risks through a well-planned strategic approach to integrating recovery measures, preventing and mitigating risks, and identifying vulnerabilities are a priority to lessen and/or deter socio-political issues in order to build global resilience and reduce risk.

1.2 Defining the acceptable level of risk

In the context of socio-political risks and decision-making the process of identifying the level of risk, expressed in terms of the likelihood of an event and its consequence is part of the strategic management framework (Marolla, 2016). A description of the likelihoods and consequences to define the level of risk is fundamental to developing a risk management strategy to minimize and deter stressors or shocks that compromise the stability of the strategy (Rollason et al., 2011; Marolla, 2016)., ISO 3100 classifies risk evaluation as a framework to compare the results of the risk analysis with risk criteria and to determine if the level of risk is acceptable, allowable, or intolerable. The priority is given to intolerable risks. It is impossible to treat every risk, and there is a possibility that high implementation costs might offset the benefits or risk reduction achieved. The methods of reducing risks are evaluated and the actions to investigate new management measures are put in place. The integration of the likelihood and consequence in the previous step presents the "unmitigated risk": risks that are not diminished or moderated in intensity or severity. After implementing existing management measures in the assessment, identifying risk priorities that need immediate attention take place (Rollason et al., 2011). The appreciation of the sociopolitical context embedded in risk resilience practice in conflict and post-conflict settings become crucial to develop and implement an efficient decision-making process to mitigate global risks considering all factors of impacts and potential risks, in addition to adaptive resilience and mitigation strategies that are not mere recommendations in reports but instead direct tangible actions toward the problem, which is vital for the success of any risk assessments framework.

The assessment of the potential socio-political risks entails the developing of an evaluation of potential future effects of stressors – in this context, stressors are any impact or event that affect the present situation and requires adjustment or coping strategies on the part of the affected individual or organization (APA, 2021).

- The framework for the assessment has to highlight issues presented by socio-political factors affecting decisions and exacerbating existing risks. The challenges and limitations faced by developing a comprehensive evaluation include the following issues (Confalonieri et al., 2007): Limited region-specific projections of changes in exposure of importance to hazards
- The consideration of multiple, interacting, and multi-causal outcomes
- The difficulty of attributing socio-political outcomes to political instability, legal and regulatory constraints, local product safety and environmental laws, tax regulations, local labor laws, trade policies, and currency regulations, in addition to economic disruptions, environmental issues and climate change.
- The difficulty of generalizing socio-political outcomes from one setting to another, when many risks have important local dynamics that cannot easily be

represented in simple relationships; limited inclusion of different developmental scenarios in risk projections
– The difficulty in identifying risk-related thresholds for social equity and political stability.
– Limited understanding of the extent, rate, limiting forces, and major drivers of severe events including socio-political factors affecting decision-making (Marolla, 2018; Confalonieri, et al., 2007).

1.3 Socio-political contingency management

Risk management strategies present a semi-structure framework for action that allows simple and complex structures to operate without constraining. International standards are ideal to address risk because they require no reservations regarding the reuse of the standard and provide multiple implementations according to specific conditions, likelihoods, consequences, and level of risks. Henceforth, assessing socio-political impacts with a risk management strategy presents multiple scenarios; planning for different outcomes and provides the basis to foresee alternative views of the future impacts addressing different patterns of the key variations of such risks (Marolla, 2016). The dynamics of global risks that affect society functioning and balance are diverse and requires a comprehensive macro and micro-strategic approach considering the local forces effects (supply chain disruptions, political instability, etc.), and the emerging global risks such as cyber-attacks, climate change and pandemics, to identify uncertainty (or undesirable certainty, unreliability) as a potential event that could occur. The process of observing and gathering quantitative and qualitative data such as indicators of status, estimates of probability, or frequencies of past occurrence and expert opinions is an integral part of the contingency management plan for socio-political risks (Strang, 2018). Developing a plan and sticking to it is not viable because the impact of climate events, and the complexity of our physical and social systems, requires a comprehensive strategic thinking and planning. Leaders of megacities need to integrate synergies into existing institutional mechanisms, creating incentives for sustaining innovation. A strategic planning involves priority cross-cutting initiatives into rapid adaptive and flexible actions. Leaders must learn quickly about what actually works and what needs to be done to improve risk processes and practices (Marolla, 2016). The strategic frameworks can assist policy-makers to prevent the far-reaching effects of global risks, as we have the resources, determination, and leadership to address the severity of the imperilment. The success of deterring the aforementioned risks and its impact on the well-being of the population depend on how rapidly and efficiently global adaptation and mitigation strategies are implemented. World leaders need to find a common ground of understanding this critical issue, as our survival depends upon the immediate actions of all parties involved. The fundamental approach to the adverse risks posed by local and global risks to the world's welfare is management, which requires a comprehensive and all-inclusive sustainable management and strategic planning approach. The analysis, projections, processes for improvement, and objectives for leadership change will enable the organizations' leaders to take bold and innovative approach to the uncertainties they face. These actions should prioritize protecting the ecosystem and natural resources, and promoting social and economic opportunities. This integral relationship provides the tools to critical planning closely related to a sustainable organization development focus on value creation. The following framework provides a forward-thinking approach, confronts and tackles those issues, and sits at the core of setting up a concrete method and direction to achieve specific goals.

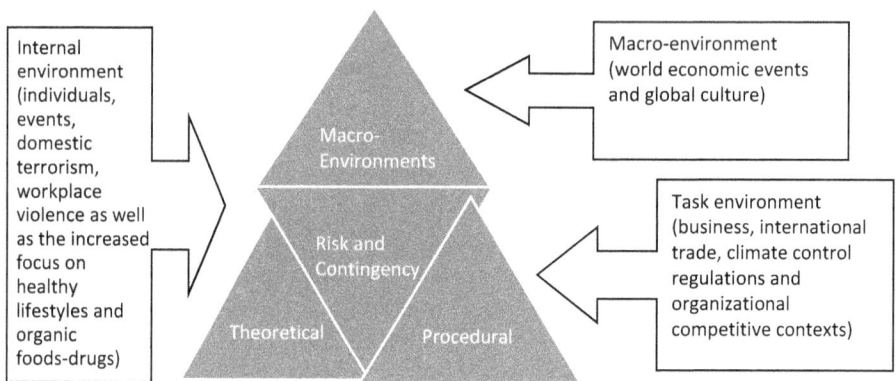

Figure 1.1: Socio-political risk-contingency models (Adapted from Strang, 2018).

Three levels of analysis are shown on the outside, namely: macro-environment (world economic events and global culture), task environment (business, international trade, climate control regulations and organizational competitive contexts), and internal environment (individuals, events, domestic terrorism, workplace violence as well as the increased focus on healthy lifestyles and organic foods-drugs) (Strang, 2018). As the complexity of the global economic environment, social tension and environmental issues exacerbate the existing risks and create new ones, the elements of the strategic planning highlight risk, contingency, uncertainty, probability, and crises with culture and socio-political ideology considerations and effective political risk analysis to identify the implications of social, political conditions for each particular event.

Functional socio-political changes occur in all functions of all the structural components of society (Gafiatulina, et al., 2018). Socio -political changes are a complex multi -level process of socio -political and socio-cultural dynamics covering all spheres of society and present an environment of social and political stability.

Consequently, the private and public sector facing uncertainties must recognize the importance of:
a) Integrating a broader set of risks into management decisions, and
b) Developing expertise in measuring the impact of social and political issues performance (Bekefi & Epstein, 2006).

Making effective decisions to limit exposure to risks and its effects can be informed by a wide range of analytical approaches for evaluating expected risks and benefits, recognizing the importance of governance, ethical dimensions, equity, value judgments, economic assessments, and diverse perceptions and responses to risk and uncertainty.

1.4 Addressing the full spectrum of the socio-political risks

Risk management serves to identify potential opportunities, and then manage and take action to prevent adverse effects. It also emphasizes the probability of events and their consequences, which are measurable both qualitatively and quantitatively (Pojasek, 2010' Marolla, 2018). These characterizations also apply to global shocks such as climate change and health hazards (pandemics) and planning evaluations (Jones and Preston, 2010; Sommer & Marolla, 2020). A risk management framework addresses the full spectrum of challenges in areas such as planning, strategy, operations, finance, and governance and addressing social inequality, environmental issues. It also recognizes the specific needs of the organization's different departments and functions as well as the potential impacts of parallel threats and events. The systematic analysis and management of risks through a well-planned strategic approach to integrating recovery measures, preventing and mitigating risks, and identifying vulnerabilities are a priority o lessen risks impacts.

Organizations building a comprehensive strategic management plan must apply specific context addressing its activities.
– Identify critical objectives and targets (stemming from the organization's vision and mission) that must be achieved.
– Remove impediments or interruptions that could deter the achievement of organizational objectives and targets.
– Allow the organization to understand the probable outcome of controls and other mitigation strategies for dealing with impediments or interruptions.
– Allow the organization to understand how it can continue to achieve its critical objectives and targets should interruptions occur.
– Create criteria and/or triggers for implementing crisis and emergency response, continuity response, and recovery response procedures.

- Ensure that staff and management understand their roles and responsibilities both during normal operations and when a major disruption may occur.
- Ensure that there is a clear understanding throughout the organization of what accountabilities and responsibilities are in place when there is an emergency or a major stakeholder issue, and ensure that this understanding remains current.
- Build consensus and commitment to the requirements, implementation, and deployment of business sustainability and continuity, which are integrated as part of the routine way the organization conducts its business (Pojasek, 2007). Currently, the COVID19 pandemic, climate change, and cyber-terrorism, just to mention a few, pose a threat to the stability of the institutions and the well-being of population. The absence of risk management and continuity management systems to cope with socio-political threats is leading to hazard-induced disasters and instability. A methodology for developing and implementing the Australian/ New Zealand Risk Management Standard – AS/NZS ISO 31000 on the effects of socio-political threats would enhance the local and national capacity for effective actions. ISO 31000 supports a unique management approach to initiating steps that manage risk more effectively and developing a cohesive method to presenting adaptive strategies across cities around the world. International guidelines can help cities plan how to recover from sudden external risks (e.g., severe weather events) and the more gradual external risks (e.g., sea-level rise, pandemics, and shifting disease patterns). This then becomes a fundamental component of frameworks for strategic management and evaluating adaptation and mitigation programs to address risks (Marolla, 2016). While organizations have been conducting risk assessments for years, many still find it challenging to obtain their real value. A strong business case that applies Risk Management ISO 31000 and the business continuity management system standard (ISO 22301) and recommends a systems view of risk assessment and proactive approach to risk management through a shared response at local and international levels would become increasingly important to measuring vulnerabilities of the system. The resilience of communities and disaster risk management are addressed utilizing British Standard 65000 (Organizational Resilience) and the ISO 37101 Sustainable Development of Communities frameworks. They establish a common practice for using, creating, interpreting, and analyzing the city's operations while confronting its vulnerabilities and disaster-risk management strategies and presenting a solid foundation for continuous improvement. This enhances crisis management and business continuity management practices by integrating these into a wider resilience plan. Indeed, such an approach aims at taking into consideration all potential risks, from a terrorist attack, other intentional releases, accidents or naturally occurring diseases, so as to be prepared to handle all crisis situations in relation to social and political risks.

1.5 Political risk management

Political risks can be determine by local or international threats impacting many areas of the business such as business license, the ability to operate, move funds, compete on work, or result in disrupting stress and tension being placed upon the organization. While operating internationally, it is important to for leadership teams, at all levels, to understand the risks presented by hostile governments, the implications of social instability, chaos, and how to best prepare for and prevent, respond to, manage, and then transition and recover from such threats. When embedded to the strategic management planning of the organization, continuity management systems can provide an important tool to cope with political instability.

Continuity management plans apply the 'Plan-Do-Check-Act' (PDCA) cycle. This involves planning, establishing, implementing, operating, monitoring, reviewing, maintaining and continually improving the effectiveness of operation.

The following are considerations for assessing a business continuity management plan:
- Historical: What types of drastic political events have occurred within its jurisdictions?
- Geographic: What could happen in your organization considering its geographical location and the organization' vulnerabilities?
- Structural: What could affect the functional ability of the organization's operations that are core to the stability and sustain growth?
- Human Factors: How the event is triggering detrimental impacts on people's abilities to function? (Adapted from Security and Resilience, 2019; Marolla, 2016).

Strategic management aims to prevent operations from grinding to a halt; while business continuity management planning ensures that local and national leaders will respond judiciously to the circumstances. A continuity management approach contributes to a more resilient society. The following key components are considered when developing and implementing a continuity management system plan:
I. Policy
II. People with defined responsibilities

Management processes relating to:
- policy
- planning
- implementation and operation
- supply chain
- performance assessment
- management review
- continual improvement process

- documentation providing auditable evidence
- Any business continuity management processes relevant to the organization (Societal security, 2011; Marolla, 2018).

Table 1.1: Principal Component Analysis (Nesset, et al., 2019).

Political Risk Components	Principal Components				
	Legal	Tension	Conflict	Policy	Uniqueness
Bureaucracy quality	**0.859**	0.133	0.094	0.218	0.118
Corruption	**0.829**	0.133	0.186	0.200	0.221
Democratic accountability	**0.723**	0.063	0.040	−0.305	0.378
Ethnic tension	0.113	**0.805**	−0.104	0.009	0.328
External conflict	0.005	−0.162	**0.860**	0.015	0.233
Government stability	−0.037	−0.042	0.004	**0.870**	0.239
Internal conflict	0.328	0.384	**0.606**	0.414	0.206
Investment profile	0.404	0.303	0.237	**0.539**	0.399
Law and order	**0.789**	0.322	0.205	0.096	0.223
Military in politics	0.426	0.353	**0.665**	0.006	0.252
Religious tensions	0.249	**0.785**	0.203	0.111	0.268
Socioeconomic conditions	**0.568**	0.326	0.062	0.471	0.345

Notes: Loadings and uniqueness. The rotated component matrix, using varimax with Kaiser Normalization, is estimated out of the disaggregated political risk index (International Country Risk Guide). Loadings in boldface are referred to as 'heavy loadings' in the text, using 0.5 as cut-off.

Mahmoudi, et al. (2021), stated that principal component analysis (PCA, in abbreviation) is a "multivariate approach that converts several correlated variables into several linearly uncorrelated variables named principal components". PCA aims to find the directions of maximum variance in high-dimensional data and projects it onto a new subspace with equal or fewer dimensions than the original data in a lower-dimensional subspace (Kherif, & Latypova, 2020). As shown in Table 1.1, a principal component analysis method is used with emphasis in bureaucracy quality, corruption, democratic accountability, law and order and socioeconomic conditions, all of which measure the quality of a country's legal system and its consequences (Howell, 2011; Nesset, et al., 2019).

1.6 Social risk management

Social Risk Management (SRM) instruments contribute to the efficient assessment of social risks in its various forms and are highlighted as follows:
i.   enhance individual and social welfare in a static setting;
ii. contribute to economic development and growth from a dynamic perspective; and
iii. serve as crucial ingredients for effective and lasting poverty reduction. All three dimensions are interrelated (Holzmann & Jorgensen, 2001).

The main elements of the social risk management framework consist of:
–   Risk management strategies (risk reduction, mitigation and coping);
–   Risk management arrangements by level of formality (informal, market-based, and publicly provided or mandated), and
–   Actors in risk management (from individuals, households, communities, NGOs, market institutions, government, to international organizations and the world community at large). (Holzmann & Jorgensen, 2001).

When facing social and political risks we need to understand that they cannot be avoided but are manageable. Risk is constantly evolving. Understanding risk and vulnerabilities and proactively planning to minimize these risks is crucial to business continuity and employee and community safety.

1.7 Resuming "Normal Operations" during and after a crisis and being proactive for the next emerging risk

There are ten important points of action that determine how the organization's system will preserve or restore critical functions. The system's quick resumption of normal operations after a severe disruptive event will affect the entire system's recovery.
1. Establish an emergency planning team: Workers from all levels and departments must be included in the team, focusing on those with expertise vital to the daily system's operation. Is this done proactively, and is in place on a standing basis not awaiting a crisis before beginning operation?
2. Identify who is in charge: It is important to identify who is in charge during a risk event and ensure that all employees know who that person or position is. Establish a procedure for succession of management if that position or leaders are not available at the time of the impact.

3. Examine the system's operation and activities: Identify internal and external operations that are important for the recovery and continuation of the organization' system and different departments.
4. Identify an alternate location: Important consideration is necessary to identify a different location to run the operations and/or different jurisdictions within the system's operations.
5. Develop collaboration and viable assistance between "like" departments or location where the organization's unites operates to share facilities.
6. Plan for citizens with special needs: Always include in your plan a set of specifications to treat and meet the needs of residents with special needs or disabilities.
7. Evacuation plan: Develop an evacuation plan for every location that houses your system's operations. It is important to identify how notice will be given: an alarm, intercom, phone call, siren, etc. All employees and staff must be aware of where to assemble in the event of an evacuation or emergency occurrence.
8. Shelter in place-plan: Develop a shelter in place-plan for every location of your system's operations, to be used in dealing with a crisis. All staff members should know where the shelter is located and have access-plan to reach the location.
9. Communication plan: Identify how the organization's employees and staff will be advised of the emergency plan and the mechanisms by which these will be communicated in the event of a crisis. List the communication tools in order of preference, emphasizing the most effective way for communication to the least effective according to the situation.
10. Emergency contact list: The emergency contact list identifies how to contact relevant staff in the event of a service interruption or an uncontrollable event affecting the entity and/or population. This will include the technical means whereby relevant staff will receive communications in order to respond in the most effective manner.
11. Write a plan: Document and update your organization's continuity management system plans at least once a year
(Adapted from Security and Resilience, 2019; Marolla, 2016).

There are at least three basic reasons why disasters are political in nature. First and most important, disasters affect people. The impact it has on people is a determinant of what a disaster entails and its effect on the organization (The U.S. Emergency Management Institute of the United States, 2020). Therefore, it is important to have a communication channel between leaders and employees to safeguard the well-being of the workforce. Getting the right workforce in place and ready to proactively adapt to new situations is an investment, and provides an effective way to diagnose and treat emerging risks.

1.8 The continuity of the organization

As business continuity management strategies place a core function on the preparation for a disaster, and post disaster recovery of operations, a network of coordinated services must be ready to take action to operate during and following the disaster. Organizations are as effective and resilient as the communities and regions where they are located and the plans in place to coordinate functions. The organization's network needs to be available to provide services for the community, which is the safety-net of the entire system. Therefore, individuals and communities need to have the aforementioned services available. The foundation for increasing resilience is risk management. Increasing resilience involves a series of steps to understand, identify and reduce risk to adapt in the face of adversity (Marolla, 2016; Pojasek, 2017).

1.9 Establishing the context and setting objectives

To set the objectives of a risk management assessment, the location and scope of the study and the operating processes in the area under threat have to be established. An assessment seeks to identify and investigate risks to describe the actions that are required to attain the following objectives:
1. The potential impact on (i.e., damage to)
2. A particular value (e.g., infrastructure) from
3. A threatening process (e.g., social chaos, political revolution) (Marolla, 2016; Rollason et al., 2011)

As a consequence of impacts, the economic, social, and environmental elements where the strategic framework applies must also be included in the assessment. Risk criteria are also important considerations for the framework. Likelihoods and consequences scales and their combination in the current conditions must be included when defining the acceptable risk level. The organization's leaders should determine what that level is and then identify tolerable and intolerable risks (giving priority to the latter) that need to be addressed according to local and global conditions (Rollason et al., 2011). Risk modeling techniques are increasingly used by many governmental and private entities to evaluate exposure to crises. Assessing and comparing different types of risks from adverse impacts becomes fundamental in understanding and minimizing their impacts and recovering quickly after the event's occurrence on the balance of probabilities. Socio-politics has recently emerged as a dimension which moderates the culture or risk. The unknown global threats present a fear culture and uncertainties of place and time. 'Fear culture' has emerged primarily as the anxiety of an unknown global terrorist attack coupled with a reduction of human rights (Korstanje & Strang, 2018).

There are three central risk modeling technique inputs:

- Hazards – Severe events impacting a territory can present uncertainties about its hazard occurrences and the affecting area exposure. Existing knowledge of past events on a local or global context afford a tangible concept of the intensity and frequency of what is expected.
- Exposure – Location and geographical distribution of the territory that will be affected by a potential event need to be mapped. An account of human occupation and physical assets has to be performed. Particular components (e.g., geometric shape of exposed elements, economic value, human occupation and location) must be identified to differentiate the exposure.
- Vulnerability – Exposed elements susceptibility or probable conduct is directly linked to the level of hazard. Risks can be differentiated and analyzed by the intensity and the frequency of the impacts. Hazard parameters can be established by analyzing and understanding past records of events and risk modeling probabilities. The nature, magnitude, frequency, and intensity can help determine the level of the hazard (World Bank, 2012). Consequently, hazard models, which are based on a set of assumptions that should be conveyed to the model user, may present a reasonable account of complex dynamics and evolution addressing many factors such as social inequity, taxation, government inefficiencies, and climate change. Socioeconomic trends assist populations and can also show their exposure to vulnerabilities and provide a clearer picture of the risks. Social and political factors affect hazard characteristics. Therefore, analysis of the long-term unequal influence over decisions made by political bodies, and the unequal outcomes of those decisions, in addition to social injustice is essential for an understanding of the probabilities under a risk assessment of vulnerabilities, while considering important factors such as urbanization and economic growth, lifestyle changes, income inequality, and demographics (Bapuji, H., & Neville, L., 2015; Marolla, 2016). The effective response to and recovery from global risks involves taking prior actions before the event strikes. A proactive approach must be established along with planning for the likelihood of an event that has the capacity to interrupt the organization's operations and impinge on the well-being of the population and financial institutions. It is necessary to emphasize the personal commitment of the leaders to dismiss the thought that "it won't happen here." Therefore, preparedness means being proactive and planning. That is the essence of efficient business continuity planning (Marolla, 2018).

1.10 Global risks and impacts- a risk management approach to decision-making

Global risks have been added to the private and public companies to their possible impacts on their risk management strategy. The strategic decision making process adding these information and different scenarios which identify and classify global risks follow the risk assessment main groups: Economic, Environmental, Geopoliti-cal, Social and Technological. The approach includes chronic societal concerns, such as immigration and border violations, and those that are generally not related to homeland security national preparedness, such as health hazards, and political, economic, environmental, confiscation, expropriation or nationalization of assets, and societal trends that may contribute to an uncertain risk environment (e.g., demographic shifts, economic trends). The six elements to consider while conducting your analysis are:

Political risk analysis
- Political decisions
- Political developments
- Socio-economic inequalities

And **societal fragilities**
- Economic
- Environmental
- Social
  (Makariou, et al., 2020).

The first step is to developing a comprehensive socio-political risk analysis and evaluates it from different perspectives, accordingly to the present and future evaluations of risks. Socio-political risk is a cluster of risks within economic, social, cultural, and environmental dimensions and requires a research analysis in order to overcome the challenges to prevent potential disasters.

1.11 Conclusion

While planning for disasters within the social and political dimension in both the public and private sectors is drawing more attention and while the quality of the risk planning processes and the plans themselves is improving, a challenge remains to recognize the interdependencies of the risks and to develop a methodology to effectively manage them. Postmortem analyses of many socio-political disaster risk events have indicated that individual entities often do well within the limited scope of their expertise, but when systemic performance is assessed, more holes exist

(Marolla, 2016). The greater challenge existed when hidden policy and resource allocation and coordination issues surfaced. Perhaps the most important step in recognizing these interdependencies is ongoing communication among all relevant parties. This not only includes normal ongoing communications and meeting at professional gatherings, but more substantively sharing plans and even participating in drills to exercise those plans. Risk management and continuity management systems provide a culture of continual improvement, establishing business continuity policy and objectives that align with the organization's objectives (ISO 22313, Security and resilience. 2020). This may all foster a program aimed at monitoring, predicting, and preventing extreme risk events, with the definition of new objectives of integrated development, involving societal inequalities, and political disruptions affecting the organization's performance, its culture and its people. A new and interesting approach should be taken, combining the development of a set of common adaptive measures, with a focus on socio-political-related disasters, creating the potential for organizations to consider a strategic plan that brings the strategy under a universal framework: Risk management.

A second step, more as part of the planning process itself, is to implement a structured methodology aimed at triggering ideas and identifying issues. Quantifying the effects of socio-political risk is challenging due to a lack of organization-level data on exposure and vulnerabilities to political risks and on the type of political issues firms may be most concerned about (Hassan, et al., 2019). Henceforth, forward-looking organizations create infrastructures resilient enough to eliminate or reduce the impact of disasters. The important point is that moving forward, strategic planners so they can develop and implement solutions that more effectively address future socio-political crisis events. As megatrends are transforming the landscape of socio-political risk, organizations must develop a framework that is broad enough for most companies to apply but suggests specific actions (Rice & Zegart, 2018). As presented in this chapter, understanding, analyzing, and mitigating risks that cannot be eliminated, and putting in place a response capability with a step by step process of continuity management system that enables effective crisis management and continuous learning is a must for the current social and political environment. Risk management strategies present a semi-structure framework for action that allows simple and complex structures to operate without constraining. International standards are ideal to address risk because they require no reservations regarding the reuse of the standard and provide multiple implementations according to specific conditions, likelihoods, consequences, and level of risks.

References

APA (2021). Stressor definition. Accessed Nov. 3, 2021. https://dictionary.apa.org/stressor

Bapuji, H., & Neville, L. (2015). Income inequality ignored? An agenda for business and strategic organization. Strategic Organization, 13(3), 233–246. https://www.jstor.org/stable/26369274

Bekefi, T., & Epstein, M. (2006). Rice University Management Accounting Guideline. Published by The Society of Management Accountants of Canada and The American Institute of Certified Public Accountants. ISBN 0-87051-656-6.

Confalonieri, U. et al. (2007). Human health. In M. L. Parry, O. F. Canziani, J. P. Palutikof, P. J. van der Linden, and C. E. Hanson (Eds.), Climate change 2007: Impacts, adaptation and vulnerability. Contribution of Working Group II to the fourth assessment report of the Intergovernmental Panel on Climate Change (pp. 391–431). Cambridge: Cambridge University Press.

Hassan, T., Hollander, S., van Lent, L., & Tahoun, A. (2019). Firm-Level Political Risk: Measurement and Effects. NBER Working Paper No. 24029 November 2017, Revised June 2019 JEL No. D8, E22,E24,E32,E6,G18,G32,G38,H32.

Holzmann, R. (2001). Social Risk Management: A New Conceptual Framework for Social Protection, and Beyond. International Tax and Public Finance, 8, 529–556, 2001. Kluwer Academic Publishers.

Howell, L. D. (2011). International country risk guide methodology. Retrieved from http://www.prsgroup.com/wp-content/uploads/2012/11/icrgmethodology.pdf

ISO 22313, Security and resilience. (2020). Guidance on the use of ISO 22301.

Jones, R. N., and Preston, B. L. (2010). Adaptation and risk management. Working Paper No. 15, Centre for Strategic Economic Studies, Victoria University, Melbourne.

Kherif, F., & Latypova, A. (2020). Principal component analysis. In Machine Learning (pp. 209–225). Academic Press.

Mahmoudi, M.D., Heydari, M., Qasem, S., Mosavi, A., Band, S. (2021). Principal component analysis to study the relations between the spread rates of COVID-19 in high risks countries, Alexandria Engineering Journal, Volume 60, Issue 1, Pages 457–464, ISSN 1110-0168, https://doi.org/10.1016/j.aej.2020.09.013.

Marolla, C. (2018). Information and Communication Technology for Sustainable Development (1st ed.). CRC Press. https://doi.org/10.1201/9781351045230.

Marolla, Cesar. (2016). Climate Health Risks in Megacities: Sustainable Management and Strategic Planning. CRC Press. Taylor and Francis Group.

Makariou, P., Karabela, A., & Tsetoura, I. (2020). The American College of Greece. Risk Evaluation and Political Risk Analysis.

Maximiliano, Korstanje & Strang, Kenneth David. (2018). Comparing the Socio-Political Ethics of Fighting Terrorism with Extreme Self-Defense in USA: An Exploratory Insight. International Journal of Risk and Contingency Management. 7. 1–19. 10.4018/IJRCM.2018010101.

Natalya Kh. Gafiatulina 1, Andrey V. Rachipa 2, Gennadiy A. Vorobyev 3, Valery V. Kasyanov 4, Tatyana M. Chapurko 5, Irina I. Pavlenko 6, Sergei I. Samygin. (2018). Socio -Political Changes As A Socio -Cultural Trauma For The Social Health Of Russian Youth. Modern Journal of Language Teaching Methods ISSN: 2251-6204.

Nesset, A., Bøgeberg, I., Kjærland, L., Molden, L. (2019). How Underlying Dimensions of Political Risk Affect Excess Return in Emerging and Developed Markets. Journal of Emerging Market Finance 18 (1) 80–105. Institute for Financial Management and Research DOI: 10.1177/0972652719831540.

Pojasek, R. B. (2007). A framework for business sustainability. Environmental Quality Management, 17(2), 81–88. https://doi.org/10.1002/TQEM.20168.

Pojasek, R. (2017). Organizational Risk Management and Sustainability: A Practical Step-by-Step Guide. CRC Press Taylor & Francis Group.

Rice, C., & Zegart, A. (2018). Managing 21st. Century Political Risk. Harvard Business Review.

Rollason, V. et al. (2011). Applying the ISO 31000 risk assessment framework to coastal zone management.

Security and Resilience – Business Continuity Management Systems. ISO 22301:2019. ISO (the International Organization for Standardization). Accessed December 18, 2021. https://www.iso.org/obp/ui/#iso:std:iso:22301:ed-2:v1:en.

Societal Security: Business Continuity Management Systems. ISO 22301. (2011). from http://www.iso.org/iso/catalogue_detail?csnumber=50038.

Sommer, A. & Marolla, C. (2020). Risk Management and Business Continuity Systems to Cope with Public Health Risks-A Challenge to Public Health Systems. https://www.academia.edu/44427424/Risk_Management_and_Business_Continuity_Systems_to_Cope_with_Public_Health_Risks_A_Challenge_to_Public_Health_Systems.

Strang, K. (2018). Socio-Political Risk-Contingency-Management Framework for Practitioners and Researchers. DOI: 10.4018/978-1-5225-4754-9.ch007

The U.S. Emergency Management Institute of the United States. Federal Emergency Management Agency. (2020). Access January 23, 2022. https://training.fema.gov/hiedu/docs/hazdem/the%20politics%20of%20disaster.doc

World Bank. (2012). Improving the assessment of disaster risks to strengthen financial resilience. Washington, DC: World Bank.

Hugh Gash

2 Socio-political risk management: Psychological aspects

2.1 Introduction

Risk management is about assessing uncertainty and understanding how we make choices is part of this process. This chapter examines psychological factors that influence individual decisions in ways that deviate from what might expected from a thorough or "objective" analysis of problems. These include heuristics, risk intelligence, cognitive styles, and emotional issues associated with identity.

Heuristics or short cuts in cognitive processing may work but their effectiveness may depend on context in unknown ways. Risk intelligence is defined in terms of how good individuals are at understanding the likelihood their judgments are correct. Cognitive styles were considered by Messick (1982) as heuristics at the level of how an individual thinks and show stable variations in the processes used. Cognitive styles considered here include: (1) complexity simplicity, (2) use of previous memories (levelers vs sharpeners), (3) impulsivity-reflectivity, and (4) field dependence/independence, a measure of the influence of context. There are individual differences in the complexity of cognitive structures used, how they are differentiated and integrated. Levelers tend to overuse past memories with a consequent tendency to underestimate differences, whereas sharpeners focus on differences. Impulsivity-reflectivity is measured on tasks as a contrast between accuracy and speed of responses: impulsive people are faster but less accurate than reflective people. Field independent-people are better at filtering out contextual details. Lastly, individuals may be influenced by emotional issues such as deep personal needs and by the views of their social group.

In what follows heuristics are introduced and key themes are considered that have implications for understanding how people think about uncertainty. This is followed by a section on risk intelligence. The chapter then considers behaviors influenced by personal needs and by social groups. The conclusion outlines implications.

2.2 Introducing heuristics

Heuristics are central in understanding human cognition. This is especially the case for thinking about uncertain social and political events where understanding the implications of decisions are important for risk management. The study of heuristics in the past century shows a slowly emerging recognition of the importance of psychological factors in making choices in uncertain contexts where estimating probabilities can play an important role.

In the USA during the 1940s and 1950s, expected utility theory (EUT) was an accepted model of economic thinking. EUT is based on the idea that individuals value commodities or money in terms of their use, and importantly that such judgments were rational and stable. Such judgments involve comparisons and Thurstone (1927) had shown that comparisons fluctuate for individual psychological reasons like distraction and judgment errors and had extended his studies of comparisons to the economic domain. Moscati (2016) reviewed early attempts by American psychologists to study subjective judgments of economic utility under risky conditions in the 20th century.

In these experiments the utility of money was measured using preferences between gambles on small amounts of money. The studies described by Moscati (2016) supported the experimental measurability of utility and EUT. There were some initial criticisms of the validity these laboratory studies and of their applicability to actual commodities. To overcome these objections, Von Neumann and Morgenstern (1944) imposed a number of constraints or axioms in their studies of individual perception of utility in the laboratory and showed that under these conditions EUT was preferred (Moscati, 2016 p.4 ff). These constraints were that the individual:

– has clear preferences in gambles;
– understands the probabilities involved (simple or complex);
– does not distort probabilities subjectively;
– only benefits from the gambling payoffs rather than the gambling itself (extrinsic motivation rather than intrinsic motivation).

These experiments confirmed the individual variability in the results, so indicating limits to the stable objective reasoning proposed by EUT. While these laboratory studies were performed with small numbers of subjects, they pointed to the advantages of studying EUT in the laboratory. They revealed features of the difference between mathematical and psychological probabilities, with bettors overvaluing low probabilities and undervaluing high probabilities. In addition, the studies showed that economic decisions were influenced by psychological variables such as willingness to take risks. Allais (1953) also challenged the stability of EUT judgments, arguing that human values and subjective probability estimates influenced economic decisions. However, Moscati's (2016) review concluded that EUT continued as the dominant theory until the 1970s when the psychological complexity of human decision making was recognized as fundamental in economic decisions. Of course, psychological elements play a role in all sorts of judgments and decisions, not just economic ones.

Laboratory studies on economic themes continued from the 1940s and the importance of two sets of studies were recognized in the 2002 Nobel Memorial Prize Awards in economics. The first set of studies emphasized economic issues. Smith began his Nobel prize-winning work in his university classes on "a series of experimental games designed to study some of the hypotheses of neoclassical competitive market theory." (1962, p 111). A subsequent paper on induced value theory (1976) was mentioned in the Nobel citation (NobelPrize.org). Tversky and Kahneman were responsible for the second set of studies on psychological dimensions in economic decision making. Tversky died in 1996 aged 59 and did not receive the Nobel Prize as it is not awarded after death. The Nobel Prize to Kahneman mentioned ".. having integrated insights from psychological research into economic science, especially concerning human judgment and decision-making under uncertainty": In Smith's case it mentioned ".. having established laboratory experiments as a tool in empirical economic analysis.." (NobelPrize.org).

In the following section a number of influences on cognitive choices are considered. These include difficulties understanding probability, some examples of heuristics, and the perception of loss and gain.

2.3 Key issues in understanding how thinking influences risky decisions

Probability. In Moscati's review (2016) of EUT laboratory experiments, one concern was how well subjects in the experiments understood how to calculate probabilities. Assessing probabilities is central in risk taking and Bayes' theorem is a basis of statistical inference and describes probability as degree of belief linked to evidence. Bayes' theorem can be outlined in this way:

> The probability of two events, A and B, occuring jointly can be written as P(A ∩ B). This is found two ways:
>
> (1) the mariginal probability of A, P(A), multiplied by the conditional probability of B when A is true, P(B | A)
>
> $$P(A \cap B) = P(A)P(B \mid A)$$
>
> and using
>
> (2) the marginal probability of B, P(B), multiplied by the conditional probability of A when B is true, P(A | B)
>
> $$P(A \cap B) = P(B)P(A \mid B)$$
>
> From (1) and (2), we find:
>
> $$P(A \mid B) = P(A) P(B \mid A) / P(B)$$

Shweder (1977) noted that people tend to use likeness to estimate co-occurrence because correlation and contingency are complex concepts. The difficulties with correlation arise as it is a relationship between two variables, and in this way a second-order concept. Contingency is complex as in estimating P(A | B) there is a tendency to ignore other relevant probabilities such as P(not A | B), and P(A | not B). As an

Table 2.1: Correlation-Relevant Frequency Information on the
Relationship between a Hypothetical Symptom and a
Hypothetical Disease in 100 Supposed Patients (Shweder, 1977).

		Disease		
		Present	**Absent**	**Total**
Symptom	Present	37	33	70
	Absent	17	13	30
	Total	54	46	100

example, Shweder (1977) considered what happened when nurses were asked if there
was a relation between having the symptom (A) and having the disease (B) (what is
P(A | B)) with the figures in Table 1. He discussed an experiment by Jan Smedslund
(1963) with the figures in Table 1 showing how adults without statistical training
focus on joint occurrences of the symptom and the disease. The well-known statistical
cliché "correlation does not imply causation" is basic to Shweder's (1977) documentation of magical thinking and resemblance as a prevalent cognitive tool. Also, it lays
the ground for understanding the adoption of fake news by groups of like-minded individuals who propagate incorrect facts, for example, about vaccines and the benefits
of social isolation that can lead to public health risks.

Tversky and Kahneman (1974) list common misunderstandings about statistics
and probability that influence judgments. These include: (1) insensitivities to sample
size, (2) ignoring prior probabilities and (3) ignoring phenomena like the levelling effect of large samples. In a small hospital, for example, it is more likely that the number of female babies born will be over 60% on any given day than is the case in a big
hospital where a larger number of babies are born. (4) Understanding and applying
"regression to the mean" to everyday examples also poses challenges. (5) Many people
may be tempted to think that previous events will influence subsequent events, on a
roulette wheel for example. Research on human judgment and decision making by
Evans (2011) provides additional evidence that humans are not good at thinking
clearly about risky choices and probability.

Common heuristics. A major achievement in Tversky's and Kahneman's research
was revealing the details about how people depart predictably from rationality in
their judgments (Kahneman 2012). Tversky and Kahneman (1974) measured the effects
of three specific heuristics, **representativeness, availability – and adjustment/
anchoring.** Stereotypes are a form of "representativeness". For example, in one study
people were given a personality description that included shy, helpful and tidy. They
were asked: is this person likely to be a farmer, salesman, airline pilot, librarian, or
physician? Respondents tend to ignore both the frequency of these jobs in the populations and also ignore information concerning sample size. In one example,

people were told that Linda is 31, single, outspoken and clever. If participants were asked whether it is more probable that she works in a bank, or works in a bank and is a feminist, more people responded that she worked in a bank and is a feminist. This is known as the conjunction error as from a statistical point of view each added detail lowers the probability that the judgment is correct and has been linked to belief in conspiracy theories and belief in the paranormal (Brotherton & French, 2014).

People use the availability of examples to assess probability. Tversky and Kahneman (1974) described how **"availability"** is influenced by how examples are accessed from memory. For example, people were shown two lists of men and women with well-known personalities distributed though the names listed. One list contained more well-known men than the second one that contained more well-known women than the first. They were asked if the lists contained more men or women. Their responses were influenced by the numbers of well-known men or women in the lists because they remembered the well-known personalities more easily. In another example, if people were asked to judge the relative frequency of works beginning with r, compared to words in which the third letter was an r, they judged that there were more words beginning with an r as this is an easier task. In the stock market domain, Barber, Odean and Zhu ((2009) show that individuals invest on the basis of previous good returns and also high volume or attention-grabbing stocks. Availability also may restrict an individual's search for new information about stocks by focusing on past experience rather than on emerging trends. As an example of an **"anchor"**, they note that students given 5 seconds to calculate $(8 \times 7 \times 6 \ldots 1)$ and $(1 \times 2 \times 3 \ldots 8)$ guess that the first grouping is larger. The five seconds limit may have been critical, but the result showed a clear preference. Ariely et al. (2006) show that individuals often do not know how to evaluate goods (prices of computer equipment) or experiences (entry fee to a poetry reading) and that their judgments are influenced by their first experience of an event or product that provides an anchor. Khan et al. (2017) have demonstrated that each these heuristics influence stock market trading with influence moderated by education and experience. Anchoring exerts a biasing effect on financial and business decision making by influencing estimates of a firm's future success in terms of earning forecasts. Investors are influenced by representativeness in failing to consider sample size when evaluating stocks, and availability influences the visibility and attractiveness of known products.

Perception of loss and gain. The 1974 Tversky and Kahneman published *Prospect Theory: An analysis of decision under risk* in *Econometrica*. It was a key paper in establishing their reputation (Kahneman, 2012). The theory depends on variations in how individuals perceive losses. Some people prefer certainty to risk taking when the gain is certain, but when the risk of loss is high, they willingly gamble. In addition, people judge losses and gains in terms of the personal significance of the sums of money involved. The results reported in this paper show that choice is not just about maximum utility or gain. Loss aversion has generated a lot of research with some detractors but research continues to support the principle that losses impact decision making more than gains (Mrkva et al., 2019).

The isolation effect, previously mentioned in Allais's work, shows that people react differently to identical choices that are presented in different forms, so demonstrating the powerful effects of context on decision making. For example, telling a patient that a heart operation will have 80% change of success will be more likely to help patients decide to undergo the operation than telling them that they have a 20% change of dying. The complexity and uncertainty mean that decision making does not depend only on careful weighing of evidence but will depend also on heuristics and personality. The form or the optics of how information is presented is part of social conventions in relation to people's feelings. People naturally want to avoid losses and danger. Engemann and Yager (2018) have proposed a comfort model for decision making. In this model each possible decision is evaluated by comparison with the worst case scenario so that comfort is derived from the comparisons. Evaluating each scenario in this way provides a summary measure of the future with comfort as a measure of satisfaction.

Kahneman (2012) distinguished between fast thinking and slow thinking. Fast (system 1) thinking is intuitive and emotional and uses heuristics provides a solution to problems without carefully assessing additional information. Slow (system 2) thinking is more thoughtful and logical. Illustrating the effect of affect, Johnson and Tversky (1983) showed that reports of accidents increased estimates of frequencies of risks and undesirable events and this tendency was independent of the type of risk. Further, an account of a happy event produced a comparable decrease in judgment of risk frequency. The advantages of this positive approach are illustrated by Keller et al. (2006) who in a series of experiments showed that (negative) affect can increase the perception of the availability of risks when risk information was provided over a long time period (30 years) in comparison to risk information provided over just one year. Recent work on this phenomenon refers to an "affect heuristic" providing additional details about how affect influences both perception of risk and of benefit and their interrelations (Västfjäll et al. 2014; Skagerlund et al. 2020). In this work the relation between risk and benefit (high risk being associated with low benefit) is shown to depend on how individuals feel about the risks and benefits. If feelings towards the activity are favourable the risks are judged as low and benefits as higher. In addition, Västfjäll et al. (2014) showed that this effect varied by domain and participants who were reminded of an experienced danger (the 2004 tsunami in Thailand) demonstrated an increased recognition of social benefits (friends and charity) and personal goals. Keller et al. (2006) who in a series of experiments showed that (negative) affect can increase the perception of the availability of risks when risk information was provided over a long time period (30 years) in comparison to risk information provided over just one year.

In addition to heuristics, the mind filters experience in other ways. For example, Downes (2012) describes how one unconsciously frames experience into distinctions (diametric spaces) or relationships (concentric spaces). This strategy seems at a different and prior level to discussions of heuristics, however its effect like heuristics is to intuitively frame an experience as inclusive and sympathetic to relationship or as excluding by making distinctions. In this sense it seems closely associated with the heuristic of representativeness involved in stereotyping. This type of unconscious framing seems to play a major role in the political discussions where group cohesion is more important than analysis.

Recent research on heuristics. Hertwig and Pachur (2015) noted that while the approaches described above indicate how decision making may be influenced by heuristics, the view taken in the 1970s assumed that heuristics provided less than perfect solutions to problems caused by human irrationality associated with an accuracy-effort trade-off. Many events are complex and we have limited knowledge about what may happen, in these cases research has shown that using heuristics have advantages over more complicated strategies (Hertwig et al., 2015). Examination of the use of different heuristic strategies under varying conditions such as domain, amount of information and the problems' complexity shows that a heuristics' effectiveness depends on its match with the "environment" (this influences bias) and on the amount of information available (influencing variance) (Hertwig et al., 2015). Calculating bias assumes a true function and is the difference between the derived algorithmic function and the "real function". Error depends on bias, variance and noise (random error). Variance is the difference between the mean and the individual measures, that is, a measure of the range of the measurements.

The current literature on heuristics is extensive and biases have been shown to apply in a wide variety of tasks (Hertwig et al., 2015). Schirrmeister et al. (2020) have analyzed the use of heuristics in foresight and scenario processes in assessing future conditions. Schirrmeister (2020) and her colleagues suggest that the psychological literature focuses on precise details and while providing clarity does not offer clear guidance on ways of overcoming biases. The literature on scenario processes, however, provides good illustrations of ways to help companies overcome the inclination to focus on familiar parts of their experience and to benefit from the possibilities inherent in creatively imagining the future.

2.4 Risk intelligence

The study of risk intelligence provides another dimension to understand people's choices in uncertain conditions. Risk management and risk intelligence are well integrated in business culture and in using the scenario processes just mentioned (above). Evans (2012) developed a test of risk intelligence based on an individual's awareness or understanding of the reliability of their probability estimates. People who take the test are asked to estimate the accuracy of judgments that are either right or wrong. As such it measures variation in degrees of awareness that judgments might be wrong.

An early definition of risk emphasized the importance of distinguishing between incalculable uncertainty and calculable risk (Knight, 1921, as cited in Evans (2012)). Evans (2012) argues that this difference is really about ways probabilities are calculated. It is not that some types of events have incalculable probabilities, rather in some cases the calculations present significant challenges. For example, the risk of calculating probabilities in relation to coin tossing is a simple process in comparison with the uncertainty of calculating probabilities in relation to complex events like identifying winners in horse races, or calculating business risks and stock market investments.

Evans' approach is primarily cognitive and so avoids emotional issues such as appetite for risk or confidence in uncertain conditions. In defining risk intelligence, Evans did not compare subjective probability estimates with actual estimates. He emphasizes that his interpretation of probability is subjective following in the tradition of Jacob Bernoulli and Evan's measure prioritizes degrees of belief and not objective facts about the world. Evans used a form of calibration testing that involves assessing the likelihood of what one knows rather than measuring how much one knows. Here is an example about weather forecasting:

> Over the course of a year, you collect 365 estimates, for each of which you have also indicated whether it did, in fact, rain or not. Suppose that you estimated the chance of rain as 0 on 15 days. If you are well calibrated, it should have rained on none of those days. Again, if there were 20 days which you assigned a 0.1 probability of rainfall, it will have rained on 2 of those days if you are well calibrated. (Evans 2012, p. 608)

Evans (2012) contrasted the experience of probability estimates of weather forecasters and doctors and noted that the former used probability estimates on a daily basis and had clear feedback for each estimate. Doctors on the other hand, he surmised, were under no such obligation with their diagnoses and so did not have the benefit of constant feedback. Evans (2012) concluded that we have a lot to learn from gamblers and weather forecasters to make better decisions in various aspects of our lives.

The early intelligence tests included items based on memory, mathematics and language. The meaning of intelligence was contrasted with the tests used in psychology following Boring's (1923) article *"Intelligence as the Tests Test it."* Carroll (1993) summarized 20th research on intelligence testing with a hierarchical three level system with generalized intelligence at the top, a set of less generalized factors, and specific abilities at the lower level. Gardner (1993) broadened our understanding of the specific abilities by including a number of cognitive skills including bodily-kinesthetic, musical, interpersonal and intrapersonal intelligence as well as the previously recognized verbal-linguistic logical-mathematical and visual-spatial intelligences. However, Eysenck (2009) argued that Gardner's approach is too loose, allows too many specific abilities and also that Gardner's dimensions are inter-correlated. Risk intelligence as described by Evans (2012) may be considered as another significant dimension of human cognitive function with the interesting difference that it is a meta-cognitive skill as it involves thinking about a thought or judgment.

The ability to cope with risk is not just a cognitive skill, it also requires emotional stability. Evans (2012) and von Neumann et al (1944) both noted this. Recently, Craparo et al. (2018) published a subjective risk intelligence scale (SRIS) that moves beyond estimating probabilities accurately and identifies other abilities that play a role in risk taking. Craparo with his colleagues developed this new test because they found that previous studies on risk (1) had neglected opportunities related to risk, (2) had not viewed the subjective perception of risk in terms of probability estimates, and (3) had neglected the emotional side of risk taking. The SRIS was developed using measures of self-efficacy, emotional intelligence, coping strategies and the "big five" personality traits (openness, conscientiousness, extraversion, agreeableness and emotional stability, Rammstedt & John, 2007). The psychological dimensions that emerged in the SRIS were imaginative capacity, problem solving self-efficacy, emotional stress vulnerability, and attitude (+/−) to uncertainty (Craparo et al. 2018). McGhee et al. (2012) found that some of these personality dimensions (extraversion, openness to experience and low conscientiousness) were related to high risk-taking as early as late childhood. While Craparo et al. (2015) had shown persistent and maladaptive gambling is associated with impulsive risk taking, measures of impulsivity were excluded from SRIS for statistical reasons.

The SRIS (Craparo et al. 2018) provides evidence that extraversion and emotional stability are highly correlated with imaginative capability, and problem solving self-efficacy. It would be interesting to know how Evans' measure of risk intelligence relates to the SRIS and whether each as a role in risk management. At the time of writing the SRIS was validated on a Russian sample by (Kornilova & Pavlova 2020) and will be used in a forthcoming study on addiction (Craparo, 2021).

2.5 Cognitive styles as determinants of cognition

Cognitive styles have been described as high level heuristics and defined as "information processing regularities that develop in congenial ways around underlying personality trends" (Messick 1982 p. 4). Various styles express features related to thinking about uncertainty. For example, Messick discusses cognitive complexity versus simplicity, leveling and sharpening, reflection and impulsivity, and field independence-dependence. Cognitively complex individuals seem most effective at using dissonant information. Leveling and sharpening relate to how differences are managed in memory. Levelers tend to overuse past memories with a consequent tendency to underestimate differences, whereas sharpeners focus on differences. Impulsivity-reflectivity is readily associated with dimensions of risky behavior and is measured on tasks as a contrast between accuracy and speed: impulsive people are faster but less accurate than reflective ones. As such it is associated with Kahneman's (2012) fast and slow thinking. Field independent people are more analytic, self-referencing and impersonal than field depend ones who are more socially sensitive and not so good at filtering out contextual details.

The cognitive styles mentioned in this section are stable ways individuals approach problems and that influence the ways that they think. As dimensions concerning differences in thinking processes, they are related to each other and to thinking about uncertainty. For example, Guilford (1980) saw field independence and complexity as related, impulsivity is a feature of problem gambling, and heuristics that ignore differences operate a form of leveling. Also thinkers that prefer complexity are likely to be wary of fast thinking.

2.6 Risks due to the need for personal consistency

An individual's thinking and judgment may be influenced by her need for (1) intra-individual consistency and (2) inter-individual consistency, each important to one's sense of self and one's identity that by definition is resistant to change (Gash 2014). An individual's sense of self-efficacy is related to emotional stability (Craparo et al., 2018). In the second case, an individual's identity is linked to how they are viewed in their social group (Gash, 2014). Inter-personal consistency is very much part of political party involvement with its risks and opportunities.

It is worth noting that calculating uncertain outcomes in both gambling and politics each depend on stable agreed rules. The internet gambling environment has enabled circumventing rules via match fixing (Andreff, 2017). Also, information gathered illegally from Facebook on individual choices enabled new forms of political manipulation exploited lucratively by Cambridge Analytica (Kaiser, 2019 & Wiley 2019). In what follows gambling is shown to meet intra-personal needs for risk and excitement, and populist politics meets intra-personal identity needs with inter-personal group support.

Gambling. Parke et al. (2019) showed that gambling satisfied needs for; mastery, detachment, self-affirmation, risk and excitement, and affiliation. Poker satisfied the needs for challenge, self-affirmation and affiliation more than gambling on sports. While affiliation is related to inter-personal needs, challenge and self-affirmation can be considered as being primarily about intrapersonal needs. Detachment which is clearly about intra-personal needs was measured with items about relaxation, stress release and escaping from one's problems. Playing slot machines had higher satisfaction on detachment than betting on sports. Finally, poker players and sports gamblers were slightly but significantly happier than those with different gambling preferences.

Gambling on cockfights in Bali was described by Geertz (2005) as "deep play" as risks arising from the size of the bets out-weight possible gains. The cockfighting rituals allow resolution of these conflicts and economic damage is avoided because fights and bets are organized so that over a series of fights losses tend to equal out. Geertz attributed part of the sport's popularity to psychological tensions arising in Balinese society due to unresolved interpersonal conflicts. Bateson (1958) made similar comments about the opportunities for resolving rivalries between the Squire and villagers in English cricket matches. Each of these examples takes "fair play" for granted and it is worth noting that part of the appeal of some blood sports like badger bating in Ireland (Viney, 1985) and bull fighting in Spain (Iliopoulou & Rosenbaum, 2013) is that it is primarily about male identity and dominating the animal.

Politics. Populism is defined as "[. . .] a thin-centered ideology that has three core concepts (the people, the elite, and the general will) and two direct opposites (elitism and pluralism)" (Mudde & Rovira Kaltwasser, 2012, p. 9). In the Brexit debate in England, complexity was avoided and fast thinking emphasized in the three word political slogans chosen by a political advisor: The People's Government; Take back control: Get Brexit Done! The simple solutions are often too simple. McWilliams (2021) described the complex details of the political arrangement agreed to ensure a hard border is avoided between the North of Ireland and the Republic of Ireland. Lack of detail can appeal and Unionist politicians claim the hard border is needed to ensure the North of Ireland is no different from England. However, details count and the overall political agreement balances varying political requirements. Here the risks involve a return to the violence of a generation ago. Populist politics as expressions of the people's will lack detail and are examples of fast thinking. There are dangers to democracy from populist politics due to certainty about the justice of their cause and frustration with Government:

> Ironically, by advocating an opening up of political life to non-elites, populism's majoritarian, anti-elite thrust can easily promote a shrinkage of 'the political' and cause a contraction of the effective democratic space. (Mudde et al. 2012, p. 22)

The effective democratic space contracts and discussion is blocked when minds are inflexible. Populists believe fake news, conspiracy theories and reinforce their views effectively using social media (Reusswig, 2020). This is a significant risk for socio-political risk management as it facilitates division, making community and discussion impossible as there is no "consensual community" (Maturana 1988, p. 34). Therefore, when discussions begin, the unconscious immediately prioritizes difference and division (Downes, 2012).

Insistence on politically correct choices demonstrates focused exclusionary demands making discussion impossible. Finding a suitable translator of Amanda Gorman's poem read at President Biden's inauguration is a high profile example of this. So far, a Dutch and a Catalan professional have withdrawn or been rejected as translators (APF Barcelona, 2021).

The important role of personal variables in political affiliation have been deepened in work on ideological attitudes in a recent study using large numbers of cognitive tasks (37) and personality surveys (22) (Zmigrod et al. 2021). The research demonstrates the overwhelming importance of personality and cognitive profiles of participating subjects in understanding ideological attitudes, particularly in comparison with demographic variables. Nationalism and conservatism were related to low scores on strategic information processing (including cognitive flexibility) and high scores on caution (in perceptual decision-making). Dogmatism was related to impulsive tendencies and a slower capacity to accumulate evidence (Zmigrod et al., 2021). The findings show how ideas suggested above regarding the importance of personal styles in determining how decisions are made can be extended to the political domain.

2.7 Future directions

This chapter outlined ways subjective dispositions influence decision making in uncertain conditions. These included heuristics, cognitive styles and risk intelligence. Increased challenges to managing risk arise in unstable risky contexts such as sports betting. Andreff (2017, 2020) has outlined the extent of cheating in sports, part of what he calls "the dark side of sport". Populist politics raises the problem of how to deal with risk in the context of strongly held views like denying science and climate change. World views involving identity exclude others, value division, and make it difficult to discuss differences. In such a context there is a need to find ways of weighing and qualifying competing arguments as seeking compromise is not viable (Reusswig, 2020). Risk has opportunities as well as dangers, this chapter has highlighted ways cognition influences decision making that need careful attention in risk management.

References

Allais M. (1953). Le comportement de l'homme rationnel devant le risque: Critique des postulats et axiomes de l'ecole Américaine. Econometrica 21: 503–546. https://doi.org/10.2307/1907921

Allport, G. (1939). Personality: A Psychological Interpretation. New York: Henry Holt.

Andreff, W. (2017). Complexity Triggered by Economic Globalisation – The Issue of On-Line Betting-Related Match Fixing. Systems 2017, 5, 12; https://doi.org/10.3390/systems5010012

Andreff, W. (2020). An Economic Roadmap to the Dark Side of Sport. Volume lll: Economic Crime in Sport. Palgrave Pivot: Springer Switzerland. https://doi.org/10.1007/978-3-030-28615-6

APF Barcelona. (2021). 'Not suitable': Catalan translator for Amanda Gorman poem removed. The Guardian. 10 March. https://www.theguardian.com/books/2021/mar/10/not-suitable-catalan-translator-for-amanda-gorman-poem-removed

Ariely, D., Lowenstein, G., and Prelec, D. (2006). Tom Sawyer and the construction of value. Journal of Economic Behavior & Organization, 60, 1–10. https://doi.org/10.1016/j.jebo.2004.10.003

Barber, B.M., Odean, T., and Zhu, N. (2009). Systematic noise. Journal of Financial Markets, 12 (4), 547–569. https://doi.org/10.1016/j.finmar.2009.03.003

Bateson, G. (1958). Naven. Stanford, CA: Stanford University Press.

Becker, L.D., Bender, N.N., & Morrison, G. (1978). Measuring impulsivity reflection: A critical review. Journal of Learning Disabilities, 11 (10), 626–632. https://doi.org/10.1177/002221947801101004

Boring, E. G. (1923). Intelligence as the tests test it. New Republic, 36, 35–37.

Brotherton, R., & French, C.C. (2014). Belief in conspiracy theories and susceptibility to the conjunction fallacy. Applied Cognitive Psychology, 28, 238–248. https://doi.org/10.1002/acp.2995

Carroll, J.B. (1993). Human cognitive abilities: A survey of factor analytic studies. New York: Cambridge University Press.

Craparo, G. (2021). Personal communication.

Craparo, G., Alessio, G., Iraci Sareri, G., & Pace, U. (2015). Personality and clinical dimensions of pathological gamblers. A pilot study. Mediterranean Journal of Social Sciences, 4 (6), DOI: 10.5901/mjss.2015.v6n4s3p612

Craparo, G., Magnano, P., Paolillo, A., & Constantino, V. (2018). The subjective risk intelligence scale. The Development of a new scale to measure a new construct. Current Psychology, 37(4), 966–981. https://doi.org/10.1007/s12144-017-9673-x

Downes, P. (2012) The Primordial Dance: Diametric and Concentric Spaces in the Unconscious World. Oxford/Bern: Peter Lang.

Engemann, K.J., & Yager, R.R. (2018). Comfort decision making. International Journal of Uncertainty, Fuzziness and Knowledge-Based Systems. Vol. 26, Suppl. 1 (December 2018) 141–163. https://doi.org/10.1142/S0218488518400081

Evans D. (2012). Risk Intelligence. In: Roeser S., Hillerbrand R., Sandin P., Peterson M. (Eds.) Handbook of Risk Theory. Springer, Dordrecht. https://doi.org/10.1007/978-94-007-1433-5_23

Eysenck, M.M. (2009). Fundamentals of psychology. New York: Psychology Press.

Gardner, H. (1993). Multiple Intelligences: The Theory in Practice. New York: Basic Books.

Gash H. (2014). Constructing constructivism. Constructivist Foundations 9(3): 302–310. Available at https://cepa.info/1077

Geertz, C. (2005) Deep play: Notes on the Balinese Cockfight. Daedalus, 134 (4), 56–86

Gopnik, A., Glymour, C., Sobel, D., Schulz, L., Kushnir, T., & Danks, D. (2004). A theory of causal learning in children: Causal maps and Bayes nets. Psychological Review, 111, 1, 3–32. https://doi:10.1037/0033-295X.111.1.3.

Guilford, J. P. (1980). Cognitive styles: What are they? Psychological Measurement, 40, 715–735. https://doi.org/10.1177/001316448004000315

Hertwig R. & Pachur T. (2015). History of heuristics. In: Wright J. D. (Ed.) International encyclopedia of the social and behavioural sciences. Volume 10. Second edition. Elsevier, Amsterdam: 829–835. http://dx.doi.org/10.1016/B978-0-08-097086-8.03221-9

Iliopoulou, M.A., & Rosenbaum, R.P. (2013). Understanding blood sports. Journal of Animal & Natural Resource Law, 9, 125–140.

Johnson, E. J. & Tversky, A. (1983). Affect, generalization, and the perception of risk. Journal of Personality and Social Psychology, 45, 20–31. https://doi.org/10.1037/0022-3514.45.1.20

Kahn, H.H., Naz, I., Qureshi, F., & Ghafoor. (2017). Heuristics and stock buying decision: Evidence from Malaysian and Pakistani stock Markets. Borsa Istanbul Review, 17(2),97–110.

Kahneman D. (2012). Thinking, fast and slow. Penguin, London.

Kaiser B. (2019). Targeted: My inside story of Cambridge Analytica and how Trump, Brexit and Facebook broke democracy. Harper Collins, London.

Keller, C., Siegrist, M., Gutscher, H. (June 2006). "The Role of Affect and Availability Heuristics in Risk Analysis". Risk Analysis. 26 (3): 631–639. https://doi.org/10.1111/j.1539-6924.2006.00773.x

Kornilova, T.V., & Pavlova, E.M. (2020). Risk intelligence scale and its relationship with risk readiness and emotional intelligence. Counselling Psychology and Psychotherapy, 28 (4), 59–78. https://doi.org/10.17759/cpp.2020280404

Knight, F.H. (1921). Risk, uncertainty and profit. University of Michigan Library, Michigan, 2009 edition.

Long, B. (2020). Why Irish problem gamblers need a regulator. www.rte.ie/2020/0430/1135874-gambling-addiction-regulator-ireland/ (8.5.2020)

Maturana H. R. (1988). Reality: The search for objectivity or the quest for a compelling argument. Irish Journal of Psychology 9(1): 25–82. https://cepa.info/598

McGhee, R.L., Ehrler, D.J., Buckhalt, J.A., Phillips, C. (2012). The relation between five-factor personality traits and risk-taking behavior in preadolescents. Psychology, 3(8),558–561. https://doi.org/10.4236/psych.2012.38083

McWilliams, M. (2021). North's status under Belfast Agreement is an inconvenient truth. *Irish Times*, 25 February, https://www.irishtimes.com/1.4494167

Messick, S. (1982). Cognitive styles in educational practice. Paper presented at the American Educational Research Association, New York 1982. ETS Report Series. DOI: doi.org/10.1002/j.2333-8504.1982.tb01299.x

Moscati I. (2016). Measuring the economizing mind in the 1940s and 1950s: The Mosteller-Nogee and Davidson-Suppes-Siegel experiments to measure the utility of money. History of Political Economy 48 (Supplement 1): 239–269.

Mrkva, K., Johnson, E.J., Gächter, S., & Herrmann, A. (2020). Moderating Loss Aversion: Loss Aversion Has Moderators, But Reports of its Death are Greatly Exaggerated. Journal of Consumer Psychology, 30(3),407–428. https://doi.org/10.1002/jcpy.1156

Mudde C. & Rovira Kaltwasser C. (2012). Populism: corrective and threat to democracy. In (Eds.) Mudde C. & Rovira Kaltwasser C. Populism in Europe and the Americas: Threat or corrective for democracy? (pp. 205–222). Cambridge University Press, Cambridge. https://doi.org/10.1017/CBO9781139152365.011

Neumann, J. von, & Morgenstern, O. 1944. *Theory of Games and Economic Behavior*. Princeton: Princeton University Press.

Nobel Prize Economic Sciences. (2002, October 9). https://www.nobelprize.org/prizes/economic-sciences/2002/summary/

Parke, J., Williams, R.J., Schofield, P. (2019). Exploring psychological need satisfaction from gambling participation and the moderating influence of game preferences. International Gambling Studies, 19(3),508–531. https://doi.org/10.1080/14459795.2019.1633381

Rammstedt, B., & Johm, O.P. (2007). Measuring personality in one minute or less: A 10-item short version of the big five inventory in English and German. Journal of Research in Personality, 4(1),203–212. https://doi.org/10.1016/j.jrp.2006.02.001

Reusswig, F.A. (2020). De- and re-constructing sustainable development. Constructivist Foundations, 16(1),30–32. https://cepa.info/6807

Schirrmeister, E., Göhring, A-L., Warnke, P. (2020). Psychological biases and heuristics in the context of foresight and scenario processes. Futures and Foresight Science, 2(2), e31. (doi.org/10.1002/ffo2.31)

Shweder, R. (1977). Likeness and likelihood in everyday thought: Magical thought in judgments about personality. Current Anthropology, 18(4): 637–658.

Siegrist, M., & Árvai, J. (2020). Risk perception: Perceptions of 40 years of research. Risk Analysis, 40, 3, 2191–2206. https://doi.org/10.1111/risa.13599

Skagerlund, K., Forsblad, M., Slovic, P., & Västfjäll, D. (2020). The Affect Heuristic and Risk Perception – Stability Across Elicitation Methods and Individual Cognitive Abilities. Frontiers in Psychology, 11, 970. https://www.frontiersin.org/articles/10.3389/fpsyg.2020.00970/full

Smedslund, J. (1963). The effect of observation on children's representation of the spatial orientation of a water surface. The Journal of Genetic Psychology: Research and Theory on Human Development, 102(2), 195–201. https://doi.org/10.1080/00221325.1963.1053274

Smith, V.L. (1962). An experimental study of competitive market behavior. Journal of Political Economy 70 (2), 111–137. http://dx.doi.org/10.1086/258660

Smith, V.L. (1976). Experimental economics: Induced value theory. The American Economic Review, 1976, 66 (2), Papers and Proceedings of the Eighty-eighth Annual Meeting of the American Economic Association (May, 1976), pp. 274–279

Thurstone, L.L. 1927. A Law of Comparative Judgment. *Psychological Review* 34:273–286. https://www.encyclopedia.com/arts/educational-magazines/smith-vernon-l-1927

Tversky A. & Kahneman D. (1974). Judgment under uncertainty: Heuristics and biases science. Science 185(4157): 1124–1131. https://doi/10.1126/science.185.4157.1124

Västfjäll, D., Peters, E., and Slovic, P. (2014). The affect heuristic, mortality salience, and risk: domain-specific effects of a natural disaster on risk-benefit perception. Scand. J. Psychol. 55, 527–532. https://doi.org/10.1111/sjop.12166

Viney, M. (12 November 1985). Ecowatch. *Irish Times* page 11. https://www.irishtimes.com/newspaper/archive/1985/1112/Pg011.html

Wylie C. (2019). Mindf*ck: Inside Cambridge Analytica's plot to break the world. Penguin, London.

Zmigrod, L., Eisenberg, I.W., Bissett, P.G., Robbins, T.W., & Poldrack, R.A. (2021). The cognitive and perceptual correlates of ideological attitudes: a data-driven approach. Phil Trans. R. Soc. B. 376: 20200424. https://doi.org/10.1098/rstb.2020.0424

Saquib Hyat-Khan

3 Human resources: Endogenous political risk

3.1 Introduction

The majority of research and literature in Human Resource Management (HRM) focuses on organizational effectiveness, organizational culture, employee well-being, and how HRM makes a positive contribution to an organization (Beer, Spector, Lawrence, Mills & Walton, 1984).

As organizations evolve to address the multiplicity of risks witnessed in the past few decades resulting from new technologies, financial crises, terrorism, cybercrime, and cross-border conflicts, a host of Enterprise Risk Management (ERM) tools and frameworks have emerged to accompany the ISO 31000:2009 Risk management principles and guidelines (International Organization of Standardization (IS), 2009). These tools and frameworks tend to focus primarily on universally understood financial and physical risks while largely ignoring the HRM function and its processes, particularly as it pertains to identifying risk beyond those prescribed by domestic labor laws such as hiring practices, discrimination, health, safety, and sexual harassment. It should be of no surprise then that individuals like Dr. Charles Lieber (Harvard University), Edward Snowden (Booz-Allen), Shelly Adelson (Sands Hotel & Casino), Jeffrey Skilling (Enron) and others have emerged as examples of internal-risk. What joins them together is that they all not only created political risk for their organizations, but they were also once prospective candidates that went through the HR screening processes at their respective institutions.

The focus of this paper is to review the literature over the past two decades to assess the gaps in HRM practices for identifying political risk and to identify potential research in this domain. Both theoretical and empirical articles have been identified and reviewed with an aim toward evaluating weak governance in the Human Resources sector which serves as a critical and poorly understood source of political risk to an organization.

3.2 Risk and political risk

There is no single widely accepted definition of the term "risk" in academic literature (Lehtiranta, 2014; Hagigi & Sivakumar, 2009). 'Uncertainty' in otherwise what might be perceived as predictable outcomes in a business operation, is interchangeably used as an alternative for discussing risk (Hagigi & Sivakumar, 2009). Other definitions of risk span across a spectrum ranging from potential negative outcomes

https://doi.org/10.1515/9783110731217-003

due to a deficit in predictability within business to others that present risk as either positive or negative outcomes of variability (Jablonowski, 2006; Jaafari, 2006; Osipova & Eriksson 2013). Aven (2010) asserts that risk comprises three intertwined actions, an occurrence, symptoms, and uncertainties. This is a commonly adopted definition in business that recognizes the existence of symptoms, either positive or negative, and related uncertainties insofar as HRM.

Historically, modern business risk management perspectives began coming to the forefront of business management between 1955 and 1964. Initially associated with equities, insurance and financial institutions, the perspectives grew into what is commonly understood as 'operational risk management' practices (Dionne, 2013). Today, managing business risk is solely viewed through multiple lens across business functions, e.g., economics, finance, treasury management, accounting, strategy, behavioral science, regulatory compliance, and information systems (Elahi, 2013).

In the broader business risk management literature, there is growing acceptance around human capital being the most critical risk in a business (Hinton, 2003), and that the risk management discipline is attuned to the fact that "human resources [related] loss" can significantly cripple an organization's ability to execute its business strategy (Nickson, 2001, p. 26). Given the discipline of risk management recognizes the relevance of human resources risks, two decades ago, Nickson (2001) argued for merging the Human Resource management field with risk management contending that, "Risk management is about mitigating risk and protecting resources. What is the most valuable resource of any company? Its people" (Nickson, 2001, p.25). In view of Nickson's argument contending that as human resources inherently involve uncertainty, and considering risk management's main focus is uncertainty, melding both risk management and HRM is critical.

At an overarching level, risks can be conceptualized in terms of their origin; exogenous (external to the organization) or endogenous (within the firm). Endogenous risks were seen to cover issues such as management attitudes, culture, and organizational practices and as such, the human resources of the firm and the associated uncertainties inherent in these (Hagigi & Sivakumar, 2009). Alternately, Dionne (2013) categorized risk and suggested that within the operational risk category, issues relating to employees (such as employee errors) should be considered. In these types of contexts, human resources are often acknowledged as an element of organizational risk, albeit in a limited way.

Considering how little control businesses have over the environments within which they operate (e.g., volatile economies, unpredictable actions of governments, competitors, clients, and suppliers), one would think companies would pay especially close attention to the one thing they can control – the quality of people they hire. Rarely does HRM engage on the topic of political risk management or "how appropriate ways of employing managing and developing the workforce will not only result in enhanced organizational outcomes but also mitigate operational risks." (Becker et. al. 2015). Daily one hears or reads about an executive saying that "people are our most important asset," yet the same executives usually do not know how best to evaluate the right people for the jobs or how to keep them from becoming disgruntled once they are working in the organization. Neither they nor their organizations know how to assess what the jobs require within the context of their organization's strategic vision, and which human characteristics would be required for optimally performing in those jobs for the duration. As a result, their companies do not know how to hire, motivate, engage, and develop the best candidates for the organization's future. Demotivated, disengaged, disgruntled employees pose a huge internal risk to an organization. They can create a stressful workplace environment by negative comments influencing the feelings and productivity of co-workers, clients, and suppliers thereby adversely affecting the brand reputation of the company. They create political risk for the company.

Human beings are an organization's most reliable resource for protecting it and helping it achieve its goals. Their experiences, worldviews, egos, judgments, values, and skills make the difference between success and failure. Bhattacharya and Wright (2005, 932) state that "any investing in human assets, from the decision to acquire (employ), develop, motivate, or retain employees, carries with it uncertainty regarding the future return." The onus therefore falls upon the HRM discipline to understand political risk.

A focus on political risk management within HRM has received limited attention across management journals and reviews (Becker, K., & Schmidt, M. 2015). Political risk inside an organization can be defined as potential harm to a business arising from an employee's political behavior. Political behavior entails operating or behaving in a manner that aims to, directly or indirectly, influence individuals in a workplace to alter the status quo for gaining, maintaining, aligning, or solidifying power for meeting one's personal, not the organization's, objectives. Every employee is also a potential political actor. In this context, the disgruntled employee is a political actor that is concerned with the social hierarchy and its underlying ideals that uses a language consisting of authority, humor, ideology which poses a unique challenge to an organization who needs to understand the fundamentals of an alternative mindset in order to identify it at the time of hiring, or address as it develops through making passive aggressive comments and/or mannerism styles visible, while keeping in mind cultural nuances. Whereas the human element is implied in some frameworks, in the risk management sphere, particularly *how* the human poses potential political risk, the question remains as to whether or not there is widespread recognition of a reconceptualization warranted on the wide range of political risks that human resources present in an organization, as well as how effective HRM practices can mitigate these risks? This paper addresses these questions, undertaking a review of the extent to the gaps in the literature and how the HRM function should be assisted with a reconceptualization of its role, especially in light of evolving technologies that enable political behavior.

3.3 Perspectives on HRM and political risk management

A large portion of Becker et al.'s analysis presents the existing literature as focusing on human resources management practices which analyze: i) specific human resources related risks; ii) specific HRM practices that create (or minimize) risk as an adoption of such practices, and iii) how HRM and risk management ought to be integrated as 'systems' instead of individual practices (Becker et. al., 2015). The literature takes into consideration how the internal audit and regulatory compliance functions within organizations perceive, drive awareness, and address risk management through operational risk management and enterprise risk management practices, which encompass sub-categories such as financial risk management, supply chain risk management, cyber risk management, etc., however, fall short of addressing the most important element, i.e., people risk.

It is important to note that HR practitioners have a herculean task in front of them as they must ensure compliance with a myriad of domestic and international federal statutes and regulations for implementing such. Of a total one hundred and ninety-three countries, the Society of Human Resources provides HR Country Guides for twenty-four (of forty-three) European nations, four (of seventeen) Middle Eastern nations, two (of fifty-three) African nations; five (of thirty-three) Asian nations, four (of twenty) South American nations. The multi-dimensionality and complexity associated with adherence and enforcement and implementation of government regulations is multiplied, especially for those organizations that operate in more than one country, in one region and, globally in multiple countries within multiple regions e.g., financial institutions, pharmaceuticals, diversified consumer products and consulting firms that hire and deal with multi-cultural and faith related matters in the workplace in some of the highest populated, politically volatile nations in the world.

In the United States, for instance, the United States Department of Labor (USDOL) administers and enforces more than one hundred and eighty federal laws. The mandates and regulations that ensure implementation are events that are audited by regulators which cover many work environment activities (USDOL). None of the events addresses endogenous political risk. As seen in the following list, most of the statutes are applicable to businesses, job seekers, workers, retirees, contractors, and grantees.
1. Wages and Hours
2. Workplace Safety and Health
3. Workers' Compensation
4. Employee Benefit and Security
5. Unions and their Members
6. Employee Protection
7. Uniformed Services Employment and Reemployment Rights
8. Employee Polygraph Protection

9. Garnishment of Wages
10. Family and Medical Leave Act
11. Veterans' Preference
12. Government Contracts, Grants, or Financial Aid
13. Migrant and Seasonal Agricultural Workers
14. Mine Safety and Health
15. Construction
16. Transportation
17. Plant Closings and Layoffs
18. Posters
    (Summary of Major Laws of the USDOL – U.S. Department of Labor, 2021)

In the United States there has been an evolution in regulatory oversight, through more than fifty-five acts and amendments however, none address political risk management or provide guidance to HR practitioners on matters pertaining to anything other than routine workforce development, workplace equity, workplace flexibility & leave, to workplace health care and workplace immigration related matters. The absence of any such regulation all but ensures that HR practitioners operating under these regulations will themselves focus scant attention to developing political risk management strategies.

In light of the above, Figure 3.2 shows the extent of Becker et al.'s (2015) contribution toward assessing the advancement of understanding human resources risks, according to which eight key HR risks, along with specific organizational or HRM practices, give rise to risks that might emerge as a result of adoption of such practices – or how the use of such practices minimizes risk.

The broad range of themes above demonstrate potential risk areas relating to human resources and identify future research directions for the two areas of risk management and HRM. In her book, *Corporate Confidential*, Cynthia Shapiro (2005) states, "HR's primary function is not to help employees, it is to protect the company from its employees." Human Resources is the entry, oversight, and exit point for employees and suppliers, i.e., contractors, consultants, and HR vendors in an organization; as such, exposes the organization to both positive and negative outcomes. The available literature, however, gives short shrift to how HR/HRM practices create *political risk* for an organization.

3.4 Political risk in an organization

The failure to consider endogenous risk is not just present in governmental regulations, it is also noticeably under-discussed in the literature. As depicted in Table 3.1, Condoleezza Rice and Amy Zegart's (2018) well known book identifies ten categories of political risk.

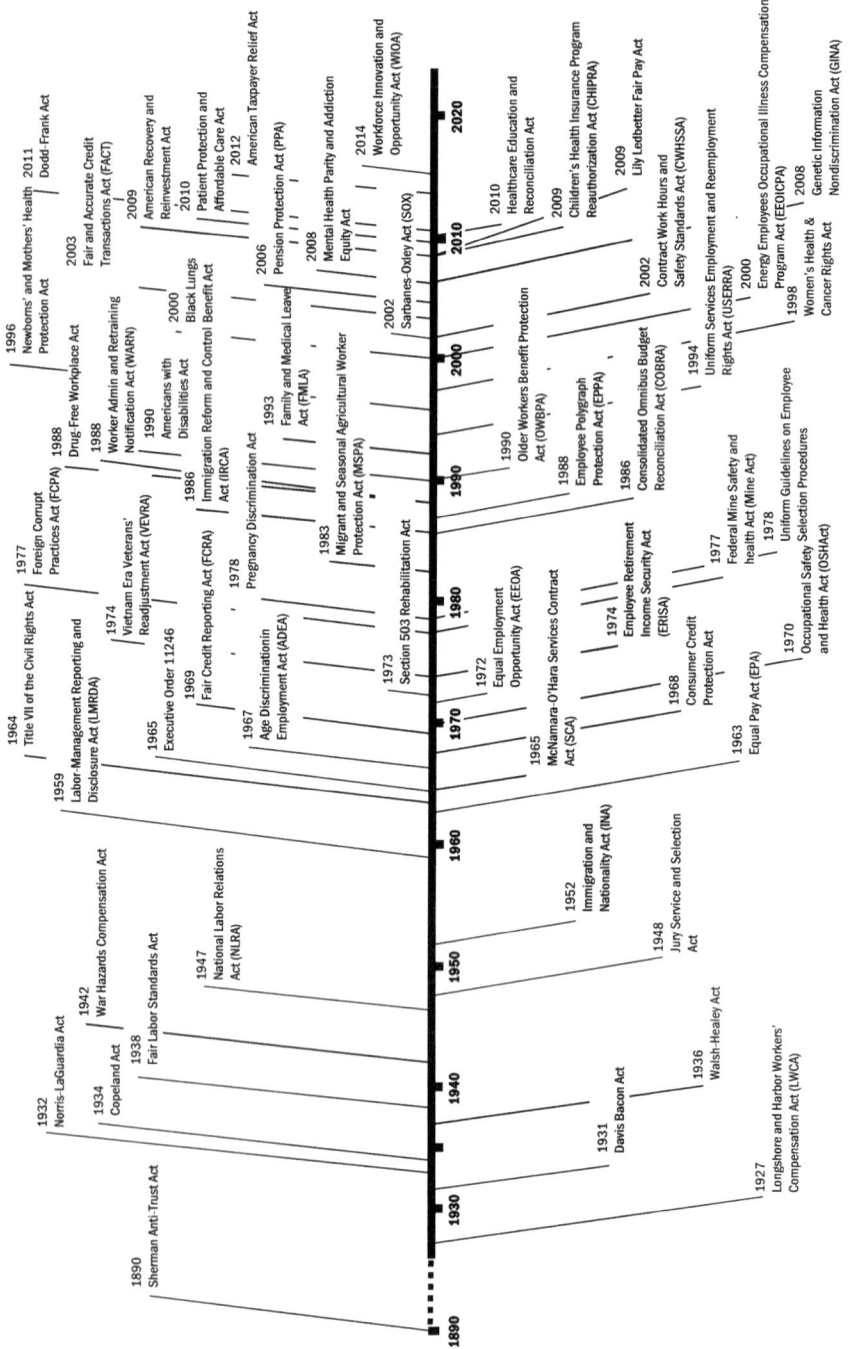

Figure 3.1: US Federal Statutes and Regulation Guiding Human Resource Management.
Source: US Federal Statutes. Society for Human Resource Management (SHRM)

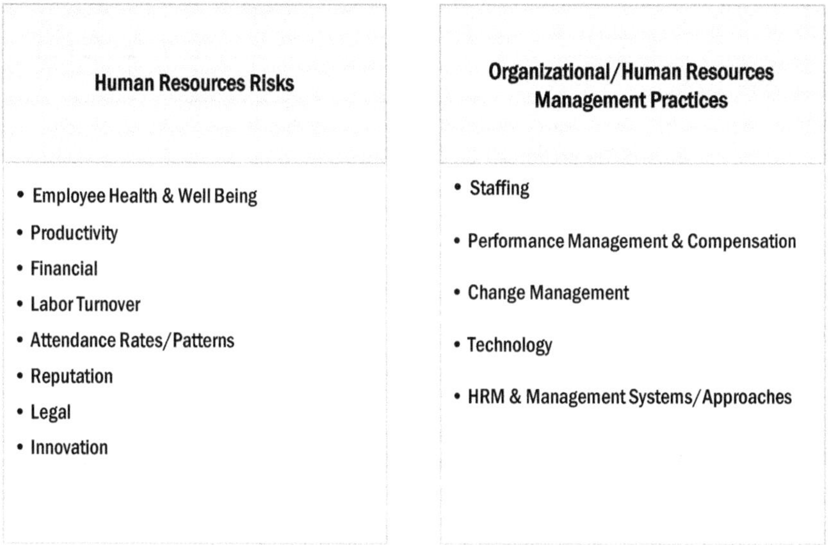

<table>
<tr><td>**Human Resources Risks**</td><td>**Organizational/Human Resources Management Practices**</td></tr>
<tr><td>

• Employee Health & Well Being

• Productivity

• Financial

• Labor Turnover

• Attendance Rates/Patterns

• Reputation

• Legal

• Innovation
</td><td>

• Staffing

• Performance Management & Compensation

• Change Management

• Technology

• HRM & Management Systems/Approaches
</td></tr>
</table>

Figure 3.2: Human Resources Risks & Organizational/HRM Practices.
Source: Becker, Karen, Michelle Smidt, A risk perspective on human resource management: A review and directions for future research, Human Resource Management Review (2015)

Table 3.1: Political Risks.

No.	Political Risk Type	Examples
1.	Geopolitics	Interstate wars, great power shifts, multilateral economic sanctions, and interventions.
2.	Internal conflict	Social unrest, ethnic violence, migration, nationalism, separatism, federalism, civil wars, coups, revolutions.
3.	Laws, Regulations, Policies	Changes in foreign ownership rules, taxation, environment regulations, national laws.
4.	Breaches of contract	Government reneging on contracts, including expropriations and political motivated credit defaults.
5.	Corruption	Discriminatory taxation, systemic bribery.
6.	Extraterritorial reach	Unilateral sanctions, criminal investigation, and prosecutions.
7.	Natural resource manipulation	Politically motivated changes in supply of energy, rare earth minerals.
8.	Social activism	Events or opinions that "go viral," facilitation collective action.
9.	Terrorism	Politically motivated threats or use of violence against persons, property.

Table 3.1 (continued)

No.	Political Risk Type	Examples
10.	Cyber threats	Theft or destruction of intellectual property, espionage, extortion, massive disruption of companies, industries, governments, societies.

Source: Rice, C., & Zegart, A. B. (2018).Political risk: How businesses and organizations can anticipate global insecurity. Twelve

Climate change and economic risks are omitted intentionally for analytical reasons. In the case of climate change, for instance, they argue that while it directly affects global agricultural production, ecosystems and the livelihood of populations living in low-lying coastal areas, it is more of a 'risk multiplier' than a risk category unto itself in that it creates circumstances that invoke social activism which in turn lead to political actions. Economic risks on the other hand, are exogenous by nature, mandated by regulators for companies to routinely examine. Rice et al (2018) argue that the focus of their work is centered on "how political actions affect businesses," and political risks that are "out there." They admit that it is "important to underscore that sometimes the biggest political risks come from within", and how organizations pay too little attention to their own corporate cultures and practices, failing to address the underlying root of endogenous risks that are best understood by and fall under the purview of HR in an organization (Rice et al, 2018).

Organizations tend to view internal operations in a traditional business management sense shrouded underneath certain 'standard operating procedures' (SOPs) that are somewhat universal. Political risk variables can be examined in PEST (Political, Economic, Social and Technological) assessments however, the political domain is strictly viewed through an exogenous lens, analogous to climate and beyond management's purview. As with climate, an unpredictable-until-foreseeable event, loss can be insured or perhaps even avoided in certain cases, but management's prescience in such situations faces limitations from a competence standpoint. The C-Suite in an organization does not have a Chief Meteorology Officer in its ranks or, in light of having a limited exogenous view only toward political risk, a Chief Political Risk Officer. HR's function is to identify, interview, screen and introduce candidates that fit a specific job description, then introduce the candidate to the hiring manager. In their book *Execution*, Larry Bossidy and Ram Charan (2002) write leaders "may not know enough about the people they're appointing." They go on to say that leaders, "may pick people with whom they're comfortable, rather than others who have better skills for the job . . . leaders aren't personally committed to the people process and deeply engaged in it." Political risk, in a company, is created through employee actions that are motivated by self-interests, i.e., political behavior, which would cause harm, or create hazard, in the form of revenue or reputation loss for the employer. Political behavior is defined as activity in which an individual engages to preserve her/his self-interest(s) and aims to achieve through influencing another person or group behavior. The most important risk facing companies, therefore, is *endogenous* that invokes political actions by staff and the lack of systematic understanding or management focus on these. After the hiring manager approves of the candidate, HR's function goes on to then make, discuss and negotiate an offer with the candidate. In light of the Employee Polygraph Protection Act (EPPA) that went into effect in 1988 in the United States – which applies to most private employers and not Federal, state, and local government agencies – most organizations' HR hiring practices do not take into consideration human psychology elements. The EPPA prohibits most[1] private employers from using lie detection tests. It is not until the candidates are hired, and during the course of employment, that in order to meet ongoing staff development requirements on a check-the-box basis, will enterprise-wide programs, questionable in and of themselves, such as personality/temperament type tests, e.g., Myers-Briggs and/or Keirsey, get rolled out by Training Departments (a subset function of HRM) to understand how staff perceives their environment and how they would react in specific situations.

There is a lack of empirical evidence pointing toward founders of organizations creating more or less political risk as compared with their staff, or leaders and employees of well-established companies creating such. Our experience shows that in startups to small companies, the organizational structures are flatter and with fewer employees, the founders, being the mascots of their companies, tend to lend themselves to constant scrutiny in the media (especially for those companies newly listed in the capital markets) and thereby more prone to creating political risk as opposed to executives from established companies where the interacting with the outside world requires training and multiple layers of internal approvals which makes it harder to have oneself heard, as in the case of Edward Snowden.

3.5 Case studies

In 2010, fourteen suicides occurred at a Foxconn plant in China. Foxconn, a Chinese company, manufactures approximately forty percent of the world's consumer electronics, including components for the iPhone, PlayStation 4, and Xbox One. Instead of drawing attention to HR/HRM practices, the suicides shone a spotlight to the poor 'labor conditions' at the factory. Investigations revealed that many of the

---

1 Subject to restrictions, the EPPA permits polygraph (a type of lie detector) tests to be administered to certain job applicants of security services firms (armored car, alarm, and guard) and of pharmaceutical manufacturers, distributors, and dispensers. It also permits testing of certain employees who are reasonably suspected of involvement in a workplace incident, e.g., theft, embezzlement, etc., that resulted in specific economic loss or injury to the employers. Where permitted, the EPPA examiner must be licensed if required by a state in which the test is conducted and must be bonded or have professional liability coverage (USDOL).

suicides were committed in protest of the work conditions. This not only created endogenous risk for Foxconn, but also exogenous (supplier) risk for Foxconn's clients, e.g., Apple, H-P, that conduct annual audits of their suppliers. Suicide is a symptom of endogenous political risk in an organization as it highlights a cause, the management team's inability to be attentive to the needs of its employees.

In that same year, the U.S. Commodity Futures Trading Commission (CFTC) released the results of an investigation that revealed the actions of certain rogue bankers involved in an international scheme in which their employers, leading global financial institutions, e.g., Deutsche Bank, Barclays, and UBS, were identified as having colluded to illegally manipulate interest rates for profit. Specifically, the bankers identified involved rigging the Libor (London Interbank Offered Rate).[2] In conspiring to artificially manipulate the Libor high or low, the bankers had the power to raise the value of their investments by millions of dollars with just a couple of emails. The financial effect as a result of the scandal, including total costs to states, cities, and other municipalities as high as US$6 billion, led to massive fines for the banks involved and substantial reform of how the Libor is determined. Regulators fined the banks more than US$9 billion, and administration of the Libor was shifted to the ICE Benchmark Administration. In such organizations that are under pressure to deliver consistent shareholder value, HR is accountable for developing the criteria, driving, and for ensuring employee adherence to the organization's culture.

On Sept. 7th, 2017, Equifax, the largest credit reporting agency in the United States disclosed that its internal systems had been hacked and as such, had failed to ensure protection of critical personal and financial information of more than one hundred and forty-five million US citizens – almost half of the United States' population – possibly the most important crisis facing the country today, more so than Covid-19, climate change and cyber-risk combined; and posing extreme political risk for decades to come. Franscesci-Biccheriai stated that, "information contained in the files accessed by hackers included names, dates of birth, Social Security numbers, addresses, and, in about 209,000 cases, credit card numbers [. . .] an earlier incidence, a former IT staff member reported that "someone had programmed files to be inappropriately wiped on multiple servers – an act of internal sabotage." (Vice, 2017). The breach and a multiplicity of similar IT governance related issues reported at the executive management level, raises eyebrows about Equifax's enterprise wide HRM practices.

In August 2019, WeWork, the office sharing real estate company, filed an S-1 form with the Securities and Exchange Commission for converting itself into a public company. A list of red flags, such as massive losses, questionably expensive

---

2 The average interest rate calculated, based on estimates submitted from a panel of global banks, used as the main benchmark for global lending rates.

lease agreements, unnecessarily complex corporate structure, and along with an all-male board of directors brought CEO Adam Neumann's integrity under the spotlight that invited further scrutiny into the company's leadership practices. Further scrutiny into Neumann's lifestyles and idiosyncratic behaviors eventually led to the IPO's collapse bringing further disrepute to the brand. Among numerous vagaries and derelictions, Neumann illegally transported cannabis in his private jet across international borders and encouraged excessive alcohol consumption in professional settings. Amid a storm of negative press, WeWork slashed its valuation from US\$47 billion to US\$10 billion, ousted Neumann, and laid off 2,400 employees – nearly one-fifth of its workforce. HR was fully aware of Adam Neumann posing political risk for WeWork and was remiss in ousting him.

Among the myriad of sexual conduct allegations aimed at senior executives at companies such as Harvey Weinstein (founder of Miramax), Roger Ailes (Chairman & CEO of Fox News), Les Moonves (Chairman & CEO of CBS Corporation), Andy Rubin (Google) thereby creating political risk for their organizations, no industry remains untouched by employees (at all levels) within an organization. In large pharmaceutical companies, Martin Shkreli (CEO Turing Pharmaceuticals), Michael Pearson (CEO Valeant Pharmaceuticals), Heather Bresch (CEO Mylan) all found guilty of corporate misconduct. In the fintech services industry, endogenous political risk that spilled over to suppliers and regulators, became visible when German mobile payment and worldwide banking services provider, Wirecard, once valued at US\$27B collapsed as a result of CEO Markus Braun's (a former KPMG consultant) announcement stated that the organization was missing US\$2.1B, highlighting not only the organization's internal HRM practices, but also those of German financial regulators and big five auditing and consulting firm EY (Ernst & Young).

Anyone who has ever been responsible for hiring, managing, and firing employees knows that there is a myriad of possibilities to sift through when dealing with human nature. Hiring a candidate into a job requires HR to first acknowledge its own biases and motivators in doing so. A mismatched hire poses political risk for an organization. Although leaders know intuitively that they are facing a problem, most choose to not make it a priority to do anything to enforce governance. Issuing directives to source the right-fit talent requires HR to know how to execute on doing so. In an attempt to get the gorilla off of their backs, HR will demonstrate an inability to deal with capacity issues by resorting to outsourcing the tasks of screening, hiring, even interviewing to so-called professional recruiters, HR consultants, employment agencies, artificial intelligence applications, thereby injecting exogenous political risk into the hiring process. Suppliers, that are not vetted on their own understanding of political risk nor on their application of such within their own hiring processes, are awarded contracts by leading companies to screen, interview, and shortlist on behalf of their clients. Exemplary of the adage: the blind leading the blind.

Research shows that, in practice, an organization's decisions to outsource are contextually drive, and not completely rational (Vernon et al., 2000). Cooke et al. (2005) confirm that the empirical literature available on the topic is fairly sparse and fragmented. Bossidy and Charan suggest that "leaders need to commit as much as forty percent of their time and emotional energy, in one form or another, to selecting, appraising, and developing people" (Bossidy and Charan, 2002). Such commitment from leaders is personally time-consuming as it requires giving continuous feedback, having meaningful conversations on-demand, and exposing oneself to critical judgment.

Relying on traditional interviews for spotting individuals that would not pose political risk for an organization requires focusing less on the chronology and roles in a candidate's career, and more knowing how to ask the right questions in order to discern how an individual perceives the world outside of the work environment. Even ethics and personality tests fall short in their efficacy to provide reliable insight into an individual's self-interests that affect their loyalty toward the employer. Whitney Martin posits that the strongest personality assessments to use in a hiring context are ones that measure stable traits, are normative in nature, evaluate a candidate's openness, that demonstrate high reliability (Martin, 2014). However, such evaluations are limited to a point in time only and in order to be effective, must be consistently rolled out on a bi-annual or annual basis.

3.6 Conclusion

Although practitioner journals currently do not offer much in the way of research findings or focus in this area, now is a particularly good time to increase research coverage and push content through social media that targets HR practitioners. Another recommendation is that journals which traditionally present only "HR" knowledge look to expanding coverage so as to include research and implementation issues related to political risk management. Other areas to bridge the vast knowledge gaps between the latest research and mainstream HRM knowledge would be to research practitioners' educational backgrounds and correlate to biases and beliefs recognizing that HR managers graduate in a wide array of educational disciplines that do not expose the student to political risk management.

A practical conclusion to this chapter is to impress upon the concept of an enterprise-wide political risk management strategy. Organizations ought to be aware about the issue in terms of a series of ongoing actions that result in embedding self-awareness and mindfulness among and, about all employees by HR. A political risk management strategy would imply developing multi-tiered and cultural-nuance aware HRM governance parameters that strike a balance between an understanding of how information security, risk transference and external relations building measures cross-influence each other and how such ought to align with shareholder tolerance for the organizations' market expansion strategies in light thereof. When exploring approaches to parametrizing HR governance through a political risk lens, HR practitioners and executive management ought to be mindful of knowing how to ask the right questions, e.g., "How aware are we about *factors* that cause political risk?" to "How can we ensure all employees digest and embody a level understanding of what constitutes political risk behaviors and acts for both themselves and our organization?"

HR practitioners ought to consider informing potential new candidates and existing employees with litigation information facing their organization. This would help encourage transparency and openness by HR to foster political risk awareness among employees about the ramifications of staff behaviors and actions.

Lastly, HR practitioners would be supported well in this area, not by the Big Four consulting firms, but management consulting firms with no audit style restrictions or conflicts of interest. Firms that can provide independent counseling uniquely positioned to deliver organizational decision-making techniques that provide not only structured but intellectually liberating safe-to-fail environments that help employees explore political risk by leveraging state-of-the-art platforms (e.g., crises simulations, on-demand scenario driven response systems, etc.) to introduce and enhance awareness among staff members at all levels and across various functions within an organization throughout an organizations' life cycle.

References

Adler, P. S. (2003). *Making the HR outsourcing decision*. Fall: MIT Sloan Management Review 53–60.

Alewell, D., Hauff, S., Thommes, K., & Weiland, K. (2009). *Triggers of HR outsourcing decisions – an empirical analysis of German firms*. The International Journal of Human Resource Management, 20(7), 1599–1617.

Ansari, S. M., Fiss, P. C., & Zajac, E. J. (2010). *Made to fit: How practices vary as they diffuse*. The Academy of Management Review, 35(1), 67–92.

Aven, T. (2010). *On how to define, understand and describe risk*. Reliability Engineering & System Safety, 95(6), 623–631.

Barney, J. (1991). *Firm resources and sustained competitive advantage*. Journal of Management, 17(1), 99–120.

Becker, K., & Schmidt, M., A risk perspective on human resource management: A review and directions for future research, Human Resource Management Review (2015), http://dx.doi.org/10.1016/j.hrmr.2015.12.001

Beer, M., Spector, B., Lawrence, P.R., Mills, D.Q., & Walton, R.E., (1984). *Managing human assets*. New York: The Free Press.

Benko, C., & Volini, E. (2014). *What it will take to fix HR*. Harvard Business Review. https://hbr.org/2014/07/what-it-will-take-to-fix-hr.

Bharadwaj, S. S., & Saxena, K. B. C. (2010). *Service providers' competences in Business Process Outsourcing for delivering successful outcome: An exploratory study*. Vikapla, 35(3), 37–53.

Bhattacharya, M., & Wright, P.M. (2005). *Managing human assets in an uncertain world: Applying real options theory to HRM*. International Journal of Human Resource Management, 16(6), 929–948. http://refhub.elsevier.com/S1053-4822(15)30001-2/rf0070.

Bossidy, L., Burck, C., & Charan, R. (2011). *Building Block Three. Why the Right People Aren't in the Right Jobs*. Execution: The discipline of getting things done. Random House.

Brewster, C., Sparrow, P., & Vernon, G. (2011). International human resource management. London: CIPD.

Bryman, A., & Bell, E. (2011). Business research methods. New York: Oxford University Press.

Cappelli, P. (2011). *HR sourcing decisions and risk management*. Organizational Dynamics, 40(4), 310–316.

Christopher, D., & Tanwar, A. (2012). *Knowledge management in outsourcing environment: People empowering people*. The IUP. Journal of Knowledge Management, 10(2), 61–86.

CIPD (2005). Outsourcing human resources – a framework for decisions. London: CIPD.

CIPD (2009). HR outsourcing and the HR function Threat or opportunity? Survey Report June. London: CIPD.

Conklin, D. W. (2005). *Risks and rewards in HR business process outsourcing*. Long Range Planning, 38(6), 579–598.

Cooke, F. L., & Budhwar, P. (2009). *HR offshoring and outsourcing: Research issues for IHRM*. In P. Sparrow (Ed.). Handbook of international HR research: Integrating people, process, and context. London: Blackwell.

Cooke, F. L., Shen, J., & McBride, A. (2005). Outsourcing HR as a competitive strategy? A literature review and assessment of implications. Human Resource Management, 44(4), 413–432.

Cox, T. (1991). *The multicultural organization*. The Academy of Management Review, 5(2), 34–47.

Dionne, G. (2013). *Risk management: History, definition, and critique*. Risk Management and Insurance Review, 16(2), 147–166.

Dowling, P. J., Festing, M., & Engle, R. (2013). *International human resource management*. London: Thompson learning.

Elahi, E. (2013), *Risk management: the next source of competitive advantage*, Foresight, Vol. 15 No. 2, pp. 117–131. https://doi.org/10.1108/14636681311321121

Evans, P., Pucik, V., & Bjorkman, I. (2011). *The global challenge: Frameworks for international human resource management*. New York: McGraw Hill.

Franceschi-Bicchierai (2017), *Equifax Was Warned*, (https://www.vice.com/en/article/ne3bv7/equifax-breach-social-security-numbers-researcher-warning)

Galanaki, E., Bourantas, D., & Papalexandris, N. (2008). *A decision model for outsourcing training functions: Distinguishing between generic and firm-job-specific training content*. The International Journal of Human Resource Management, 19(12), 2332–2351.

Glaister, A. J. (2014). *HR outsourcing: The impact on HR role, competency development and relationships*. Human Resource Management Journal, 24(2), 211–226.

Glaser, B. G. (2013). *Staying open: The use of theoretical codes in GT*. The Grounded Theory Review, 12(1), 3–8.

Gospel, H., & Sako, M. (2010). *The unbundling of corporate functions: The evolution of shared services and outsourcing in human resource management*. Industrial and Corporate Change, 19(5), 1367–1396.

Grimshaw, D., & Miozzo, M. (2009). *New human resource management practices in knowledge-intensive business services firms: The case of outsourcing with staff transfer*. Human Relations. Studies Towards the Integration of the Social Sciences, 62(10), 1521–1550.

Hagigi, M., & Sivakumar, K. (2009). *Managing diverse risks: An integrative framework.* Journal of International Management, 15(3), 286–295. http://refhub.elsevier.com/S1053-4822(15)30001-2/rf0225

Hayes, J. (2014). *The theory and practice of change management.* New York: Palgrave MacMillan.

Hern, C., & Burke, R. J. (2007). *Outsourcing: Enhancing the experience of transitioned employees.* The Journal of Industrial Relations and Human Resources, 9(2), 29–48.

Hinton, M. (2003) Managing the Human Resource Risk. *Franchising World,* 2, 58–60.

Jaafari, A. (2001). *Management of risks, uncertainties, and opportunities on projects: Time for a fundamental shift.* International Journal of Project Management, 19(2). 89–101.

Jablonowski, M. (2006). *Precautionary risk management: Dealing with catastrophic loss potentials in business, the community and society.* Palgrave Macmillan.

Kessler, I., Coyle-Shapiro, J., & Purcell, J. (1999). *Outsourcing and the employee perspective.* Human Resource Management Journal, 9, 5–19.

Khanna, S., & New, J. S. (2005). *An HR planning model for outsourcing.* Human Resource Planning, 28(4), 37–43.

Klaas, B. S., McClendon, J., & Gainey, T. W. (2001). *Outsourcing HR: The impact of organisational characteristics.* Personnel Psychology, 52(1), 113–136. Management, 24(4), 511–531.

Lawler, E. E., & Boudreau, J. W. (2009). *What makes HR a strategic partner?* People and Strategy, 32(1), 14–22.

Lehtiranta, L. (2014), *Risk perceptions and approaches in multi-organizations: A research review 2000–2012.* International Journal of Project Management, 32(4), 640–653.

Lilly, J., Gray, D., & Virick, M. (2005). *Outsourcing the human resource function: Environmental and organizational characteristics that affect HR performance.* Journal of Business Strategies, 22(1), 55–73.

Martin, W. (2014). *The Problem with Using Personality Tests for Hiring.* Hiring and Recruitment. Harvard Business Review (https://hbr.org/2014/08/the-problem-with-using-personality-tests-for-hiring)

Nickson S. (2001). *The human resources balancing act.* Risk Management, 48(2), 25–29.

Oliver, C. (1992). *The antecedents of deinstitutionalization.* Organization Studies, 13(4), 563–588.

Osipova, E., & Eriksson, P.E. (2013). *Balancing control and flexibility in joint risk management: Lessons learned from two construction projects.* International Journal of Project Management, 31(3), 391–399.

Personnel Today (2015). *HR outsourcing: a sophisticated, innovative future?* Retrieved March 05, 2016, from https://www.personneltoday.com/hr/how-the-hr-outsourcing-market-became-more-sophisticated/.

Prouska, R., & Cooke, F. L. (2006). *Global trends and the challenges to the HR profession.* Human Factors, 1(2), 17–25.

Reichel, A., & Lazarova, M. (2013). *The effects of outsourcing and devolvement on the strategic position of HR departments.* Human Resource Management, 52(6), 923–946.

Rice, C., & Zegart, A. B. (2018). *Political risk: How businesses and organizations can anticipate global insecurity.* Twelve.

Ruth, D., Brush, T. H., & Ryu, W. (2015). *The use of information technology in the provision of HR compensation services and its effect on outsourcing and centralization.* Journal of Purchasing and Supply Management, 21, 25–37.

Saunders, M., Lewis, P., & Thornhill, A. (2009). *Research methods for business students.* Harlow: Pearson.

Shapiro, C. (2005). *Chapter Two: Are You Making Executive Sized-Mistakes?* Corporate Confidential: 50 Secrets Your Company Doesn't Want You to Know—and What to Do About Them. St. Martin's Griffin. New York.

Society for Human Resources Development. Employment Law. *Federal Statutes, Regulations and Guidance.* https://www.shrm.org/resourcesandtools/legal-and-compliance/employment-law/pages/federal-statutes-regulations-and-guidance.aspx

Silverman, D. (2007). *Doing qualitative research: A practical handbook.* SAGE Publications Limited.

Sparrow, P., Brewster, C., & Harris, H. (2004). *Globalizing human resource management.* London: Routledge.

Strauss, A., & Corbin, J. M. (2008). *Basics of qualitative research: Techniques and procedures for developing grounded theory.* SAGE Publications Limited.

Sturdy, A. (2004). *The adoption of management ideas and practices: Theoretical perspectives and possibilities.* Management Learning, 35(2), 155–179.

Truss, C., Gratton, L., Hope-Hailey, V., Stiles, P., & Zaleska, J. (2002). *Paying the piper: Choice and constraint in changing HR functional roles.* Human Resource Management Journal, 12(2), 39–63.

Ulrich, D. (1996). *The human resource champions: The next agenda for adding value and delivering results.* Boston: Harvard Business Review Press.

Ulrich, D. (2014). *Do not split HR – at least not Ram Charan's way.* Harvard Business Review. https://hbr.org/2014/07/do-not-split-hr-at-least-not-ram-charans-way

Ulrich, D., & Brockbank, W. (2009). *The HR business-partner model: Past learning and future challenges.* People and Strategy, 32(2), 5–7.

United States Department of Labor. *"Summary of the Major Laws of the Department of Labor."* https://www.dol.gov/general/aboutdol/majorlaws

United States Department of Labor. (December 2016). eLaws Advisors. Employment Law Guide, Other Workplace Standards: Lie Detector Tests. "Employee Polygraph Protection Act of 1988 * (EPPA)29 USC §2001 et seq.; 29 CFR Part 801)" https://webapps.dol.gov/elaws/elg/eppa.htm

Vernon, P., Brewster, C. (2000). European Trends in HR Outsourcing. United Kingdom: William M. Mercer.

Weick, K. E. (2012). *Organized sensemaking: A commentary on processes of interpretive work.* Human Relations; Studies Towards the Integration of the Social Sciences, 65 (1),

Williamson, O. E. (1979). *Transaction cost economics: The governance of contractual relations.* Journal of Law and Economics, 22(2), 233–261.

Williamson, O. E. (2007). Transaction cost economies: An introduction. Discussion Paper. www.economicsejournal.org/economics/discussionpapers/2007-3/count+&cd=4&hl=en&ct=clnk&gl=de

Wray, G. N. (1996). *The role of human resources in successful outsourcing.* Employment Relations Today, 23(1), 17–23.

Wright, P. M., Stewart, M., & Moore, O. A. (2011). *The 2011 CHRO challenge: Building organizational, functional, and personal talent.* Cornell Centre for Advanced Human Resource Studies.

Jeanne Sheehan

4 Beyond lip-service: Content clouds, 10-K filings, cyber risk and the electric grid

4.1 Introduction

In the spring of 2021, two major companies operating in the United States were hit by back-to-back ransomware attacks. The first attack shuttered Colonial Pipeline; one of the nations' largest oil pipelines which runs 5,500 miles from the Texas Gulf to New England and serves major portions of the eastern coast. The shutdown sparked widespread fears of a gas shortage and led to both an increase in oil prices and panic buying up and down the Atlantic seaboard (Uren, 2021).

Shortly after, JBS Foods – one of the world's largest meat suppliers – fell victim to cyber criminals who demanded a similarly exorbitant payout. The attack forced the company to temporarily halt production at its U.S. plants and led to both price increases and panic buying.

While the Colonial and JBS attacks received a good deal of media attention, these companies were not alone. Around the same time, the Metropolitan Transportation Authority (MTA), the nation's largest transit authority which serves the New York City metro area, suffered its third and most significant attack (Goldbaum et al., 2021). And earlier in the year, it was discovered that there was an unsuccessful attempt by cyber criminals to poison the water supply in Oldsmar, Florida. The Oldsmar attack came on the heels of another major cyber-attack – the SolarWinds hack – that was uncovered in December of the previous year. In that instance, hackers were able to intrude on and leverage software made by SolarWinds – which serves 18,000 customers – to infiltrate and compromise at least nine U.S. federal agencies and more than one hundred private sector companies, including some operating in the energy and electric sector (The SolarWinds, 2021).

What is notable about all these attacks is that each targeted key sectors of America's infrastructure – oil, food, transportation, water, energy, and electricity. In striking critical industries, these hackers showed not only how vulnerable the nations' infrastructure is but how disruptive and potentially deadly a successful attack might be. While the Colonial and JBS attacks were short-lived and only briefly disrupted some American's – more inconvenience than crisis; nevertheless, for many they portended much more deadly and consequential attacks to the nation's infrastructure. As Rick Tracy, Chief Security Officer and Product Manager at Telos Corporation said, "imagine a similar attack on the power grid in the dead of summer. How many heat-related deaths might occur in the hottest parts of the country (quoted in Walton, 2021)?"

It is this type of fear that, in the wake of these attacks, ultimately seemed to catch the attention of not just of the public and media, but those at the highest levels of government. Shortly after the pipeline attack, President Biden became the first president in American history to speak publicly about the threat of ransomware. At the same time, he announced the creation of a cyber-security task force within the Department of Justice (DOJ) to investigate the growing number of attacks, specifically focusing on the risks to America's critical infrastructure and national security.

The seriousness that these threats were being taken was reinforced by FBI Director Christopher Wray who compared the spate of cyber-attacks against the U.S. to the 9/11 terror attacks. He stated, "there are a lot of parallels, there's a lot of importance, and a lot of focus by us on disruption and prevention (Viswanatha et al, 2021)." He went on to confirm that the number of reported incidents to his agency show that ransomware attacks in the U.S. had tripled over the last year (Baker, 2021).[1]

There is no question that these incidents cast an unprecedented level of governmental, public, and media attention on cyber-attacks. To this extent they were, in the words of Tobias Whitney, vice president of Fortress Information Security, 'eye-opening.' A "wake-up call to the rest of the critical infrastructure industries," Whitney said, "to really make sure we are not just giving lip service to these issues (quoted in Miller, 2021)."

But are critical infrastructure industries taking these threats as seriously as Whitney and other experts suggest they should? And if so, how seriously? How does the threat of cyber-attack rank when compared with other critical risks these organizations are facing? This article sets out to provide answers to these questions by focusing on one of the most vulnerable infrastructure sectors – energy, and in particular, the electricity segment. First, however, it is important to look at where cyber threats fit within our traditional conception of 'political risk.'

4.2 Re-conceptualizing political risk to meet 21st century threats

In "Note on Political Risk Analysis" Heidi Deringer and Jennifer Wang (1997, 1) define political risk as a "broad concept" that refers "to the possibility that political decisions or events in a particular country will cause foreign investors there either to lose money or fail to capture their expected returns." They (1997, 1) go on to argue that it "arises from the vagaries of governmental action: from policy changes, leadership changes, nationalization of private property, expropriation of foreign holdings, civil strife, currency inconvertibility, or even war."

---

1 It is remains difficult to determine exactly how many cyber-attacks have taken place in the United States because there is no centralized agency that tracks them, consequently, many continue to go unreported (Shue, 2019).

Writing more than two decades later, Condoleezza Rice and Amy Zegart (2018a; 2018b) take issue with this type of definition, which they describe as outdated because of its limited conception of risk generators. In the 21st Century, they argue, no longer is the threat merely from governmental actors, but political actors more broadly defined. "Political risk," they (2018a, 3) write, "is essentially the probability that a political action will significantly affect business –whether positively or negatively." They go on to note that they (2018a, 3) chose the phrase 'political action,' as opposed to 'government action,' in an effort to "highlight the growing role of risk generators outside the usual places like capitals, army barracks, and party headquarters."

Rice et al's contributions in this area should be applauded. Not only do they recognize the need to expand risk generators beyond the traditional scope of governmental actors, but they also highlight something critical to this series, that the impact is not only potentially negative, but positive as well (Engemann et. al., 2021).

Despite this, as we examine it from the perspective of 21st century threats such as ransomware and cyber-attacks, their reconceptualization falls short in two areas. The first, is its tendency to focus on the motives of the actor. Rice et al. (2018a, 3) describes their re-definition as "radical" because the generator is no longer merely a government or governmental entity, but a political action coming from any actor who is politically motivated (i.e., documentarians, terrorists, etc.). Unfortunately, by linking the new definition to motive, they run into a conundrum long noted by post-structuralists and find themselves with a definition that is not as modern or all-encompassing as they claim.

In another realm, John Searle (1993) famously argued that 'truth' is independent of motive. In a similar vein, a more 'radical' conception of risk fit for the 21st Century should resist the tendency to find political risk only in cases where the motive of the actor is known. In short, political risk should be independent of the motives of the generator if only because motive is perennially difficult to know and often changing.

Consider, for instance, ransomware attacks of the type we witnessed with Colonial and JBS. Under Rice et al.'s (2018a) definition of risk, the motive of the hackers (i.e., the generators) would have to be 'political' for these attacks to qualify as creating 'political risk' for these organizations. Yet in the case of Colonial, that type of designation is difficult to assess. The U.S. government has attributed the attacks to a group called DarkSide believed to be operating in Eastern Europe, but not, as far as officials have acknowledged to date, connected with the Russian government or any governmental or political body. More importantly, shortly after the attack, DarkSide addressed the shutdown and explicitly noted that they were not politically motivated. As they wrote on their web site: "we are apolitical, we do not participate in geopolitics, do not need to tie us with a defined government and look for our motives. Our goal is to make money (quoted in Javers, 2021)." The veracity of this statement aside, it underscores how difficult it is to attribute motive, as well as how easy it would be to imagine information and evidence coming forward in the future which refutes their claims.

It is for this reason that as we think about ransomware attacks in particular, it makes sense to avoid tying the existence of political risk to the motives of the generator. In the DarkSide example, there are cases where an actor may be motivated by something other than politics or, alternatively, their motives may be unknown, unknowable, unclear, or mutable. Nevertheless, their actions can and do present political risk to an organization. The issues in these instances are not necessarily the motives of the actors, but rather the state of the political environment in which they are operating – in these cases, an atmosphere that allows them to engage in behavior which creates political risk for an organization.

Consider the example of a company that is interested in setting up a factory in a country where the risk of kidnapping is high. In this scenario, you can postulate the 'kidnappers' are not motivated by politics but rather by economic interest. Most risk analysts would agree that any company looking to establish business interests in that geographical area would accept a certain amount of political risk. In this case, the hypothetical political risk stems not from the motives of the kidnappers, but rather the state of governance (or lack thereof) on the ground in the country in which they are operating.

The same is true in the case of a ransomware attack. If we accept their claim as fact just for purposes of this hypothetical scenario, we can adopt the assumption that a group of hackers like DarkSide may not be politically motivated. That does not mean, however, that they did not pose a grave political risk to Colonial. Just as in the case of our hypothetical kidnappers, their motives were not a factor. Instead, it the fact that the company was operating in an environment that that did not contain the proper governmental safeguards to protect them from cyber-attack. In this case the lack of governance can come from a variety of arenas including the countries or areas in which the hackers are operating and the countries or areas in which the company is operating. This may also include the failure of cyber security experts both internal to the company and/or outsourced by them, to secure the space.

The second area where both Deringer et al.'s (1997) and Rice et al.'s (2018a; 2018b) work on conceptualization falls short, particularly in the context of this volume, is that they focus almost exclusively on risks to corporations and businesses versus other types of organizations such as public sector entities, quasi-public entities, and those operating in the non-profit arena. As we focus on critical infrastructure in the U.S., we find a host of different types of organizations impacted by cyber threats. Consider that the four cyber-attacks in early 2021 were against Colonial (a privately owned company), JBS (a publicly traded company), the MTA (a public transport agency), as well as an attempted hack of a water treatment facility in Pinellas County, Florida. These examples underscore the need to consider political risk today as something that impacts not just for-profit companies, but organizations of all types (i.e., profit, non-profit, public, quasi-public, private, etc.).

In order to accommodate both modern and emerging threats in the cyber realm as they pertain to different organizations, for purposes of this paper, political risk is re-defined as: the possibility that an action by a governmental or non-governmental entity, regardless of motive, will impact an organization (i.e., profit, non-profit, public, quasi-public, private, etc.), positively or negatively. While in many cases the motivation of the risk generator may be political, it does not have to be. In these latter cases, political risk arises because the governance systems in place are unable to secure and protect an organization and its assets.

4.3 Uniquely critical: Cyber attacks & the electrical sector

In 2021 Jacquelyn Bualo and the tech-review firm TechJury.net shared startling findings regarding the number of cyber-attacks that occurred globally throughout the previous year. For instance, they determined that ransomware attacks grew by 150%, while around the world 30,000 web sites were hacked daily. In addition:
– 64% of companies worldwide have experienced at least one form of a cyber-attack
– There were 20M breached records in just March 2021
– Every 39 seconds, there is a new attack somewhere on the web
– Approximately 24,000 malicious mobile apps are blocked daily on the internet

Amongst the many industries vulnerable to these growing attacks is the energy segment. This is why many industrialized nations, including the U.S., categorize energy as a critical infrastructure sector (for a complete list, see box below). According to Presidential Policy Directive 21 [PPD-21], critical sectors are defined as those whose "assets, systems, and networks . . . are considered so vital to the United States that their incapacitation or destruction would have a debilitating effect on security, national economic security, national public health, or safety or any combination thereof (16 Critical Infrastructure, NDA)."

16 critical infrastructure sectors in the U.S.[2]
1. Chemical Sector
2. Commercial Facilities Sector
3. Communications Sector
4. Critical Manufacturing Sector

---

2 Similarly, in its April 2021 "Annual Threat Assessment" the U.S. Office of the Director of Intelligence (ODNI) cautioned that countries like China have the capacity to "launch cyber-attacks that, at a minimum, can cause localized, temporary disruptions to critical infrastructure within the United States (Annual Threat, 2021; Miller 2021)."

5. Dams Sector
6. Defense Industrial Base Sector
7. Emergency Services Sector
8. Energy Sector (whereas sector includes electricity, oil, and natural gas segments)
9. Financial Services Sector
10. Food and Agriculture Sector
11. Government Facilities Sector
12. Healthcare and Public Health Sector
13. Information Technology Sector
14. Nuclear Reactors, Materials, and Waste Sector
15. Transportation Systems Sector
16. Water and Wastewater Systems Sector

The CISA's assessment is supported by the World Economic Foundation (WEF) who in their 2020 Global Risks Report listed cyber-attacks on critical infrastructure sectors, including energy, as the fifth top risk (Granados, 2020).

Unlike most other sectors, however, energy is not only described as vital but "uniquely critical" to the extent that it enables most of the other critical sectors (16 Critical Infrastructure, NDA). If power were disrupted for a long period of time over a large swath of the nation, it could have a cascading impact because almost all of the other critical systems would be negatively impacted including communications, financial, information technology, transportation, water, etc. This helps explain why the three segments that make up the energy sector – electricity, oil, and natural gas – are among the most frequent targets of and uniquely vulnerable to cyber-attacks. As Gib Sorebo et. al. (2020) write, cyber-attacks on critical infrastructure are always a serious threat, but particularly when it comes to the electricity sector because of the potential for "devastating cascading effects" which can result in "loss of life, economic costs, and industrial disruption, among other severe consequences."

This is not just supposition. In their study of cyber risk in the electric power grid, Steven Livingston et al. (2018) notes that the U.S. energy grid has become one of the three most targeted sectors for cyber intrusion. According to a 2016 report of incidents by sector, twenty percent of the reported attacks in the United States that year were against the energy sector (National Cyber Security, 2016). Speaking before a House Appropriations subcommittee in early 2018, then Energy Secretary Rick Perry placed the number of attempted attacks at "hundreds of thousands" per day (quoted in Siegel, 2018). The remark prompted a top Democrat on the Senate Energy Committee, Sen. Maria Cantwell (WA) to urge the federal government to do more to

---

3 Similarly, in its April 2021 "Annual Threat Assessment" the U.S. Office of the Director of Intelligence (ODNI) cautioned that countries like China have the capacity to "launch cyber-attacks that, at a minimum, can cause localized, temporary disruptions to critical infrastructure within the United States (Annual Threat, 2021; Miller 2021)."

protect the U.S. power grid. "Our energy infrastructure is under attack," Cantwell said. "it's under cyberattack and we need to do much more to protect it as a national critical asset (quoted in Siegel, 2018)."

Throughout the COVID-19 pandemic, the threat of cyber-attacks on critical infrastructure, particularly the electricity grid in the U.S. has only increased. As Manny Cancel, senior vice president of the North American Electricity Reliability Corporation (NERC) and CEO of the Electricity Information Sharing and Analysis Center (EUSAC) said, the sector saw an "unprecedented" increase in cyber threats during the pandemic (quoted in Miller, 2021). He attributed the increase to the fact that actors from nation states to cyber criminals were growing increasingly capable of launching such attacks, and that throughout the pandemic, an increasing number of employees in that sector were working from home (Miller, 2021). Cancel's assessment of the vulnerability of the sector was underscored by a General Accounting Office (GAO) report released in early 2021 which concluded that the:

> U.S. electricity grid's distribution systems – the parts of the grid that carry electricity to consumers – are becoming more vulnerable to cyberattacks, in part because of the introduction of and reliance on monitoring and control technologies (Electricity Grid, 2021).

The report went on to note that while the U.S. Department of Energy is working on the energy sector portion of the national cybersecurity strategy, it has focused its efforts on the grid's generation and transmission, as opposed its distribution systems. According to the GAO report, the "potential impacts from such attacks" is still "not well understood (Electricity Grid, 2021)."

This sector is not just increasingly under attack in the U.S., but around the world. A 2021 Cyber Threat Ranking Table from Hiscox, for instance, found that the energy sector in the United Kingdom was the most at risk of a cyber-incident (The Hiscox, 2021; Hurst, 2020). This comports with findings from other nations over the last several years. In the 2016 Threat Report by the Australian Cyber Security Centre (ACSC), the energy sector was identified as the area with the highest number of reported cyber incidents with 18 percent reported, as compared the next largest sector – banking and financial at 17 percent, followed by communications at 12 percent (Frewin, 2017).

As Table 4.1 shows, in the last decade, cyber-incidents impacting the energy sector have been reported world-wide including Australia, the European Union, Iran, Japan, Saudi Arabia, the Ukraine, United Kingdom, and the United States, just to name a few (Sorebo et al., 2020).

Perhaps the most well-reported of these were the two separate information technology [IT] and operational technology [OT] cyberattacks in the Ukraine. In December 2016, hackers infiltrated an electric transmission station north of Kiev and successfully blackened out about one-fifth of the capital's total power (Greenberg, 2017). This was the second such attack on the Ukraine's power grid. The first, that occurred a year earlier, caused power outages at three regional electric power distribution

Table 4.1: Sample of Cyber Incidents Impacting the Energy Sector Around the World (2009–2020).

2010	Iran	Stuxnet affects centrifuge control systems, causing malfunction, destruction and significant political consequences
2012	Saudi Arabia	Shamoon virus shut down 30,000 control systems, erasing data on hard drives and causing severe damage
2014	United States	Brute-force attack used to hack passwords on utility network
2015	Ukraine	Black Energy attack on Ukraine energy companies left 225,000 citizens without power
2017	European Union	Virtual wiretapping of unencrypted traffic from transmission operator in UK passing through routers in Northern Ireland and Wales
2017	Saudi Arabia	Trisis/Triton penetrated the safety systems of a petrochemical plant to sabotage operations and trigger an explosion
2019	United States	Firewall firmware vulnerabilities used to cause denial of service attacks, affecting utility control center
2020	European Union	Ransomware attack strikes large utility, supposedly stealing 10 TB of sensitive data, with a threat to expose it if not paid a ransom

Source: Adapted from Sorebo et al, 2020, p. 5, Figure 1; Livingston et al, 2018, p. 4

companies (Oblenergos) and impacted approximately one-quarter of a million customers who were left without power for hours in the middle of the winter (ICS Alert, 2016). Those attacks, which U.S. and other cyber security experts have attributed to Russia, were noteworthy because they "set an ominous precedent for the safety and security of power grids everywhere (Zetter 2016)." After the second attack, ESET Security Research Robert Lipovsky argued, "If this is not a wakeup call, I don't know what could be (quoted in Greenberg, 2017)."

As Lipovsky noted, the Ukrainian shutdowns showed the world just how vulnerable this sector is to actors with the skills to mount cyber-attacks (Greenberg, 2017). Tucker Bailey et. al., highlights three characteristics that help explain why the electrical power sector is uniquely vulnerable to cyber-threats. First, is the increase in the number and type of actors focused on mounting cyber-attacks against utilities for a variety of reasons. This includes, but is not limited to nation-states, organized criminals, hacktivists, and individual hackers. Second, the utilities "attack surface" is not only large but increasing as a result of their geographic and organizational complexity, as well as the "decentralized nature of many organizations' cybersecurity leadership (Bailey, 2020)." A fact that harkens back to the definition of political risk being intimately related to an absence or failure of governance. Finally, and not widely discussed, is the fact that this sector contains the rare interdependency between the physical and cyber infrastructure that leaves the organizations that control them particularly exposed (Bailey, 2020). These factors, coupled with the exposure during the pandemic noted by Cancel, and the increasing number of actors with the skills, interests and capabilities of launching these types of attacks, leave the electricity segment of the energy sector uniquely vulnerable.

4.4 Research design & method: Using content clouds to sample 10-K filings

Content Clouds as a Method of Exploratory Qualitative Data Analysis With this understanding of the increasing risk cyber-attacks pose to a sector that is defined as both uniquely vulnerable and critical, this study sets out to measure how seriously those who control the electricity segment in the U.S. take this threat. Where does it rank in comparison to other threats these organizations face? Do the people in charge of the companies that run the electric grid identify cyber-attacks as a serious threat to their core business practices as we are often led to believe?

In order to address these questions, this chapter relies on an unobtrusive method of exploratory qualitative data analysis and visualization via the creation of content clouds. Julie Cidell's (2010, 514) describes the use of content clouds as "a type of visualization that summarizes the contents of a document by depicting the words that appear most often in larger, darker type within the cloud." While Cidell's work is focused on geography, the use of this method as a form of qualitative data analysis makes sense across multiple disciplines because content clouds provide a useful way to summarize and compare information from a host of documents. Moreover, any material that can be examined using content analysis can be visualized through the generation of content clouds.

As Cidell (2010) notes, this approach is particularly useful when the research is exploratory and inductive. While there has been a good deal of research in the areas of cyber- attacks and cyber-risk, there has been significantly less examination when it comes to the specific questions at issue in this study. Given the amount of attention cyber threats have generated in the press of late, there is a gnawing supposition that those operating critical infrastructure sectors would take it seriously; but just how seriously and how it compares to other threats they face and other risks to their business operations is yet unknown. As a result, this inductive and exploratory approach is advisable in that it allows for investigation without expectation and hypothesis. Rather than presupposing answers to the research questions, this study begins at the bottom of the research circle with the data and based on the findings, induces an explanation or theory to make sense of the findings.

The web site FreeWordCloudGenerator.com was used to generate the content clouds for this study. It is one of a number of cloud generators, but chosen because it was free for noncommercial use. It removes (or allows for inclusion of) stop words, numbers, and special characters, while providing an ease of use for simple visualization projects. It allows for visualization of files larger than 500 kilobytes which was necessary given the size of the Risk sections of the 10-K filings for the companies included in this sample.

Content: 10-K Filings in the U.S. publicly traded companies are required by the Securities and Exchange Commission (SEC) to file 10-K reports.[4] These annual reports are designed to help keep investors informed of a company's financial performance, as well provide them with the time and information they need to make investment decisions. This legal requirement was initially part of the Securities Exchange Act of 1934 but has been amended over the years. In 2004, the SEC passed the "Final Rule" which gave corporations 75-days, as opposed to the original 90-days, after the end of the fiscal year to file their reports. This was the case for any company issuing shares available for public trade (Public Float) of at least $75 million; those with over $700 million in public float only have only 60-days to file.

A typical 10-K filing includes several sections that focus on an overview of the company's main business operations, products, and services, select financial data, management decisions and analysis, financial statements, supplementary data and most critical to this study, risk factors. This last section, generally included in SECTION 1A, was made mandatory by the SEC in the mid-2000s in order to ensure that investors and shareholders are aware of risks facing the company with the understanding that this was critical to making investment decisions. The SEC determined that if an investor is to take a risk and invest in a company, they are entitled to know all potential risks facing the organization in the near future.

Sample The risk portion (1A) of the last set of 10-K filings of a sample of electric companies in the U.S. was used in an effort to determine where cyber-attacks rank in the context of risks facing these organizations. In order to determine which companies would be included in the sample, MergentOnline.com was used. MergentOnline offers a good deal of data on companies and corporations across the world. As their web site notes, this includes "company financials, descriptions, history, property, subsidiaries officers and directors" among much else. Using Mergent's advanced search function, I was able to isolate active U.S. utility companies. By specifying the Industry Classification Benchmark (ICB) code 65101015, I was able to identify the sixty-nine (69) listed as "conventional electricity utilities." Based on this list, I sampled more than a quarter (26%) of the Risk sections (1A) of their latest 10K filings (February 2021, for the Fiscal Year ending December 31, 2020). These filings were found via either MergentOnline or the SEC's Edgar search engine (https://www.sec.gov/edgar/search/).

---

4 The U.S. is not unique in requiring this type of filing, other countries require similar type of information to be made publicly accessible as well. In the United Kingdom, for instance, since 1844 the Companies House has listed financial information. In Canada the System for Electronic Document Analysis and Retrieval (SEDAR) is used to ensure investors' awareness. Similar systems are used in countries worldwide, including Belgium, China, and Germany, among many others.

Table 4.2: Conventional Electricity Companies Sampled (U.S., Public, Active, 2020).

Company Name	SIC Code	Exchange	Ticker	Customers (M)	Employees	Revenue ($B)	Shareholders
AES Corp	4911	NYS	AES	2.5	8,200	10	3,771
Allete Inc	4931	NYS	ALE	185,000**	1,322	1	20,000
Alliant Energy Corp	4931	NMS	LNT	1	3,375	3	23,282
Connecticut Light & Power	4911	NBB	CNLTN	1.2	1,381	4	1
Consolidated Edison Co. NY	4931	N/A	N/A	3.4	12,477	11	N/A
Consumers Energy Co.	4931	NYS	CMSPRB	2	7,617	6	1
Dominion Energy Inc	4911	NYS	D	7	17,300	15	130,000
DTE Energy Co	4911	NYS	DTE	3.5	10,600	13	47,485
Edison Intl/Southern Cal Edison	4911	NYS	EIX	14	13,351	14	27,353
Entergy Corp	4911	NYS	ETR	2.7	13,400	11	22,817
Exelon Corp	4931	NMS	EXC	10	32,340	34	91,240
NextEra Energy/FPL	4911	NYS	NEE	5.6	14,000	17	16,080
PG&E Corp	4931	NYS	PCG	16	24,000	19	46,536
Public Service Enterprise Group Inc	4911	NYS	PEG	2.3	12,788	10	54,220
Southern Co.***	4911	NYS	SO	8.54	27,700	21	107,362
Tennessee Valley Authority	4911	NYS	TVC	10	9,989	10	N/A
Virginia Electric & Power	4911	NL	N/A	2.4	6,000	8	1
Xcel Energy	4931	NMS	XEL	5.8	11,367	12.3	52,689
				97.95	227,207	219.3	642,838

*All data expressed in these columns are approximations/estimations, rounded, and based on publicly available data & company filings

**in thousands

***Holding Company, holding company provides electric service to customers in 3 Southern states via is subsidiaries (Alabama Power Company, Georgia Power Company, and Mississippi Power Company, Co.)

Source: Compiled from information publicly available and accessible on MergentOnline

A complete list of the conventional electricity companies sampled for this study are included in Table 4.2. The sample includes some of the largest public and active electric utility companies in the U.S. as measured by revenue and number of customers, as well as a geographic cross-section.[5] In total, in 2020, the 18 companies sampled serve approximately 97.95 million customers, employed over a quarter of a million people, and generated roughly US$219B in revenue.

4.5 Findings

Do Cyber-Attacks Make the Risk Section? An Aggregated View. It is difficult to determine how seriously the largest electric companies in the U.S. are taking the threat of cyber-attack. One measure, may be the amount of money companies are spending, per year, on protection. Another example, reflected in this study, is how prominently the threat is featured in their 10-K filings in comparison to other risks. If these organizations are taking the threat as seriously as many experts today suggest they should, it stands to reason that it would be featured prominently in the Risk sections of their 10-K filings. In order to make this determination, the Risk (1A) section of the last 10-K filings (2021) of each of the companies sampled was examined and compiled into a content cloud.

Figure 4.1 shows the content cloud portrays the general pattern of what risks matter most to the sample of 10-K filers included in this study. The words that appeared most often in the risk portion of their 10-k filings are displayed in larger, darker type. In this instance, the top fifty (50) words are included.

In total, 5,389 distinct words were used in this portion of these filings. As Table 4.3 shows, the top ten terms used were: operations, financial, costs, energy, results, including, utility, business, facilities, gas. Across the filings, these terms were used between 534 and 954 times. As we continue further down the list to include the top-25 words used, the remainder include power, results, companies, customers, generation, impact, affect, ability, risks, operating, capital, regulatory, subject, nuclear, and condition.

Notably, as Figure 4.1 and Table 4.4 show, none of the terms associated with cyber threats, attacks, or ransomware made it into the top 50 of the most frequently used terms.

While cyber-risk related terms do appear, they do so with far less frequency and much further down the list than other words. As Tables 4.3 & 4.4 show, 'cyber' related terms not only failed to make the top 50 most-used terms, but they do not even make the top 150. 'Cyber' is the only term to crack the top 450 in fact, coming

---

5 The sample includes 9 of the 10 largest utility companies by revenue, 2014; as well as a sample of the leading electric utilities based on number of customers, 2019 (Leading Electric, 2021).

Figure 4.1: Content Cloud aggregated of Risk Section of 10-K Filings of 18 U.S. Electrical Companies.

Table 4.3: Most Frequently Used Words in Risk Sections of 10-K Filings Sampled.

Ranking (#)	Frequency (N)	Word
1	954	Operations
2	908	Financial
3	829	Costs
4	742	Energy
5	664	Results
6	604	Including
7	601	Utility
8	597	Business
9	553	Facilities
10	534	Gas
11	531	Power
12	521	Result
13	489	Companies
14	485	Customers
15	470	Generation
16	465	Impact
17	462	Affect
18	462	Ability
19	456	Risks
20	455	Operating
21	455	Capital
22	443	Regulatory
23	402	Subject
24	393	Nuclear
25	389	Condition

Table 4.4: Placement and Frequency of Cyber-Attack Related Words (and their variants) Used in Risk Sections of 10-K Filings Sampled.

Ranking (#)	Frequency (N)	Word
178	106	cyber
472	42	Cybersecurity
1449	9	Cyberattacks
1657	7	cyber-attacks
2351	4	Ransomware
2702	3	Cyberattack
3312	2	Cybercrime
3581	2	cyber-security

in at 178 on the list with 98 mentions across the aggregated filings. This was followed much later by 'cybersecurity' (and its variant, 'cyber-security') which are used 44 times (ranking 472 and 3581 respectively).

Much further down the list are 'Cyberattacks' (and its variants 'cyber-attacks' and 'cyberattack') which are used a total of 19 times. While ransomware attacks on utilities have become common place, as it pertains to risks faced by these electric companies, it was mentioned only 4 times in the context of Risk across all eighteen filings making it 2351 on the list. Likewise, the word 'cybercrime' was used only twice.[6]

A Similar Pattern at the Individual Level Figure 4.2 shows the content clouds for a sub-sample of five corporate filings mapped by approximate size (as measured by customer base). The general pattern of most frequently used words varies across the risk sections of these filings [see Table 4.5]. Despite this, there are two terms that appear in the top 10 of all five of these filings – 'financial' and 'operations'. This is followed by the term 'costs' which appears in the top 10 of three of the filings (PG&E, Southern, and Exelon). While not in the top-10, the term also ranks high in the other two filings, coming in the top-25 for TVA (ranking 22) and the top-20 for NextEra (ranking, 16).[7]

As in the case of the aggregated data filings, when examined individually, the sub-sample demonstrates little concern or discussion of cyber-threats. As Table 4.6 shows, the two most frequently used cyber-threat terms across the sub-sample were 'cyber' (used 27 times in total) and 'cyber-security' (used 15 times in aggregate).

---

6 Other key terms checked did not appear, for example the common 'distributed denial of service (s)' or 'ddos'.

7 If combined with the variant 'cost' in all cases, the frequency of usage increases a good deal. This is also true for the other words reflected as the data mapping software does not combine those in the calculation.

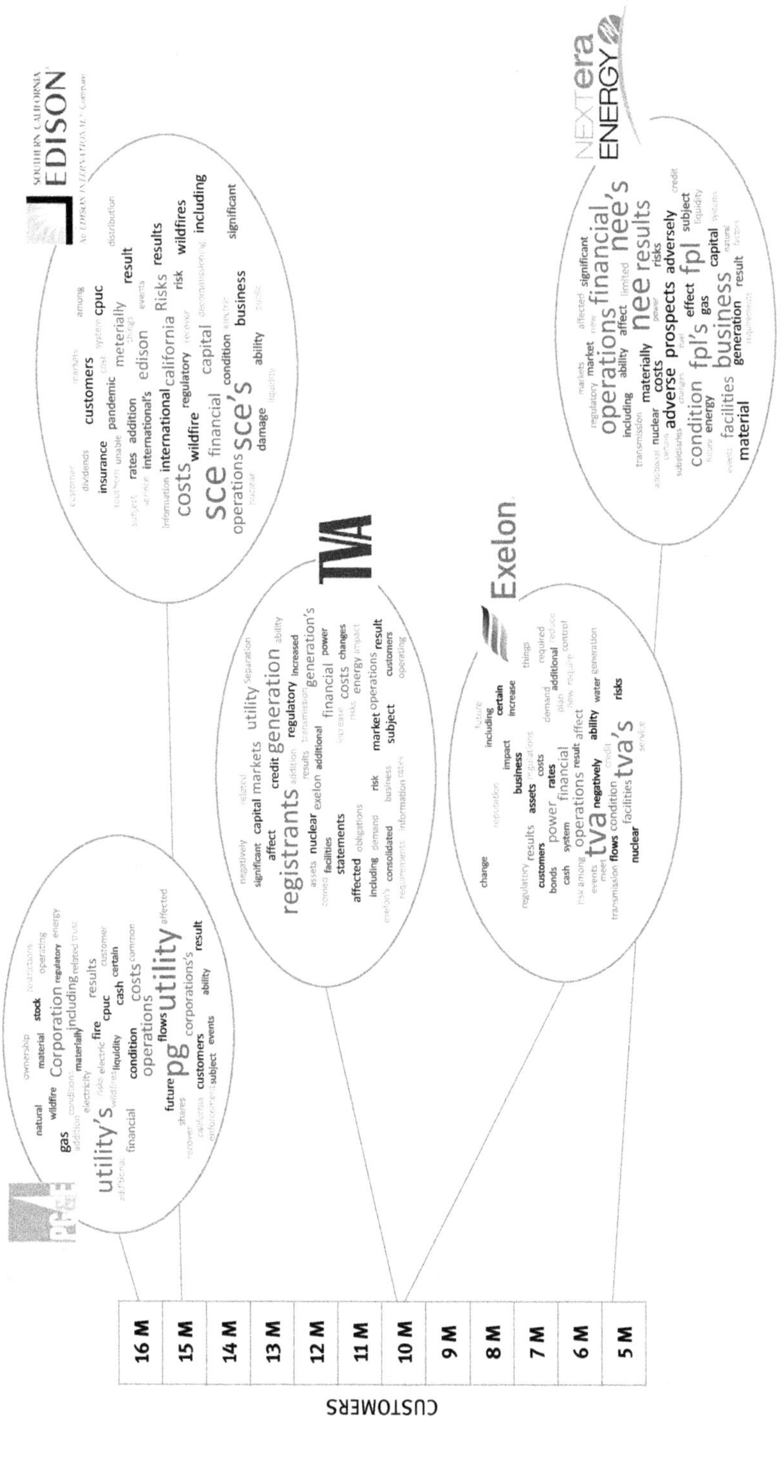

Figure 4.2: Content Clouds of Risk Section of 10-K Filings of a Sub-sample of Electrical Companies.

Table 4.5: Most Frequently Used Words in Risk Sections of a Sub-Sample of Electrical Companies.

Ranking (#)	PG&E	Southern	TVA	Exelon	NextEra
1	utility	Sce	tva	registrants	nee's
2	pg	sce's	tva's	generation	nee
3	utility's	*Costs*	operations	utility	fpl
4	corporation	Edison	power	**financial**	fpl's
5	*costs*	financial	financial	*costs*	financial
6	corporation's	Risks	results	generation's	**operations**
7	**financial**	**operations**	condition	exelon	business
8	**operations**	california	facilities	markets	results
9	including	materially	cash	energy	condition
10	results	capital	affect	**operations**	facilities

Table 4.6: Frequency (#) of Cyber-Attack Related Words (and variants) in Risk Sections of Sub-sample.

	cyber	cyberattack(s)/cyber-attack(s)	ransomware	cybercrime/ cyber-crime	cybersecurity
PG&E	9	2	0	0	0
Southern	6	0	1	0	6
TVA	8	0	0	0	4
Exelon	2	1	0	0	5
NextEra	2	4	0	0	0
Total	27	7	1	0	15

Interestingly, the term 'ransomware' only occurred once in this section of the risk filings sub-sampled (Southern California/Edison), while 'cybercrime' and its variants were not used at all.

Not Even Lip Service In the wake of the Colonial attack, many security experts said that at the very least, they hoped it served as a "wake-up call." As Tobias Whitney argued, it is more important than ever that those working in critical infrastructure sectors are taking these threats seriously and not just paying "lip service to these issues (quoted in Miller, 2021)."

The findings of this study do not allow us to conclude whether the electrical companies sampled are taking the threat seriously. They do, however, show that cyber threats are not prominently featured as a risk to their organizations in their most recent 10-K filings. To this extent, the findings suggest that the situation is even worse than Whitney may have imagined. Far from paying lip service to the issue, the electric companies hardly even mention the threat of cyber-attacks – at least not in the risk sections of their 10-K filings. Given how much these issues are in the public consciousness this year, the results are astounding.

If cyber threats and ransomware attacks are as existential a threat to the U.S. as we are often told, and if electrical sector is indeed both uniquely vulnerable and critical, one would hardly know it based on a reading of their latest 10-K filings. Few people would imagine that in 2021, the term ransomware would be mentioned only four times in the risk sections of the 10-K filings of the U.S.'s largest electrical companies sampled for purposes of this study. Instead of cyber and ransomware, the risks that are the focus of these companies' attention are financial, operations, and costs.

Inducing an Explanation for the Findings In the wake of the pipeline attack, President Biden established a DOJ cyber-security task force to investigate the growing number of attacks and in particular the risks posed to America's critical infrastructure. During a June 2021 news briefing, task force Deputy Director Lisa Monaco spoke in no uncertain terms about the danger cyber and ransomware threats present to those in critical infrastructure sectors:

> the threat of severe ransomware attacks pose a clear and present danger to your organization, to your company, to your customers, to your shareholders, and to your long-term success. So, pay attention now. Invest resources now. Failure to do so could be the difference between being secure now, or a victim later (quoted in "Justice Department," 2021).

This type of stark warning came just a few months after most of the electrical companies sampled in this study submitted their latest filings to the SEC. While it is difficult to know why these organizations did not highlight these risks, one possibility is that these filings reflected fiscal year 2020. Perhaps, the 2021 attacks have served as a wake-up call and future research may find that the filings next year differ substantially from their predecessors in this regard.

Another possibility is that the Risk sections of the 10-K are viewed as a place to focus on financial as opposed to other types of risks. It may be strange, particularly given the amount of ransom asked in the Colonial and JBS hacks, to imagine that these companies do not see the attacks as a potential financial risk. One reason for this may be the recent growth in cyber liability insurance. The research firm AdvisorSmith found that in 2020, U.S. businesses with cyber insurance paid an average annual premium of $1,485 (Pattison-Gordon, 2021). While more research needs to be done in this area, it may be that this type of investment substantially diminishes the amount of financial risk a company may sustain during an attack; to this extent, if they see the Risk section of the 10-K as a place to discuss major financial risks, premiums of this level, may be an indication as to why ransomware attacks are not seen as a major financial risk, particularly when compared with other threats facing these companies.[8]

---

8 It is also worth noting that some clarification may be in order from the SEC regarding what types of risks are appropriate for this section of the 10-K.

4.6 Conclusion

Traditional conceptions of political risk tended to focus on the risks to "for-profit" companies. An earlier section of this paper referenced the need to broaden this view to include public entities, quasi-public entities, public, and non-profit organizations. This is underscored in the case of cyber and ransomware attacks on electrical companies and other critical infrastructure in the U.S. As cyber insurance options continue to grow and more organizations take advantage of them, it is possible to imagine that while disruptive in the short term, these attacks do not pose as much risk to these organizations as other types of threats (i.e., regulation). Despite the recent media narrative, these organizations are cognizant of the major risks they are facing, and as disruptive as cyber-attacks may be, they do not rise to the top.

Viewed from another perspective, when focusing on the electrical companies, we are looking at the wrong organization to begin with. The industries most at risk when it comes to cyber and ransomware attacks on critical utilities are not private companies, but the public entities, governments, and quasi-governmental organizations. These entities are charged with serving and protecting the public's health, safety, and well-being, as well as the protecting state/nation from internal and external attack. These are their top priorities, whereas the primary responsibilities of the electrical companies differ substantially. And in the 21st Century, this goal cannot be accomplished sans a fully functioning grid. In their 2020 report on how best to deter attacks against the electrical grid, Anu Narayanan et al. underscored just how essential it is to U.S. national security that the grid be secure:

> The U.S. Department of Defense (DoD) increasingly relies on electric power to accomplish critical missions. As a result, ensuring that forces and facilities have access to a reliable supply of electric power is critical for mission assurance. However, DoD does not directly manage its supply of power; most of the electricity consumed by military installations in the continental United States comes from the commercial grid – a system that is largely outside of DoD control and increasingly vulnerable.

Defense and security are critical, but only one reason that disruptions of the grid presents such a serious threat to the public sector – from the U.S. federal government to all state, county and local governments. Imagine, the threat posed to the country by a massive, coordinated attack that took down the grid for a substantial period of time. During a 2015 hearing before the Senate Committee on Homeland Security, former Central Intelligence Agency Director James Woolsey explained the potential impact in stark terms. When asked by Chairman Ron Johnson (WI) to "describe what happens to society when the grid is down for [a] very long time (quoted in "Protecting" 2015)?" Woolsey said:

> There are essentially two estimates on how many people would die from hunger, from starvation, from lack of water, and from social disruption. One estimate is that within a year or so, two-thirds of the United States population would die. The other estimate is that within a year

or so, 90 percent of the U.S. population would die. We are talking about total devastation (quoted in "Protecting" 2015).

The ninety percent death estimate is based on a 2008 government study and the threat from this type of attack has only increased since that time. Based on this scenario, when we reference the political risk of cyber and ransomware attacks, it is important to look at not just the risk from the perspective of the electrical companies, but public sector organizations such as the federal government, the CIA, Homeland Security and the states agencies. It is these organizations – not the electrical companies themselves, whose top priority is to protect the health, safety, welfare, and well-being of citizens. Do the electrical companies face risk as a result of these attacks? Absolutely, but the degree of risk differs. The fact is that cyber and ransomware attacks may not be at the top of their priority list when it comes to risks being addressed. In the case of the public sector, the risks are more substantial.

In *Political Risk,* Rice et al (2018b, 192–195) provides a framework for understanding the differential nature of these risks. In their discussing of risk mitigation, the authors note that prioritization is key to mitigating risk. Since no organization can protect itself against all risks, mitigation requires understanding (a) what assets are most valuable (i.e., what are their priorities), (b) what assets are most vulnerable, and (c) focusing attention on the highest value assets that are most vulnerable. As Table 4.7 shows, this is the quadrant labeled 'top priority' where the most vulnerable and most valuable assets intersect.

Table 4.7: Rice et al Matrix of Value & Vulnerability.

	Lower Vulnerability	Higher Vulnerability
Lower Value	Low priority	Medium priority
Higher Value	Medium priority	**Top priority**

Source: Rice et al, 2018b, p. 195

If we apply this matrix to the electrical companies, it is possible that their understanding of the most valuable and vulnerable assets does not place cyber and ransomware attacks in the top priority quadrant. In the worst-case scenario, they can be insured to survive a widespread attack. The same cannot be said of the threat from extreme weather. The Texas blackout that occurred during the winter of 2021 was just another example in a long line of reminders that climate-driven, extreme weather is increasingly putting stress on the U.S. power system and much needs to be done to ensure that the power grid can withstand extreme weather events which will become more common place in the future. Several months later, in the wake of another summer of devastating wild fires on the West Coast, Pacific Gas and Electric Company, the largest natural gas and electric utility in the U.S. which serves 16 million people in Northern and Central California, announced that it was planning to bury 10,000 miles of power lines at an estimated cost of $20 billion (Blunt, 2021). As we reflect on what might be included in the utilities "high priority" quadrant, these types of concerns likely make the list.

In contrast, public entities such as the Department of Defense or City of New York, have very different priorities and vulnerabilities which, as a result, may make these types of attacks a key priority. In the case of the latter, public safety and health are among the city's top priorities and given how vulnerable the grid is to attacks and the devastating consequences that might ensue, these types of attacks become a top priority.

While this is a new area for exploration, future research might consider in future filings whether electrical companies and other utilities should begin to identify these types of attacks a more prominent feature? Alternatively, it would be important to gain a better understanding of the nature of the risks they feel are important to cover in these filings (i.e., merely financial for instance?) They should also do a comparison of the Value/Vulnerability Matrices for utility companies versus public/quasi-public sector organizations. If the political risk of cyber-attacks is greater for public versus private entities, then it is incumbent on the government to take the necessary steps to ensure that those commercial entities charged with managing our energy supply are regulated to a degree that they are required to pay more than just lip service to this threat.

References

"16 Critical Infrastructure Sectors." (NDA). *Cybersecurity and Infrastructure Security Agency (CISA). Identifying Critical Infrastructure During COVID-19 | CISA.*

"Annual Threat Assessment." (2021). "Annual Threat Assessment of the U.S. Intelligence Community." *Office of the Director of National Intelligence.* April 9, 2021. ATA-2021-Unclassified-Report.pdf (dni.gov)

Bailey, Tucker, Adam Maruyama and Daniel Wallance. (2020). "The energy-sector threat: How to address cybersecurity vulnerabilities." *McKinsey and Company.* November 3, 2020. The energy sector threat: How to address cybersecurity vulnerabilities | McKinsey.

Baker, Sinead. (2016). "FBI Director Christopher Wray compared the latest spate of ransomware attacks against the US to 9/11." *Yahoo News.* June 4, 2021. FBI Director Christopher Wray compared the latest spate of ransomware attacks against the US to 9/11 (yahoo.com)

Blunt, Katherine. (2021). "PG&E, in Reversal, to Bury Power Lines in Fire-Prone Areas." *Wall St. Journal.* July 21, 2021.

Bulao, Jacquelyn. (2021). "How Many Cyber Attacks Happen Per Day in 2021." *TechJury.* June 17, 2021. https://techjury.net/blog/how-many-cyber-attacks-per-day/

Cidell, Julie. (2010). "Content clouds as exploratory qualitative data analysis," *The Royal Geographical Society.* Vol. 42, No. 4. December 2010, pp. 514–523.

Deringer Heidi and Jennifer Wang. (1997). "Note on Political Risk Analysis." *Harvard Business School.* 9-798-022. September 17, 1997.

Electricity Grid. (2021). "Electricity Grid Cybersecurity: DOE Needs to Ensure Its Plans Fully Address Risks to Distribution Systems." *General Accounting Office (GAO)*, GAO-21-81. March 18, 2021. Electricity Grid Cybersecurity: DOE Needs to Ensure Its Plans Fully Address Risks to Distribution Systems (gao.gov)

Engemann, Kurt J. and Rory V. O'Connor, Ed. (2021). *Project Risk Management: Managing Software Development Risk*. Berlin: De Gruyter.

Frewin, Heath. (2017). "Protected Assets – Energy and Cyber Security." *Energy Insider*. Energy Networks Australia. February 23, 2017. Protected Assets – Energy and Cyber Security | Energy Networks Australia.

Goldbaum Christina and William K Rashbaum. (2021). "The M.T.A. Is Breached by Hackers as Cyber attacks Surge." *New York Times*. June 3, 2021. https://www.nytimes.com/2021/06/02/nyre gion/mta-cyber-attack.html

Granados, Emilio Franco. (2020). "The Global Risks Report." *Insight Report*, 15th Edition. World Economic Forum. WEF_Global_Risk_Report_2020.pdf (weforum.org)

Greenberg, Andy. (2017). "'Crash Override': The Malware That Took Down a Power Grid." *Wired*. June 12, 2017. Crash Override Malware Took Down Ukraine's Power Grid Last December | WIRED.

Hurst, Aaron. (2020). "Energy sector most at risk of cyber incidents, Hiscox analysis reveals." *Information Age*. October 14, 2020. Energy sector most at risk of cyber incidents, Hiscox analysis reveals (information-age.com)

ICS Alert (IR-ALERT-H-16-056-01). (2016). "Cyber-Attack Against Ukrainian Critical Infrastructure." February 25, 2016. *Cybersecurity & Infrastructure Security Agency* (CISA). Cyber-Attack Against Ukrainian Critical Infrastructure | CISA.

Javers, Eamon. (2021). "Here's the hacking group responsible for the Colonial Pipeline shutdown." *CNBC*. May 10, 2021. Hacking group DarkSide responsible for Colonial Pipeline shutdown (cnbc.com)

"Justice Department announces Seizure of Millions in Ransomware Paid to Colonial Pipeline Hackers." (2021). *Yahoo News*. June 7, 2021. https://news.yahoo.com/justice-department-an nounces-seizure-millions-160440847.html

"Leading Electric Utilities Based on the Number of Customers in the United States 2019." (2021). *Statista*. Largest U.S. utilities by number of customers 2019 | Statista.

Livingston, Steven, Suzanna Sanborn, Andrew Slaughter, and Paul Zonneveld. (2018). "Managing Cyber Risk in the Electric Power Sector." *Deloitte Insights*. DI_Managing-cyber-risk.pdf (deloitte.com)

Miller, Maggie. (2021). "Colonial Pipeline attack underscores US energy's vulnerability." *The Hill*. May 10, 2021. Colonial Pipeline attack underscores US energy's vulnerability | TheHill.

Narayanan, Anu, Jonathan William Welburn, Benjamin M. Miller, Sheng Tao Li, Aaron Clark-Ginsberg. (2020.) "Deterring Attacks Against the Power Grid." *Rand Corporation*.

National Cybersecurity and Communications Integration Center. (2016). FYI 2016 Incidents by Sector as reported in Livingston, Steven, Suzanna Sanborn, Andrew Slaughter, and Paul Zonneveld. (2018). "Managing Cyber Risk in the Electric Power Sector." *Deloitte Insights*, p. 2, fn. 4. DI_Managing-cyber-risk.pdf (deloitte.com)

Pattison-Gordon, Jule. (2021). "What Can Government Do as Cyber Insurance Costs Increase." *Government Technology*. July 14, 2021. What Can Government Do as Cyber Insurance Costs Increase? (govtech.com)

"Protecting the Electric Grid From the Potential Threats." (2015). Hearing Before the Committee on Homeland Security and Governmental Affairs, United States Senate, 114th Congress, S. Hrg. 114–483. July 22, 2015. U.S. Government Publishing Office. – PROTECTING THE ELECTRIC GRID FROM THE POTENTIAL THREATS OF SOLAR STORMS AND ELECTROMAGNETIC PULSE (govinfo.gov)

Rice, Condoleezza and Amy B. Zegart. (2018a). "Managing 21st Century Political Risk." *Harvard Business Review*. May–June 2018. https://hbr.org/2018/05/managing-21st-century-political-risk

Rice, Condoleezza and Amy B. Zegart. (2018b). *Political Risk: How Businesses and Organizations Can Anticipate Global Insecurity*. New York: Hachette Book Group.

Searle, John R. (1993). "Rationality and Reason. What is at Stake?" *Daedalus*. Fall 1993. 122, 4. Searle – Rationality and Realism, What Is at Stake | Copyright Law | Law (scribd.com)

Shue, Craig. (2019). "Should Cities Ever Pay Ransome to Hackers?" *Wall St. Journal*. September 17, 2019. https://www.wsj.com/articles/should-cities-ever-pay-ransom-to-hackers-11568772120

Siegel, Josh. (2018). "Rick Perry boasts new cybersecurity office can handle Russian targeting of US grid." Washington Examiner. March 20, 2018. Rick Perry boasts new cybersecurity office can handle Russian targeting of US grid | Washington Examiner.

Sorebo, Gib and Thomas Duffey. (2020). "Cyber Resilience in the Electricity Industry: Analysis and Recommendations on Regulatory Practices for the Public and Private Sectors." *World Economic Forum*. July 2020. WEF_Cyber_Resilience_in_the_Electricity_Ecosystem_Policy_makers_2020.pdf (weforum.org)

The Hiscox Cyber Readiness Report, 2021. (2021). *Hiscox*. The Hiscox Cyber Readiness Report 2021 | Hiscox UK.

The SolarWinds Cyber-Attack. (2021). "The SolarWinds Cyber-Attack: What You Need to Know." Executive Overview. *Center for Internet Security*. March 15, 2021. The SolarWinds Cyber-Attack: What You Need to Know (cisecurity.org)

Uren, Tom. (2021). "Colonial Pipeline Cyberattack Exposes Serious Vulnerabilities." *The Maritime Executive*. May 27, 2021. https://www.maritime-executive.com/editorials/colonial-pipeline-cyberattack-exposes-serious-vulnerabilities

Viswanatha, Aruna and Dustin Vulz. (2021). "FBI Director Compares Ransomware Challenge to 9/11." *Wall St. Journal*. June 4, 2021. https://www.wsj.com/articles/fbi-director-compares-ransomware-challenge-to-9-11-11622799003?mod=e2twp

Walton, Robert. (2021). "Colonial Pipeline hack highlights grid disruption risks even with IT-focused cyberattack, analysts say," *Utility Dive*. May 11, 2021. Colonial Pipeline hack highlights grid disruption risks even with IT-focused cyberattack, analysts say | Utility Dive.

Zetter, Kim. (2016). "Inside the Cunning, Unprecedented Hack of Ukraine's Power Grid." *Wired*. March 3, 2016. Inside the Cunning, Unprecedented Hack of Ukraine's Power Grid | WIRED.

Steven Michels

5 The risk of climate change and extreme weather

5.1 Introduction

The Earth's climate is changing again. The difference this time is that it is happening relatively quickly and that one species is mostly responsible for it. The prevailing consensus is that we need to keep the increase to 1.5 degrees Celsius or less, a figure we could pass early in the 2030s or even as soon as 2024 (McKibben, 2021). The coronavirus pandemic was largely beneficial insofar as it slowed economic activity and bought us some time. But the result could very well be negative since we have not been using that time wisely. We could also experience a post-pandemic boom that could push the planet past its breaking point.

No plans have been proposed much less implemented to meet this emergency – even the much-heralded Paris Agreement of 2016 falls short of what is needed and lacks any enforcement mechanism. Although we are uncertain about how significant the increase in global average temperatures will be and how that increase will manifest itself, it is very likely that the impact will hit poor and indigenous peoples soonest and strongest. And since we have already begun to see the effect of climate change in the form of extreme weather, the future we have been dreading is already here.

The reasons why we have gotten to this point are numerous but also obvious. Economists have been negligent to an astonishing degree in excluding environmental costs from their models and forecasts. Even though it favors the pursuit of wealth as a normative goal, the discipline is too focused on a narrow cost-benefit analysis, which has come to dominate environmental policymaking (Heinzerling, 2018). Relatedly, business leaders are too focused on profit margins to think about the long-term viability of their industries and seem to be banking on their ability to move assets to safer locations to shield themselves from any consequences.

Political institutions also incentivize short-term thinking over sustainability and stewardship. Politicians are rewarded at the ballot box for what they can deliver in the present, not for the future harms they can avoid. Climate is not simply a free-rider problem, with some benefiting from their inaction, or a tragedy of the commons, where commonly held lands are neglected. It is a distributive-conflict problem, in that large coalitions have emerged to oppose actions they fear will harm their interests (Meyer, 2021). In that sense, the outsized influenced that economic elites have in democratic politics has warped the accountability structure for elected officials.

Scientists too have, albeit inadvertently, aided to the problem, in that they have devoted a great deal of time and attention to predictive modeling, attempting to discern the exact magnitude of development on the climate, rather than building a broad consensus around information that is actionable. In so doing, they have set the standard for information and knowledge too high, which has permitted skepticism and confusion about the nature of the problem and what needs to be done about it (Sutton, 2019).

The pandemic, which exacerbated the problem of inequality, also revealed serious gaps in the infrastructure related to public health and social services and the willingness of elected officials to do what is necessary in favor of what is popular or perceived to be popular in response to a crisis. In the United States in particular, masks and vaccines have become as politicized as climate science has been in previous decades. The pandemic also pulled the curtain down on the prevailing wisdom for some of our inaction – namely, that the human brain was to a certain extent unable or unwilling to graph the magnitude of the problem. For the psychologist Daniel Kahneman, climate change is the perfect threat since it is distant and uncertain but requires clear and immediate sacrifices (Marshall, 2014). Yet the pandemic has shown that humans can also be incapable of appropriately responding to immediate and clear threats, even when the sacrifices are minimal and temporary. This is especially true in 'loose cultures', which tend to favor openness and individual creativity over order and coordination (Rose, 2021).

The numbers related to managing climate risk bear this out. A recent survey from Ipsos of people from thirty markets from around the world found that only four percent knew that the previous six years had been the hottest on record, with incorrect answers underestimating the impact of climate change. This is also true for strategies. The survey identified recycling as the most-mentioned individual-level action to combat climate change, with 59 percent of people identifying that as a top option. In fact, only 11 percent named having one fewer child (the most effective action) in their top three, while 17 percent named not having a car, and 21 percent named avoiding one long-distance air travel, the second and third most-effective measures. Only respondents in Belgium, Germany, the Netherlands, and Sweden were more likely than average to identify long-distance travel as an effective measure (Perils, 2021). Clearly, we need to get better at managing climate-related disasters and extreme weather events, but the public first needs to more fully comprehend the scope and magnitude of the issue.

The short answer to the question of climate is sustainable development. In its landmark 1987 report, Our Common Future, the World Commission on Environment and Development defined sustainable development as 'development that meets the needs of the present without compromising the ability of future generations to meet their own needs' (World Commission, 1987). As the Commission notes, we have not only the ability but also the responsibility to do what needs to be done. And we are quickly discovering that we have no other option. The more the risk has been ignored, the fewer options we will have and the more aggressive responses must become.

The purpose of this chapter is to explain how to manage risk related to climate change and extreme weather by transforming economic development, planning, and social policies. As Bahadur et al. put it, 'Transformation is a not a capacity but rather an approach to holistically and fundamentally build, reshape and enhance people's capacity to adapt to, anticipate and absorb shocks and stresses' (2015). While the risk can never be eliminated completely, it can be greatly reduced and much more must be done if we are to avoid the worst of its effects.

To organize possible strategies, we will follow Bahadur et al. (2015) and break down resilience of social systems into three types of responses – adaptive, anticipatory, and absorptive, capacity. Since how we categorize responses might vary according to community context, especially one facing an immediate threat, the categories are not mutually exclusive and indeed build on one another. Indeed, the categories are more complementary than hierarchical, with each community and country needing an appropriate combination of short-term responses and long-term planning and investment.

5.2 Adaptive capacity

Adaptive capacity is the extent to which social systems are altered to meet the various risks related to climate change and extreme weather, including making adjustments after events. It also involves actions designed to minimize the likelihood that hazards will occur and mitigating negative outcomes when they do. Government officials, for example, could use data related to changing rainfall patters to modify drainage systems. The same data could be used by farmers to change the crops they produce (Bahadur, et al. 2015). Moreover, adaption involves learning from repeated events to rebuild in a manner that is less vulnerable and more resilient (Manyena et al., 2011) to avoid getting trapped in a cycle of vulnerability (Becchetti and Castriota, 2011). This type of resilience requires deliberation and planning, especially after conditions change, and is more often and perhaps best practiced during non-emergencies.

One essential area of focus is the food system, which as currently constructed is unsustainable in several ways. The United Nations Food Programme estimates there are 931 million tons wasted ever year, with 61 percent of that resulting from households (Food Waste). If this waste were a country, it would rank third, behind China and the United States, in greenhouse gas emissions (Promoting Sustainable Lifestyles). In sum, about 8–10 percent of greenhouse gases are the consequence of wasted food (Mbow et al., 2019). One recent study found that the average person wastes a total of 727 calories per day, which is roughly 25 percent of the calories humans have available for consumption (Verma, et al., 2020). Perhaps the most staggering revelation from the study is that we are wasting more food than we used to – a 38.2 percent increase since 2003. Unsurprisingly, food waste is largely a product of affluence, which in part explains some of the trend, and unless this pattern changes, lesser developed countries will adopt the same wasteful practices as the more-developed parts of the world. Loss related to transportation is especially pronounced in developing countries and will require infrastructure to correct. But given that households are responsible for such a large portion of the loss, consumer awareness is also a key component in making the necessary corrections.

How we choose to eat also affects the climate. Perhaps the most impactful change will be a reduced reliance on animal-based protein, which is terribly inefficient. Although it is well-known issue, world-wide meat consumption has been increasing, especially in lesser-developed countries, which have come to see meat as an important measure of status or class. Many people are simply unwilling to go without meat, even when better alternatives exist and even though people in well-off countries continue to eat enough protein for daily requirements even after animal-based protein is removed from their diets. The loss of micronutrients is of greater concern than protein-deficiency for vegetarian diets and should be given more attention. We also need to educate and incentive against food and beverages like coffee, tea, soda, alcohol, and chocolate, which can require a significant amount of cropland but produce little or no nutritional content (Macdiarmid and Whybrow, 2019). To that end, we need to stop feeding food to our food be smarter about what we produce and consume.

Water is another essential area for adaptive resilience, some of which is related to food production. We need to increase the availability and reliability of water by developing new techniques for collection, storing, and dispensing through dams, farm ponds, and public tanks in agricultural areas (Sikka et al., 2017). Also essential to transforming water systems is drainage and more efficient irrigation systems (Naresh et al., 2017). This could include drip irrigation, hydroponic or other low-use systems, especially for urban agriculture.

The twenty-first century will very much be 'the century of cities' (Yigitcanlar and Inkinen, 2019), which in addition to agricultural areas, are also an important element of risk management and sustainable development. Cities are responsible for 78 percent of the world's energy use and 60 percent of greenhouse gases, even though they cover only 2 percent of the surface of the planet. By 2050 another 2.5 billion people will be living in cities, making city planning essential to any sustainable development strategy (Cities and Population, 2021).

Unfortunately, the concept of a 'smart city' has too infrequently placed environmental concerns at the forefront, focusing instead of matters of good governance, infrastructure modernization, and digital technologies, among other innovations. Songdo, South Korea is widely touted as the smartest city in the world, but, apart from social concerns, it has also been highly criticized for its environmental standards (Townsend, 2013). Although there are some exceptions (e.g., Vancouver, Copenhagen, Vienna), 'the environment is afforded a rather more marginal role in the smart city than one would expect from comparable sustainable city concepts and initiatives' (Joss, et al., 2019). To reduce the impact of cities on the climate, UN-Habitat, UNEP, the World Bank, and Cities Alliance have established the Joint Work Programme to bring environmental-conscious development more fully into city planning processes. In Hangzhou, China, for example, this led to a bike-sharing system, which significantly alleviated road traffic and improved air quality. And in Jamaica, this meant a communications initiative for residents. Moving forward, 'smart' must mean sustainable much more so than it has to this point.

Cities run the risk of congestion, pollution, and terrible inefficiencies with regard to how people get around. But areas with dense populations also bring with them the opportunity for great advancements. One recent study of Australia's four largest cities found that cities had policies and standards for access, but there was great variation among the goals and how that access was measured. And given the disparity, it was not possible to assess the relative effectiveness of each system. It is also essential that access is mapped to discern any spatial inequities, which will direct areas of future investment and development (Arundel, et al., 2017). The goal should be to increase the percent of the population with easy access to public transportation, especially for the elderly and people with disabilities.

A systems-level look at climate will also focus more extensively on the treatment of women and girls. For example, around three billion people use fires or kerosene, biomass, or coal stoves, which, in addition to climate change, are serious health hazards that disproportionately affect this part of the population. As the group responsible for a large portion of domestic work, women and girls also suffer from exposure to household pollution, resulting in 1.8 million premature deaths in 2016 (Progress, 2020). Yet, as deputy secretary-general of the UN, Amina J. Mohammed noted at the Climate and Development Ministerial Meeting in March 2021, women and girls, who make up 80 percent of those who are displaced by climate disasters, are often shut out from the processes that could prevent future crises. Giving proper attention to the education and treatment of women, in addition to being the just and equitable thing to do, has important spillover effects in terms of adaptive capacity.

Some have suggested a carbon-pricing solution to alter the current incentive structure and make the changes necessary to eliminate the severest of consequences related to the climate. But as Rosenbloom et al. (2020) detail, the focus should be on transforming the system, not correcting for a market inefficiency. Moreover, the urgency of the situation demands rapid progress, which the rigidity of current economic structures make exceedingly difficult. There is also the political question of how such a regime can be implemented in a manner that is effective. To that end, Rosenbloom and his coauthors suggest a 'sustainability transition policy' as a more viable alternative. The focus here is not on the market, but on technical and sociological solutions related to energy, inequity, food, and industry. Carbon pricing might be part of the mix, but a transition policy is a comprehensive solution that is more focused on replacing inefficient technologies and infrastructure, increased support for innovation, reforming planning processed and the rules of the market, to create new social norms and practices. As a result, this approach would be able to quickly reduce emissions, transform systems in a fundamental way, develop responses that are context appropriate, and navigate sometimes-murky political waters.

In her speech at the Ministerial Meeting, Mohammed also observed that, although resilience and adaptation as a 'moral, economic and social imperative', only one fifth of climate finance is dedicated to it. She went on to offer five practical actions to address the climate emergency, which she wanted to see put in place by the end of the year: (1) a doubling of the public finance devoted to climate action from 2021–2025 and also a 50 percent increase from development banks; (2) more efficient and simpler access to climate support; (3) an increase in existing disaster-related financial instruments, in addition to new ones designed to increase resilience; (4) developing countries must have access to the tools and instruments they will need to incorporate climate risk management into planning and other processes; and (5) greater support for local and regional adaptation projects in the most vulnerable locations (Mohammed, 2021).

Put most simply, development that is not sustainable is not really development. Progressives and environmentalists have focused too much on the negative risk, without sufficient attention to positive risk. Indeed, most mitigation efforts are also goods unto themselves. It is not just that we are avoiding negative consequences, but getting development and energy right means the economy is becoming more sustainable, and we would also get to enjoy the benefits of cleaner, healthier, and more equitable living as a result.

5.3 Anticipatory capacity

Unlike adaptive capacity, which focuses on ever-changing risks and long-term planning, anticipatory capacity deals with specific and more immediate threats. This form of resiliency involves planning and preparedness to predict and minimize the impact of specific hazards related to climate change and extreme weather. This is also contrasted with absorptive capacity and the reactive behaviors that occur after an event (Bahadur, et al. 2015). The goal is to protect lives and limit the social, economic, and physical consequences of weather events.

Anticipatory capacity, for example, could involve using early-warning systems for droughts or cyclones or geospatial data for preemptive measures to reduce the impact of disturbances (Fankhauser et al., 1999). This would include emergency planning and preparedness exercises, for example moving goods and services or putting in place or plans to assist the most vulnerable in the population before such events (Kellett and Peters, 2014). In the case of flood risk, this could involve making public evacuation routes and sharing flood management plans that include responsibilities for designated individuals (Asian Development Bank, 2009).

Increasing temperatures, the change in precipitation patterns, and the increase of extreme events related to climate change already begun to affect food security, especially in parts of the Mediterranean that have seen warming and drying. At the same time, harvest yields in higher latitudes have seen an increase in crop yield in recent decades (Mbow et al., 2019). Even where availability is not affected, prices will almost certainly increase. To prepare, agriculture practices need to improve erosion control and increase organic matter in soil, better land management, and genetic modifications for drought and heat. Food systems should also be diversified to include integrated production and a more heterogeneous diet.

Many risks related to climate are overlapping, especially in food and water, which can require bolder interventions but can also limit anticipatory planning options. This is especially true given the estimates surrounding food production, which will need to increase by about 50 percent by 2050 to meet the growing population (The Future of Food and Agriculture, 2018). As a remedy, some have pointed to 'sustainable intensification' that is, using technology and new approaches to increase the productive capacity of agricultural areas. Some techniques have the added benefit of carbon sequestration (Jat el al., 2016). While not prescriptive with regard to the particular innovation, it does require that an ecosystem is preserved and that all aspects of food production are sustainable. Governments needing farmers to adopt agroecological practices should also make available low-cost loans or micro financing, insurance, or contingency funds (Mbow et al., 2019).

Migration and conflict are other specific threats, which is often related to food insecurity. We have already seen an uptick in international migration (International Migration Outlook, 2017). Changing patterns of precipitation has already been linked to food security in eight countries (Warner et al., 2012) and migration, permanent and seasonal, has already been linked to droughts and land degradation (Gray, 2011). Floods and droughts can affect the availability of food and water, which can cause families to flee a region. But becoming displaced is itself a cause of food insecurity, especially when migration-related conflict occurs. This too disproportionately affects the poor, in particular women and children. Already fractured regions, like Central Asia and North and Central Africa, are especially vulnerable (Buhaug, 2016).

Just as women and girls have a strong role to play in absorptive capacity and the creation of food infrastructure, food insecurity will also disproportionately affect poorer communities and will disproportionately affect women, another reason why gender equity needs to be at the forefront of any risk management plan. Women, not surprisingly, are less likely to have access to land and other essential elements of food production (Thompson, 2018). Women are also more likely to be affected by spikes in prices, especially in regions where cultural norms expect women to reduce consumption when other family members are in need (Vellakkal et al., 2015). Women need to be at the table to set the standards for what sustainable development and food security looks like.

Many anticipatory activities have additional positive risks. Irrigation ditches created to withstand storm surges, for instance, can also increase farm production and reduce deforestation and soil erosion (Tanner et. al., 2015). More generally, these activities have the added benefit of increasing a community's independence and ability to coordinate it activities. Moreover, climate change and extreme weather can affect the quality and the quantity of food available for consumption, especially staple crops, which is a serious concern for lesser-developed regions. Importing food from far away means that communities are too reliant on certain sources, which can be detrimental in the wake of a weather emergency, whereas eating locally grown food reduces the environmental cost of transporting food long distances. This is especially true in areas that have insufficient transportation infrastructure. This is especially true in areas that have insufficient transportation infrastructure.

To help us to better determine where our attention and investments should be and prioritize our action plans, we also need better data. For example, the 17 Sustainable Development Goals (SDG), established by the United Nations' Department of Economic and Social Affairs in 2015, outlines the need for developed and developing countries to partner in a comprehensive plan to end poverty and increase economic growth, while protecting the environment and addressing climate change. Yet the related SDG indicators outline an action plan for cities focused on sustainable development and health, many of which are inconsistent with the SDGs and are insufficiently focused on the structural and policies changes required to bring about the stated outcomes.

Similarly, a framework set by UN Habitat included indicators related to interventionist policies but failed to consider important health indicators (Giles-Corti, Lowe, and Arundel, 2020). Plans must include not only comprehensive goals, but adequate tracking of outcomes. As Mohammed (2021) puts it, 'Risk information is the critical first step for risk reduction, transfer and management'. At the same time, planners and public officials need to be mindful when gathering and analyzing the data needed to build or renovate infrastructure and related practices that they are modest in their standards. They should not, for instance, make the same mistake as many climate scientists have made in demanding and working toward perfect knowledge (Sutton, 2019). Data will always be incomplete and imprecise, but at some point it needs to be actionable.

Relatedly, there also needs to be more integrated studies related to the nexus of food, energy, and water that would focus on local and regional monitoring and modeling (Van Gaelen et al., 2017) and public and private partnerships, especially among industry, government, and the academy to gather data and form policy (Scanlon et al., 2017). Such an approach would need to be founded on the notion that demand for resources could still be greater than what sustainable methods can produce (Benton et al., 2018).

If addressing the issues of food and water is foremost a problem for science and technology, migration and conflict require multilateral diplomatic and economic solutions, if only to protect and support for the millions who will find themselves needing to flee their homes to survive. Both will require a substantial increase in financial support and collaboration and will include additional political risks.

5.4 Absorptive capacity

Building anticipatory capacity is largely a product of adaptive capacity falling short. If we had done what needed to be done in the 1970s and 1980s, we would not need to speak about anticipatory capacity or absorptive capacity, except in the case of natural disasters and accidents. Similarly, the more our anticipatory measures fall short, the more we will require reactive and costly absorptive measures. In that sense, we will come to rely more and more on what should be our last line of defense against climate change and extreme weather events.

Unlike anticipatory capacity, which deals with preparedness, absorptive capacity refers to the period during and after disasters and weather events (Bahadur, et al., 2015). The most visible form of resilience, it focuses on the ability of communities to use existing resources and skills to effectively manage the impact of such events. The goal here is to increase the ability of social and economic systems to serve as a buffer and to withstand weather disturbances.

In practice, this means deploying tangible and intangible resources to help communities survive and preserve their quality of life. Financial resources, which are essential to maintaining essential functions and rebuilding infrastructure in the aftermath of an event, are especially useful. This can take many forms, including governments having in place social programs or issuing insurance payments. These mechanisms are most effective when preset triggers have been put in place to release collective loans and other savings programs (Bastagli and Harman, 2015). On the private side, donor networks, especially international networks and other support services, are essential in times of crises.

We will need large-scale financial incentives build resilience through urban planning, architecture, forest management, seawalls, and other projects that increase absorptive capacity, rather than just trying to make the future less bad. We need to think beyond tax breaks to more psychological or emotional incentives – guilt can work, but pride would be better – that can be part of our everyday lives and might have more of an impact on some people (Met, 2021). Half-measures designed to limit the impact on the environment need to give way to measures designed to build resilience for the more-distant future.

The financial costs of disasters and weather events on households especially impacts children (Becchetti and Castriota, 2011), so having created mechanisms for easy credit will ease the impact of families and children when the stresses and shocks arrive. Micro-credit and other forms of disaster relief are valuable tools that can help with absorptive capacity (Doocy et al., 2005). Diversity in assets also increases a community's resilience. Business leaders will need to look past the profit motive and immediate self-interest and do what the emergency requires.

This will also be a test of the integrity and competence and responsiveness of public officials. Since the market is not made for crises, governments and other relief agencies need to monitor the disbursement of funds to protect against corruption, theft, and price gouging. As we witnessed time and time again with the COVID-19 pandemic, elected officials are quick to shirk their responsibility and good sense when their leadership is met with resistance. We have also seen instances where that resistance is more than just rhetorical, with the attempted kidnapping of the governor of Michigan, in response to her aggressive but sensible management of the health crisis. To be effective, public officials need to rely on and defer to scientists and public health officials to assess the scope of the situation and determine the best path forward, especially when it is unpopular.

The lack of absorptive capacity can have long-term implications for a community's ability for development, including anticipatory or adaptive planning. From a risk management perspective, absorptive capacity is the easiest to estimate because the extent of the risk is mostly known. On the other hand, since the crisis has already come, it is too late to initiate any preventative or mitigation measures. The goal should be to become resilient without the need of a disaster.

What is more, building back better cannot mean building back the same, regardless of the strong cultural and political incentives to do so. Rebuilding is an opportunity for more sustainability, not an excuse for repeating the same mistakes. If we do not sufficiently attend to matters of adaptive capacity, the more we will find ourselves lurching from one crisis to the next, always reacting and never doing what is needed to develop in a way that provides for and prepares future generations.

5.5 Conclusion

The impact of human development and behavior is more than merely a matter of quality of life, although that will be readily apparent. We are running the risk of fundamentally altering the living patterns of large parts of the planet and displacing millions, especially the poor and ingenious peoples. There is also likely to be an increase in political strife and violence, as states vie for territory and resources.

Although the situation is serious, all is not lost. It is a risk we are capable of managing, even if we are decades behind. Perhaps the most important thing we can do is to stop focusing on the costs of whatever adaptive measures we deploy or consider. Resilience can be costly, but the cost of doing nothing is far greater. A recent study of sea-levels and flood maps showed that $8 billion of the $70 billion total cost from 2012's Hurricane Sandy, which walloped the East Coast of the United States, could be attributed to human impact (Strauss, et al. 2021). Similar results were found related to the 2019–2020 brush fires in Australia, which were exacerbated by climate change by 30 percent or more (Oldenborgh, et al., 2021). There is much more of this to come.

The problem, as we have discussed, is that market capitalism and popular governments include strong incentives for short-term thinking. One significant obstacle to building resilience has been the capitalist ideology and rhetoric surrounding regulation and green planning as somehow at odds with development. As Naomi Klein details in her 2014 book *This Changes Everything*, we need to stop pitting the environment against the economy in a zero-sum game. Sustainability and resilience needs to be the foundation for any development strategy.

At the same time, we need to operate on a scale that matches the problem. The time for incrementalism and kicking the can down the road has long passed. Meeting the moment will require a culture shift in how people, especially people in developed states, imagine their relationship with the natural world. We cannot be so focused on material goods, imagined conveniences, and petty pleasures that we are unwilling to take the actions necessary to avoid climate catastrophe. For too long, many of our conclusions about climate action have fallen into two camps: actions that are too big and therefore impossible or actions that are too small and therefore insignificant. It is true that any one thing will not be enough, but that does not mean that small actions should be disregarded.

Large-scale mobilization is required to elect climate-aware officials and hold them accountable for the laws and the policies they put in place. Democratic institutions must be strong and vigilant enough to control the market and make sure not only that future development is sustainable but that wasteful activities are either ended or drastically scaled back. If a distributive-conflict problem is at the heart of climate inaction, then larger coalitions will need to be created on the other side to tip the balance from short-termism and extractivism in favor of resilience and sustainability. In policy terms, we need a Green New Deal on a global scale.

We also need to be aware of how political borders are either irrelevant or harmful to resilience strategies. Economic actors have used the limits of political reach to exploit natural resources and maximize profits, but the climate does not recognize interstate boundaries. We need governments to act through alliances and international organizations vehicles for risk management and collective action.

Moreover, getting on the right side of climate should be a huge incentive for business leaders who are not motivated by wanting to do the right thing but should want to future-proof their bottom line. Getting out in front will mean they can avoid the most extreme government regulation when or if it happens. Unsustainable businesses will have the pressure of not being able to recruit and retain the best talent. There is the added incentive of avoiding boycotts and public backlash, especially with high-profile accidents.

We should also be aware of the magnifier effects of equality. The positive risks associated with a sustainable approach to development are consistent with the values of humanitarian and political liberalism. Yet women and girls, as we have seen, suffer the most in the wake of any particular crisis, receive the least attention and support in preparation for climate-related threats, and yet are also the least equipped to influence the direction of sustainable development activities. Getting right with how we treat marginalized and exploited populations, including the poor and indigenous peoples of the world, is the single most important element of managing the risk related to climate change and extreme weather. It is not a stretch to say that if we can do right by them, we can do right by the planet.

Education is an essential precondition for any nation or community to support the regulatory regimes and financial policies required to build adaptive capacity (Bengtsson, Barakat, and Muttarak, 2018). Worldviews matter. The vision of the future might not be precise, but it should focus the public on how climate change might affect them and their families. It should also include what each person could be doing, even when those actions could be considered to be a sacrifice.

'The main challenge', says UN Environment Programme's Tim Christophersen, 'is the lack of human imagination; our inability to see a different future because we're staring down this dystopian path of pandemic, climate change, biodiversity loss. But the collective awareness that we are in this together is a huge opportunity' (Rose, 2021). Too often our creativity is used for innovations that are more wasteful. Think of difficult-to-recycle K-cups that fuel individual coffee makers; synthetic clothing, which releases plastic every time it is washed; and the packaging from processed foods (Good, 2021).

Even so, our plans and the messaging related to them need to be positive. 'We're not going to change humanity by saying, "Everything has to be less"', says Ties Van der Hoeven, the co-founder of the Weather Makers, a firm of Dutch engineers who are implementing an eco-restoration plan for the Sinai peninsula. 'No, we have to do *more* of the *good* things'.

References

Arundel, J., et al. (2017). Creating liveable cities in Australia: Mapping urban policy implementation and evidence-based national liveability indicators. Centre for Urban Research, RMIT University Melbourne.

Asian Development Bank (2009). Understanding and Responding to Climate Change in Developing Asia. Manila, ADB.

Bahadur, A.V., et al. (2015). The 3As: Tracking Resilience across BRACED. BRACED Knowledge Manager Working Paper. ODI, London.

Bastagli, F., Harman, L. (2015). The role of index-based triggers in social protection shock response. London: Overseas Development Institute.

Becchetti, L., Castriota, S. (2011). Does microfinance work as a recovery tool after disasters? Evidence from the 2004 tsunami. World Development. 39(6),898–912.

Bengtsson, S.E.L., Barakat, B., and Muttarak, R. (2018). The role of education in enabling the sustainable development agenda. New York: Routledge.

Benton, T.G., et al. (2018). Designing sustainable landuse in a 1.5 °C world: the complexities of projecting multiple ecosystem services from land. Current Opinion in Environmental Sustainability (31): 88–95.

Buhaug, H. (2016). Climate change and conflict: Taking stock. Peace Econ. Peace Sci. Public Policy, 22, 331–338.

Carpenter, S., Walker, B., Anderies, J.M., and Abel, N. (2001). From Metaphor to Measurement: Resilience of What to What? Ecosystems. 4(8),765–81.

Cities and Pollution. (2021). United Nations, https://www.un.org/en/climatechange/climate-solutions/cities-pollution, Accessed 4 April 2021.

Doocy, S., Teferra, S., Norell, D., Burnham, G. (2005). Credit program outcomes: coping capacity and nutritional status in the food insecure context of Ethiopia. Social Science & Medicine. 60(10): 2371–2382.

Fankhauser, S., Smith, J.B., Tol, R.S.J. (1999). Weathering climate change: some simple rules to guide adaptation decisions. Ecological Economics. 30(1),67–78.

Food Waste Index Report. (2021). United Nations Food Programme.

The Future of Food and Agriculture: Alternative Pathways to 2050. (2018). Food and Agriculture Organization of the United Nations, Rome, Italy.

Van Gaelen, H., et al. (2017). Bridging rigorous assessment of water availability from field to catchment scale with a parsimonious agro-hydrological model. Environmental Modeling and Software (94): 140–156.

Gelfand, M.J., et al. (2021). The relationship between cultural tightness–looseness and COVID-19 cases and deaths: a global analysis. The Lancet Planetary Health. 5/3, March 1.

Giles-Corti, B., Lowe, M., and Arundel, J. (2020). Achieving the SDGs: Evaluating indicators to be used to benchmark and monitor progress towards creating healthy and sustainable cities. Health Policy 124: 581–590.

Global report on urban health: equitable healthier cities for sustainable development. (2016). World Health Organization.

Good, K. (2021). 5 Convenient Inventions That are Killing the Planet. OneGreenPlanetcom. Accessed 8 May 2021.

Gray, C.L., (2011). Soil quality and human migration in Kenya and Uganda. Glob. Environ. Chang., 21, 421–430.

Heinzerling, L. (2018). Cost-nothing Analysis: Environmental Ethics in the Age of Trump. Colorado Natural Resources, Energy, and Environmental Law Review. Vol 30:2.

International Migration Outlook. (2017). Organisation for Economic Co-operation and Development. OECD Publishing, Paris, France.

Jat, M.L., et al., (2016). Climate change and agriculture: Adaptation strategies and mitigation opportunities for food security in South Asia and Latin America. Advances in Agronomy, Vol. 137 of, 127–235.

Joss, S.; et al. (2019). The smart city as global discourse: Storylines and critical junctures across 27 cities. J. Urban Technol 26.

Kellett, J., Peters, K. (2014). Dare to prepare: taking risk seriously. London: Overseas Development Institute.

Klein, N. (2014). This Changes Everything: Capitalism versus the Climate. Simon & Schuster. New York, NY.

Levine, S. Ludi, E., Jones, L. (2011). Rethinking Support for Adaptive Capacity to Climate Change. London: ODI.

McKibben, B. (2021). How 1.5 Degrees Became the Key to Climate Progress. The New Yorker, April 21.

Macdiarmid, J.I, and Whybrow, S. (2019). Nutrition from a climate change perspective. Proceedings of the Nutrition Society 78, 380–387.

Manyena et al. (2011). Disaster resilience: a bounce back or bounce forward ability? Local Environment: The International Journal of Justice and Sustainability. 16(5),pp.417–424.

Marshall, G. (2014). Understand faulty thinking to tackle climate change. New Scientist. August 13.

Mbow, C., et al. (2019). Food Security. In: Climate Change and Land: an IPCC special report on climate change, desertification, land degradation, sustainable land management, food security, and greenhouse gas fluxes in terrestrial ecosystems.

Met, A. (2021). It's time to get creative with climate incentives. Quartz. April 20.

Meyer, R. (2021). An Outdated Idea Is Still Shaping Climate Policy. The Atlantic. April 20.

Mohammed, A. (2012). Opening Remarks at the Climate and Development Ministerial Meeting. March 31.

Naresh, R., et al. (2017). Water footprint of rice from both production and consumption perspective assessment using remote sensing under subtropical India: A review. International Journal of Chemical Studies (5): 343–350.

van Oldenborgh, G.J. et al. (2021). Attribution of the Australian bushfire risk to anthropogenic climate change. Natural Hazards and Earth Systems Science. 21: 941–960.

Our Common Future. (1987). The World Commission on Environment and Development. Oxford University Press.

Perils of Perception: Environmental Perils. (2021). Ipsos. April.

Progress on the Sustainable Development Goals: The Gender Snapshot. (2020). United Nations Entity for Gender Equality and the Empowerment of Women (UN Women) and Department of Economic and Social Affairs (DESA).

Promoting Sustainable Lifestyles, UN Environment Programme. (2021). https://www.unep.org/regions/north-america/regional-initiatives/promoting-sustainable-lifestyles [accessed 28 April 2021]

Rose, S. (2021). 'Our biggest challenge? Lack of imagination': the scientists turning the desert green. The Guardian. March 20.

Rosenbloom, D., et al. (2020). Opinion: Why carbon pricing is not sufficient to mitigate climate change – and how 'sustainability transition policy' can help. Proceedings of the Natural Academy of the Sciences of the United States of America. April 21, 117(16) 8664–8668.

Scanlon, B.R., et al. (2017). The food-energy-water nexus: Transforming science for society. Water Resources Research (53/5): 3550–3556.

Sikka, A.K., Islam, A., and Rao, K.V. (2017). Climate-Smart Land and Water Management for Sustainable Agriculture. Irrig. Drain., 67–81.

Strauss, B.H. (2021). Economic damages from Hurricane Sandy attributable to sea level rise caused by anthropogenic climate change. Nature Communications. Volume 12.

Sutton, R. (2019). Climate Science Needs to Take Risk Assessment Much More Seriously. American Meteorological Society. September.

Tanner, T., et al. (2015). Unlocking the 'triple dividend' of resilience. Washington, D.C. and London: GFDRR, World Bank and Overseas Development Institute.

Thompson, M.S. (2018). Critical perspectives on gender, food and political economy. In: Handbook of the Political Economy of Gender Elias, J. and A. Roberts (eds.). Edward Elgar Publishing, Gloucestershire, UK, pp. 470–485.

Townsend, A.M. (2013). Smart Cities: Big Data, Civic Hackers, and the Quest for a New Utopia. WW Norton & Company: New York, NY.

Ulrichs, M., Slater, R., Costella, C. (2019). Building resilience to climate risks through social protection: from individualised models to systemic transformation. Disasters 43(S3): S368–S387.

Vellakkal, S. et al. (2015). Food price spikes are associated with increased malnutrition among children in Andhra Pradesh, Journal of Nutrition 145 (8), 1942–1949

Verma M., de Vreede L, Achterbosch T, Rutten M.M. (2020). Consumers discard a lot more food than widely believed: Estimates of global food waste using an energy gap approach and affluence elasticity of food waste. PLoS ONE 15(2).

Warner, K., T. Afifi, K. Henry, T. Rawe, C. Smith, and A. De Sherbinin. (2012). Where the rain falls: Climate change, food and livelihood security, and migration. Boekenplan, Where Rain Falls Project, CARE France, Paris, France.

Yigitcanlar, T., Inkinen, T. (2019). Geographies of Disruption: Place Making for Innovation in the Age of Knowledge Economy. Springer: Cham, Switzerland.

Yigitcanlar, T., Han, H., and Kamruzzaman, M. (2019). Approaches, Advances, and Applications in the Sustainable Development of Smart Cities: A Commentary from the Guest Editors. Energies, 12, 4554.

Cathryn F. Lavery

6 Socio-political risks associated with sexual harassment, assault and gender discrimination among institutions of higher education

6.1 Introduction

In 2007, Tarana Burke first used *"Me Too"* to help survivors of sexual assault on college and university campuses across the United States know they were not alone; and to help unite the cause of changing the climate of sexual violence across institutions of higher education (Feloni, 2009). In 2017, actress Alyssa Milano tweeted using the hashtag *#MeToo* as a response to a *New York Times* article in reaction to the Harvey Weinstein accusations. This went viral and global (Harris, 2018). Suddenly, *#MeToo* became a global social movement and propelled forward from not only the university systems, but to the entertainment and arts world, and politics. Within a few days, 45% of Facebook users identified at least one family member or friend with the hashtag (CBS News, 2017). Within this rapid-fire move, the conversation moved to include not only sexual assault, but harassment, gender discrimination, racism discrimination, sex/race discrimination, child sexual abuse and intimate partner and workplace violence (Harris, 2018).

Although the movement served to empower women, the LGBTQIAP groups, and children globally, what was also brought to light was the inevitable culture clashes seen world-wide involving vastly different definitions and interpretations of sexual assault and abuse, discrimination, and harassment (Harris, 2018). This had a tremendous impact into various work cultures within higher education, as well as public and private sectors. The increasing social and political risks dealing with *#MeToo* were either not thoroughly considered or resulted in serious backlash within these environments for both victims and alleged perpetrators (Bower, 2019). This has created more ambiguity, fear, and threats of retaliation within work and educational environments (Bower, 2019).

Additionally, universities and colleges around the world were catastrophically hit by the Coronavirus pandemic (2020). In the United States, some were forced to closed due to financial hardships, loss of tuition revenue and compounded factors affecting most institutions of higher education prior to the pandemic. Any movement and measures which were focused stemming out of *#MeToo* were sidelined. Then, *The Black Lives Matter* movement took precedence. In wake of George Floyd's tragic death and the resulting criminal trial of Derek Chauvin (Greene et al. 2019), priorities on university campuses shifted and the #MeToo movement slipped into the background. Due to shutdowns no social protests allowed to continue publicly, court cases focused on rape and sexual harassment were remanded to remote conferences, the shutdown brought new unanticipated problems for victims and with the media focus on the global pandemic, the fuel needed to escalate the power of the movement was cut (Jeydel, 2020).

With the new administration of President Biden, issues of sexual assault, harassment and sex and race discrimination are slowly moving back to center stage at institutions of higher education nationally. However, there are many lagging and undefined points regarding uniformity in policies and although the United States has a foundation in policy format with *Title IX,* this is not an issue that crosses countries and cultures. With global social unrest from marginalized population groups, the emergence of countries from lockdowns and fifteen months of fear, uncertainty, and anxiety, this is the time for universities internationally reexamine policies of sexual harassment, discrimination, and violence in the hopes to protect, create awareness and more importantly, mitigate financial and criminal risks and liabilities. By examining current trends politically and socially, University stakeholders can design new policies to protect themselves amid ongoing crises while creating better interconnected systems of information, policies, and procedures to enhance their environments for students, faculty, staff, and administrators.

6.2 The United States and the federal government's title IX

The Civil Rights Act of 1964 was created to end any discrimination based on race, color, sex, religion, and one's national origin pertaining to employment (OASAM, 2021). However, it did not set protective shields against gender discrimination on public education systems or federally assisted (funded) programs. This directly comprised if high school and collegiate programs in athletics. Prior to President Nixon's official signature into law, only about 1% of college budgets went towards women's sports. In high schools, male athletes had the advantage, out numbering females 12:1 (Busuvis, 2016).

During President Nixon's Administration in 1972, Title IX was signed into law. The original purpose was to forbid any type of sex discrimination in educational programs and activities that receive any federal funding. This was originally targeted to ensure equal opportunity and funding for women's sports at schools (Busuvis, 2016). The purpose of Title IX not only was to ensure equity for genders involving funding assistance, but it also extended to foster and promote respectful, safe, and secure university/college environments. The American Association of the University of Women (1992) conducted a report entitled, How Schools Shortchange Girls. It examined how socioeconomic statues more than other variables predict educational and professional outcomes for women. It stressed how gender, race and class are interrelated. The report highlighted that self-esteem outcomes for women ranged based on race, ethnicity, class, and physicality, even though educationally they were on even footing. This clearly confirmed the interconnectedness of issues and emphasized the benefits of Title IX for students (AAUW, 1992). It was established so that students, faculty, and all staff could be protected against incidents of sex-based discrimination and sexual harassment, which includes sexual violence, relationship violence and acts of stalking.

6.3 The evolution of title IX from financial issues to rape in the United States

If Title IX in the United States were to help keep schools in check regarding sex discrimination in athletics, how did it become applied to sexual assault across college campuses? Even further how did university campuses evolve into their own courts when examining occurrences of sexual violence and intimate personal violence?

During the late 1960's, 1970's and 1980's we saw the development of the second wave of feminism in this country and internationally. Initially in the United States, we saw the beginnings post World War II when women in the United States had been out in great numbers in the workforce, and now encouraged, if not remanded back into the home to their tradition societal sex roles, Internationally, in 1967, the *International Alliance of Women Congress* was held in London, United Kingdom. A proposal had been moved forward to study and evaluate women in respective countries. This was led by the United Nations Commission on the Status of Women (ECO-SOC, 2010). Organizations worldwide evaluated the conditions of women in the workplace and home and urges countries to establish their own National Commissions on the subject (ECOSOC, 2010).

There was also movement on the issues of domestic violence and sexual assault. Beginning in the 1970's with Brownmiller's (1975) publication, *Against Our Will: Women, Men & Rape*, the United States became part of our national agenda. Brownmiller's assertion was that men benefited from acts of sexual violence because the threatening nature of rape and its acts kept women subordinated. Her work discussed the acts of acquaintance and marital rape at a time when those typologies of the crime did not even exist in American language and criminal law (Brownmiller, 1975; Beneke, 1982). This work had a huge impact on reshaping laws against marital rape and gave people a new social and legal understanding of rape. Brownmiller helped transform rape from an "expression of sexuality to an expression of power" (Brownmiller, 1975, 5). Her research also brough controversial attention on the international scene with descriptions of rape in wartime as "a weapon of terror" and resulting merely as collateral damage from conflict (Beneke, 1982, 13).

Rape myths are considered false beliefs about sexual violence, rapists, and survivors. There has been extensive research conducted regarding the impact of rape myths and how they can influence law enforcement, attorneys. Judges, juries, rapists and even victims themselves. They originated from cultural stereotypes beginning in the United States with traditional gender roles. The jurist Matthew Hale sustained the concept rape myths through legal writings which later were supported in the American Court systems for decades (Geis, 1978). Although the issue of rape myth acceptance was investigated post-Brownmiller's work, there were many criminologists and social scientists pointing out misconceptions of sexual violence, for example, that victims were "asking for it" and that men rape due to uncontrollable desires. Martha Burt (1980) in her research on rape myth acceptance defined them as "prejudicial, stereotyped and false beliefs about rape, rape victims and rapists" which create "a climate hostile to rape victims (Burt, 1980, 217). Timothy Beneke's *Men on Rape* (1982) addressed the cultural emphasis on rape myths and the range of viewpoints that men had on sexual violence eat the time of publication. He addressed the use of negative and violent connotations about women through the English American language and how that reinforces stereotypes.

Susan Estrich wrote *Real Rape* (1987) after she had been raped in the 1970's by a stranger. The police at the time asked her if she knew the perpetrator. When she said no, the reply was "Oh, then you were really raped" (Estrich, 1988). Her book led to the movement of reconceptualizing sexual violence. Thus began the advocacy movement attacking rape myths, one of which is that rape can only exist if committed by a stranger and highlighting the epidemic of rape on college campuses. What was brought out of the shadows was not only the inadequate response by the criminal justice system to sexual violence (stranger rape, acquaintance/date rape, gang rape, and marital rape) but how insufficient colleges and universities were handling these types of complaints. More so, what they were not doing to raise awareness and prevent this crime. Even today, we know that between 85–90% of sexual assaults on college campuses are committed by perpetrators known to the victim (RAINN, 2020).

6.4 Jeanne Clery and the 1991 campus crime act

The rules of Title IX officially alerted permanent in 1986 with the rape and murder of Jeanne Clery on Lehigh University's campus (Pennsylvania, USA). Although the crime was perpetrated by a stranger, Ms. Cleary's parent became strong advocates of criticizing American campuses regarding students' safety issues. They founded Security on Campus and led the crusade to change domestic law resulting in the legislative reform, the 1991 Clery Campus Crimes Act. On one regard, campuses had to recognize the problem and scop of rape in their environment and were now required to fully disclose yearly crime rates. Colleges were forced to take preventive measures to protect students and face possible legal liabilities when faced with these incidents (Graham & Konaradi, 2018). However, problems are still evident today. Rape is still underreported, many cases are considered he said/she said, and complicated factors involving student freedom, alcohol and drugs makes complaints difficult to sort. Additionally, there are complicated relationships between campuses and local law enforcement agencies. Complex situations have significantly increased due to the response and inclusion of the criminal justice system, the financial and social impact on universities from legal suits focused on and negative media exposure (Graham & Konradi, 2018).

The Supreme Court first linked the concept of sexual violence to sexual harassment in a 1979 Title IX case involving a medical student at the University of Chicago (Zirkel, 1998). And later raised the Title IX liability bar for schools with *Gebser v Lago Vista* (1998) applying the deliberate indifference standard. This meant that if a school was aware of an act of harassment or violence and ignored it, the school is liable for damages in a civil lawsuit (Zirkel, 1998). This resulted with colleges and universities trying to cover themselves legally by being more aware of the social problem of rape, supporting victims, creating sexual assault response teams, and moving forward with misconduct policies and training for faculty, staff, and students (Zirkel, 1998).

6.5 The dear colleague letter of 2011 and the normalizing of rape culture on American campuses

The Dear Colleague Letter (U.S. Department of Education, 2011) was disseminated to 7000 schools in response to questions and confusions surrounding the Department of Education, the Office of Civil Rights and issues pertaining to Title IX. The letter took a specific tone including sexual assault statistics indicating one in five women are victims of completed or attempted sexual assault while in college (U.S. Department of Education, 2011). In the letter, the definition of harassment and hostile environments is reiterated. It explained that a formal complaint is not a necessary requirement to trigger an investigation. Meaning if the school has any knowledge of possible harassment and sexual violence occurring, they are required investigate and include local law enforcement authorities if there are signs of criminal conduct/behavior. The letter also elaborates on issues of confidentiality for the victim's safety and offered concrete examples for institutions of learning to formulate programming for prevention, awareness, and safety. The letter advocated for a Title IX Coordinator to be available for students, faculty and staff which regards to filing a complaint and for oversight on procedures. There were additional details and guidance for assisting complainants and alleged perpetrators regarding safety in dormitories, classes and walking around campuses (Richards, 2020).

In 2013, The United States reauthorized the *Violence Against Women Act*, and revised Clery to expand on issues of sexual violence to include: Intimate partner/ dating violence and stalking (Wu & Denby, 2020). Other forms of conduct include bullying and/or hazing, electronic/social media harassment, any gender-based discrimination, sexual racism, and retaliatory actions from the complainant (Richards, 2020). New measures also expand for campuses to off campus housing, immediate areas (a perimeter) outside the campus, to internships, to study abroad programs (Wu & Denby, 2020).

6.6 Examining issues of sexual harassment on American University and college campuses

Sexual harassment is defined as: "Unwelcome sexual advances, requests for sexual favors, direct or indirect threats or bribes for sexual activity, sexual innuendos and comments, sexually suggestive jokes, unwelcome touching or brushing against a person, pervasive displays of materials with sexually illicit or graphic content, and attempted or completed sexual assault" (Beavers and Halabi, 2017, 558). Sexual harassment, like any form of sexual violence can have long lasting effects and extends to victims feeling like outcasts or the potential to self-blame. Many acts of sexual harassment are covert, thus making physical evidence of the act visible. Claims are situational, verbal with an emotional impact that significantly affects the victim (Beavers & Halabi, 2017). Many victims do not report the incident due to stigmatization and retaliatory actions. Within institutions of higher education, examples of sexual harassment impact the academic and learning experience of students, faculty, and staff. The educational environment becomes a harmful one. It can be a primary obstacle for individuals to obtain educational and professional goals. Many victims of sexual harassment leave their institution without completing degrees (Petersen and Ortiz, 2016).

Dr. Martin Philbert, Chief Academic Officer (Provost) for University of Michigan was terminated by the University in 2019. Dr. Philbert, originally hired as a faculty member in the sciences, was under investigation where he was accused of sexual harassment of multiple women, including graduate and colleagues over seven years. In November 2020, University of Michigan reached settlement for over 9 million dollars with the women, who documented suffering sexual, emotional, and psychological abuse by Dr. Philbert (Svrluga, 2020).

The Association of American Universities released results from a 2019 study on their Climate Survey on Sexual Assault and Misconduct. Over 181,700 students from

33 institutions of higher education participated. This was a follow-up to their 2015 campus climate survey. The rate of non-consensual contact or contact occurring despite the inability to consent rose to 26.4% with undergraduate female students. Overall, rates for nonconsensual sexual contact with women or those in the LGBTQIAP communities were higher than for men (AAU.edu, 2019). In April 2013, at Columbia University in New York City, Ms. Emma Sulkowicz, was a senior (4th year student) majoring in visual arts filed a complaint with University administrators requesting her fellow seniors, Paul Nungesser, from Germany, be expelled from the University alleging he had raped her in her dormitory room in August of 2012 (Young, 2017). After a campus investigation, Nungesser was found not responsible for the alleged incident. Following the outcome of that investigation, Sulkowicz filed a report against Nungesser with the New York Police Department (NYPD). After the District Attorney's office met with students and university officials did not pursue criminal charges. who did not pursue charges, Ms. Sulkowicz produced for her senior thesis, a performance piece entitled, *Mattress Performance (Carry that Weight)?* This involved the student carrying a dormitory mattress around campus representing the "burden rape victims carry" every day. It also was a statement in response to Columbia's handling of the complaint. In 2015, Mr. Nungesser filed a Title IX gender discrimination lawsuit against Columbia and various stakeholders alleging the University facilitated gender discrimination resulting with Ms. Sulkowicz receiving academic credit for the project and thus encouraging permissive behavior which resulted in bullying behavior by other students, forcing him to leave the institution (Young, 2017). Although initially dismissed, Mr. Nungesser refiled, and Columbia settled with non-disclosure amendment (Young, 2017).

Other studies have shown that Studies have also shown that fraternity men are three times more likely to commit an act of sexual assault than those who are not involved in Greek life. This can be in part due to the social status Greek life represents and it is easier to dominate and control those who are new to campus life (Sanday, 1996). Greek life are social organizations found notably at American and Canadian institutions of higher education whose goal is to provide unification through groups where they may live together and form social and professional networks after leaving the college environment. Greek life is formed with the use of Greek letter organizations and separated usually by gender into creating sororities and fraternities (Sanday, 1996). Research has consistently shown in the United States that affiliations with Greek organizations has led to increased amounts of sexual assault and harassment on college campuses (Valenti, 2014). According to Seabrook, et al. (2016, men who belong to fraternities are 3 times more, likely to commit acts of sexual violence than other college men.

It was noted a significant increase that students indicated a better knowledge base about sexual harassment and sexual violence that in earlier studies. Additionally, there was an increase on the knowledge of policies and procedures on their campuses with respect to sexual assault and reporting (AAU.edu, 2019). American and

Canadian Universities have also revamped their approach in programming to include "Bystander Intervention" training programs. This type of programming, which is applicable to students, faculty, staff, etc. at schools' teachings individuals the tools and empowers them to intervene and/or stop the inappropriate conduct occurring (Bannon & Foubert, 2017). Examples include buddy systems for students when they attend parties or implementing policies at campuses for information sharing and knowing when to report. It is a form of prosocial behavior that can have a beneficial impact on stopping sexual violence at colleges and universities (Evans, et al., 2019).

6.7 Sexual assault on university campuses internationally – enabling rape and victim blaming

Whereas the United States has continued updating terms and guidelines for universities, the international front is vastly different. Acts of sexual violence and victimization are handled quite differently and with less uniformity than the United States (Kalra & Bhugra, 2013). The United Kingdom and throughout Europe a structural systemic violence of sexual aggression exists. Although countries differ on definitions of university rape based on the demographics and nature of their campuses, the problem is still prevalent. For example, in the UK, since 2017, universities have paid off students to essentially "gag" students while trying to control any criticism and negative media attention on their institutions and forcing the victims to sign non-disclosure agreements (NDAs) (Bennett, 2019). It has been noted that students have been threatened with expulsion, retaliatory actions by campuses and women felt they were treated more like an inconvenience, than a priority (Bennett). The student group *Project Warwick Women* (2021) which has organized sit ins in protest over the University handling of the 2018 *"Rape Chat"* scandal, where women were targets of a chat groups where men had discussed violent sexual actions about them (Millard, 2019). The University's handling of the event had been considered misguided and protesters believe Warwick has created a "a culture of fear" for women and has demonstrated their ambivalence and lack of support when dealing with victims of sexual violence (Millard 2021).

Across Spain in 2020, prior to the pandemic, there were specific incidents of rape and harassment that spawned a country wide protest (Jones, 2021). In April of 2021, three men, noted "The Sabadell Wolfpack" were convicted and sentenced to thirteen years for the rape of an 18-year-old woman in Sabadell, Spain (Jones, 2021). The "Wolfpack case: was given in reference to a gang rape in Pamplona during the running of the bulls' festival in 2016. That year 16 men were arrested at San Fermin Fiesta and investigations ranged from incidents of rape, attempted rape, and sexual assaults (Jones, 2021). Although the crime was not committed on a university campus, it supports the statistics of victimization of college-age women and the support of a rape prone culture. On the cusp of #MeToo, there was an outcry for an overall and reexamination of Spain's sexual crimes and legislation (Jones, 2021).

France, the topic of sexual harassment and rape demonstrate the systemic violence immersed in their culture. For many, rape and sexual harassment are more of a "rite of passage" (Rose, 2016). Regarding institutions of higher education, the French university system is loosely organized and is not seen as a focal point of socialization among students. In fact, there is little evidence of college communities, which is in stark contrast to many campuses in the United States (Rose, 2016). Greek systems do not exist, and clubs are more targeted to disciplines, not social networking. Students live in off campus housing and have meals off site. Their legal interpretation of rape is complex. A rape charge is possible if there is evidence of "force, threat, violence or surprise"(Rose, 2019). If not, it can be tried under a lesser offense/charge. This evidentiary issue applies to children as well as France does not have a legal age of consent (Rose, 2016). Currently, otherwise it is tried as the lesser offense of sexual assault. That applies to children as well, as France has no legal age of consent. Currently there are bills working through parliament regarding status of minors. However, France's interpretation of rape has maintained serious for French students. Recent accusations towards alleged perpetrators of sexual assault at *Sciences Po*, an esteemed university directed towards political science, government administration and civics, was recently highlighted as an institution where students have been exposed to high rates of sexual assault and even threats of retaliation and attitudes of indifference by university administrators (Rose, 2016).

In 2016, Cologne Germany was under a microscope from the New Year's Eve, where 1,000 women accused men of sexually groping, molesting and assault took place, and the Mayor of Cologne suggested women adopt "a code of conduct" to help prevent this behavior. Interpretation of this comment lend to accusations of victim-blaming and perpetuating a rape culture within the country (Yan & Mazloumsaki, 2016). According to Stewart (2021), Catherine Serou attending The State University of Nizhny Norgorod, near Moscow, Russia went missing after June 15th, 2021, and her body was soon after discovered, murdered by a young man.

Northern Ireland has been noted as having a problem with rape culture (WRDA, 2018). In 2017 in Belfast, a restaurant, *Ribs and Bibs* advertised a cheap lunch with the slogan, '*ya can beat the wife but ya can't beat a 5-pound lunch!*' (Pollack, 2019). Initially, the management of the business tried to downplay and focus on the humor by posting to viewers on social media to '*get a life, it's a bit of wit*' (Pollack, 2019). What is so shocking is that with Northern Ireland in 2016, Public Safety of Northern Ireland cited receiving a particularly high level of IPV calls (averaging one call every 18 minutes). Although a backlash, comprehending that a person believed that it was ok to use domestic/intimate partner violence was a good risk as a marketing tool for advertising and public relations, is astonishing, and indicative that sexual harassment and violence against women has not been treated with the same level of awareness and prevention.

In 2021, the Police in Northern Ireland were outed on Twitter after passing leaflets out to University students and linking alcohol to rape. Comments on the flyers included: The flyers messages leaned toward "victim-blaming," which outraged students and local women's groups in Ireland (Taylor, 2021). Victim blaming is the perception that a victim of a crime is somehow responsible for the crime occurring and could have been in control of the outcome (Fox & Cook, 2011). There has been historical as well as and current prejudice towards survivors of sex crimes, sexual harassment, and intimate partner violence due to the possible relationship status of perpetrator and victim prior to the commission of a crime. It also is directly correlated with rape myths and the idea that women are somehow responsible for their own victimization due to how the look, dress, and react (Bieneck and Krahe, 2011).

The PSNI have issued an apology and investigating why the flyers were distributed and identified they were old flyers. The leaflets made comments for example as "Alcohol is the number one drug for rape. How much have you already taken?" (Taylor, 2021). "We have identified the source of these leaflets as being shared in error by the authorities," the spokesperson said (Taylor, 2021). A representative of *the Rape Crisis Network* in Northern Ireland said the re-emergence of the flyers and their distribution on university campuses is "unfortunate" (Taylor, 2021). It is evident that the PSNI did not measure the social and political risks on many levels. First, the decision to recycle old flyers after the social movements against sexual violence and the global impact on rape and sexual harassment. Second, that they would not anticipate a backlash. In this instance, the consideration that moving forward with this activity may have a lasting stain on PSNI, especially with young women.

Amnesty International recently released data of a study featuring 1000 participants of college-age in the Netherlands (2021). According to results, 1 in 10 women have been raped by the time they complete college – with most perpetrators being someone they knew or met before (Cluskey, 2021). "What's most shocking is that so many students are becoming the victims of rape in such a short period of their lives, typically the three or four years while they're studying", said Dagmar Oudshoorn, the Director of Amnesty Netherlands (Cluskey, 2021). More troubling is that only a small percentage of the students assaulted were aware of who they should approach in their educational institutions to help them in the immediate aftermath. With 3% claiming they reported the crime to "a university mentor", while 40% claimed they never told anyone at the university about what occurred (Cluskey, 2021).

In a subsequent interview Martine Goeman, an Amnesty International representative, stated about the results, "While of course universities and colleges are not responsible for the rape, they could certainly do more to help the victims and to create an environment where this is unacceptable. That is particularly true because in the majority of cases revealed, the attackers were known to the victims, from a party or a date, for instance. We are not talking about strange men hiding in the bushes." (Cluskey, 2021). Again, a pattern seen across Europe was identified in this study as well. There is a substantial difference between female students and male regarding perceptions about sexual assaults. Thirty seven percent of males indicated a woman was more likely to be a victim of rape if she wore sexually suggestive clothes, Twenty-five percent of women agreed. Even more significant is that 6% of males surveyed believed a kiss after a date meant consent for sexual intercourse (Cluskey, 2021).

6.8 What are the sociopolitical risks to colleges and universities?

Rape culture has become increasingly normalized not only in American society, but around the world. Mismanagement by college and university administrators happens not only due to the negative views enforced by social media and news organizations surrounding our criminal justice system, but also the perception that colleges and universities protect their own reputations over their students (Wu & Denby, 2020). Rape culture is accepted and has been in many cultures and societies for a long time. It is unrealistic to suggest that colleges and universities can change the mindset of students in addition to preventing the actions of sexually aggressive individuals. In U.S. culture, we have seen examples supporting rape myths and victim blaming. The 1977 movie, *Looking for Mr. Goodbar*, highlighted at the time in America, women's confusion about independence, sexual freedom, mental health and understanding sexual violence through the character of Teresa Dunn (played by actress Diane Keaton). Many interpreted the main character as being mentally ill and not acting like a "proper" woman, thus an active participant in her own murder (Gubar, 1987). In 1986, the rape and murder of Jennifer Levin by Robert Chambers (i.e., The Preppie Killer) was when media instigated anger from women's groups, suggesting Jennifer Levin's social status, sexuality and alcohol use were the main contributors of her death. Not the individual who strangled her and watched her die. Victim blaming has been an ongoing theme within our society. Victim blaming, whether in entertainment or real-life criminal cases reinforces and normalizes a rape supportive culture. It is an accepted understanding within the criminal justice discipline that sexual violence is based on elements of power, control, anger, and domination (Zeisler, 2019). Additionally, as with violence, people appear to be desensitized to a rape supportive culture (Zeisler, 2019).

Unfortunately, from cases mentioned and many more, universities and colleges deal with cases of sexual assault and sexual harassment poorly and their victims (whether students, staff, or faculty) are often left to deal with on their own, not given appropriate information on procedures and policy or are pressured into not pursuing criminal and/or civil remedies (Hingston, 2021; Rice & Zegart, 2018). In some instances, the alleged perpetrator many be suspended or moved off a campus, there may be a closed hearing or alternative sanctions that are not always binding, as they do not occur in a criminal courtroom (Graham & Konradi, 2018).

University and college administrators are at serious risk, if they do not put procedures in place and adhere strictly to policy as dictated by the institution. Mitigating risks for institutions of higher education today is crucial. In the United States we have seen a significant drop of enrollment numbers with admissions (Hingston, 2021). For many schools, tuition revenue is paramount (Hingston, 2021). The coronavirus pandemic, low birth cohorts and high tuition rates have put additional stresses for college campuses to survive.

6.9 Considerations for universities and colleges in efforts to combat sexual harassment and assault: The impact of sociopolitical risks

According to the *Center of Disease Control and Prevention, The National Center for Injury Prevention and Control* and the *Division of Violence Prevention* (November 2016), recommendations were made to provide a framework to combat sexual harassment and violence on campuses. These recommendations include: a comprehensive prevention strategy that targets the campus' infrastructure and bridges into community partnerships to execute successful rape prevention and sexual harassment strategies (Dills, et al., 2016). Focusing on the audiences including students, faculty, and staff of the campus. Looking at these groups to develop effective programming, campaigns, and messages through the academic and social environment of the school. Encourage the campus administrators to create community partnerships with all stakeholders invested in the institution's success. By building these bridges within the community, it will naturally generate continuous sustainability. Finally, it is recommended to conduct ongoing evaluations and assessments to discover what works, what does not, thereby honing policies and procedures to construct a safe environment (Dills, et al., 2016).

Recognizing and acknowledging that sexual violence in any form is a global social and health problem and must be prioritized on every college and university campus. By doing so, University members can begin to mitigate the sociopolitical risks they may be faced with if every there is an incident (or multiple ones) on their campuses. The approach as discussed in the previous paragraph takes from the social-ecological model. This means building efforts stemming from individual actions to cooperating and growing relationships within the community. The ultimate result being that this will change societal attitudes amidst a rape supportive culture and result in solid prevention efforts and clear policies and practices regarding sexual violence (Mackenzie, 2010).

When dealing with sexual harassment, post-*#MeToo* movement, Universities across the global need to be aware of all the social and political risks they face when dealing with a sexual harassment case or worse. Major known risks for universities around the globe are familiar; student recruitment, retention, financial sustainability, organizational sustainability, solid infrastructure and means of reasonable business continuity (Rice & Zegart, 2018). However, within these basic categories, universities need to strategically plan and anticipate for potential social and political crises that can impact one or all threats that previously believe was controlled or managed effectively.

6.10 Sexual harassment and assault complaints – mitigating the risks

Even though universities have attorneys, human resources and in the United States, Title IX Coordinators in place, this does not mean there will be negative consequences for the institution. Schools must not only prepare their student body for potential dangers, but faculty and staff as well. We have seen from *#MeToo* the power of social media and the impact it can have on institutions reputation. Even international schools, though loosely organized in structure and camps life (in some ways similar to development to community colleges in the Unted States) must still be proactive in programming, accessing counseling or help and have a solid hierarchical chain of command for reporting and oversight of the situation or case. Goals of the universities are to mitigate, when possible, not hide the issue under the carpet. That simply brings more negative attention and the strong probability of a backlash on the institution. Faculty, staff, and peer leaders should undergo and maintain training not only on procedures but on bystander tactics and not feel pressured about any retaliatory measures that they may face as a consequence. High level administrators must be opened to working with community leaders and law enforcement does not judge a situation from their own perception and assess it from the mindset of "what is best for the university". This viewpoint will only backfire in the 24 hour-news cycle and global social media outlets existing today. It is not enough to just have institutions of higher education plan for civil lawsuits, NDAs, and plug in programming to cover the bases. University and college campuses all over the globe should work to layout the groundwork for fundamental uniformity with codes and guidelines so that any member of the Academy (students, faculty, staff, and members of administration, etc.) have an understanding that they are and will be protected by incidents of sexual aggression and violence.

6.11 Recommendations to help prevent sociopolitical risks regarding sexual harassment and assault on your campus

It is crucial for institutions of higher education to layout policies and procedures regarding incidents of sexual harassment and aggression (including cyber bullying, off campus events, traveling abroad, internships and externships, etc.). These policies need to be readily available on websites, in cooperative agreements with internship and community partners and discussed amongst potential students and parents. There has been a long practice of diminishing crime around and on a college campus for fear it would hurt a school's reputation. Now is the time to embrace what the rates are and how the university is taking steps to protect not only their student population, but all population groups on their campuses. Highlight proactive programs like Bystander Intervention, *Take Back the Night* rallies. Have open discussions on the global impact of sexual harassment and assault and openly discuss how it impacts all genders and sexual identities and orientations.

A survey from 2019 by the association of American Universities found that 27% of US female college seniors experienced some form of unwanted sexual contact and/or sexual violence within their four years at college (AAU, 2019). The Rape, Abuse, Incest National Network (RAINN) found that most acts of sexual violence indicated that they were committed by "the conscious decisions of a small percentage of the community to commit a violence crime" (RAINN, 2020). This infers that that a significant issue of rape involves repeat offenders. In the United States, RAINN recommended a three-tier approach for colleges and universities to prevent and raise awareness of sexual violence, thereby mitigating risks for campuses. The first is to advocate bystander intervention and trainings. This will empower members of the campus community to be involved and respond when confronted with sexual violence. The second is to employ risk reduction techniques by promoting ongoing training on the education of sexual assault on campuses and empowering students, faculty and administrators with awareness and teaching s on personal safety. Finally, to train and education on an ongoing basis the legal ramifications and factors associated with sexual violence, especially on discussions with regard to consent and use of alcohol and drugs (RAINN, 2020). These approaches emphasize campus transparency and reduce sociopolitical risks for campuses.

University systems should partner with local law enforcement. Although most campuses have their own security personnel, it is imperative that they work directly with local enforcement for information sharing, collaborative efforts, and programs, and creating community ties is only beneficial for schools. Collaborating with student groups and integrating programming with campus security and student government. Throughout the world there has been a growing "Us versus Them" them among citizens and law enforcement. Internationally as well as in the United States it corresponds with government interventions and decentralization of enforcement (Beck, 2016). That feeling transcends to college environments. By Institutions taking the lead and integrating how campus safety measures are beneficial and service students well, it fosters a sense of public and personal safety.

Universities need to monitor social media outlets carefully. They need to have their finger on the pulse of events and happenings at their campuses. If incidents occur, it is better to be open about them and not attempt to squash or deceive the public. Attorneys for Universities and Colleges need to be aware and receive training and updates on practices regarding issues of sexual harassment and sexual aggression. From examples given and many more easily found, the pattern has been for schools to take either a "no-accountability" outlook or a more bellicose tone about the incident. Neither perspective benefit anyone, especially not the institution.

In August 2021, two major events occurred in the United States involving sexual harassment and rape and highlight how the sociopolitical risks need to be considered and ongoing throughout not only universities but within government agencies. Both examples show a lack of consideration for social and political risks at an agency/university level as well as social and reputational. If certain factors had been taken into consideration and were ongoing with assessment and a focus on areas of risk reduction, the outcomes, could have been preventable at best, or their impact minimized with such severe consequences.

A lawsuit was filed against Brown University in Providence, Rhode Island which students have accused the school of allegedly being dismissive and uncaring to students who have come forward to report acts of sexual assault and harassment (Associated Press, 2021). One attorney for the women who filed the suit though that in the post #MeToo movement, this behavior was apathetic and indifferent and reflective of the University's lack of concern for their students' safety and wellbeing. The complainants accused Brown University of a poor response procedure to their complaints and that this is a direct violation of Title IX policies. This resulted not only in negligence but "an intentional infliction of emotional distress" (Associated Press, 2021). They also accuse the University that policies and training on sexual misconduct do not meet the federal standards (Associated Press, 2021).

New York State's former governor, Andrew Cuomo resigned in disgrace based on the findings of an investigation conducted by New York State's Attorney General, Letitia James and two outside attorneys (Klepper, 2021). Accusations made by 11 women that the former governor Cuomo inappropriately touched, made repeated references about their physical appearances and sexually suggestive comments, were highlighted, validated by the investigation, led to Cuomo's resignation, and opened him up to other possible civil and criminal investigations (Klepper, 2021). Cuomo's reaction and denial immediately showed a lack of accountability and understanding on his part. His response severely backfired for him. Once considered an advocate and leader on women's rights, these accusations showed a broader culture of abuse and how sexual harassment is at its root, an expression of power and control. If the Governor of New York State had been proactive about his alleged behavior and monitored himself and gave a different commentary regarding the comments and allegations made against him, there may have been a vastly different outcome. If his immediate staff around him raised awareness, identified his behavior if deemed inappropriate, and correlated it to the negative consequences (i.e., his political future, his administration and legacy), perhaps the public would have seen a different path for Andrew Cuomo (Klepper, 2021). The ability of holding one's behavior accountable and related to their actions is easier when one continuously assesses the risks, not only to the person, but their position, their agency and how it would impact those around you. Considering one's reputation, stigma, career staining and permanent effects on those affected by you can drastically reduce and mitigate the consequences. The significance of weighing out social and political risks, however, should not only be considered by those maintaining leadership, but it should also be examined at every level of leadership – extending from university/college leadership to peer-based college activities/organizations like fraternities, sororities, residential life, and athletes.

It is understood that rape is social and public health problem. Even with all the initiatives, social and political movements, the statistics of sexual violence around universities and college campuses remain high. Victimization of people is the highest between 16–26 (Booth, et al., 2014). Sexual harassment in the college setting with students, faculty and staff remains a constant occurrence. Policies such as Title IX should be monitored and supported by higher education institutions. Further, it is recommended that all universities and colleges, whether in the United States, Europe, Online should establish universal policies in relation to sexual harassment and assault. Whether it occurs on or off campus, or online, protections should be put in place for all students. This would help secure policies and protections for students studying abroad as well. It is within the best interests of institutions of higher education to pay closer attention to the social and political risks they face when confronted with an incident involving harassment or rape. By taking steps to mitigate, preparing, and educating their administrators, faculty, employees, and students, it will create and nurture a safer, successful atmosphere for all.

References

Association of American Universities (AAU) (October 2019). The 2019 AAU campus climate survey on sexual assault and misconduct. URL retrieved: "https://www.aau.edu/newsroom/press-re leases/aau-releases-2019-survey-sexual-assault-and-misconduct" AAU Releases 2019 Survey on Sexual Assault and Misconduct | Association of American Universities (AAU)

American Association of University Women (AAUW). (1992). *How Schools Shortchange Girls*.

Anderson, G. (May 2020). Location based protection. *Inside Higher Ed*. Retrieved from: New Title IX regulation sets location-based boundaries for sexual harassment enforcement (insidehighered.com).

Associated Press. (August 2021). Brown University accused in lawsuit of failing to protect women from sexual misconduct. NBC News. URL retrieved: Brown University accused in lawsuit of failing to protect women from sexual misconduct (nbcnews.com)

Bannon, R.S. & Foubert, J.D. (2017). The bystander approach to sexual assault risk reduction: Effects on risk recognition, perceived self-efficacy, and protective behavior. Violence and Victims, 32(1), 46–59.

Beck, C. (July 2016). Relationship-based policing. The Police Chief. URL retrieved: http://www.police chiefmagazine.org/magazine/index.cfm?fuseaction=display&article_id=4209&issue_id=72016.

Beneke, T. (1982) Men on rape. New York, NY: St. Martin's Press.

Bennett, R. (April 2019). British universities spend £87m "gagging staff. *The Sunday Times*. URL retrieved: British universities spend £87m 'gagging staff' | News | The Times

Bieneck, S. & Krahé, B. (June 2011). "Blaming the Victim and Exonerating the Perpetrator in Cases of Rape and Robbery: Is There a Double Standard?". *Journal of Interpersonal Violence*. 26, 9, 1785–1797. doi:10.1177/0886260510372945.

Beavers, J.M., & Halabi, S.F. (2017). Stigma and the Structure of Title IX Compliance. The Journal of Law, Medicine & Ethics, 45, 558–568.

Boothe, M. A. S., Wilson, R. M., Lassiter, T. E., & Holland, B. (2014). Differences in sexual behaviors and teen dating violence among Black, Hispanic, and White female adolescents. *Journal of Aggression, Maltreatment & Trauma*, 23, 1072–1089. doi:10.1080/10926771.2014.964436.

Bower, T. (September-October 2019). The #MeToo backlash. Harvard Business Review. Retrieved: The #MeToo Backlash (hbr.org).

Brownmiller, S. (1975), Against our will: Men, women, and rape. New York, NY: Simon & Schuster.

Burt, M. R. (1980). Cultural myths and support for rape. Journal of Personality and Social Psychology, 38, 217–230. doi:10.1037/0022-3514.38.2.217.

Buzuvis, E.E. (2016). On the basis of sex: Using Title IX to protect transgender students from discrimination in education. Wisconsin Journal of Law, Gender, and Society, 29. URL retrieved: https://hosted.law.wisc.edu/wordpress/wjlgs/files/2014/07/Buzuvis-Article.pdf.

CBS News (October 2017). More than 12M "Me Too" Facebook posts, comments, reactions in 24 hours. URL Retrieved: https://www.cbsnews.com/news/metoo-more-than-12-million-facebook -posts-comments-reactions-24-hours/.

Cluskey, P. (2021). One in 10 female third-level students in Netherlands has been raped. Irish Times. URL retrieved: One in 10 female third-level students in Netherlands has been raped – report (irishtimes.com).

Dills J, Fowler D, Payne G. (2016). Sexual violence on campus: Strategies for prevention. Atlanta, GA: National Center for Injury Prevention and Control, Centers for Disease Control and Prevention. URL retrieved: Sexual Violence on Campus: Strategies for Prevention (cdc.gov).

ECOSOC (July 2010). *Economic & social council focuses on social issues, human rights. Economic & Social Council 2010 Substantive Session*, 44th & 45th Meetings, UN Press, 6448. URL retrieved: "https://press.un.org/en/2010/ecosoc6448.doc.htm" Economic and Social Council Focuses on Social Issues, Human Rights | UN Press.

Estrich, S. (1988). Real reform? *Harvard Law Review*, 101, 8, 1978–1983. https://doi.org/10.2307/1341445.

Evans, J. L, Burroughs M.E. Knowlden, A.P. (2019). Examining the efficacy of bystander sexual violence interventions for first-year college students: A systematic review. Aggression and Violent Behavior, 48, 72–82.

Feloni, R. (April 2009). The founder of #MeToo explains why her movement isn't about 'naming and shaming,' and shows how she is fighting to reclaim its narrative. Business Insider. Retrieved: Me Too Movement Founder Tarana Burke Says It Needs a Narrative Shift (businessinsider.com).

Fox, Kathleen A.; Cook, Carrie L. (November 2011). Is knowledge power? The effects of a victimology course on victim blaming". *Journal of Interpersonal Violence*. 26, 17, 3407–3427. doi:10.1177/0886260511403752.

Geis, G. (1978). Lord Hale, witches, and rape. British Journal of Law and Society, 5, 1, 26–44. Wiley Publishing.

Gill, G. & Rahman-Jones, I. (July 2020). Me too founder Tarana Burke: Movement not over. Retrieved: Me Too founder Tarana Burke: Movement is not over – BBC News.

Graham, R.D. and Konradi, A. (2018), "Contextualizing the 1990 campus security act and campus sexual assault in intersectional and historical terms", *Journal of Aggression, Conflict and Peace Research*, Vol. 10 No. 2, pp. 93–102. https://doi.org/10.1108/JACPR-05-2017-0284.

Greene, L. S. and Buckner Inniss, L., Crawford, B. J. & Baradaran, M., Ben-Asher, N., Capers, B. I., James, O. R. and Lindsay, K. (August 2019). Talking about Black lives matters and #MeToo. *Wisconsin Journal of Law, Gender & Society*, 1.

Gubar, S. (1987). Representing Pornography: Feminism, Criticism, and Depictions of Female Violation. *Critical Inquiry*, *13*(4), 712–741. http://www.jstor.org/stable/1343526

Harris, A. (October 2018). She founded me too. Now she wants to move past the trauma. The New York Times. Retrieved: She Founded Me Too. Now She Wants to Move Past the Trauma. – The New York Times (nytimes.com).

Hingston, S. (2021). The pandemic exposed our broken higher-education system. It's also given us a chance to make things better. *Philadelphia Magazine*. URL retrieved: The Pandemic Exposed How Broken the College Admissions Process Is (phillymag.com).

Jeydel, A. (May 2020). Keeping the #metoo movement relevant during the pandemic. Fair Observer. URL retrieved: How to Keep the #MeToo Movement Relevant During the Pandemic (fairobserver.com).

Jones, S. (April 2021). Three men sentenced in Spain's 'sabadell wolf pack' in gang-rape trial. The Guardian. URL retrieved: Three men sentenced in Spain's 'Sabadell wolf pack' gang-rape trial | Spain | The Guardian

Kalra, G., & Bhugra, D. (2013). Sexual violence against women: Understanding cross-cultural intersections. *Indian journal of psychiatry*, *55*(3), 244–249. https://doi.org/10.4103/0019-5545.117139.

Klepper, D. (August 2021). Cuomo's drive to dominate led to his success, and his downfall. *Brooklyn Daily Eagle*. URL retrieved: https://brooklyneagle.com/articles/2021/08/23/cuomos-drive-to-dominate-led-to-success-and-his-downfall/.

MacKenzie, Megan. (2010). Securitizing sex? *International Feminist Journal of Politics* 12.2, 202–221.

Millard, E. (February 2019). A 'duty of care' for sexists – no wonder Warwick students are furious. The Guardian. URL retrieved: A 'duty of care' for sexists – no wonder Warwick students are furious | Eloise Millard | The Guardian.

Office of the Assistant Secretary for administration and Management (OASAM). (2021). Legal highlight: The Civil Rights Act of 1964. URL retrieved: Legal Highlight: The Civil Rights Act of 1964 | U.S. Department of Labor (dol.gov).

Perraudin, F. (October 2019). #MeToo two years on: Weinstein allegation 'tip of iceberg,' say accusers. The Guardian. Retrieved: #MeToo two years on: Weinstein allegations 'tip of iceberg', say accusers | #MeToo movement | The Guardian.

Peterson, A., & Ortiz, O. (2016). A Better Balance: Providing Survivors of Sexual Violence with "Effective Protection" Against Sex Discrimination Through Title IX Complaints. Yale Law Journal, 125, 7.

Pollack, S. (September 2019). Ireland has a rape culture': Woman who was assaulted calls for more victim protection. *The Irish Times*. URL retrieved: 'Ireland has a rape culture': Woman who was assaulted calls for more victim protection (irishtimes.com).

Rape, Abuse &Incest National Network (RAINN) (2020). College sexual violence: Statistics. URL retrieved: HYPERLINK "https://www.rainn.org/statistics/campus-sexual-violence" Campus Sexual Violence: Statistics | RAINN

Rice, C. and Zegart, A. (2018). Political risk: Facing the threat of global insecurity in the twenty-first century. London, United Kingdom: Weidenfeld & Nicolson.

Richards, A. J. (September 2020). Title IX campus sexual assault cases: New updates to know about. *Georgia Crime*. URL Retrieved: Title IX updates – You need to know these updates to Title IX if you are accused of a sexual assault on campus (georgiacrime.com).

Rose, L. (July 2016). Lost in translation: Rape culture at college in France. *Frenchly*. URL retrieved: Lost in Translation: Rape Culture at College in France – Frenchly.

Sanday, P.R. (1996). Rape-prone versus rape free campuses. *Violence Against Women*, 2, 2, 191–208.

Seabrook, R. C., Ward, L. M., Giaccardi, S. (2016). Why Is Fraternity membership associated with sexual assault? Exploring the roles of conformity to masculine norms, pressure to uphold masculinity, and objectification of women. *Psychology of Men & Masculinity*, http://dx.doi. org/10.1037/men0000076.

Stewart, W. (June 2021). Ex-convict confesses to raping & stabbing former US marine whose body was found in a russian forest. *Daily Mail*. URL retrieved: Ex-convict confesses to raping and stabbing former US marine whose body was found in Russian forest | Daily Mail Online.

Syrluga, S. (November 2020). University of Michigan reaches settlement with women who reported sexual harassment by former provost. Washington Post. URL retrieved: Settlement reached in sexual harassment case against Martin Philbert the former provost of the University of Michigan – The Washington Post.

Taylor, J. (2021). Police flyers linking rape to alcohol intake were given to students 'in error', source says. *Independent*. URL retrieved: Police flyers linking rape to alcohol given to students 'in error' | The Independent

United States Department of Education. (April 2011). Dear colleague letter: Sexual violence. UDDOE & Office of Civil Rights.URL retrieved: Dear Colleague: From Assistant Secretary for Civil Rights, Russlynn Ali (PDF).

Valenti, J. (September 2014). Frat brothers' rape 300% more. One in 5 women is sexually assaulted on campus. Should we ban frats? *The Guardian*. URL retrieved: Frat brothers' rape 300% more. One in 5 women is sexually assaulted on campus. Should we ban frats? | Jessica Valenti | The Guardian.

Women's Resource & Development Agency (WRDA). (2018). Northern Ireland has a problem with rape culture. *Bold Women Blogging*. URL retrieved: Northern Ireland has a Problem with Rape Culture – Women's Resource and Development Agency (wrda.net).

Wu, S. & Denby, B.L. (2020). Do the new Title IX regulations endanger students when off-campus? University Business. URL retrieved: Do the new Title IX regulations endanger students when off-campus? | (universitybusiness.com).

Yan, H. & Mazloumsaki, S. (January 2016). Cologne, Germany: Hundreds of sexual assault charges from New Year's Eve. *CNN*. URL retrieved: Cologne, Germany: Hundreds of sexual assault charges | CNN.

Young, C. (July 2017). Columbia student: I didn't rape her. The Daily Beast. URL retrieved: Columbia Student: I Didn't Rape Her (thedailybeast.com).

Zeisler, A. (November 2019). Dead wrong. *Bitch Media*. URL retrieved: "The Preppy Murder" Revisits a Shameful Perversion of Justice | Bitch Media.

Zirkel, P.A. (1998). Teacher-on-student sexual harassment: Monkeying around? *Phi Delta Kappen*, 80, 2, 171–172.

Kimberly Spanjol and Paolo Zucca

7 Biophilia, one health, and humane education: Mitigating global risk through embracing humanity's interconnection with the natural world

7.1 Introduction: Biophilia

The most erroneous stories are those we think we know best – and therefore never scrutinize or question. Stephen Jay Gould

Humans are an interconnected part of the natural world, and in order to acquire and maintain the health of our species we must not forget our evolutionary origins. Since ancient times, poets, philosophers and scientists have celebrated the inextricable bond between humans, non-human animals and the environment.

The psychoanalyst Carl Jung stated that *"every person needs to have a piece of garden, although small, to remain in contact with the earth and therefore with something deeper in himself"*. Karl Popper, one of the 20th century's most influential philosophers of science, considered *"the science of nature, together with music, poetry and painting, as the greatest realization of the human spirit"*. According to Konrad Lorenz, Nobel laureate in medicine and physiology and founder of modern ethology, *"the missing link between animals and the real human being is most likely ourselves"*. The acquisition of greater awareness and sensitivity toward nature and our interconnection with other species is an integral element of a disease prevention process that mitigates otherwise insurmountable risks to public health and wellness. This also facilitates an evolution toward becoming a more humane species that can ensure the survival of life on our planet. We must move from an *"anthropocentric alienation"* to an *"ecosystem integration"* approach, where humanity is in balance and interconnected with all other living beings, rather than perched in a self-appointed superior position atop a fabricated social hierarchy.

The term biophilia (*bio* – life, living and *filia* – friendship, passion, tendency) was used for the first time by the psychoanalyst Erich Fromm in his 1973 book *The Anatomy of Human Destructiveness* to indicate a psychological orientation and attraction towards all that it is alive and vital. In 1984, E.O. Wilson, a Harvard biologist and the father of sociobiology, assigned a more evolutionary and ecological meaning to the term biophilia. According to his Theory of Biophilia, the human species possesses *"an innate attraction on a biological basis for nature and for all its forms of life"* (Wilson, 1984). This interest is the product of the co-evolution between humans, non-human animals, and the environment. It is a process in which non-humans and nature were key actors that enabled the human species to evolve (Kellert, 1997).

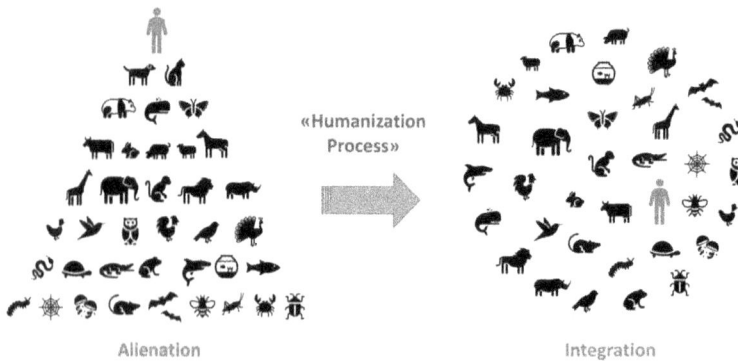

Figure 7.1: The Humanization Process.
Source: One Health (2022). World Health Organization. URL Retrieved: https://www.who.int/news-room/fact-sheets/detail/one-health.

The beginning of the evolutionary history of our ancestors took place in Africa, the continent from which the colonization of the entire planet began. It is impossible in the context of this chapter to exhaustively deal with the complex phenomenon of the evolution of the human species. However, in the context of an evolutionary approach to health promotion and education, it is important to remember what an anomaly the current epoch actually is. Our solitude as a species is a relatively recent event in the five-million-year history of human lineage. Scientists have discovered at least 15–20 different species from which ancestral humans descended, and many of these species have lived and inhabited Planet Earth at the same time, developing and adapting to different ecological niches. Until 30,000 years ago there has likely not been a time period when there have been less than at least two – and sometimes as many as five – species of hominid sharing our planet simultaneously (Dunbar, 2004). Certainly "humanity" has developed more than once, and many branches of this evolutionary tree have been lost to extinction, leaving no traces or descendants. If 30,000 years ago, *Homo sapiens* shared the earth with *H. neanderthaliensis* and *H. floresiensis*, why has our species alone remained? The explanations could be multiple: a greater adaptive plasticity to environmental changes, the development of linguistic and technological skills more sophisticated than other species, and perhaps the natural evolution of consciousness may constitute the pillars that led to the overwhelm of other species of *Homo* and to our present isolation. Many use this isolation as a pretext to justify a detachment from the natural world and from our ancestral proclivity and need to interact with nature and acknowledge our interconnection with the natural world. Humanity is at great risk to think that cultural and technological progress makes our species immune to evolutionary influence (Pievani, 2006). Our species needs exposure and growth in environments rich with natural stimuli throughout its ontogenesis in order to optimally develop physically, psychologically and cognitively. The rapid loss of awareness of this need that has happened over the last few decades consequently generates our behavior as an *"invasive and lethal species"* for all other living beings on this planet. We are extremely efficient at destroying habitats and assaulting nature without awareness, care, or acknowledgement of harm, rather than protecting the planet we coexist with. This has led to the Zoonosecene, the new geological epoch of intensive breeding, wildlife exploitation, antibiotic resistance and pandemic disease, following the Anthropocene (Zucca 2020).

Why, despite the evidence and consequences of our predatory relationship with nature in a world we have failed to coexist in, do we continue to behave in a self-destructive way? Biophilia is not a single instinct, but rather a pack of learning rules that can be analyzed separately (Wilson 1984). When humans are removed from the natural environment, these biophilic learning rules are not replaced by new rules adapted to artificial environments. These rules remain atrophic and persist throughout generations, but do not manifest themselves in the artificial environment into which human society has projected itself. Our species' lack of exposure to the natural world during delicate phases of development is the cause of many chronic pathologies that plague us, and for this reason the mitigation of global risk through transformation of humanity's relationship with the natural world must start from the inclusion of the One Health concept in every school's curricula as well as government, industry, corporate, and nonprofit entities (Wilson 1984; Kellert 1997; Zucca et al. 2021).

7.2 One health

> *Between animal and human medicine, there is no dividing line – nor should there be.* Rudolf Virchow

The COVID-19 pandemic dramatically illustrates humanity's need to expand care and compassion toward non-human animals in our relationships and interactions with them. The likely zoonotic origins of the virus and factors leading to the pandemic implicate underlying causes related to a lack of environmental and animal protection, as well as connected human rights abuses. Human consumption of wild animals, the legal and illegal wildlife trade, live animal markets, human and non-human animal exploitation in industrialized animal agriculture, and disproportionate prevalence of the virus in minority populations all highlight the intersections of harm that are relevant to the root causes of the virus (Shapiro, 2020). While widespread concerns have focused on human-centered harm, it is the harm that our species perpetrates toward other animals that led to the COVID-19 pandemic. The One Health model acknowledges that most diseases have roots in the interactions of humans and non-human animals, and encourages alliances across human, animal, and environmental health sectors (Deem, Lane-deGraaf, & Rayhel, 2019).

The origins of the *One Health* model lie in the unitary vision of modern medicine introduced by the German scientist Rudolf Virchow, who argued since the latter part of the 19th century that *"between human and animal medicine there is no dividing line – nor should there be"*. Virchow, unanimously considered the father of modern pathology, was also the first to understand the importance of the human/animal interface as a source of infectious disease. He coined the term "zoonoses" to describe the phenomena of disease transmission from animals to humans. Starting from these scientific foundations, over decades, many scientists have contributed to the development of a unified vision of health. This unified vision includes not only humans, but other animals and the environment as well – that lead to the theoretical framework known as "One Health".

One Health is defined as a cooperative, multisectoral and interdisciplinary approach that operates at a global, national, regional and local level. The aim of the One Health model is to improve human health by monitoring the human-animal- environmental interface (CDC, 2021; Khan et al., 2021). This approach views the health of humans, non-human animals and ecosystems as an interconnected network, rather than as unrelated entities to be addressed individually. Key concepts of One Health include viewing the health of all species as needing to be balanced, focusing on assessment and disease prevention rather than exclusively on treatment and promoting a strong collaborative endeavor between human and veterinary medicine (McMahon et al., 2018; CDC 2021; Khan et al., 2021; Zucca et al., 2021). An accurate application of a One Health approach must include all of these key concepts. In order to accomplish this, physicians and veterinarians must emerge from the isolation of healthcare units and practices and collaborate to best understand and protect the health of humans, domesticated and free- living animals, and the environment. *"Medicus"* must abandon pathways of increased specialization to instead embrace a generalist approach that includes other disciplines such as ecology. In fact, the One Health approach demands that the treatment of human and animal diseases not be solely based on symptomatic therapy. Instead, one must delve deeper into the diagnostic process, searching for the causal factor that originates the *"morbus"* through a broader vision of disease – one that encompasses an understanding of the complex ecosystem represented by the human-animal-environment interconnection. This etiological diagnosis can only be obtained through study of the *"ecology of the pathogens"*, defined as a declination from the classic discipline of pathology toward a One Health perspective. Evidence supports Virchow's assertions that employing a pragmatic and preventative One Health approach to endemic zoonoses is more equitable and effective than exclusively treating human cases of disease (Cleaveland, et al., 2017).

On a cautionary note, the One Health model should not be somehow misused to further cause harm to non-human animals through culling, hunting, or otherwise attempting to reduce their numbers or eliminate them in a short-sighted and erroneous attempt to "protect human health". The One Health framework requires that human behaviors which increase risks to both human *and* non-human animal health be addressed and corrected. To be clear, the model advocates for a "collaborative, multisectoral, and transdisciplinary approach – working at the local, regional, national, and global levels – with the goal of achieving optimal health outcomes recognizing the interconnection between people, animals, plants, and their shared environment" (Centers for Disease Control website, retrieved May 2, 2021). The growing application of the One Health model can play a role in rebalancing human relationships with other animals and nature, thereby promoting true health for all.

7.3 Biological risks and zoonoses

The real voyage of discovery consists not in seeking new landscapes, but in having new eyes.
Marcel Proust

A zoonosis (from the Greek word: ζῷον zoon "animal" and νόσος nosos "disease") is any disease or infection that can be transmitted from vertebrate animals to humans. The war between humans and disease is as old as the evolutionary history of the species itself. The consequent antagonistic co-evolutionary dynamic can be explained by the Red Queen Hypothesis: a model in evolutionary biology that explains the role of sexual reproduction in response to parasites (including virus and bacteria). The model name comes from a statement that the Red Queen made to Alice in Lewis Carroll's *Through the Looking-Glass*, a sequel to *Alice's Adventures in Wonderland* in her explanation of the nature of Looking-Glass Land: "*Now, here, you see, it takes all the running you can do, to keep in the same place*". Hosts (humans) must constantly evolve, adapt and proliferate in order to survive while facing parasites that want to kill them. In fact, sexual reproduction, although biologically costly, has spread among species because those that use this reproductive strategy are able to improve their genotype in changing conditions and offer greater genetic variability in offspring that reduces the risk of infection. More than 70% of the 1,700 infectious diseases that affect humans come from animals. COVID-19, Ebola, HIV, SARS, MERS, Swine and Avian flu, Zika, and other pandemics started from sporadic phenomena limited to rural areas and went on to become global emergencies. Emerging zoonoses are a growing threat to global health and have caused astronomical economic damage in the past 20 years because they have tremendous impacts on public health, 'livestock' economies, and wildlife conservation (Cleaveland et al. 2001, Lo Iacono et al. 2016, Beirne 2020, Zucca et al. 2021, Zucca 2021a).

Why has this co-evolutionary equilibrium between human and parasites that has – while experiencing variable epidemics and mortality – predominantly allowed our species to survive, now more frequently favoring parasites and putting our survival at risk? As quoted by Marcel Proust: "*The real voyage of discovery consists not in seeking new landscapes, but in having new eyes*". COVID-19 is not the root problem, but rather a symptom of a much wider human-nature imbalance of which we ourselves are the cause.

In fact, the lack of exposure to the natural world of humans during the delicate phase of development increases our propensity as a species for ecological destruction, generates a lack of knowledge about biological risks and amplifies the negative effects of cognitive-ecological biases. The spread of these systematic errors is practically ubiquitous and most, if not all, Governments and Public Health stakeholders are at risk of error due to these biases since it is a generalized phenomenon neither correlated with intelligence nor with other specific cognitive ability (Zucca 2022).

Human survival depends on an etiological diagnosis of the causal factors favoring the rapid onset and emergence of potentially lethal zoonoses for our species. The current repeated and frequent onset of pandemics can be directly attributed to the irresponsible behavior of humans. The creation of widespread domestic animal farming that indiscriminately uses antibiotics on intensive breeding farms, the destruction of forests, the legal and illegal animal trade, and the consumption of wild animals are all factors that cause the insurgence of lethal human diseases (Zucca 2020). If the human species wants to increase its chances for survival, we must act on the root causes of the human-nature imbalance. The symptomatic therapeutic approach for any specific zoonosis only serves to alleviate suffering in the short term. If symptomatic therapy is not followed by a drastic reduction in the exploitation of nature, our species will continue to race toward extinction.

Any effort to effectively mitigate this global risk must have a starting point. Urgent measures must be put in place to reduce our assault on nature and consequently reduce the risk of new pandemics. The One Health framework can be used as a guide – however, it can be quite challenging to apply this approach to zoonotic spillover control because One Health is based on a very broad and interdisciplinary theoretical framework (Zucca et al. 2021). If spillover management activities are considered through the lens of the One Health Cycle, we can understand how this approach integrates and optimizes the spillover management process (Zucca et al. 2021) as reported in Figure 7.2.

A pathogen control process is a series or set of activities that interact to produce benefits to people and animals. The classic models of zoonotic disease prevention include three steps: monitoring, detection and control. We can increase our disease prediction capacity by inserting a fourth step named "early prediction" thanks to the development of big data and artificial intelligence. Unfortunately, all these steps are still not enough in light of the current situation. A recent school-based survey on zoonotic risk that was conducted in six countries (Italy, Austria, Slovenia, Germany, Mauritius and Japan) with 656 adolescents revealed that 28.96% of the students did not know that many diseases affecting humans come from animals, while a further 32.16% of the students did not know what zoonosis is. The circularity of the One Health concept related to the transmission of diseases from animals to humans and vice-versa was not well understood by a large percentage of the adolescents surveyed, with 31.40% and 59.91% of wrong responses, respectively (Zucca et al., 2021). Results indicated that future generations are not prepared for a pandemic, nor are

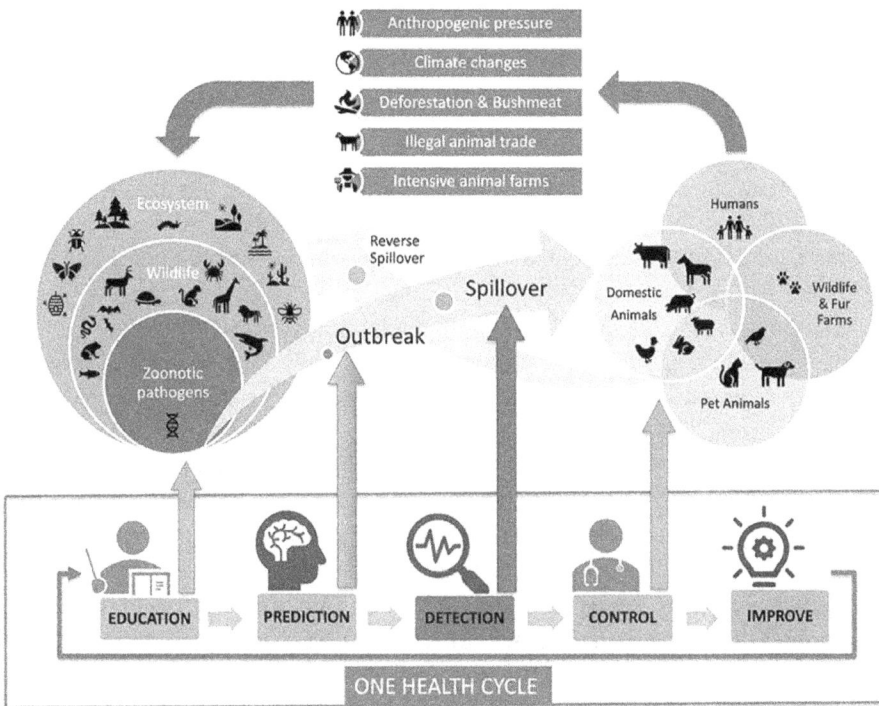

Figure 7.2: One Health Cycle.

they aware of the biological and zoonotic risks to which they are and will be exposed to. On a positive note, the research also revealed that they seem to learn quickly. In order to reduce our negative impact on nature and consequently reduce the risk of new pandemics, a first important step is to be sure that the One Health model is presented to all learners through education (the "early education" step of the One Health Cycle).

7.4 Human interaction with nature: Speciesism and entangled victimization of humans, non-human animals and the environment

It does not do to leave a live dragon out of your calculations if you live near one- J.R.R. Tolkien

Nature and non-human animals are victimized directly and indirectly on a mass scale in multiple ways through dangerous and short-sighted systemic harms that intersect with human exploitation. The scope and size of these interconnected harms centered on the commodification of non-human animals and the degradation of the natural world is enormous. Industries and individuals that profit from using other animals for food, experimentation, human companionship, entertainment, sport, and testing harm non-humans directly and indirectly as collateral damage – and drive the victimization of humans and nature. The legal and illegal trade of animals and their parts, mass deforestation and habitat destruction, privatization of natural resources and land grabs, intensive animal agriculture, and the bushmeat trade are just some examples of devastatingly damaging and risky routine practices.

Non-human animals and nature are predominantly valued in terms of human perspectives and experiences, and humans are typically illogical in their relationships with other animals. This is reflected in ethical double standards that are the social norm and allow humans to care for some animals while participating in standard practices and consumer patterns that drive exploitation of other animals. Willful blindness rooted in human exceptionalism allows our species to see without witnessing as interconnected systems of mass media, corporate interest, education, public policy, and law collaborate to shape predominant attitudes, language, and behavior toward some humans, other animals and nature. Historical and current human moral attitudes perpetuate successful indoctrination of perceiving some humans, animals and nature as commodities for use and exploitation (Kasperbauer, 2018). This widespread phenomenon is reflected in all human social institutions and can be attributed to speciesism, the view that members of one species are morally more important than members of other species in the context of their needs and interests (Ryder, 2004, Singer, 2009).

A speciesist worldview promotes the objectification of other animals and nature as mere resources that can in certain cases be regulated for human trade and use. Other animals may be somewhat protected primarily depending on their varying relationships with humans. Gruen (2015) instead advocates for an "entangled empathy" which focuses on responsible and responsive care that acknowledges the complex relationships humans engage in with other animals. These complex relationships also result in our shared victimization. Therefore, our species must also acknowledge this entangled victimization with other animals that is largely ignored and socially condoned, reflected in the legality of many harmful practices that are generally perceived as normal, natural, and necessary for human survival and well-being (Joy, 2011). Reality is quite the opposite, and these belief systems pose continued global risk to all humanity as well as other species. Even when acts perpetrated against non-human animals and nature are criminalized, laws are often inadequate and insufficiently enforced due to widespread corruption as well as denial of the victim and minimization of the victimization, rendering them effectively meaningless.

The emotional inner life of non-human animals, while scientifically well-documented and part of a rapidly growing knowledge base, is not adequately reflected in laws that are stated to protect them (Beckoff, 2008). Laws and policy regulating the treatment of other animals vary on a spectrum from a negative state of *"illfare"* (a term coined by Sztybel 2006) to a defined optimal state of *"welfare"*. Currently, existing legislation typically attempts to address animal welfare, but few laws enable true protection and even fewer recognize any rights of other animals (Wise, 2000; Zucca, 2009). Laws addressing animal *"illfare"* would help to reduce harms and risks facing humans as well as non-human animals (Sztybel, 2007).

Anthropocentrism can be used interchangeably with humanocentrism, the concept of human supremacy or exceptionalism, that drives speciesism and the tendency to consider humans as being separate from nature and other animals. This allows our entangled victimization to remain largely hidden as the treatment of other animals and the environment as nothing more than inexhaustible commodities for human use without repercussions persists. This is evident, for just one example, in the number of animals slaughtered and consumed globally for food, which is estimated to be approximately 70 billion (Faunalytics, 2018). According to UNFAO, low estimates of the numbers of aquatic animals killed for human consumption, while they remain unrecorded, were anywhere from 790–2,300 billion in just the decade between 2007 and 2016 (UNFAO, 2020). These harms are not limited to physical injury or death, and also include mental and emotional distress. Animal agriculture and commercial fishing are also associated with significant environmental harms that impact wildlife through pollution, intensive land and water use that drives deforestation and greenhouse gas emissions that fuel the climate crisis, and routine practices that kill non-target animals – for example, the killing of wild "livestock" predators, "bycatch" and "bykill" (Almiron et,al., 2016; Chai et.al. 2019; Hunt, 2015; Inoue, 2017; Kemmerer & Doop 2015; Reynolds et. al., 2014). Noske's (1989) concept of the Animal Industrial Complex highlights how efficient, legal, and state-sanctioned systematic harms perpetrated by humans against non-human animals and nature, as well as oppressed humans, are enabled through inter-related transnational corporations, government policy, science, and individual acts. Economic, cultural, social and affective dimensions of this system support the commodification of animals and nature on a global scale.

Almiron (2016) exemplified the Animal Industrial Complex by highlighting interconnections of the animal agriculture industry with other global industries. Consider that producers of GMO seeds grow crops that are treated with fertilizers and herbicides from the chemical industry to feed to animals used for food. This feed is treated with medicines produced by the pharmaceutical industry after being tested on other non-human animals in an effort to control disease rampant in commercial animal feeding operations (CAFOs) so that animals can be packed as tightly together as possible. The bodies, parts, and products of non-human animal female reproductive processes in the form of milk and eggs are farmed and transported through state-maintained infrastructure – from slaughter to market – through fuel provided by the oil industry. These products are then marketed through mass media to drive consumer demand (Nibert, 2016). Other aspects of these systems are less obvious and sustain the system through state-involved legislation such as 'animal welfare' and food safety laws, infrastructure that facilitates the transport of 'animal products', and the purchasing of them to feed hospital patients, students, prison inmates and others in public care, while also providing financial subsidies for 'livestock' farming (Almiron, 2016). Publicly funded media promotion and direct advertising by corporations have been very successful in normalizing and stimulating increased, daily 'animal product' consumption (Nibert, 2016).

The perpetuation of these systems through imagery and rhetoric has become so ingrained in individual and cultural identity and reinforced via emotional attachments – that *preferences* are no longer seen as *choices*, even when other less harmful options exist. Instead, despite extreme risks, these visible and invisible systems are interpreted as an integral part of being human. Any scrutiny of them is often attacked, despite the scale of harm and entangled victimization of humans, non-human animals, and the environment perpetrated (Fiddes, 1991; Adams, 2004; Stewart and Cole, 2020). This ensures the smooth operation and continued profitability of transnational corporations that depend on state-maintained infrastructures, subsidies, and legal frameworks as well as media and marketing representations that minimizes their tremendous risk and harm. This entangled victimization creates unsustainable global risk.

Humanity must move forward with a new way of seeing and interacting with other animals and the natural world to which our species is inextricably linked. Despite exposure of these harms that are widely available and easily researched, scant media attention and cognitive dissonance perpetuates their invisibility (Freeman, 2016). Therefore, deeply exploring, highlighting, and effectively communicating the affective dimension of the Animal Industrial Complex and the interconnecting social structures that construct demand for "animal products" through education and presentation of alternative choices and replacement behaviors is crucial toward interrupting this largely unscrutinized and extraordinarily dangerous behavior that continues to threaten all life.

7.5 A biophilic humane education: Steps toward connecting the disconnect and increasing prosocial attitudes, behavior, and policy

Human beings, who are almost unique in having the ability to learn from the experience of others, are also remarkable for their apparent disinclination to do so. Douglas Adams

A comprehensive understanding of intersectional harms, expanded notions of empathy, and entangled victimization that includes non-human animals and the environment is essential toward protecting humanity as well as other animals and nature. Our species' interdependence on other animals and the natural world requires this.

While individual and systemic biases toward other species and nature persist, evidence supports that shifts in attitude and behavior can be learned (Ascione 2001; Itle-Clark & Comaskey, 2020; Weil, 2006; Zucca et. al., 2020). While all human groups have different patterns of thought, emotion, and behavior driven by specific antecedents and consequences unique to their individual social, geographic, and political contingencies, practices can be applied to shape prosocial attitudes and behavior in meaningful ways. Regardless of differences in culture and place, it is imperative for all of humanity to follow indigenous knowledge practices that raise awareness of the interconnection of all life that cultivate increased empathy and compassion for other humans, animals, and the earth (Bruchac, 2014). Human moral attitudes and cognitions impact emotions and behaviors that are required to reduce global risks to social, political, and economic security. Transforming and delivering educational and training discourse widely and across disciplines and sectors is crucial. This education should not be limited to young learners, and should be applied broadly in higher education, the public sector, and industry across disciplines and fields (Spanjol, 2020). Humane Education and humane pedagogical best practices provide practical tools toward developing the perspective taking, critical thinking, and problem-solving skills needed to accomplish this overwhelming endeavor and manage the risks that humanity faces in the 21st century (Itle-Clark & Comaskey, 2020; Weil 2006). Human moral attitudes shaped by past histories and current practices of dominion and oppression, selfishness and greed, short-term thinking and consumerism, and a disregard of empathy and compassion have led to an anthropocentric blindness and victimization of less powerful humans and the natural world (Kasperbauer, 2018). While present circumstances appear bleak, evidence supports that common human attitudes and beliefs which inherently entitle our species to these moral priorities over others seems to appear late in development, and are therefore very likely socially acquired – implying that they can be unacquired as well (Wilks et.al., 2021). Default systems of indoctrination that have long been in place to teach humans that marginalized people, other animals, and planetary health have diminished importance are social constructions. In order to move toward alternative ways of thinking and being, a clear alternative model must be presented in order for learners to recognize options in commonly taught human-centered thought and behavior patterns. Humane Education can be examined as an alternative approach that provides eco and biocentric values and aligned behavior to emphasize respect for the interdependence of all life. Relevant to humanocentric concerns, expanding empathy toward non-human animals also appears to increase the capacity for greater empathy toward other humans as well (Ascione, 2001).

Humane education is defined as learning which is inclusive of compassion and empathy toward people, animals, and the planet and the interconnection among the three (Academy of Prosocial Learning, n.d.; Association of Professional Humane Educators, n.d.; Humane Education Advocates Reaching Teachers, 2019; Weil 2006).

Furthermore, Humane Education and Pedagogy uses education to nurture respect for all living beings and examines the intersection of social justice issues with a focus on identifying *systemic* problems and solutions. An examination of the "true price" of humanity's relationship with other species and how it impacts all stakeholders in terms of human rights, animal protection, and environmental stewardship is key. The focus is on systemic solutions, asking learners to explore any alternative behaviors that will cause less harm and promote prosocial outcomes (Weil, 2006).

While ethics, character education, and moral growth and development have long been a focus of educators, and even mandated by law in many places, clear teaching approaches including the examination of implicit and explicit biases and related behavior have been addressed only relatively recently in educational settings due to successful social justice work and movements (Itle-Clark & Comaskey, 2020). Successful social justice activism shapes educational interventions and procedures, and in turn education further shapes and evolves social justice movements. Harmful human-animal interactions and relationships, within and outside of educational settings, have been largely ignored and not interpreted as a social justice issue. Addressing and recognizing the plight of non-human animals as an intrinsic element of social justice discourse that should be included in educational settings has been proposed by humane education models alone. As explained by Itle-Clark & Comaskey:

> Within a humane approach to education (a humane pedagogy), species is an intersecting identity in the same way that other forms of stratification such as race, class, age, and gender are. The privileges or disadvantages inherent of each intersecting component become equally valid. . . The providence of human-kind is linked to humane work and the development of the prosocial traits that create a world in which all living beings are afforded the ability to live as they were meant to, in a fair and comfortable way. In order for this to occur, society must continue to provide humane education and most importantly, to expand the framework of how this education is delivered so the lessons are fair and equitable, without bias toward human or animal-kind, and designed to support each learner (p.10).

Itle-Clark & Comaskey go on to provide a comprehensive account of the evolution of moral education models and the predominant exclusion of animals. A humane pedagogy empowers learners to identify their values and align their behavior in accordance with them through critical thinking, perspective taking and reflection. Implementing a humane pedagogy can help learners identify the processes of their thinking to reveal implicit and explicit biases behind the creation of their values, attitudes, morality, and ethics. Humane education principles and methods must be applied broadly and beyond the classroom to forge an alternative way of thinking, being, and solving social problems and formidable risks to humanity moving forward.

Our education and other socially constructed systems are products of our inequitable shared histories, increased privatization and corporate incursions (Urban, Wagoner, Gaither, 2019). All of these systems intentionally and unintentionally perpetuate moral blind spots that minimize the inherent worth of certain humans, non-human animals and the environment and lead to the maintenance and cultivation of further implicit and explicit bias against them. These systems are varied, violent, and oppressive, and nearly every human, if not all humans, participate in them as there are few apparent or easy alternatives. This is the case regardless of human status and victimization within these systems that are birthed from fabricated social hierarchies. Examining biases toward non-human animals and the natural world provides a unique opportunity to practice awareness, deep examination, and possible transformation of attitudes and systems that are the products of cultural and structural violence – and the root cause of all social harms perpetrated against other animals, including other humans, and the environment (Galtung, 1969).

Education and training play a central role in developing leadership and moral behavior in our complex, rapidly changing, knowledge-based society. Moral growth does not always fit neatly into established disciplines, and educators in all settings need essential theory and formative research to support them in creating curriculum and applying methods to effectively expand ethical development, social responsibility, civic engagement, and other prosocial behaviors. Without these compassionate guidelines, ethical people largely turn a blind eye to the everyday commodification and exploitation of other animals and the natural world. Widely held implicit biases prevent educators and learners *in all settings* from including animal and planetary concerns in the vast majority of teaching environments. Our individual and collective empathy is dampened regularly as we ignore the exploitation of nature that maintains, reinforces, and expands oppressive power structures and occurs with most of our consent and collaboration (Joy, 2011; 2019). It is not only morally imperative that institutions of formal and informal learning and teaching recognize and illuminate these ethical blind spots; it is imperative for the survival of our species. These blind spots are at the root of widespread and systematic human caused suffering inflicted on animals, the environment, and ultimately, ourselves. Our anthropocentric worldview can possibly spur compassion for other creatures when we reject the single focus and willful blindness that has thus far kept us on a steady path toward destruction and cruelty. A true anthropocentric worldview would accept the reality that human well-being and survival is interconnected and entangled with consideration and care of other species.

Ideological shifts in discourse and thought required for this type of trans-discipline cultural, societal, economic and political transformational change has a starting point that has been developing over decades through the interdisciplinary field of Human-Animal Studies (HAS). A steadily increasing group of scholars across fields provide frameworks to include new ways of thinking, learning and training. Shapiro's (2020) comprehensive work examining the past, present and possible future of this field notes a wide variety of involved disciplines that include the following:

animal law – anthropology – biosemiotics – communications – conservation – criminology – cultural studies – development studies – education – environmental studies – geography – history – literary studies – performance studies – philosophy – political theory and science – psychology – religion – semiotics – social zooarchaeology – sociology – urban studies – women's and gender studies (p. 814).

As Shapiro (2020) notes, "given the sixth great extinction, global warming, and ocean pollution, our obligation to animals has never been timelier and more compelling". The resources we need to consider other species and a collaborative and compassionate existence exist and are growing. Applying research and findings from the rapidly growing field of Human Animal Studies that are delivered through a Humane Education framework and pedagogical best practices to teach, train, and develop public policy and practice can ensure that they are implemented ethically and with consideration and care toward the health of all humans, other animals, and our environment.

7.6 Interconnected harm impacts humans, non-human animals and the environment: A discourse of entangled victimization in the zoonosecene

> You can often change your circumstances by changing your attitude. – Eleanor Roosevelt

Reducing risk of human extinction calls for a transformation of humanity's perception of our relationship with nature and other animals. Relearning our patterns and interactions with other animals and nature is extraordinarily challenging. Dominant language and imagery across cultures shapes human perception regarding whether or not other animals and nature are even worthy of our attention. Michel Foucault's (1926–84) theories of power-knowledge and discourse are helpful to understand how power and knowledge are interrelated. This is represented in the majority of language and imagery regarding most non-human animals and nature that is intrinsically harmful. Language and imagery shapes knowledge of who is labeled and perceived as victim and makes them more vulnerable to further harm by making the harm itself nearly impossible to recognize because the victim is considered unworthy of concern. Humans also dehumanize and justify harm perpetrated toward other humans through these processes. For example, throughout history humanity's views of non-human animals as subordinate to humans has made comparing people to 'dogs', 'rats' or 'pigs' a tool to reduce their moral worth through the process of dehumanization, making it acceptable to victimize and harm them (Almiron et.al., 2016; Kasperbauer, 2018; Plous, 2003). At its most extreme, animal-based name-calling has been used to render the victims of genocide as deserving of violence such as Nazi propaganda comparing Jews with lice or rats, or describing Tutsis as 'cockroaches' prior to their victimization in the 1994 Rwandan genocide Almiron et. al., 2016; Kasperbauer, 2018). Human moral attitudes are shaped by language and imagery that promote the victimization of non-human animals and nature by powerful, economically motivated social systems.

Foucault argued that power is productive rather than repressive – that it instigates action rather than stops action. Foucault applies this argument to the experiences of criminals in nineteenth-century prisons in *Discipline and Punish*, arguing that the goal of prisons at that time was not to stop criminals from perpetrating crime – rather their purpose was to produce 'docile bodies' (1991, p. 138). Docility equaled utility, and a corrective penal regime could remake someone into a productive working citizen that was an asset rather than a burden to society. As knowledge of each prisoner was produced, responses of the regime could be altered to secure and gain more power. The interconnection of power and knowledge could then be applied to networks of state social systems and institutions such as military, legal and justice systems, schools, hospitals, and more to create "useful citizens" (Foucault, 1991). Almiron et. al. (2016) applies this extension to nonhuman animals in order to understand how their "usefulness" to humanity has been systematically created. This can also be applied to all human exploitation of nature. The disciplining of nature and non-human animals to serve human needs has gone to such extremes that humanity's alienation from which it is in reality an inextricable part of, has created a blindness to the harm it is itself experiencing. Power structures create and reinforce hierarchies through language, imagery, and behavior to ensure its persistence through isolation and disconnection from nature and all non-human life. This language, imagery, and behavior that objectifies other animals and nature as objects to enable their victimization has ultimately caused our own. We must create a new discourse to understand the entangled victimization of humans, nonhumans, and nature that this power structure creates and maintains.

Discourse can be defined as an authoritative system of communication, encompassing language, images and symbols. It is a central concept in the analysis of harm. Zemiology, the study of social harm, is used to analyze relationships between crime, harm and the state, and to explore relationships between power and resistance. Discourse, and arguably all forms of human communication, shape cognition, emotion, and actions that develop habitual patterns of thought and behavior – it is never neutral. A new discourse to transform harms perpetrated against nature and non-human animals requires a number of humanocentric views to transform. Namely, a true humanocentric approach must represent the reality of humanity's entangled victimization with other animals and the environment we share. This includes using intentional language, images, and practices that connects humanity to other animals and nature rather than separating us to transform mutual well-being and interconnection as normal, natural, and necessary – and to replace the current harmful predominant structures that disconnect us through ordinary social processes that create incalculable risk for humanity. Humans must move away from viewing harms against other animals and nature as inevitable, and understand that these harms impact our species directly.

Current humanocentric discourse makes it difficult to recognize nonhuman distress as resistance to the power relations we are all indoctrinated into accepting. The reduction of nonhuman animals and nature to objects for human use is perpetuated by their exploitation through capture, confinement, slaughter, dismemberment and packaging as commodities to market. An alternative discourse is needed to construct a moral view of non-human animals and nature that entangles their victimization with our own. The pervasive reach of the dominant discourse that promotes this entangled victimization is difficult to counter. However, discourse is an important analytical tool that can be used to identify how humanocentric harms are perpetuated, as well as develop alternative views to counter dominant discourses that cause harm to humans, non-human animals, and the environment (Almiron et. al. 2016; Foucault, 1991; Joy, 2019).

The Anthropocene has been a geological epoch characterized by a significant increase of the impact of human activity on our shared ecosystem. It has been a short evolutionary period, as we have now entered a new period that can be called the Zoonosecene, characterized by the increasingly frequent appearance of pandemic infectious diseases transmitted to humans by animals (zoonoses) (Zucca, 2020). Can this counter-discourse shift our relationship with nature and other animals and enable humanity to acknowledge entangled victimization and avoid extinction? As in any audit process, we cannot limit ourselves to identifying only the critical points of the system (see Table 7.1). We must also provide corrective actions to restore the functionality of the system, keeping in mind that the time available to reduce risk and restore balance is extremely limited.

Table 7.1: One Health Audit with Critical element and Corrective measures lists.

One Health Audit: Critical Elements
– Species isolation and alienation has generated a false perception that our species is disconnected from other animals and ecosystems.
– Humans consider themselves to be the most intelligent living species, but do not consider that some forms of intelligence are a secondary effect of evolution and does not necessarily constitute an evolutionary advantage – in fact, as argued here, it can prove to be extremely risky.
– Current, dominant humanocentric discourse perpetuates many cognitive biases. For example, humanity has an innate tendency to underestimate biological risks.

Table 7.1 (continued)

One Health Audit: Critical Elements
– The development of technology does not make us immune to humanity's victimization of other animals and the natural world.
– Our species in general, including policy makers and others who hold power, lack the capacity and motivation for global vision.
– It took only one of many Coronaviruses to remind humanity of its evolutionary weakness and to highlight how we must quickly stop exploiting other animals and the planet in order to prevent the extinction of our species.
– The repeated and frequent onset of pandemics can also be attributed to the irresponsible and harmful behavior of humanity. In particular, the creation of enormous and intensive animal domestication for consumption, the indiscriminate use of antibiotics on concentrated animal feeding operations, the destruction of forests for agriculture and illegal logging, the legal and illegal pet and wildlife trade, and the trafficking, warehousing, slaughtering and consumption of wild animals are all causal factors leading to the insurgence of lethal human diseases.
– The COVID-19 pandemic is only a symptom of more widespread issues that are the root causes related to the assault of human activities on other animals and our ecosystem.
– The more we increase the human-animal interface, the more the health risks to which we are exposed increase.
– It is a false notion that other zoonotic diseases are waiting their turn and will not emerge as we confront SARS-CoV-2.

One Health Audit: Corrective Measures
– From a medical viewpoint, it is useless treating the symptoms of a patient without eliminating the causes of the illness simultaneously, because true healing cannot occur. Similarly, it is useless developing ever more powerful antibiotics or increasingly sophisticated vaccines unless we reduce the assault by our species on other living beings. We must restore the balance and recognize the interconnection between our species, other animals, and ecosystems.
– We must recreate and implement a truly humanocentric discourse toward health prevention and treatment. We have to shift from reacting to symptomatic rather causal solutions and recognize and act on the knowledge that humanity's victimization is entangled with the harm we perpetrate against other animals and the environment we share.
– There are currently more than 1,000 outbreaks of High Pathogenicity Avian Influenza in Europe alone. Several people have died due to avian influenza virus spillovers during the recent past months and some countries such as Russia are already developing a test system and vaccine for Avian flu. Recombination between human and avian flu viruses could easily generate a new pandemic with a 60% mortality rate, making coronaviruses seem mild in their devastation. Policy makers must act NOW to shift discourse and focus on transforming root causes that facilitate the resurgence of new pandemics. Our species will not be able to survive another and possibly concomitant pandemic.

Table 7.1 (continued)

One Health Audit: Critical Elements
–   The mitigation of global risk through a transformed relationship between humanity and the natural world can start with the widespread inclusion of the One Health model on micro and macro levels that is rooted in scholarship from the robust and developing field of Human-Animal Studies and applied through Humane Education and Pedagogical best practices in education, government, corporate, health care, media and other entwined systems.
Available resources and training institutes such as The Academy of Prosocial Learning, Humane Education Coalition, Institute for Humane Education, academic think tanks such as Animals and Society Institute, and data repositories such as Faunalytics offer a wealth of information to assist in developing ethical educational opportunities and public policy that can reduce and hopefully eliminate the entangled victimization of humans, non-human animals, and the environment that is causing unprecedented global risk and harm of the Zoonosescene (see Appendix 1 for a list of suggested resources).

Source: One health (2022). URL Retrieved: https://www.who.int/health-topics/one-health#tab=tab_3.

7.7 Conclusion

Less powerful humans, non-human animals and the environment are victims of commodification and biases that lead to rampant abuse, exploitation, and oppression that is systematically perpetuated without adequate protection. There is relatively little awareness or acknowledgement of these harms that impact all life due to a number of reasons that include economic greed and a humanocentric, speciesist worldview – and even less understanding of how these harms directly impact human health. Education, policy, and practice rooted in Biophilia, One Health, and Humane Pedagogical frameworks as well as Human-Animal Studies scholarship promotes individual and systemic transformative relationships with the natural world that acknowledges and emphasizes humanity's deep interconnection with the well-being of other species and the environment we share. Embracing and utilizing these approaches are crucial steps toward solution-based interventions that address root causes of human, animal, and environmental harm to mitigate global biological risks and zoonoses that impact all social and political spheres. All humans, non-humans, and our environment share interconnected needs. We also share our greatest threats. To experience true global health and security, human systems across sectors must take action to place extreme value on nature in order to create a healthy and stable world.

The COVID-19 pandemic presents humanity with a significant opportunity for prosocial change and growth. This requires changing our relationships to nature, other animals, each other, and ourselves. An awareness of our interconnected finitude may propel humanity to respond to risks to its own survival that our current practices have created, and allow us to co-exist in more meaningful ways. COVID-19 has opened the door to this alternative pathway. While nature is a profound teacher, humanity must choose to respond to her lessons. This formidable endeavor demands a re-education and the immediate cooperation of us all.

References

Adams, C. J. (2004) *The sexual politics of meat: a feminist-vegetarian critical theory*. 20th Anniversary edn. New York: Continuum.

Almiron, N. (2016) 'The political economy behind the oppression of other animals: interest and influence', in Almiron, N., Cole, M. and Freeman, C. P. (eds) *Critical animal and media studies: communication for nonhuman animal advocacy*. New York: Routledge.

Ascione, F. R. (2001). Animal Abuse and Youth Violence. Juvenile Justice Bulletin. Juvenile Justice Clearinghouse.

Beirne P. (2020). Wildlife trade and COVID-19: towards a criminology of anthropogenic pathogen spillover. *British Journal of Criminology*. 2020: azaa084. doi: 10.1093/bjc/azaa084

Bekoff, M. (2008). *The emotional lives of animals: A leading scientist explores animal joy, sorrow, and empathy – and why they matter*. Novato, Calif: New World Library.

Bruchac, M. (2014). Indigenous Knowledge and Traditional Knowledge. In Smith, C. (Ed.), Encyclopedia of Global Archaeology, 3814–3824. New York: Springer.https://repository. upenn.edu/cgi/viewcontent.cgi?article=1172&context=anthro_papers

Chai, B. C., van der Voort, J. R., Grofelnik, K., Eliasdottir, H. G., Klöss, I. and Perez-Cueto, F. J. A. (2019) 'Which diet has the least environmental impact on our planet? A systematic review of vegan, vegetarian and omnivorous diets', *Sustainability*, 11(15), pp. 4110–28. doi:10.3390/ su11154110

CDC. *One Health*. (2021). CDC website. Available online at: https://www.cdc.gov/onehealth/ (accessed 06 May, 2021).

Cleaveland, S, Sharp, J., Abela-Ridder, B., Allan, K.J., Buza, J., Crump, J.A., et al. (2017). One Health contributions towards more effective and equiTable le approaches to health in low- and middle-income countries. Philos Trans R Soc London Ser B Biol Sci., 372:20160168. doi: 10.1098/rstb.20 16.0168

Cleaveland, S., Laurenson, M.K., Taylor, L.H. (2001). Diseases of humans and their domestic mammals: pathogen characteristics, host range and the risk of emergence. *Philos Trans R Soc London B Biol Sci.*, 356:991–9. doi: 10.1098/rstb.2001.0889

Cole, M. (2016) 'Getting (Green) Beef: Anti-Vegan Rhetoric and the Legitimizing of Eco-Friendly Oppression', in Almiron, N., Cole, M. and Freeman, C. P. (eds) *Critical animal and media studies: communication for nonhuman animal advocacy*. New York: Routledge.

Demm, S.L., Lane-deGraaf, K. E., & Rayhel, E. A. (2019). Introduction to one health: An interdisciplinary approach to planetary health. Wiley Blackwell.

Dunbar R. (2004) The Human Story. A new history of mankind's evolution. Faber and Faber Limited, London.

Faunalytics (2018). URL Retrieved: https://faunalytics.org/farmed-animals-fundamentals-sources/

FAO (2020). *The State of World Fisheries and Aquaculture 2020. Sustainability in action*. Rome. https://doi.org/10.4060/ca9229en

Fiddles, N. (1991) Meat: A natural symbol. NY: Routledge.

Foucault, M. (1991) *Discipline and punish: the birth of the prison*. London: Penguin Books.

Freeman, C. P. (2016) 'This little piggy went to press: the American news media's construction of animals in agriculture', in Almiron, N., Cole, M. and Freeman, C.P. (eds) *Critical animal and media studies: communication for nonhuman animal advocacy.* New York: Routledge, pp. 169–184.

Friend M. (2006). Biowarfare, bioterrorism, and animal diseases as bioweapons. In: Friend M, editor. *Disease Emergence and Resurgence: The Wildlife-Human Connection.* Reston, VA: U.S. Geological Survey, Circular 1285, p. 400.

Fromm, E. (1973) The Anatomy of Human Destructiveness. Holt, Rinehart and Winston.

Galtung, J. (1969). Violence, Peace, and Peace Research. *Journal of Peace Research, 6*(3), 167–191. https://doi.org/10.1177/002234336900600301

Gruen, L. (2015). *Entangled empathy: An alternative ethic for our relationships with animals.* New York: Lantern Books.

Hunt, C. (2015) 'Farm gone factory: industrial animal agriculture, animal welfare, and the environment', in Kemmerer, L. (ed.) *Animals and the environment: advocacy, activism and the quest for common ground.* Abingdon: Routledge, pp. 173–85.

Inoue, T. (2017) 'Oceans filled with agony: fish oppression driven by capitalist commodification', in Nibert, D. (ed.) *Animal oppression and capitalism, Volume 1: The oppression of nonhuman animals as sources of food.* Santa Barbara: Praeger, pp. 96–117.

Itle-Clark, S. & Comaskey, E. (2020). A proposal for a humane pedagogy. International Journal of Humane Education, 1 (1). Retrieved from: https://www.prosocialacademy.org/volume-1-issue-1-2020

Joy, M. (2011). *Why we love dogs, eat pigs, and wear cows: An introduction to carnism: the belief system that enables us to eat some animals and not others.* Berkeley, Calif.: Conari.

Joy, M. (2019). Powerarchy: understanding the psychology of oppression for social transformation. Oakland, CA: Berrett-Koehler Publishers.

Kanizsa, G., (1955). 'Margini quasi-percettivi in campi con stimolazione omogenea', Rivista di Psicologia, 49 (1) pp.7–30. English translation, 'Quasi-perceptual margins in homogeneously stimulated fields', in S. Petry and G. E. Meyer, (Eds). (1987), The Perception of Illusory Contours pp. 40–49, Springer: NY.

Khan, L.H., Kaplan, B., Monath, T.P., Woodall, J., Conti, L.A. (2018). *One Health initiative.* Available online at: http://www.onehealthinitiative.com/ (accessed 06 May, 2021).

Kellert, S. 1997. Kinship to Mastery: Biophilia in Human Evolution and Development. Washington, DC: Island Press.

Kellert, S. and E.O. Wilson, eds. 1993. The Biophilia Hypothesis. Washington, DC: Island Press.

Kemmerer, L. and Dopp, B. (2015) 'A fishy business', in Kemmerer, L. (ed.) *Animals and the environment: advocacy, activism and the quest for common ground.* Abingdon: Routledge, pp. 163–72.

Kasperbauer, T. (2018). Subhuman. 1st ed. Oxford: Oxford University Press.

Kim, C.J. (2011) Moral extensionism or racist exploitation? The use of holocaust and slavery analogies in the Animal Liberation Movement, New Political Science, 33:3, 311–333, DOI: 10.1080/07393148.2011.592021

Lee, C., Nguyen, A. J., Haroz, E., Tol, W., Aules, Y., & Bolton, P. (2019). Identifying research priorities for psychosocial support programs in humanitarian settings. Global Mental Health, 6. https://doi.org/10.1017/gmh.2019.19

Longo G.O. (2003) Il Simbionte. Prove di umanità futura. Booklet (ed), Milano, Italy.

Lo Iacono G, Cunningham AA, Fichet-Calvet E, Garry RF, Grant DS, Leach M, et al. (2016). A unified framework for the infection dynamics of zoonotic spillover and spread. *PLoS Negl Trop Dis.,* 10:e0004957. doi: 10.1371/journal.pntd.0004957

Lovitz, D. (2010). *Muzzling a movement: The effects of anti-terrorism law, money, and politics on animal activism*. New York: Lantern Books.

McMahon, B.J., Morand, S., & Gray, J.S. (2018). Ecosystem change and zoonoses in the Anthropocene. Zoonoses Public Health. 65:755–65. doi: 10.1111/zph.12489

Nibert, D. (2016) 'Origins of oppression, specialist ideology, and the mass media', in Almiron, N., Cole, M. and Freeman, C.P. (eds) *Critical animal and media studies: communication for nonhuman animal advocacy*. New York: Routledge, pp. 74–88.

Noske, B. (1989). *Humans and other animals*. London: Pluto Press.

One health (2022). The World Health Organization: Health topics; URL Retrieved: https://www.who.int/health-topics/one-health#tab=tab_3.

Pievani T. (2006) La teoria dell'evoluzione. Il Mulino, Bologna.

Plous, S. (Ed.). (2003). *Understanding prejudice and discrimination*. McGraw-Hill.

Reynolds, C. J., Buckley, J. D., Weinstein, P. and Boland, J. (2014) 'Are the dietary guidelines for meat, fat, fruit and vegetable consumption appropriate for environmental sustainability? A review of the literature', *Nutrients*, 6(6), pp. 2251–65. doi:10.3390/nu6062251

Rosnay, J.D. (2000) The Symbiotic Man: a new understanding of the organization of life and a vision of the future. McGraw -Hill, 2000.

Ryder, R.D. (2004). Speciesism revisited. Think, 2, 6, 83–92.

Sanders, B. (2018, October 10). *Global Animal Slaughter Statistics And Charts*. Faunalytics. https://faunalytics.org/global-animal-slaughter-statistics-and-charts/

Shapiro, K. (2020). Human-Animal Studies: Remembering the Past, Celebrating the Present, Troubling the Future, *Society & Animals*, 28(7), 797–833. doi: https://doi.org/10.1163/15685306-BJA10029

Shapiro, K., & DeMello, M. (2010). The state of human-animal studies. Society & Animals, 18(3), 307–318.

Singer, P. (2009). *Animal liberation: the definitive classic of the animal movement*. Harper Perennial.

Spanjol, K. (2020). Removing ethical blind spots in higher education: The necessity of including non-human animals in social justice discourse. In S. Itle-Clark (Ed.) Humane Education in Higher Education, WCY Humane Press, Amissville, VA.: 73–114.

Spanjol, K. (2020). Teaching process over content: Addressing underlying psychological processes and biases in learners when including non-human animals in education and social justice discourse. International Journal of Humane Education, 1(1), 66–104

Stewart, K., & Cole, M. (2020, October 23). *Meat is masculine: How food advertising perpetuates harmful gender stereotypes*. The Conversation. https://theconversation.com/meat-is-masculine-how-food-advertising-perpetuates-harmful-gender-stereotypes-119004.

Sztybel D. (2006) The Rights of Animal Persons, in "Animals Liberation Philosophy and Policy Journal", 4, pp. 1–37.

Sztybel, D. (2007). Animal Rights Law: Fundamentalism versus Pragmatism. *Journal for Critical Animal Studies*, 5(1).

Urban, W. J., Wagoner, J. L., & Gaither, M. (2019). *American education: A History*. Routledge.

Weil, Z. (2006). Power and Promise of Humane Education. New York: New Society Publishers.

Wilks, M., Caviola, L., Kahane, G., & Bloom, P. (2021). Children Prioritize Humans Over Animals Less Than Adults Do. *Psychological Science*, 32(1), 27–38. https://doi.org/10.1177/0956797620960398

Wilson, E. O. (1984). Biophilia. Cambridge: Harvard University Press.

Wise, S. M. (2000). *Rattling the cage: Toward legal rights for animals*. Cambridge, Mass: Perseus Pub.

Zucca P (2009) Benessere Animale. In Sovrano V, Zucca P, Regolin L (Eds) Il comportamento degli animali: evoluzione, cognizione e benessere. Carocci Editore, Roma.

Zucca P. (2020) The Zoonosecene: the new geological epoch of intensive breeding, of wildlife trade, of antibiotic resistance and of pandemic diseases, following the Anthropocene. *Platinum, Sole 24 Ore English edition*, **11**, 114.

Zucca, P.; Rossmann, M. C.; Dodic, M.; Ramma, Y.; Matsushima, T.; Seet, S.; Holtze, S.; Bremini, A.; Fischinger, I.; Morosetti, G.; Sitzia, M.; Furlani, R.; Greco, O.; Meddi, G.; Zambotto, P.; Meo, F.; Pulcini, S.; Palei, M. & Zamaro, G. (2021), 'What do adolescents know about One-Health and Zoonotic risks? A school-based survey in Italy, Austria, Germany, Slovenia, Mauritius and Japan', *Frontiers in Planetary Health*, doi: 10.3389/fpubh.2021.658876.

Zucca P. (2021a) *"Illegal animal trade across Europe as an organised crime: the time is up"*. Communication at the Intergroup on the welfare and conservation of animals of the European Parliament, 21 April 2021, DOI: 10.13140/RG.2.2.26063.41121.

Zucca P. (2022) *Four cognitive-ecological biases that reduce integration between Medical and Cyber Intelligence and represente a threat to cybersecurity*. Forensic Science International: Animals and Environments, 100046, ISSN 2666-9374, https://doi.org/10.1016/j.fsiae.2022.100046.

Part II: **Applications**

Giampiero E. G. Beroggi

8 A latent factor risk model for COVID-19

8.1 Introduction

The term "Pandemic" originates from the old Greeks, where "pan" means "all" and "demos" means "the people" [Qiu et al., 2017]. A pandemic affects thus all the people and, as it was witnessed for COVID-19, also the whole world [Wikipedia, 2022]. Pandemics extend over several months or years and usually come in multiple waves. The spread, duration, and extent of pandemics are characterized by high uncertainty. The decline in severity of detrimental effects might signal the end of the pandemic or merely the end of a wave; i.e., the silence before the next storm. Due to the rapidly fluctuating condition of a pandemic, pandemic risk management pertains to the field of operational risk management Beroggi and Wallace [1994].

Various risk concepts for modeling pandemics have been proposed. They all include elements of preparedness, followed by mitigation measures, response measures, and finally recovery measures. Mounier-Jack and Coker [2006] analyzed 21 national preparedness plans for pandemics. They concluded that preparation for logistic aspects were to some extend good, while response and intervention were probably inadequate. Marin-Ferrer et al. [2017] introduced an index for risk management (INFORM), meant to identify countries at risk of humanitarian crisis and disaster that would overwhelm national response capacity. Morse et al. [2012] proposed several research and surveillance opportunities and goals to move the global pandemic strategy from response to preemption. Lesmanawati [2020] developed a multifactorial risk analysis tool, called "EpiRisk". The tool allows to gain rapid insight into the potential severity of emerging epidemics. It does so by combining disease-related parameters and country-related risk parameters. By predicting the risk of emerging outbreaks in real-time, EpiRisk should provide the means for timely intervention and thus prevent catastrophic epidemic outcomes. PAHO [2020] developed a checklist for COVID-19 pandemic risk and impact management. The checklist serves as a tool for national authorities to develop or revise national pandemic preparedness and response plans to COVID-19. Roberts [2019] investigated the role of big data and the application of algorithmic processing techniques for the real-time surveillance of infectious disease outbreaks. Kyea and Hwang [2020] analyzed the causal effect of a pandemic crisis and institutional responses on social trust using empirical data during COVID-19. They concluded that trust in South Korean society, people, and the central and local governments improved substantially, whereas trust in judicature, the press, and religious organizations sharply decreased. The World Health Organization (WHO) has established in 2005 the International Health Regulations (IHR), to which 196 countries are committed to [WHO, 2021]. The IHR constitutes an international treaty to combat the global spread of diseases. Each year, the 196 countries bound by the IHR must file a self-assessment report to the WHO, stating their status of preparedness for health emergencies. However, the veracity of these self-reports can be questionable, making them possibly an inadequate tool for pandemic risk assessment and management [Guardian, 2021]. For reasons like these, world-leaders are calling for an international pandemic treaty that enables countries to be better able to predict, mitigate, and respond to pandemics in an internationally coordinated way [BBC, 2021].

8.2 Latent factor risk model

The traditional risk models for pandemic risk management are based on operational factors that affect the potentially adverse effects of a pandemic. These factors refer to preparedness, mitigation, and response aspects. They typically include the number of available vaccines, the amount of available protective equipment (e.g., face masks), and the number of available intensive care beds.

Contrary to the traditional risk models, the risk model presented here is based on latent factors (see Figure 8.1). These latent factors are used to characterize various characteristics of nations, such as the people's general health, the economic state and potential, the overall prosperity, etc. Starik and Rands [1995] identify four key factors that contribute to an organization's sustainability: economic, political, social–cultural, and ecological environments. Accordingly, three meta latent factors are identified to be included into the proposed risk model: (1) business, (2) political, and (3) population.

Business factors: Roy and Goll [2014] identify corruption (*Crr*) and social responsibility (*Rsp*) as critical economic factors to predict sustainability of nations. As an alternative measure of economic freedom, business friendliness (*Bus*) is considered in this model. Gravito Hernández and Rueda Galvis [2021] discuss innovation and patents as business success factors, suggesting that the number of patents (*Ptn*) should also be considered as a latent factor. COVID-19 has had a major impact on workers and workplaces all over the world [Kniffin et a., 2021]. Consequently, the employment rate (*Emp*) is an important latent factor to be considered for this risk model.

Political factors: Various political factors have been used in studying nations' characteristics. Bayerlein et. al (2021) analyzed how populistic governments (mis) handle the COVID-19 pandemic. They provide empirical evidence that countries governed by populistic government did get hit worse by the pandemic. Bollen [1993] proposes two method factors to subsume a large number of political indicators. These are *political liberty* (e.g., civil liberties, political participation, and personal autonomy) and *democratic rule* (e.g., electoral process and pluralism, functioning of government, and clean elections). Elff and Ziaja (2018) extend Bollen's two-dimensional concept to three and four dimensions. For the purposes of the risk model presented here, Bollen's two-dimensional model will be operationalized with the latent factors political liberty (*Frd*) and democratic rule (*Dmc*).

Population factors: The implications of COVID-19 have been linked to preexisting health conditions, such as obesity, which in turn has an effect on life expectancy [Rychter et.al, 2020]. For this reason, the two latent factors *life expectancy* (*Exp*) and *population health* (*Hlt*) are considered.

The nine latent factors introduced above can all be influenced by the stakeholders of a nation. Freeman [2010, p. 25] defines stakeholders to be "all of those groups or individuals that can affect, or are affected by, the accomplishment of organizational purpose." Business factors can be influenced by enterprises and unions, political factors can be influenced by all political stakeholders, and population factors can, to some extent, be influence by the population.

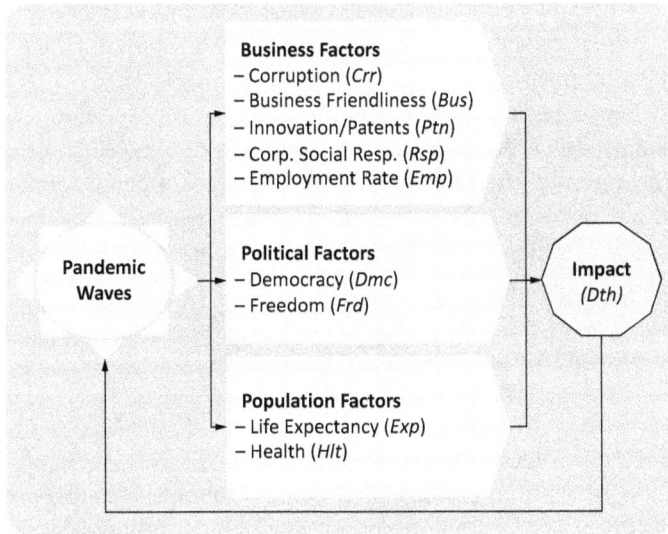

Figure 8.1: Latent factor risk model with three meta latent factors and nine latent factors.

8.3 Dimensions of latent factors risk model

8.3.1 Data collection

The data for the proposed latent factors were obtained from various online sources, which were accessed on September 24, 2020, after the first COVID-19 wave. Characteristics about the factors, their three letter abbreviations (*italic*) used as factor names, and details about the online sources are subsequently presented.

Business factors:

1. *Crr*: Corruption Perception Index (CPI), as defined by Transparency International (transparency.org/cpi). Transparency International states that the CPI scores and ranks countries/territories based on how corrupt their sector is perceived to be by experts and business executives. It is supposed to be a composite index, consisting of a combination of more than a dozen surveys and assessments. The data used in this context are the corruption scores of the nations, meaning that less corrupt nations have higher scores, while more corrupt nations have lower scores.

2. *Bus*: This variable stands for business friendliness and is recorded as the ease of doing business index (EBI). EBI is an index created jointly by Simeon Djankov and Gerhard Pohl, two leading economists at the Central and Eastern Europe sector of the World Bank Group. The data (2020) was taken from The World Bank.

3. *Ptn*: The number of patents per one million inhabitant reflects the latent factor patents. The number of patents data (2019) was taken from (https://statnano.com/report/s135). (https://www.doingbusiness.org/en/data/doing-business-score?topic=starting-a-business).

4. *Rsp*: The Corporate Social Responsibility (CSR) data (2019) were taken from the CSRHub (csrhub.com/). The CSRHub generates consensus ratings using a big data algorithm. The algorithm first aggregates 279 million data points, which then are converted into almost ten thousand metrics. These metrics are mapped into 12 areas. After normalization and weighting of the data, the country score is derived. These country scores are used as the responsibility measure.

5. *Emp*: The employment data were taken from the World Bank for the year of 2019 (https://data.worldbank.org/indicator/SL.EMP.TOTL.SP.ZS).

Political factors:

1. *Dmc*: The Democracy Index (2019) was taken from Wikipedia (wikipedia.org/wiki/Democracy_Index). The index is compiled by the Economist Intelligence Unit (EIU), a UK-based company. The purpose of this index is to measure the state of democracy in more than 100 countries.

2. *Frd*: The freedom score is assessed by Freedom House and refers to people's access to political rights and civil liberties. The score is composed of political rights and civil liberties. The data for the global freedom score were taken from the Freedom House website (https://freedomhouse.org/countries/freedom-world/scores) for the year 2020.

Population factors:

1. *Exp*: The life expectancy data were taken from Wikipedia as the UNDP data from 2018(https://en.wikipedia.org/wiki/List_of_countries_by_life_expectancy).

2. *Hlt*: As a health measure of a nation, the Global Obesity Level was taken. The data (2016) were taken from ProCon.org (obesity.procon.org/global-obesity-levels).

Dependent factor:
1. *Dth*: As the dependent or impact factor for COVID-19, the number of deaths per one million inhabitants was taken. The data were taken from Worldometer (worldometers.info/coronavirus/).

Because the data come from different sources and are generally reported by the different countries, the measurement approach and the quality of the data will also vary along these dimensions. Especially for the reported COVID-19 deaths, there could be quite some uncertainty about the data consistency and quality. Data quality and considerations for modeling and analysis have been addressed by various institutions, such as the U.S. Government Accountability Office [GAO, 2020]. Moreover, the pandemic's different dynamics around the globe is another source of limited comparability of the data. Due to these different limitations and for the sake of straightforward reevaluation of the performed analyses, no additional formatting of the reported data has been done.

8.3.2 Data cleaning

The data analysis was conducted with the R-Software [R Core Team, 2021]. Data for the latent factors identified in the risk model were collected from the referenced sources. A total of 85 countries (observations) were considered for the ten variables of the risk model. Only countries with a minimum population of one million inhabitants were considered for this purpose. For the remaining 72 countries, 5% were missing values. Discarding all countries with missing values would have left only 44 countries, which would be too few to conduct meaningful analyses. The variables *Dth*, *Crr*, *Dmc*, and *Frd* have no missing values. The variables *Bus*, and *Emp* have one missing value, *Exp* has two, *Hlt* five, *Ptn* 12, and *RSP* 19 missing values. The correlation matrix for the ten variables with the missing values and the correlation matrix for the ten variables with imputation do not differ significantly. This implies that the imputation has only marginal impact on the correlations among the ten variables. By proceeding this way, the number of complete observations could be increased from 44 to 72.

The imputation was done iteratively, starting with the factor having the least missing values. The missing values of this factor were then imputed with linear regression, where all factors without missing values served as independent factors. Thereby, *Dth* was not included in the imputation. This procedure was repeated until the missing values of all factors were imputed.

An outlier analysis revealed that there were quite some outliers for several variables. Considering the rather small number of observations (72), some of these outliers were eliminated. The criteria to include countries for the analysis were the following: *Dmc* > 5, *Hlt* > 0.05, *Exp* > 40, and *Emp* > 45. As a result, 50 nations could be used for the following data analyses.

8.4 Validation of the latent factor risk model

8.4.1 Latent factor analysis

The correlations among the impact factor *Dth* and the nine latent factors are illustrated with a correllograph (Figure 8.2), computed with the R-Package *PerformanceAnalytics* [Peterson and Peter, 2020]. On the diagonal, from top left to bottom right, in Figure 8.2, the histograms of the ten variables are shown. Below the diagonal, the scatterplots of any two of the ten variables are shown with a fitted trend curve. Above the diagonal, the correlation values (between –1.0 and +1.0) with the level of significance are plotted. Cells with at least one star (*) imply that the correlation is significant at the 5% level, while a dot (.) indicates a level of significance of 10%.

The first row shows the correlations between *Dth* and the nine latent factors. Only two latent factors (*Bus* and *Rsp*) do not have a statistically significant correlation with the impact factor *Dth* (level of significance 10%). *Dth* correlates strongest with *Exp* (34%), followed by *Hlt* (33%), *Frd* (30%), *Dmc* (29%), *Ptn* (28%), *Crr* (27%), and *Emp* (–25%). The only significant negative correlation with *Dth* stems from *Emp*. This implies that higher employment values result in lower *Dth* values, and vice versa.

The correllograph in Figure 8.2 shows, that the latent factors relating to the meta latent factor *Business* have a quite high pairwise correlations, except with *Emp*. The two latent factors referring to *Politics* (*Dmc* and *Frd*), have the highest correlation (81%). The two latent factors referring to *Population* (*Exp*, *Hlt*) have a correlation of 43%.

8.4.2 Meta latent factor analysis

The assignment of the nine latent factors to the three meta latent factors can be tested with a confirmatory factor analysis (CFA). This is done with the R-Package "sem" [Fox et al., 2020]. The results show a model Chi-square of 63,94, with 24 degrees of freedom and $p < 0.01$ (AIC = 105.94, BIC = –29.95). This implies that the model is statistically significant; i.e., the assignment of the nine latent factors to the three meta latent factors is statistically significant. The parameter estimates are summarized in Table 8.1.

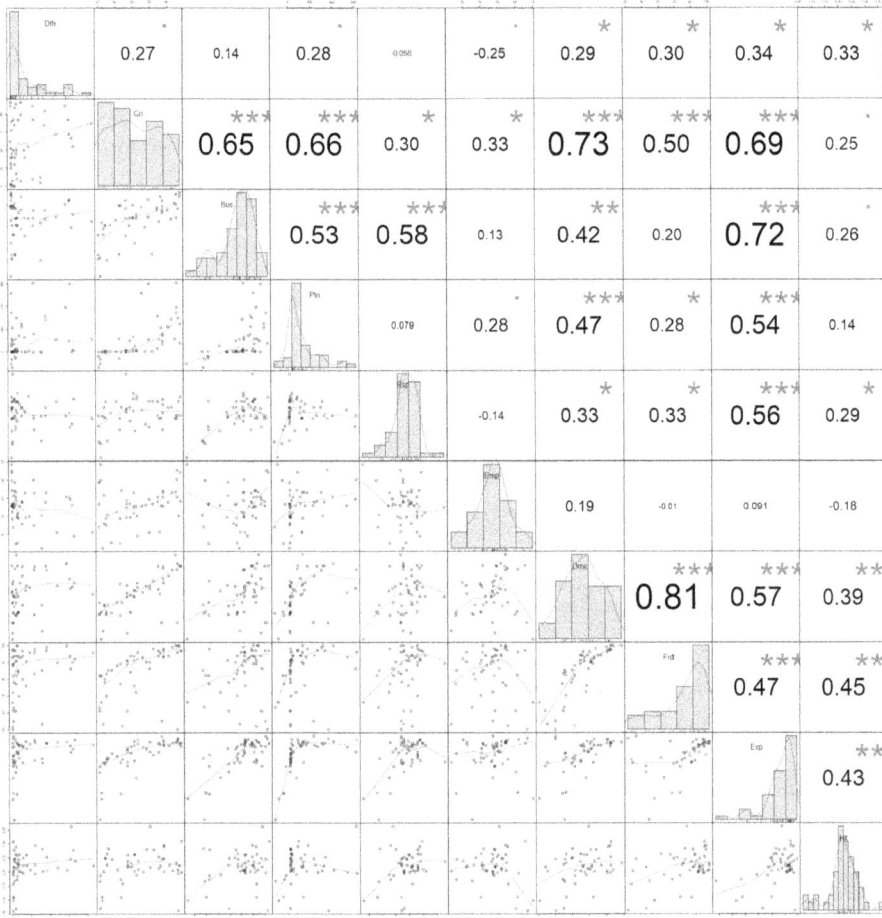

Figure 8.2: Correllograph for the impact factor *Dth* and the nine latent factors.
Note: Signif. codes: 0 "****" 0.001 "***" 0.01 "**" 0.05 "." 0.1 " " 1)

Table 8.1: Parameter estimates with confirmatory factor analysis for the grouping of
the nine latent factors (LF) to the tree meta latent factors (MLF).

Estimate	Std Error	z value	Pr(>|z|)	LF		MLF
13.54	1.78	7.60	<0.01	Crr	<—	Business
6.22	1.00	6.24	<0.01	Bus	<—	Business
113.53	21.73	5.23	<0.01	Ptn	<—	Business
2.43	0.73	3.35	<0.01	Rsp	<—	Business
1.32	0.74	1.77	0.08	Emp	<—	Business
1.29	0.14	9.45	<0.01	Dmc	<—	Politics

Table 8.1 (continued)

Estimate	Std Error	z value	Pr(>|z|)	LF		MLF
10.17	1.89	5.37	<0.01	*Frd*	<—	*Politics*
7.05	1.25	5.63	<0.01	*Exp*	<—	*Population*
0.02	0.01	2.54	0.01	*Hlt*	<—	*Population*

8.5 Predictive risk models for COVID-19

Two sets of regression models will be analyzed, one for the three meta latent factors and one for the nine latent factors.

8.5.1 Regression modeling with meta latent factors

With the R-Package "FactoMineR" [Le et al., 2008], the rotated coordinates for the three principal components are calculated. The correllograph in Figure 8.3, is calculated for the three meta latent factors and the independent variable *Dth*, using the R-Package *PerformanceAnalytics* [Peterson and Peter, 2020].

From Figure 8.3 it can be seen that *Dth* only correlates significantly with the meta latent factor *Business*. Therefore, only *Business* can be used for a predictive regression model. The result of the linear regression model is illustrated in Table 8.2.

The residual standard error is 211 on 48 degrees of freedom. The multiple R-squared is 0.0973, the adjusted R-squared is 0.0785, the F-statistic is 5.17 on 1 and 48 degrees of freedom, and the p-value is 0.02.

It can therefore be conclude that the meta latent factor *Business* is the only significant meta latent factor affecting the reported number of deaths, while the meta latent factors *Politics* and *Population* are not statistically significant. The interpretation of this result could be that business factors are directly affecting the interaction of people, while political factors (democracy and freedom) are of a more strategic nature. Population factors (life expectancy and health) can very well affect the behavior of people, but probably not to such an operational level as the business factors do.

8.5.2 Regression modeling with latent factors

At the level of the nine latent factors, four separate models are built, one for each of the three meta latent factors and one considering all nine latent factors simultaneously.

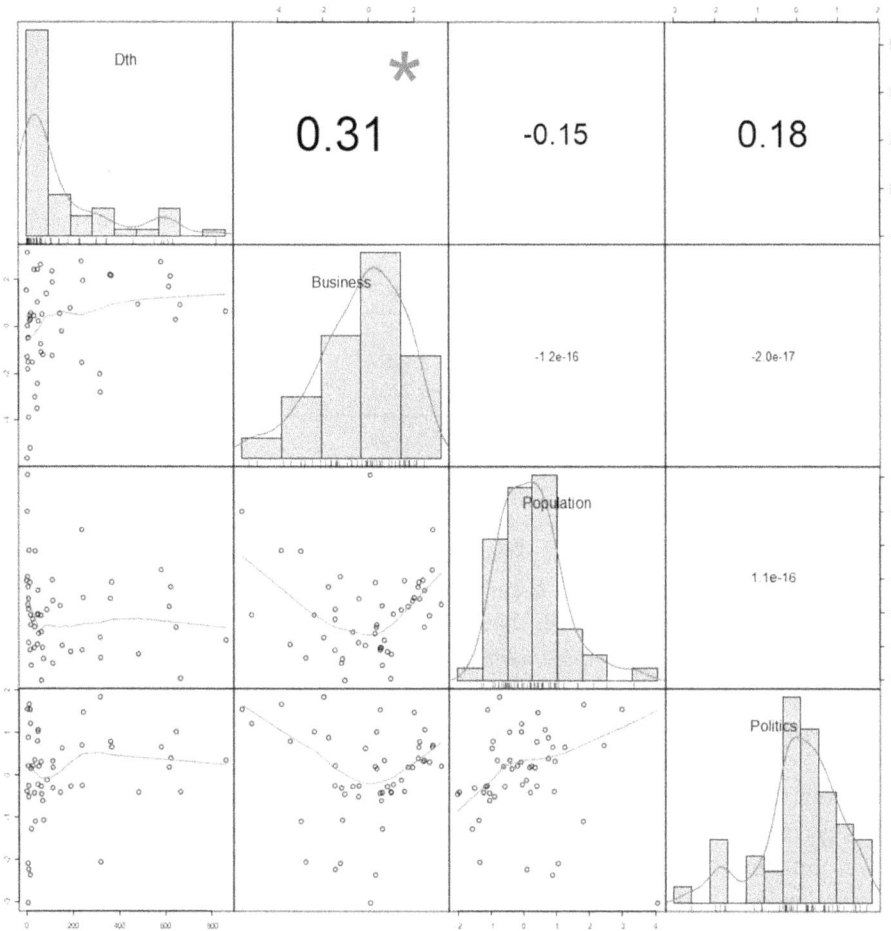

Figure 8.3: Correllograph for the three meta latent factors and the independent variable *Dth*.
Note: Signif. codes: 0 "****" 0.001 "***" 0.01 "**" 0.05 "." 0.1 " " 1

Table 8.2: Result of linear regression analysis.

	Estimate	Std. Error	t value	Pr(>|t|)
Intercept	166.1	29.8	5.58	< 0.01
Business	32.7	14.4	2.27	< 0.31

(a) Business latent factors

The initial model for the latent factors referring to *Business* is the following: *Dth ~ Crr + Bus + Ptn + Rsp + Emp*. In words: *Dth* is the independent variable, while the variables to the right of the "~" sign are the independent variables, separated by "+". This model is not statistically significant. A step-wise regression reveals the statistically significant model: *Dth ~ Crr + Emp*. Obviously, only corruption and employment are significant predictors for *Dth*. Table 8.3 shows the results of the analysis.

Table 8.3: Result of stepwise regression to predict *Dth* with only the business latent factors.

	Estimate	Std. Error	t value	Pr(>|t|)
Intercept	758.91	326.54	2.32	0.02
Crr	5.58	1.97	2.84	0.01
Emp	−16.29	5.95	−2.74	0.01

The residual standard error is 200 on 47 degrees of freedom, the multiple R-squared is 0.2, the adjusted R-squared is 0.166, the F-statistic is 5.87 on 2 and 47 degrees of freedom, and the p-value is < 0.01. This is thus a statistically significant model to predict *Dth* with two latent factors, *Crr* and *Emp*, pertaining to *Business*.

The model in Table 8.3 shows that the corruption score (*Crr*) is positively correlated with *Dth*, while the employment rate (*Emp*) is negatively correlated with *Dth*. This implies that higher *Crr* values (which means less corrupt nations), coupled with lower *Emp* values (which means a lower employment rate), lead to higher *Dth* values. In words: less corrupt nations (higher *Crr* values) with lower employment rate tend to have higher number of deaths due to COVID-19. On the other hand, more corrupt nations (lower *Crr* values) with higher employment rates tend to have lower number of deaths due to COVID-19. However, *Crr* and *Emp* have a positive correlation (33%), which implies that less corrupt nations (higher *Crr* values) have a higher employment rate (higher *Emp* values).

The relative importance of the two latent business factors entering the final model to predict *Dth* are calculated with the R-Package "relaimpo" [Grömping, 2006].

Figure 8.4 shows that the two latent business factors account for 20% of the total variability. Thereby, *Crr* is slightly more influential than *Emp*.

(b) Politics latent factors

The initial model for the latent factors referring to *Politics* is the following: *Dth ~ Dmc + Frd*. However, this model is not statistically significant. A step-wise regression leads to the statistically significant model: *Dth ~ Frd*. However, also the model with the other latent factor, *Frd* (i.e., *Dth ~ Dmc*) is statistically significant. The model with *Frd* as the independent variable has the higher adjusted R-squared (0.07), compared to the model with *Dmc* as the independent variable (0.06). Because *Dmc* and *Frd* are

Relative importances for Dth
Method LMG

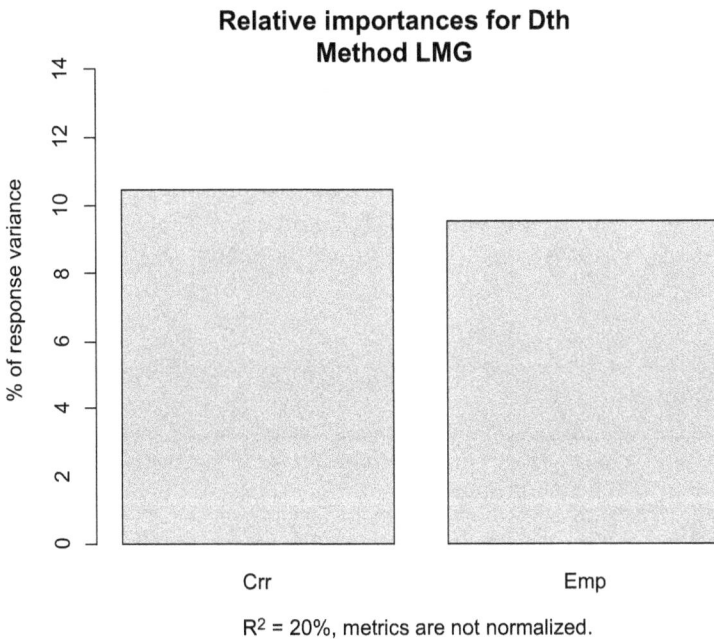

R² = 20%, metrics are not normalized.

Figure 8.4: Relative importance of the two latent business factors entering the predictive model for *Dth*.

highly correlated (81%) it is not surprisingly that only one of the two latent factors entered the predictive model. Table 8.4 shows the results of the analysis.

Table 8.4: Result of regression analysis to predict *Dth* with only *Frd* as independent variable (left) and only *Dmc* (right).

	Estimate	Std. Error	t value	Pr (>|t|)
Intercept	−225.09	183.65	−1.23	0.23
Frd	4.61	2.14	2.16	0.04

	Estimate	Std. Error	t value	Pr (>|t|)
Intercept	−254	205.6	−1.24	0.22
Dmc	54.8	26.5	2.07	0.04

For the slightly stronger model with the latent factor *Frd*, the results are the following: The residual standard error is 212 on 48 degrees of freedom, the multiple R-squared is 0.0885, the adjusted R-squared is 0.0695, the F-statistic is 4.66 on 1 and 48 degrees of freedom, and the p-value is 0.04. Although it is a statistically significant model to predict *Dth*, the model is quite weak and thus not suited to make any inference. It basically implies that nations with higher values of political freedom reported higher numbers of death. The same holds for *Dmc*. This implies that more democratic freedom tends to result in higher expected fatalities due to COVID-19.

(c) Population latent factors

The initial model for the latent factors referring to *Population* is the following: *Dth ~ Exp + Hlt*. However, this model is not statistically significant. A step-wise regression leads to the statistically significant model: *Dth ~ Exp*. Here too, the model with the other latent factor, *Hlt* (i.e., *Dth ~ Hlt*) is also statistically significant. The model with *Exp* as the independent variable has the higher adjusted R-squared (0.095), compared to the model with *Hlt* as independent variable (0.088). Table 8.5 shows the results of the analysis.

Table 8.5: Result of stepwise regression to predict *Dth* with only *Exp* as independent variable (left) and only *Hlt* (right).

	Estimate	Std. Error	t value	Pr (>|t|)		Estimate	Std. Error	t value	Pr (>|t|)
Intercept	−102.4	116	−0.88	0.38	Intercept	−745.87	369.88	−2.017	0.05
Hlt	1234.7	515.8	2.394	0.02	Exp	11.74	4.746	2.474	0.02

For the slightly stronger model with the latent factor *Exp*, the results are the following: The residual standard error is 208.7 on 48 degrees of freedom, the multiple R-squared is 0.113, the adjusted R-squared is 0.095, the F-statistic is 6.12 on 1 and 48 degrees of freedom, and the p-value is 0.02.

Because health and life expectancy are rather highly correlated (43%) it is not surprisingly that only one variable entered the final model, in this case life expectancy. Health is operationalized as the obesity level of the countries, implying that higher obesity levels lead to higher expected fatalities due to COVID-19. This confirms results reported, e.g., by Rychter et.al [2020].

(d) All nine latent factors

After looking at the nine latent factors separately, grouped into their meta level factors, an overall predictive model is derived that considers all nine factors simultaneously. The initial model for all nine latent factors is the following: *Dth ~ Crr + Bus + Ptn + Rsp + Emp + Dmc + Frd + Exp + Hlt*. This model is not statistically significant. A step-wise regression reveals the statistically significant model: *Dth ~ Rsp + Emp + Exp*. Table 8.6 shows the results of the analysis.

The residual standard error is 184.8 on 46 degrees of freedom, the multiple R-squared is 0.334, the adjusted R-squared is 0.290, the F-statistic is 7.69 on 3 and 46 degrees of freedom, and the p-value is < 0.01.

Table 8.6: Result of stepwise regression to predict *Dth* considering all nine latent factors simultaneously.

	Estimate	Std. Error	t value	Pr(>|t|)
Intercept	444.21	460.75	0.96	0.34
Rsp	−19.77	6.34	−3.12	<0.01
Emp	−16.14	5.36	−3.01	<0.01
Exp	22.10	5.20	4.25	<0.01

Corporate social responsibility (*Rsp*) has a negative coefficient (−19.77). This implies, that higher values of *Rsp* lead to lower values of *Dth*. Similarly, higher employment values (*Emp*) lead to lower *Dth* values, because the coefficient of *Emp* is also negative (−16.14). Corporate social responsibility and life expectancy have a strong social component. This suggests, that higher social scores result in lower impacts. Considering that COVID-19 has had a major impact on workers and workplaces [Kniffin et a., 2021] it seems still to be safer to have a higher employment rate, instead of avoiding workplaces.

The relative importance of the three latent factors entering the final model to predict *Dth* are calculated with the R-Package "relaimpo" [Grömping, 2006]. Figure 8.5 shows that live expectancy (*Exp*) has the strongest influence on the prediction model. The coefficient of life expectancy is positive (22.1) which implies that higher values of *Exp* lead to higher *Dth* values, while nations with lower values of *Exp* can expect lower values of *Dth*. This suggests, that COVID-19 affects primarily older people and that, consequently, nations with more older people suffer more negative impacts – a finding that has been reported since the beginning of the pandemic (CDC, 2022).

A comparison of the model considering all nine latent factors (all-factors model) with the three models derived for the three meta latent factors reveals some interesting results. The three models for the three meta latent factors are the following. *Business*: *Dth ~ Crr + Emp*, *Politics*: *Dth ~ Frd* and *Population*: *Dth ~ Hlt*. The all-factors model is the following: *Dth ~ Rsp + Emp + Exp*. Of the four latent factors that made it into the three meta factor models, only *Emp* made it into the all-factors model. Regarding the business latent factors, *Rsp* replaced *Crr* in the all-factors model. None of the political factors made it into the all-factors model. While *Hlt* was the only latent factor in the population model, it got replaced by *Exp* in the all-factors model. Quite interesting is the fact that *Rsp* has no significant correlation with *Dth* but made it anyway into the all-factors model. This is the case, because *Exp* is the most important latent factor in the all-factors model, while *Rsp* has been used to further improve the performance of the model.

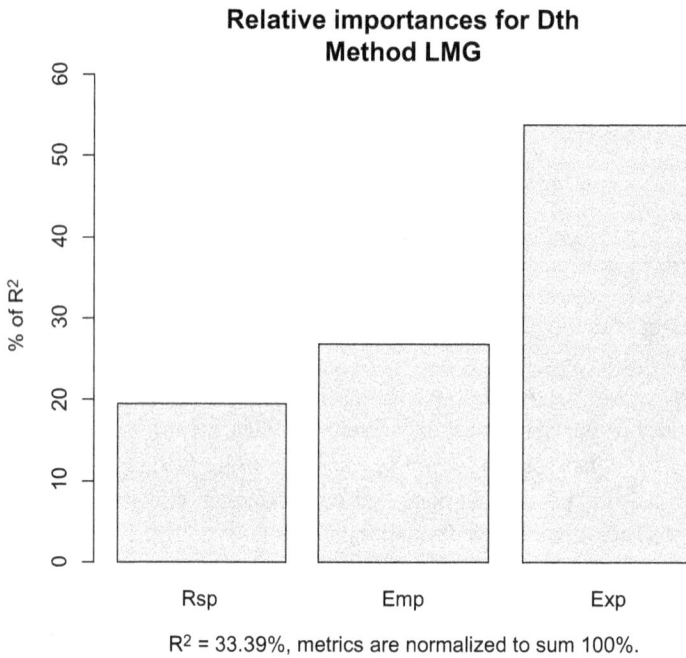

Figure 8.5: Relative importance of the latent factors entering the predictive model for *Dth*.

8.6 Post-event risk model

Finally, the learning effect of nations, as the pandemic progresses in multiple waves, is investigated. The progression of the pandemic in terms of *Dth* is shown in Figure 8.6.

The correlograph (computed with the R-Package *PerformanceAnalytics* [Peterson and Peter, 2020]) in Figure 8.7 shows that *Dth* strongly correlates among the five time periods. Pairwise correlation is highest between two neighboring periods (i.e., above the diagonal in Figure 8.7), while it slowly declines over time (i.e., towards the top right corner), starting at 0.84 in September 2020 and declining to 0.33 in January 2022. All correlations are statistically significant at the 5% level of significance. It can be concluded that the characteristics or the behavior of nations did not change substantially along the development of the pandemic.

8.7 Conclusions

A latent factor risk model was proposed to explain and predict the consequences of COVID-19 at a national level. Nine latent factors and three meta latent factors were

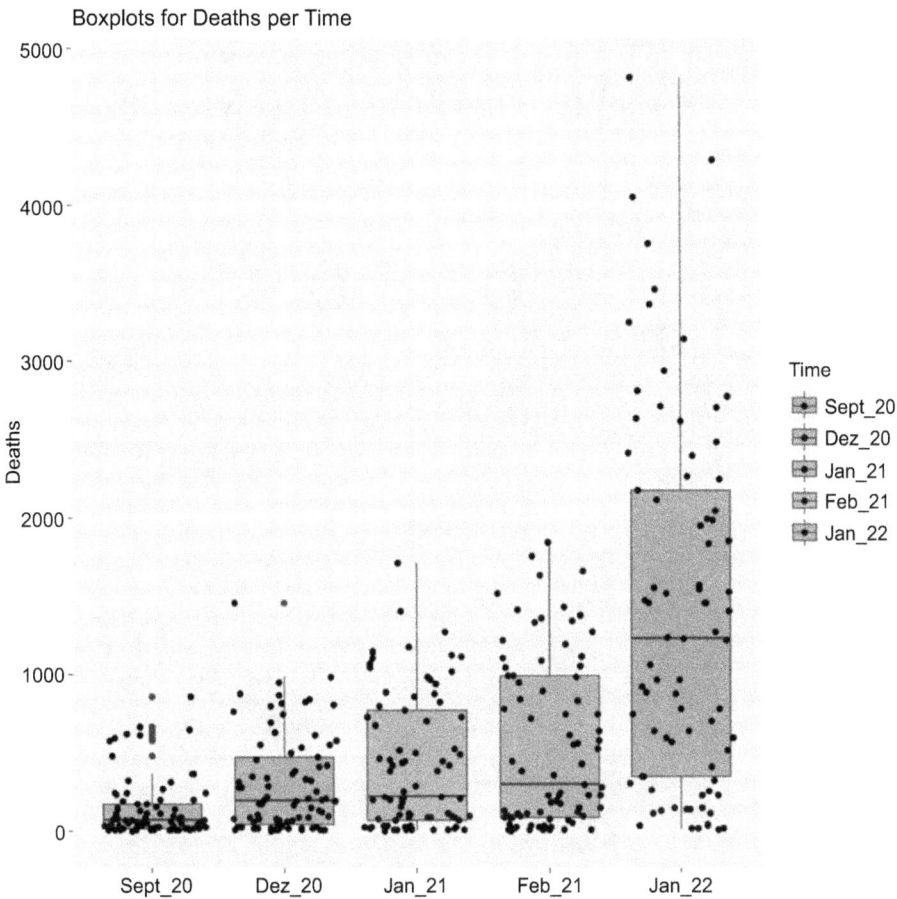

Figure 8.6: Boxplots for *Dth* at different Times.

defined. As the impact measure of COVID-19, the number of deaths per million population (*Dth*) was chosen.

The following results were obtained:

– The latent factor risk model, with nine latent factors and three meta latent factors, could be validated with empirical data.
– *Dth* can be predicted with a regression model using the three latent factors *Rsp* (corporate social responsibility), *Emp* (employment), and *Exp* (life expectancy). While higher standards of corporate social responsibility and higher rates of employment reduce the reported number of deaths, higher life expectancy has the opposite effect.
– *Dth* can also be predicted with a regression model, using only the meta latent factor *Business*, but not the meta latent factors *Democracy* and *Population*.

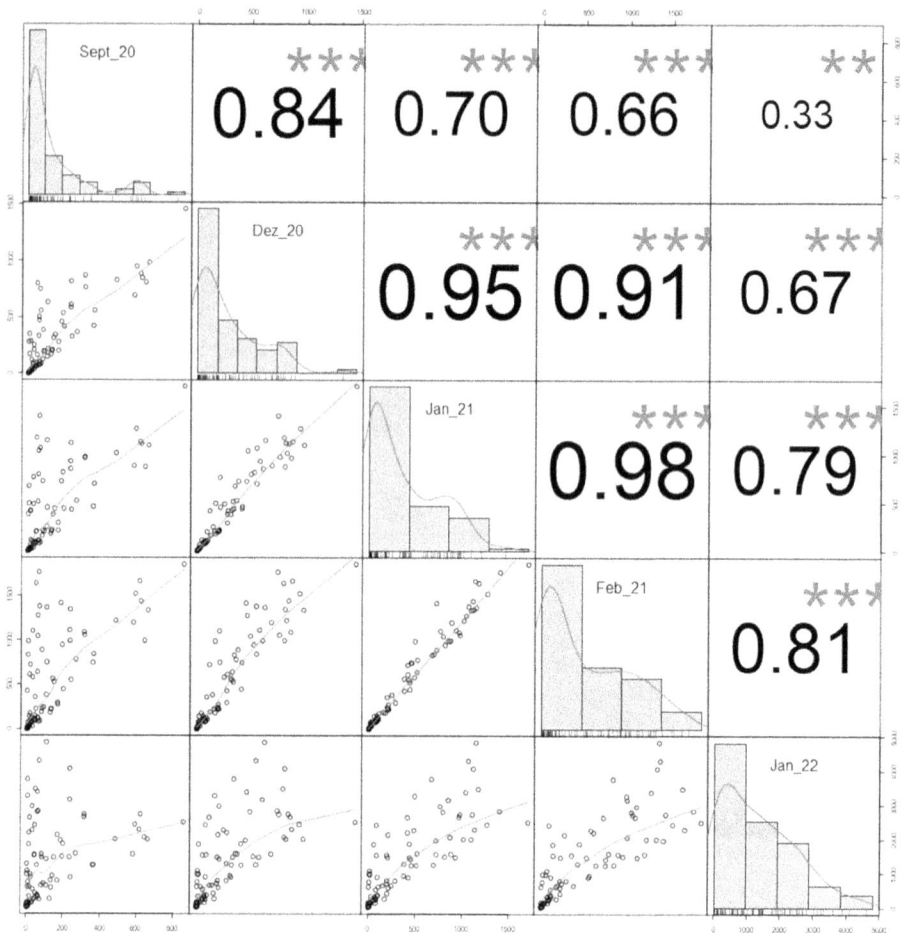

Figure 8.7: Correlograph for five time periods.

- The linear regression model considering all nine latent factors was compared to other regression techniques, based on machine learning. Basically, no improvement of the linear model could be obtained ridge regression, lasso regression, or elastic net regression.
- The results did not change significantly along the timely progression of the pandemic. This implies that nations did not alter their original influence on the latent factors as the pandemic progressed.

The analyses have also several limitations:
- The small number of nations (50) used for the analyses makes any result rather sensitive. This means that small changes regarding, e.g., the elimination of

outliers and imputation can have some impact on the results of the analyses, especially on the statistical significance of multivariate statistical models.

– The data quality and veracity of the nine latent factors as well as of *Dth* varies over the different organizations and nations. Instead of the reported number of deaths, alternative measures, such as the number of excess deaths could have been considered. However, the purpose was to analyze the publicized data, which was a primary source for public debate.

– The selection of *Dth* as the measure of consequence for COVID-19 is arbitrary. The number of infections per million population was, especially in the initial stages of the pandemic, the more important criterion to derive mitigation measures, such as curfews and shutdowns. However, the number of infections was, especially in the initial stages of the pandemic, very much dependent on the national testing strategies.

– COVID-19 hit different nations worldwide during different periods of time. This resulted in different peaks in time of the multiple waves. However, the waves were defined according to the global distribution of *Dth* from a world-wide perspective.

The proposed latent factor risk model was validated with empirical data. Regression analysis with the nine latent factors, as well as with the three meta latent factors, were performed to assess the predictive validity of the latent factor risk model. The results of these analyses provide ample evidence for face validity as well as of construct validity of the proposed latent factor risk model. Autocorrelation effects make the model also useful along the progression of the pandemic.

References

Bayerlein M., Boese V.A., Gates S., Kamin K., Kamin K., and S.M. Murshed (2021). Populism and COVID-19: How Populist Governments (Mis)Handle the Pandemic. Journal of Political Institutions and Political Economy, 2(3): 389–428.

BBC (2021). Covid-19: World leaders call for international pandemic treaty. https://www.bbc.com/news/uk-56572775 (accessed on March 30, 2021).

Beroggi G.E.G. and Wallace W.A. (1994). Operational Risk Management: A New Paradigm for Risk Analysis. IEEE Transactions on Systems, Man, and Cybernetics, 24/10, 1450–1457.

Bollen, K. A. (1993). Liberal Democracy: Validity and Method Factors in Cross-National Measures. American Journal of Political Science, 37(4), 1207–1230.

CDC (2022). Risk for COVID-19 Infection, Hospitalization, and Death By Age Group. https://www.cdc.gov/coronavirus/2019-ncov/covid-data/investigations-discovery/hospitalization-death-by-age.html (accessed on February 4, 2022).

Elff M. and Ziaja S. (2018). Method Factors in Democracy Indicators. Politics and Governance, 6/1, 92–104.

Fox John, Nie Zhenghua and Byrnes Jarrett (2020). sem: Structural Equation Models. R package version 3.1-11. https://CRAN.R-project.org/package=sem.

Freeman, R. E. (2010). Strategic Management: A Stakeholder Approach. Cambridge, UK: Cambridge University Press.

GAO (2020). Covid-19: Data Quality and Considerations for Modeling and Analysis, U.S. Government Accountability Office: https://www.gao.gov/products/gao-20-635sp, accessed January 18, 2022.

Gravito Hernández Y. and Rueda Galvis J.F. (2021), Innovation and Patents as a Business Success Factor", Journal of Economics, Finance and Administrative Science, 26/5151, 143–159.

Grömping Ulrike (2006). Relative Importance for Linear Regression in R: The Package relaimpo. Journal of Statistical Software, 17(1), 1–27.

Guardian (2021). "Italy 'misled WHO on pandemic readiness' weeks before Covid outbreak." Guardian online, accessed on March 22, 2021 (https://www.theguardian.com/world/2021/feb/22/italy-misled-who-on-pandemic-readiness-weeks-before-covid-outbreak).

Kniffin K.M. et al. (2021). COVID-19 and the Workplace: Implications, Issues, and Insights for Future Research and Action. American Psychologist Journal, 76/1, 63–77.

Kyea B. and Hwang S.-J. (2020). Social trust in the midst of pandemic crisis: Implications from COVID-19 of South Korea. Research in Social Stratification and Mobility 68, pp 1–5.

Le S., Josse J., Husson F. (2008). FactoMineR: An R Package for Multivariate Analysis. Journal of Statistical Software, 25 (1), 1–18.10.18637/jss.v025.i01.

Lesmanawati D.A.S., Veenstra P., Moa A., et al. (2020) A rapid risk analysis tool to prioritise response to infectious disease outbreaks. BMJ Global Health 5: e002327. doi:10.1136/bmjgh-2020-002327.

Marin-Ferrer M., Vernaccini L., and Poljansek K. (2017). Index for Risk Management INFORM Concept and Methodology Report – Version 2017, EUR 28655 EN, doi:10.2760/094023.

Morse S.S, Mazet J.A.K., Woolhouse M., Parrish C.R., Carroll D., Karesh W.B., Zambrana-Torrelio C., W Lipkin I., Daszak P. (2012). Prediction and prevention of the next pandemic zoonosis. Lancet 380, pp 1956–65.

Mounier-Jack S. and Coker R.J., 2006. How prepared is Europe for pandemic infl uenza? Analysis of national plan. Lancet, 367, 1405–11.

PAHO (2020). A checklist for COVID-2019 pandemic risk and impact management. Interim document – Version 1–27 February 2020. Available at https://iris.paho.org/handle/10665.2/52274.

Peterson Brian G. and Carl Peter (2020). PerformanceAnalytics: Econometric Tools for Performance and Risk Analysis. R package version 2.0.4. https://CRAN.R-project.org/package=PerformanceAnalytics.

Qiu W., Rutherford S., Mao A. and Chu C. (2017). The Pandemic and its impacts. Health, Culture and Society, Vol 9–10 (2016–2017), online: http://hcs.pitt.edu.

R Core Team (2021). R: A language and environment for statistical computing. R Foundation for Statistical Computing, Vienna, Austria. URL https://www.R-project.org/.

Roberts S.L. (2019). Big Data, Algorithmic Governmentality and the Regulation of Pandemic Risk. European Journal of Risk Regulation, 10, pp. 94–115.

Roy A. and Goll I., 2014. Predictors of Various Facets of Sustainability of Nations: The Role of Cultural and Economic Factors. International Business Review, 23, 849–861.

Rychter A.M., Zawada A., Ratajczak A.E., Dobrowolska A., and Krela-Kaźmierczak I., 2020. Should Patients with Obesity be More Afraid of COVID-19? Obesity Review, 21/9, 1–8.

Starik, M., & Rands, G. P. (1995). Weaving an Integrated Web: Multilevel and Multisystem Perspectives of Ecologically Sustainable Organizations. Academy of Management Review, 20(4), 908–935.

WHO (2021). International Health Regulations. Online, accessed on March 22, 2021 (https://www.who.int/health-topics/international-health-regulations#tab=tab_1).

Wikipedia (2022): COVID-19 Pandemic, https://en.wikipedia.org/wiki/COVID-19_pandemic, accessed on January 16, 2022.

Markus Biehl and Nisha Kulangara

9 A triadic perspective on the risks of IS outsourcing in a Software as a Service (SaaS) context

9.1 Introduction

In today's networked environment, organizations depend on their suppliers for much of the value added to their products or services. While standardized items (e.g., nuts and bolts) or services (e.g., cleaning or maintenance) can simply be purchased, the acquisition of high-value resources often requires organizations to collaborate with their suppliers (Tsay et al., 2018). This is particularly true if the organization seeks to access resources that are valuable, rare, inimitable and non-substitutable – the conditions for generating a competitive advantage (Barney, 1991). In such setups, organizations must collaborate and share information, which can expose the buyer and supplier to risks particularly when geographically removed or culturally different from one another, due to bounded rationality and the increased potential for opportunistic behavior (Williamson, 1975). As a result, many firms have more recently explored the "reshoring" of outsourced operations (Gray et al., 2013).

What happens when such a setup suddenly becomes even more complex – when organizations must engage in *triadic* outsourcing, where they need to engage with two service providers whose services to the buyer/client depend on each other (see Figure 9.1). Such complexity has recently come to the forefront with the development of Software-as-a-Service (SaaS) offerings. Instead of hosting software on the buyer's servers ("on-premise"), software is now frequently a subscription-based service, that is hosted on remote servers, i.e., in the "cloud." Cloud-based software platforms cannot be customized to suit the needs of a particular buyer as they serve a larger number of subscribers. To make this software work for the client, a configuration layer is introduced that "translates" between the cloud product and the client's interfaces to it. With enterprise-level systems, this configuration is not typically undertaken by the client as this task is oftentimes too complex. Neither is it offered by the software provider, as the software provider only provides access to the software platform and documentation, all of which is available to all its subscribers. Instead, a number of

Triadic IT services

Client

System integrator ———————— System provider

Figure 9.1: Structure of a Triadic Partnership.

consulting firms, known as "system integrators" have filled this service gap. System integrators are responsible for investigating the client's needs in terms of inputs, processes, and outputs, and then configuring access to the software platform in such a way that the client's individual needs are largely met.

For the client, this now presents an unusual proposition, where two services – those of the systems integrator and the SaaS provider – interact with each other in a context in which the actions of the provider (e.g., in the form of updates to existing or the introduction of new functionality) and the work of the integrator both impact the client's outcomes. In other words, each partner is directly impacted by the two others and can influence, and be influenced by, the others' actions (Karatzas et al., 2017). In addition, the client's choices along the implementation timeline determine how difficult it is for the integrator to achieve their mission. In short, what used to be a dyadic process for the buyer and supplier is now an ever-moving target whose outcome depends on several actors.

Unfortunately, research on the topic of triadic IS outsourcing is in its infancy. While social network analytic approaches are useful for structurally examining triads, questions of how to best manage such setups via legal (control) and social (coordination) methods are still lacking (Bastl et al., 2019). In addition, the investigation of performance impacts of triadic designs (ex-ante) and governance (ex-post) approaches is also needed (Broekhuis and Scholten, 2018; Perdikaki et al., 2015). Partnerships that involve three organizations are particularly difficult to manage as the coordination patterns are more complex (Vlachos and Dyra, 2020).

The absence of research on outsourcing triads is a significant problem as investments for such systems by medium-sized or large firms run in the millions to tens of millions of dollars each, and firms depend on the reliability of such systems and configurations for basic operations. Meanwhile, such systems are becoming pervasive in industry, Gartner predicts that by 2023, 80% of service-based firms will have a cloud-based ERP in a total market worth US$ 44 bn (Gartner, 2019). Yet, very little information is available that could guide buyers with their large financial investments, beyond the use of Service Level Agreements (SLAs).

The aim of this chapter is hence to survey which risks exist in a triadic partnership, including sociopolitical risks in cases where one or two partners stem from differing cultures or geographical regions. We also derive recommendations on how to manage those risks. We conclude with findings on how such risks may interact.

9.2 Framework

Literature on dyadic sourcing provides a good overview of the principles that also apply to triadic exchanges. Transaction Cost Theory (Williamson, 1975) and the Resource Based View (Barney, 1991, Cannon and Perreault Jr., 1999) propose a number of external determinants as well as key relationship connectors that influence project outcomes. The external determinants include market and situational conditions, whereas the relationship connectors address how the triad is governed. These determinants and connectors are summarized in Figure 9.2.

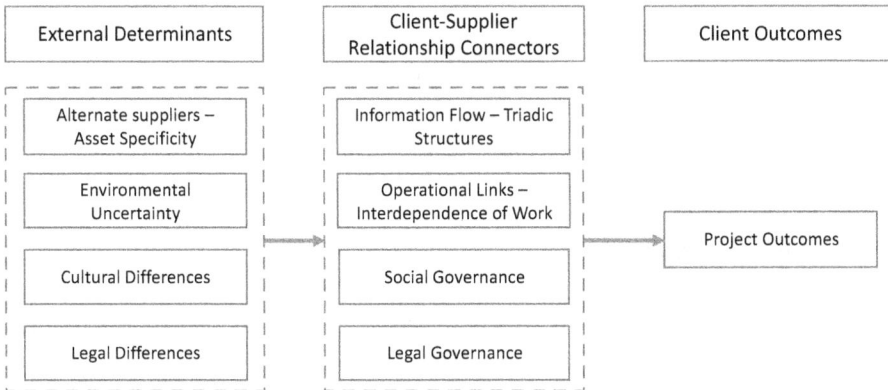

Figure 9.2: Overview of Key Determinants and Relationship Connectors (based on Cannon and Perreault Jr., 1999, 442).

The external determinants influence the client's degree of freedom with regards to the relationship. For example, if there are very few alternate suppliers or, similarly, the client must rely on assets that are highly specific to this triad, then the client's power in the relationship is low and its best approach is to look towards the full range of connectors to make the partnership work. A high degree of environmental uncertainty necessitates a different mix of relationship connectors, with some legal safeguards complemented by social governance mechanisms. Cultural differences can significantly impact how partners interpret each other's messages and behaviours, thus increasing risk as well (Hofstede, 1994). Lastly, the enforceability of (service level) contracts have implications on how the triad is governed, as a decrease in enforcing a contract prompts an increase in non-legal (relational) governance approaches.

The relationship connectors influence how the partners interact. This interaction is influenced by how the triad is structured with strong or weak communication channels, how interdependent the three partners' work is, how much the partners work toward a common goal, and a mix of legal and social governance mechanism that help set and manage expectations and ongoing issues.

We will start by discussing these relationship connectors, before showing how external determinants impact these connectors.

9.3 Buyer-supplier relationship connectors

In this section we investigate the dimensions that influence how the triadic partners interact. To discuss how information is exchanged, we first take a structural view of the triad using a network analytic approach. Second, we view the operational link-ages through the lens of the interdependence of the partners' work as interdependence is an important and complex topic in a triad that also includes a discussion of the role of adaptations by partners. To address cooperative norms, we discuss the concept of social governance within a triad, including the question of goal congruence. Finally, we briefly expose the interaction between legal and social governance.

9.3.1 Triadic structures

Li and Choi (2009) investigate service triads from a network analytic view (see Liu et al., 2017) for a great overview of social network theory). As shown in Figure 9.1, a service triad has connections between each of the three actors. That is, not only does the client interact directly with the system integrator (SI) and software pro-vider (SP), but the SI and SP also interact with each other. All parties are part of a bidirectional information flow, where all three parties supply significant inputs in the service co-production (Bastl et al., 2019). The direct interaction among all part-ners is a characteristic that differentiates service triads from manufacturing triads (Li and Choi, 2009).

If any of the three links are cut, a structural hole opens in the triad. A structural hole between the SI and SP, for example, would put the client into a bridge (coordina-tion) position and make it easier for it to control the information flow (and agenda), but would also inhibit coordination and knowledge transfer between the SP and SI, ultimately challenging the completion of the project's implementation on time and budget. This is a scenario that is unlikely to occur in a SaaS environment. The same argument can be made for any other missing link in the triad, with slightly different balances of "benefits" (e.g., control) and risks. Note that structural holes may also exist for other reasons that inhibit information flow, especially if at least one of the partners is located in a different cultural or geopolitical area.

Risk #1: Disrupted or politically controlled information flow due to structural holes in the triad

---

Bridging functions may also decay naturally over time as the other non-bridging partners can start improving connections, thus annulling the bridging function (Li and Choi, 2009). For example, as a SaaS implementation progresses, the client could establish a stronger connection with the SP, thus slowly taking over the bridging function from the SI.

Each of these scenarios has benefits and risks associated with them, depending on the role each partner plays, as outlined in more detail in the following sections. The least concerning structural hole in a SaaS environment is that between the client and SP, as long as the SI is competent and reliable; the most dangerous one is between the client and SI as it has an immediate and significant impact on project success.

As this risk overlaps with risk #3, we will examine potential mitigation strategies in the next section.

9.3.2 Interdependence of work

As alluded to above, all three partners need to be able to partake in the exchange of information and be part of service delivery, which makes the relationship interdependent (Bastl et al., 2019). In a SaaS environment, the SP must document the system's ability and the interfaces provided through its application programming interfaces (APIs – the interfaces that allows clients to retrieve or input data), along with system security and performance measures. As well, the SP will continuously improve and further develop the functionality of the system.

The client must document its own requirements – ideally after a broad consultation with its own internal or external clients in order to document existing inputs, processes, and outputs – and evaluate the potential for simplification (Gunasekaran and Nath, 1997). As is known from examples of unsuccessful ERP implementations, the attempt to make information systems fit cumbersome processes is not only time consuming and expensive, but also likely to lead to failure (Garg and Agarwal, 2014; Garg and Khurana, 2017). This is particularly true as very onerous requirements increase not only the project's complexity and the SI's work, but also the likeliness that the client's requirements cannot be satisfied with the SP's service. In short, it is important that the client adapt its requirements if its process capabilities have not already been optimized.

Finally, the SI's task is to fully understand the software platform's design and capabilities and keep up-to-date with regards to upcoming changes. This knowledge will inform the guidance it provides to the client as the latter investigates, documents, and communicates its requirements. During a fit-gap analysis, the client and SI will assess how well the platform can meet the client's needs, and how the client's inputs, outputs and processes can be simplified to narrow the gap between the software's capabilities and the client's needs. As the SI typically has the benefit of deep expertise in the client's industry through having provided the same or similar service to other clients, the SI's role in this partnership is pivotal as it bridges the client's needs and the platform's capabilities. At the same time, the SI needs to be able to recognize which idiosyncratic processes are important to the client's performance and find ways of adapting to them.

What are the risks in SaaS triads from a perspective that takes into account that the partners' work is interdependent? While the SP has a stake in the project's success, the main interaction occurs between the client and SI. While either the SI or the client may be in a more pivotal role (i.e., occupy the bridge function), some arrangements are very risky. In particular, a client whose processes or organizational change capabilities need significant support from the SI is typically best served by allowing the SI to take on the bridge function in the triad. This is even more important if the implementation represents a significant change in the way the client thinks about and interacts with the software, e.g., when moving away from legacy systems (see Figure 9.3). That is, in order to reduce the interdependency of work, the client would thus exhibit adaptability and allow the SI to occupy the bridge function. The client exerting too much power would challenge the project's success as it would make it more difficult for the SI to match up the client's processes with the platform's capabilities. Stepping back would allow the client to take advantage of the SI's experience with the SP and industry to help it align its processes and, due to the significant changes that are to be implemented, the organizational change process.

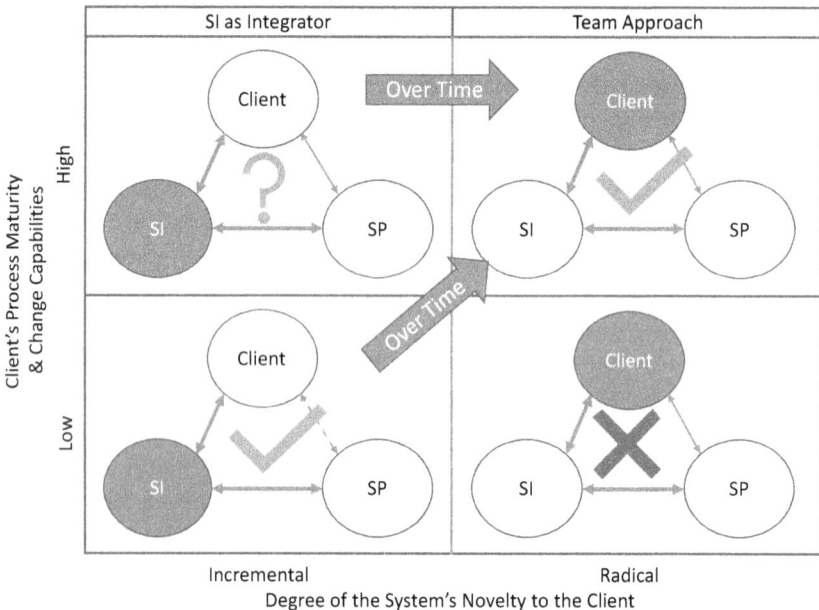

Figure 9.3: Triadic configurations (adapted from Ateş et al., 2015).

In contrast, if a client possesses simple and linear processes that serve its business outcomes, plus the ability to bring along its community through a change management process, the client may occupy the bridge function instead. While maintaining a very strong connection with the SI, the client should then also maintain a connection to the SP, to further familiarize itself with the platform's capabilities and interfaces. Note that this scenario may naturally occur over time, thus slowly shifting the bridge function from the SI to the client. According to Li et al. (2009), the bridge function naturally decays over time as the SI has no effective way to prevent repeated contact between the buyer and SaaS firm. After implementation, the SP would be in a position of leverage and, thus, the bridge would have transferred to the software supplier, making the client more dependent on the SP (Li and Choi, 2009).

Figure 9.3 shows that a third scenario is possible, with the SI occupying the bridge function even through the client possesses a high level of process maturity and change capabilities. This allows the client to enjoy the SI's experience and the onboarding of the new platform, while minimizing the risk that naturally occurs with the implementation of a new enterprise platform. In this scenario the volume of adaptations is much lower than in the other scenarios and distributed between the SI and client.

Risk #2: Client's process maturity or change management capabilities

---

Risk #3: SI's ability to match the client's needs with the software's capabilities

---

What does this mean in terms of risk? As the partners' success at delivering the service depends on what the two other partners do, the risk to successfully completing the project is very high. The risk emanating from the client and SI stand out, due to their positions in the triad. The risks can be divided into those during the implementation and steady-state phases. During implementation, for the client, managing its requirements and constantly supporting and updating and benefiting from the SI's experience will be the main goals. For the SI, retaining an up-to-date and in-depth knowledge of the platform's capabilities, properly understanding the client's needs, and its ability to find ways to configure the software and advising the client to match needs and capabilities will be critical. According to Ateş et al. (2015, 1517), "deciding on each party's level of autonomy is one of the most critical issues" in innovation projects, particularly when the project "requires a high degree of creativity on the part of the supplier." Striking a balance between control and autonomy is not always easy, however, as too much autonomy may also reduce goal congruence (see next section) and encourage opportunistic behaviour and the leakage of technical knowledge (Ateş et al., 2015).

After the implementation, the importance of the SI will diminish and, thus, the risks caused by it, meaning that most risks will come from the client side. By the time the project reaches production, the client should have developed a very good link with the SP and knowledge of the software's capabilities such that any further developments of capabilities and other changes to the platform can be managed either by the client or with occasional the help of the SI.

9.3.3 Goal congruence and social governance

Whereas the previous section investigated the triad with a view towards the interdependence of the work completed by the actors, a related topic treated in this section is the relationship complexity. In a triad, the three partners have overlapping but different goals. The client is mostly focused on its ability to service its internal and external users while containing cost and time. The SP is interested in expanding the platform's capability or improve its interfaces to better serve existing and attract new clients. The SI ultimately wants to be perceived by both the client and the SP as a capable partner as this reputation makes it easier to attract new clients. Still, the goals also overlap. First, the client wants to end up with a well-functioning information system so it can serve its customers and justify its monetary and temporal effort to its managers or other stakeholders. The SI wants the client to be satisfied with its services to increase the likeliness that the client will retain them as a trusted partner during steady-state and recommend them to other potential clients. The SP will find it easier to attract additional clients to its platform if clients and SIs use and recommend it.

A lack of goal congruence is a significant risk factor in large-scale projects. Social Capital Theory (Tsai and Ghoshal, 1998) investigates this issue and refers to goal congruence as "shared goals," and shows that they are directly linked to the outcomes of strategic purchasing initiatives (Villena et al., 2011).

Risk # 4: Lack of goal congruence between the partners

Two basic governance mechanisms exist for ensuring that a low goal congruence does not lead to an increase in the effort required to successfully complete a project. First, the three partners typically enter contractual relationships with each other, which, in the realm of information systems, includes service-level agreements and may also include three-way non-disclosure agreements. Contracts typically set out the terms of the sale, warranties and timelines, frequently also dispute resolution mechanisms and occasionally stipulations for penalties in the case of non-performance. Williamson (1975, 2002) and many others recognize, however, that contracts are rarely complete, i.e., they cannot possibly fully capture complex situations. Contract enforcement can also be expensive, time consuming (please see the section on external determinants), and damage the social structure of a relationship.

This is a major reason why, as of late, literature has investigated mechanisms based on social capital theory (Tsai and Ghoshal, 1998). Within a contracting context, social capital rests on three pillars: the patterns of connections between the parties (structural capital), shared goals and values (cognitive capital) and trust, respect and friendship (relational capital) (Nahapiet and Ghoshal, 1998). As a powerful complement to contracts, social connections can keep complex triads stable and operating "in an effortful, cooperative manner with actors overcoming any conflicting interests by developing triad-specific collaborative routines" (Vlachos and Dyra, 2020, 287).

The cognitive capital dimension captures goal congruence while the other dimensions provide mechanisms for preventing or rectifying difficulties within the triad. Social connections between the partners facilitate the socialization process between the partners, which may be formal and more traditional (i.e., task focused interactions) or informal or even personal (e.g., over a meal or a round of golf) (Cousins et al., 2006). While formal socialization occurs primarily at the day-to-day, or operational, level and is focused on contractual or partnership-level information, informal socialization often relays tacit, confidential or even personal information (Kulangara et al., 2016). Both types of socialization are effective in addressing problems and establishing or reinforcing shared values (Kulangara et al., 2015) and can be used to strengthen goal congruence. Socialization also affects relational capital, and trust in particular. Kulangara et al. (2015) showed that informal (but not formal) socialization builds trust, and that trust has a positive effect on performance, including cost and time. In contrast, formal socialization drove innovative capabilities, a dimension that is important in an SaaS implementation setting, both directly and through an improved goal congruence.

In short, both formal and informal socialization are important, albeit for different purposes. In a SaaS project, partners need to not only exchange texts and emails but also get together to hash out any problems and review what has gone well at the operational, tactical, and strategic levels.

9.3.4 The interaction between social and legal governance

Supporting the importance of social linkages, Karatzas et al. (2016) investigated a number of permutations through which legal ("formal") and social ("informal") mechanisms could effectively help govern innovative projects. According to the literature, these "different types of control are appropriate under different conditions" (Ateş et al. 2015, 1516), with uncertainty and asset specificity being the main driver for the choice. Both uncertainty and asset specificity limit the enforceability of contracts.

The customary basic legal agreement in an information systems (including SaaS) environment is the service level agreement (SLA) struck between each pair of the partners, sometimes as a more detailed document within the framework of a master service agreement (Rosencrance et al., 2021). The SLA broadly addressing the agreement's objectives, scope of services, the responsibilities of the involved parties, performance metrics and dispute resolution mechanisms and penalties (see Rosencrance et al. (2021) for more detail; Wazir et al. (2016) compare the effectiveness of different SLA structures for SaaS).

Karatzas et al. (2016), however, found that in many cases adaptations to the relationship were necessary to make it work – as discussed above. Williamson (1975) already observed the need for such adaptations may not be captured in contracts but evolves over time as the client assesses its needs – in the case of SaaS likely with the help of the SI either from the beginning or starting partly into the project. In situations with this degree of complexity it is key that, rather than resort to contractual mechanisms, partners learn about the factors that drive the need for adaptations (Madhok, 2002). Such reflective activities are not easy but a necessary skill in the context of triads that execute complex projects. In line with Karatzas et al. (2016), contract support played a positive role, while legal bonds were of minor relevance, particularly in long-term relationships.

9.4 External determinants

Referring back to Figure 9.2, this section investigates the market and situational determinants that impact triadic projects within a SaaS environment. We focus first on asset specificity and environmental uncertainty as important components that may limit the client's choice of governance activities. We will then discuss sociopolitical dimensions to address cultural and legal differences between partners.

9.4.1 Asset specificity in SaaS triads

Recall that the SaaS approach differs from a traditional software purchase in that all adjustments are made in the configuration layer. For implementing large-scale systems, most clients elect to have an SI who has deep knowledge of the platform and experience in the client's industry. This setup creates two dependencies for the client: first, on the SI's expertise and knowledge of the platform and the client's needs and processes and, second, on the platform itself as the configuration layer is, to a large degree, not usable for other platforms. That is, it would be a significant effort to switch either to a different SI during the implementation process or to a different SaaS at any point of time. Thus, both the work with the SI and the configuration layer represent investments in specific assets.

Risk # 5: Asset specific investment in the SI's knowledge of the client

---

Risk # 6: Asset specific investment in the platform's configuration layer

---

Even though the concept of asset specificity is not new, literature has not investigated it in the context of sourcing in general or software implementation in particular. In a manufacturing context, asset specificity may lead to positive outcomes such as manufacturing competitiveness (Wacker et al., 2016), organizational performance, cooperative innovation on projects, and manufacturer's innovation performance (Delbufalo, 2017). Within a SaaS context, this would mean that asset specificity could strengthen the bond particularly between the client and SI, thus deepening their cooperation and willingness to adapt, giving them the opportunity to use asset specificity to their advantage. At the same time, asset specificity is also associated with increased project performance, even though the causal links and temporal sequence are not clear at this time.

On the flipside, when asset specificity is high, the project's transactional risk increases (Dyer, 1996; Williamson, 1985). Relationship-specific investments can lead to opportunism (shirking and poaching) in outsourcing relationships (Handley and Benton, 2012), such as the SP not responding to legitimate requests from the SI or client, or the client (SI) ignoring relevant input from the SI (client). Such investments can also result in governance misalignment which, as discussed above, can negatively impact outsourcing performance (Handley, 2017). For example, a lack of shared goals could lead to the SI recommending unnecessary or perform incomplete work for the client, thus provoking suboptimal outcomes. Similarly, the client could block process adaptations in the hope that the SI would influence the SP or find other ways to accommodate the client.

How can the risks emanating from asset specificity be managed? It is advisable to refrain from becoming complacent and too comfortable with each other (Villena et al., 2011) and lean on social governance mechanisms (formal and informal socialization, information sharing) that are suited for establishing and strengthening shared goals and trust through both formal and informal socialization (Kulangara et al., 2015; Poppo and Zenger, 2002; Villena et al., 2015). This is because intuitive agreement on issues as well as professional and personal bonds make it more difficult for one of the parties to turn their back on the other and exploit the power they have gained through asset specific investments. In short, an increased amount and depth of communication – driven by both tasks and social ties – will benefit the SaaS project and its outcomes.

9.4.2 Environmental uncertainty

Environmental uncertainty deals with external risks such as market volatility and competition. It refers to unexpected, unforeseen changes in a transaction (Noordeweir et al., 1990) and is prevalent in the IS offshoring context where triads also deal with geographical, cultural, and legal differences (to be discussed further in the next sections). In the case of new projects, triadic players mainly deal with "task uncertainty." Task uncertainty refers to "the difference between the amount of information required to perform the task and the amount of information already possessed by the organization" (Galbraith, 1977, 36). In triadic situations, the number of organizations and people involved can add complexity to task identification and coordination.

Risk #7: Environmental uncertainty due to unforeseen political, social or legal events

---

Researchers have also proposed that, in dyads, higher levels of environmental uncertainty require higher levels of communication and coordination strategies (Gulati et al., 2012; Xu and Beamon, 2006) and deeper investments in relationship-specific assets such as mutual respect, trust, and commitment (Bastl et al., 2012; Handley and Benton, 2012). This should also hold for triads.

The partners should strive for clarity about how information will flow and who the boundary spanners will be within the network. As well, uncertainty can be reduced for the client by having the SI occupy the bridge function to coordinate the information flow (Handley and Benton, 2012). The client could protect itself from any opportunism from the SI or SP by having contractual safeguards (i.e., well-written master agreements and SLAs) in place at the beginning of the project. Finally, the client can lean on the synergistic impact of both relational embeddedness and contractual bonds (Poppo and Zenger, 2002) to safeguard itself from the risks of environmental uncertainty caused by market turbulence, information uncertainty within the triad, task uncertainty, and external competition.

9.4.3 Cultural differences

In a globalized environment, it is common for IS outsourcing projects to consist of virtual teams with partners residing in different social and cultural realms. (National) culture can be defined as "shared collective values that make diverse (national) human communities different or similar, and to the reasons underlying these differences" (López-Duarte et al., 2016, 397). Significant differences in culture, referred to as "cultural distance," can result in project failures. For example, some cultures are blunt and direct, which can be perceived as impolite by a team member from another culture, resulting in misunderstandings and negative team dynamics. In some cultures, it is considered unprofessional to be tardy for meetings or project deliverables while others expect it. A partnership must account for these differences. Therefore, when working in a triadic context across national borders, the client must factor in sociopolitical aspects, including differences in social (cultural) and organizational value systems, all of which can drive (or help avoid) uncertainty.

Hofstede (Hofstede, 1994) identified six unique social dimensions (power distance, individualism, masculinity, uncertainty avoidance, long term orientation, indulgence) that differentiate national cultures, the first four of which are frequently used in management. Due to these differences, the type and range of measures employed in interacting with one's partners may have to differ. As an example, using a subset of the cultural dimensions, Hofstede (1985) classified countries and regions based on their scores along uncertainty avoidance and power distance, as shown in Figure 9.4. These differences in approaches can result in very different communication patterns, interaction styles and organizational customs. For example, a client in the Well-oiled Machine category may not be comfortable with the degree of uncertainty or ambiguity its supplier from the Family category is tolerating. Similarly, the communication norms the supplier employs may be quite different from those the client is accustomed to. In the context of SaaS implementations, a Family-type SI would be more comfortable moving forward with incomplete specifications and attempt to figure those out as the project progresses, and then communicate those to their Machine-type client in a more top-down fashion. This (not uncommon) scenario increases the risk of misunderstandings and fallouts between the client and SI, thus severely challenging project success.

Risk #8: Social (cultural) differences amongst triadic partners

---

How can the differences in information flow among different cultures be handled? In IS outsourcing dyads, Poppo and Zenger (2002) found that customized contracts and relational governance (trust, respect, commitment, see above) play a complementary role instead of a substitutionary role. The project teams will have to examine the conditions (social, political, cultural context) under which it would be beneficial to have a formal or informal approach in triads, particularly when cultural and geopolitical differences between triadic players become more pronounced (Hofstede, 1994), with some partners feeling more comfortable with codified contractual bonds, others with relational bonds.

In a first step, partners should adapt contracts to mitigate some of the risks associated with socio-political or cultural differences (Poppo and Zenger, 2002). This is partly because the line of communication between the SP and client is minimal at

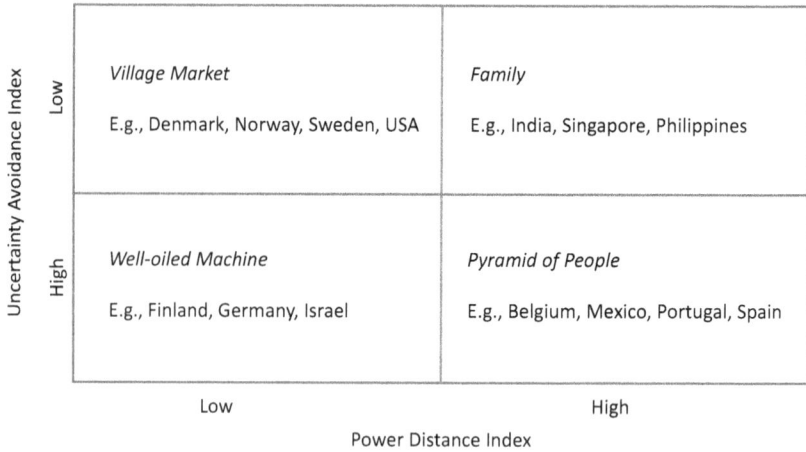

		Low	High
Uncertainty Avoidance Index	Low	Village Market E.g., Denmark, Norway, Sweden, USA	Family E.g., India, Singapore, Philippines
	High	Well-oiled Machine E.g., Finland, Germany, Israel	Pyramid of People E.g., Belgium, Mexico, Portugal, Spain

Power Distance Index

Figure 9.4: Different Cultural Approaches (adapted from Hofstede, 1985).

the beginning stages of the project, with the SI filling the communication gap. The SI would be in more frequent communication with the client and adapt an appropriate complementary approach to tilt it towards formal or informal socialization, depending on what is more effective in the cultural mix. That is, it is crucial that the SI in particular (but also the client) understand cultural differences and adapt communication styles and coordination mechanisms for smooth information flow based on the partners' socio-political norms. In such cases, having managers with relevant global exposure and prior international business experience can be a tremendous asset. Partners should also strive to maximize the compatibility between teams as compatibility is hugely dependent on the national culture of team players (Gurung and Prater, 2006).

9.4.4 Legal differences

In addition to cultural differences, a global context also requires attention to legal differences. Laws are based on differing cultural, economic, political, and social conditions (Santolaya et al., 2012). For example, a legal framework could stem from a common law tradition as in England and many Commonwealth countries, a civil law tradition as in many other European countries, or a consuetudinary law tradition, as practiced by many indigenous nations (Santolaya et al., 2012). In comparison, Chinese law, while having strong historical roots, was abolished in the 1950s and re-established slowly starting in the late 1970s. While judges in the Western hemisphere are viewed as interpreting law and are sometimes elected by the population (e.g., in the United States of Amercia), Chinese judges are considered a supervisory part of the state (Gao, 2010).

Such differences are relevant not only for legal proceedings and the enforceability of contracts but also the ability to successfully arbitrate. As national culture influences a country's legal framework and vice versa (Varner and Varner, 2014), companies must consider differences like uncertainty avoidance, communication patterns, employee rights, privacy rights or intellectual property rights (Gurung and Prater, 2006) when developing legal contracts with global partners.

Risk #9: Legal differences amongst countries in which triadic partners reside

---

While the details concerning the structure and enforceability of laws and contracts goes well beyond this chapter, various organizations provide indicators or advice on this subject (e.g., The World Bank, 2020; United Nations, 2011). For example, the World Bank (2020) provides scores that rank both enforceability and the cost of enforcing contracts. When contracts need to be drawn up or detailed questions arise, however, the help of internationally versed consultants or lawyers becomes advisable.

9.5 Conclusions

Triadic partnerships present numerous complexities to managers. The risks in triadic projects are multiplied as compared to those in dyadic projects since three, rather than two, partners, must set common goals, coordinate, adapt and align their resources to make the project successful.

This chapter investigates the main risks in triads within the context of Software as a Service. Risks can be divided into external and relationship-specific risks. External determinants influence relationship structures and execution, which in turn impact project outcomes.

While any commercial relationship needs to rest on a good legal agreement, two factors simplify the management of triads in a SaaS relationship. First, in a SaaS context, the main interaction occurs between the client and the software integrator (SI). While the client's initial decision is often based on proposals submitted jointly by the SI and software provider (SP), the bulk of the interaction is between the client and the SI. Thus, from a structural perspective, this somewhat reduces the risk within the triad, as compared to a team of three equally important partners. Please note that this insight is not generalizable to other types of triads.

Second, while there is a relatively large number of external and relationship-specific factors, all of them can be managed through three categories of activities: social and cultural aptitude, socialization, and legal bonds, with all three interacting with each other (see Figure 9.5). If all partners stem from the same culture, only two categories apply.

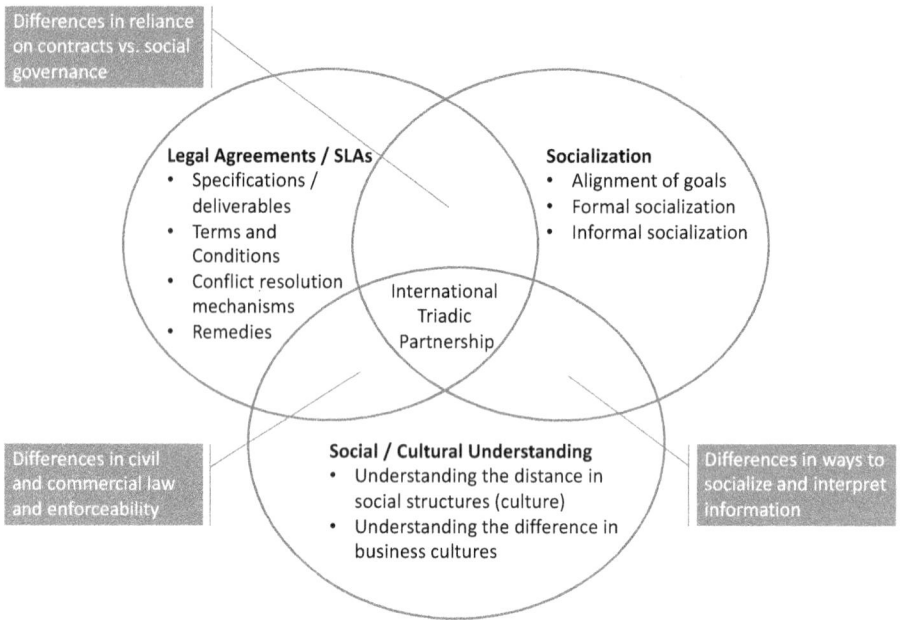

Figure 9.5: Managing an International Triadic Partnership.

How do legal and social mechanisms interact? When the triadic partners share the same culture, they need to strike a balance between contractual and social governance. Contracts, particularly service level agreements, are very important for capturing a basic understanding of the sides' obligations and potential conflict resolution mechanisms and addressing potential environmental uncertainties (Poppo and Zenger, 2002). As not everything can be captured in or foreseen for a legal agreement, however, agreements need to be complemented with social governance mechanisms. Long-term relationships in particular rely mostly on social governance (Karatzas et al., 2016), with formal governance addressing day-to-day issues and informal governance building up close relationships and building trust (Kulangara et al., 2016). Both formal and informal socialization also further the establishment of shared goals and values, which we suspect help partners resolve issues and decide who needs to adapt how much, to reach those goals, avoid negative potential impacts due to asset specificity between the client and SI. The partners thus need to find a good balance between legal and social mechanisms. New relationships may rely on fuller contracts, long-term relationships less so.

Management of a triadic partnership becomes more complicated in a cross-cultural context. Here, legal frameworks and agreements and social mechanisms must be viewed within the context of differing cultural and social norms, as the latter influence laws and their enforceability as well as the expectation for and interpretation of social interactions. If contracts are difficult to enforce, partners should shift the balance in terms of governance towards socialization, again while keeping the partners' social norms in mind. As well, the meaning of socialization and the way different cultures expect to socialize may vary depending on power distance, individualism, uncertainty avoidance or masculinity. Therefore, social mechanisms need to be considered within the framework of the partner's social system rather than one's own, and adaptations will be necessary beyond the project's specifications. Depending on the social context, a reconsideration of the weight given to legal versus social mechanisms may also be required. From a managerial perspective, the boundary spanners, i.e., the outsourcing managers who is the point of contact between triads should have considerable amount of international experience and an understanding of cultural norms influencing legal frameworks. Outsourcing managers with higher cultural IQ will contribute toward greater outsourcing success in IS offshoring triadic projects.

As many organizations now embark on the journey of changing their information systems from legacy or site-hosted to new-generation cloud hosted systems, the scenario of Software as a Service will more and more frequently emerge. This chapter will hopefully guide organizations that have to rely on two partners simultaneously for the implementation of their new systems, and perhaps use SPs or SIs located outside their own countries.

References

Ateş, M.A., Van den Ende, J., Ianniello, G. 2015. Inter-organizational coordination patterns in buyer-supplier-design agency triads in NPD projects. International Journal of Operations & Production Management 35 (11), 1512–1545. http://dx.doi.org/10.1108/IJOPM-01-2013-0036.

Barney, J.B. 1991. Firm Resources and Sustained Competitive Advantage. Journal of Management 17 (1), 99–120. https://doi.org/10.1177/014920639101700108.

Bastl, M., Johnson, M., Finne, M. 2019. A Mid-Range Theory of Control and Coordination in Service Triads. Journal of Supply Chain Management 55 (1), 21–47. https://doi.org/10.1111/jscm.12187.

Bastl, M., Johnson, M., Lightfoot, H., Evans, S. 2012. Buyer-supplier relationships in a servitized environment: An examination with Cannon and Perreault's framework. International Journal of Operations & Production Management 32 (6), 650–675. https://doi.org/10.1108/01443571211230916.

Broekhuis, M., Scholten, K. 2018. Purchasing in service triads: the influence of contracting on contract management. International Journal of Operations & Production Management 38 (5), 1188–1204. http://dx.doi.org/10.1108/IJOPM-12-2015-0754.

Cannon, J.P., Perreault Jr., W.D. 1999. Buyer-Seller Relationships in Business Markets. Journal of Marketing Research 36 (4), 439–460. https://doi.org/10.2307/3151999.

Cousins, P.D., Handfield, R.B., Lawson, B., Petersen, K.J. 2006. Creating supply chain relational capital: The impact of formal and informal socialization processes. Journal of Operations Management 24 (6), 851–863. https://doi.org/10.0.3.248/j.jom.2005.08.007.

Delbufalo, E. 2017. The effects of suppliers' trust on manufacturers' innovation capability: an analysis of direct versus indirect relationships. Production Planning and Control 28 (14), 1165–1176. https://doi.org/10.1080/09537287.2017.1350766.

Dyer, J.H. 1996. Does Governance Matter? Keiretsu Alliances and Asset Specificity As Sources of Japanese Competitive Advantage. Organization Science 7 (6), 649–666.

Galbraith, J. 1977. Organization design. Addison-Wesley Pub. Co., Reading, MA.

Gao, J. 2010. Comparison Between Chinese and American Lawyers: Educated and Admitted to Practice Differently in Different Legal Systems. Penn State International Law Review 29 (1), 129–146.

Garg, P., Agarwal, D. 2014. Critical success factors for ERP implementation in a Fortis hospital: an empirical investigation. Journal of Enterprise Information Management 27 (4), 402–423. https://doi.org/10.1108/JEIM-06-2012-0027.

Garg, P., Khurana, R. 2017. Applying structural equation model to study the critical risks in ERP implementation in Indian retail. Benchmarking 24 (1), 143–162. https://doi.org/10.1108/BIJ-12-2015-0122.

Gartner. 2019. ERP Primer for 2020 [WWW Document]. ERP Primer for 2020. URL https://www.gartner.com/document/3979797?ref=solrAll&refval=275995114 (accessed 2. 1.21).

Gray, J.V., Skowronski, K., Esenduran, G., Rungtusanatham, M.J. 2013. The Reshoring Phenomenon: What Supply Chain Academics Ought to know and Should Do. Journal of Supply Chain Management 49 (2), 27–33. https://doi.org/10.0.4.87/jscm.12012.

Gulati, R., Wohlgezogen, F., Zhelyazkov, P. 2012. The Two Facets of Collaboration: Cooperation and Coordination in Strategic Alliances. Academy of Management Annals 6 (1), 531–583. https://doi.org/10.1080/19416520.2012.691646.

Gunasekaran, A., Nath, B. 1997. The role of information technology in business process reengineering. International Journal of Production Economics 50 (2,3), 91–104. https://doi.org/10.1016/S0925-5273(97)00035-2.

Gurung, A., Prater, E. 2006. A research framework for the impact of cultural differences on IT outsourcing. Global sourcing of services: strategies, issues and challenges 9 (1), 24–43. https://doi.org/10.1080/1097198x.2006.10856413.

Handley, S.M. 2017. How Governance Misalignment and Outsourcing Capability Impact Performance. Production and Operations Management 26 (1), 134–155. https://doi.org/10.1111/poms.12609.

Handley, S.M., Benton, W.C. 2012. The influence of exchange hazards and power on opportunism in outsourcing relationships. Journal of Operations Management 30 (1/2), 55–68. https://doi.org/10.1016/j.jom.2011.06.001.

Hofstede, G. 1985. The interaction between national and organizational value systems. Journal of Management Studies 22 (4), 347–357. https://doi.org/10.1111/j.1467-6486.1985.tb00001.x.

Hofstede, G. 1994. The business of international business is culture. International Business Review 3 (1), 1–14. https://doi.org/10.1016/0969-5931(94)90011-6.

Karatzas, A., Johnson, M., Bastl, M. 2016. Relationship Determinants of Performance in Service Triads: A Configurational Approach. Journal of Supply Chain Management 52 (3), 28–47. https://doi.org/10.1111/jscm.12109.

Karatzas, A., Johnson, M., Bastl, M. 2017. Manufacturer-supplier relationships and service performance in service triads. International Journal of Operations & Production Management 37 (7), 950–969. https://doi.org/10.1108/IJOPM-11-2015-0719.

Kulangara, N.P., Jackson, S.A., Prater, E. 2016. Examining the impact of socialization and information sharing and the mediating effect of trust on innovation capability. International Journal of Operations & Production Management 36 (11), 1601–1624. https://doi.org/10.1108/IJOPM-09-2015-0558.

Kulangara, N.P., Prater, E.L., Biehl, M., Frazier, G.V. 2015. Investigation of Supply Chain Governance Mechanisms in the Manufacturing Industry. Presented at the Annual Conference of the POM Society, Washington, D.C.

Li, M., Choi, T.Y. 2009. Triads in Services Outsourcing: Bridge, Bridge Decay and Bridge Transfer. Journal of Supply Chain Management 45 (3), 27–39. https://doi.org/10.1111/j.1745-493X.2009.03169.x.

Liu, W., Sidhu, A., Beacom, A., Valente, T. 2017. Social Network Theory. In: Rössler, P., Hoffner, C.A., Zoonen, L. (Eds.), The International Encyclopedia of Media Effects. Wiley, Chichester, England.

López-Duarte, C., Vidal-Suárez, M.M., González-Díaz, B. 2016. International Business and National Culture: A Literature Review and Research Agenda. International Journal of Management Reviews 18 (4), 397–416. https://doi.org/10.1111/ijmr.12070.

Madhok, A. 2002. Reassessing the Fundamentals and Beyond: Ronald Coase, the Transaction Cost and Resource-based Theories of the Firm and the Institutional Structure of Production. Strategic Management Journal 23 (6), 535. https://doi.org/10.1002/smj.247.

Nahapiet, J., Ghoshal, S. 1998. Social Capital, Intellectual Capital, and the Organizational Advantage. Academy of Management Review 23 (2), 242–266. https://doi.org/10.2307/259373.

Noordewier, T. G., John, G., & Nevin, J. R. (1990). Performance Outcomes of Purchasing Arrangements in Industrial Buyer-Vendor Relationships. Journal of Marketing, 54(4), 80–93. https://doi.org/10.1177/002224299005400407.

Perdikaki, O., Peng, D.X., Heim, G.R. 2015. Impact of Customer Traffic and Service Process Outsourcing Levels on e-Retailer Operational Performance. Production and Operations Management 24 (11), 1794. https://doi.org/10.1111/poms.12359.

Poppo, L., Zenger, T. 2002. Do formal contracts and relational governance function as substitutes or complements? Strategic Management Journal 23 (8), 707–725. https://doi.org/10.1002/smj.249.

Rosencrance, L., Louissaint, S., Brush, K. 2021. What is a Service-Level Agreement (SLA)? [WWW Document]. Definition: Service Level Agreement (SLA). URL https://searchitchannel.techtarget.com/definition/service-level-agreement (accessed 2.2.22).

Santolaya, P., Iñiguez, D., Orozco, J., Zuckermann, Y., Balasko, R.D. 2012. Legal Framework [WWW Document]. Legal Framework. URL https://aceproject.org/ace-en/topics/lf/onePage (accessed 7.29.21).

The World Bank. 2020. Doing Business 2020 [WWW Document]. DoingBusiness. URL https://www.doingbusiness.org/en/doingbusiness (accessed 7.29.21).

Tsai, W., Ghoshal, S. 1998. Social Capital and Value Creation: the Role of Interfirm Networks. Academy of Management Journal 41 (4), 464–476. https://doi.org/10.2307/257085.

Tsay, A.A., Gray, J. V., Noh, I.J., Mahoney, J.T. 2018. A Review of Production and Operations Management Research on Outsourcing in Supply Chains: Implications for the Theory of the Firm. Production and Operations Management 27 (7), 1177–1220. https://doi.org/10.1111/poms.12855.

United Nations. 2011. Rule of Law Indicators – Implementation Guide and Project Tools.

Varner, I., Varner, K. 2014. The Relationship Between Culture and Legal Systems and the Impact on Intercultural Business Communication. Global Advances in Business Communication 3 (1), http://commons.emich.edu/gabc.

Villena, V.H., Choi, T., Revilla, E. 2015. Managing the Dark Side of Close Buyer-Supplier Relationships. Supply Chain Management Review 19 (6), 50–55. https://doi.org/10.1080/1461667022000028834.

Villena, V.H., Revilla, E., Choi, T.Y. 2011. The dark side of buyer-supplier relationships: A social capital perspective. Journal of Operations Management 29 (6), 561–576. https://doi.org/10.1016/j.jom.2010.09.001.

Vlachos, I., Dyra, S.C. 2020. Theorizing coordination, collaboration and integration in multi-sourcing triads (B3B triads). Supply Chain Management: An International Journal 25 (3), 285–300. https://doi.org/10.1108/SCM-01-2019-0006.

Wacker, J.G., Yang, C., Sheu, C. 2016. A transaction cost economics model for estimating performance effectiveness of relational and contractual governance: Theory and statistical results. International Journal of Operations & Production Management 36 (11), 1551–1575. https://doi.org/10.1108/IJOPM-10-2013-0470.

Wazir, U., Khan, F.G., Shah, S. 2016. Service Level Agreement in Cloud Computing: A Survey. International Journal of Computer Science and Information Security (IJCSIS) 14 (6), 324–330.

Williamson, O.E. 1975. Markets and Hierarchies. Free Press, New York.

Williamson, O. 1985. The economic institutions of capitalism: Firms markets, relational contracting, Journal of Economic Behavior & Organization. Free Press, New York, London.

Williamson, O.E. 2002. The Theory of the Firm as Governance Structure: From Choice to Contract. Journal of Economic Perspectives 16 (3), 171–195. https://doi.org/10.0.4.233/089533002760278776.

Xu, L., Beamon, B.M. 2006. Supply Chain Coordination and Cooperation Mechanisms: An Attribute-Based Approach. Journal of Supply Chain Management 42 (1), 4–12. https://doi.org/10.1111/J.1745-493X.2006.04201002.X.

Katherine Kinkela

10 Environmental, Social and Governance objectives and disclosures (ESG) and enterprise risk

10.1 Introduction

Environmental, Social and Governance (ESG) objectives and disclosures have gained importance in strategic planning and external communications for organizations. Because ESG goals are connected to operational processes, the structure, and metrics for measuring success for ESG initiatives includes selecting appropriate financial and nonfinancial information. ESG related disclosures must balance the need for transparency to external stakeholders with social, political and compliance risks. Environmental, Social and Governance (ESG) disclosures are reports detailing the steps that the organization has taken to meet sustainability goals. ESG disclosures demonstrate the success or failure to meet specific social goals and objectives related to sustainability (Herz, et al., 2017).

One challenge on creating ESG disclosures is that the definition of sustainability is broad:

> Yet "sustainability" has many – and often confusing or conflicting – definitions. Is it sustainability of the enterprise, thereby impacting reputation and "license to operate"? Is it about specific sustainability measures like climate control or deployment of human capital? Does it capture ESG measures? Is it all of the above? (Herz et al., 2017)

Over the past 5 years, global authorities and investors have demanded greater accountability of an organization's leadership to specific social governance goals incorporated into the strategic plan of an organization (Faris, et al., 2013).

> For many organizations, sustainability has evolved from a "feel good" exercise to a strategic imperative that focuses on economic, environmental, and social risks and opportunities which, left unattended, can potentially threaten the long-term success of strategies and the viability of business models. They understand that sustainability is not one function's domain, but a responsibility that the entire enterprise needs to own. This new perspective has raised the visibility of sustainability within the organization and prompted more meaningful discussions at the senior executive and board levels. Sustainability is no longer seen solely as a way of cutting costs or gaining efficiencies. It also can be used as a vehicle to achieve competitive advantage and growth through the positioning of products, services and brands that appeal to the organization's stakeholders. (Faris et al., 2013se)

Thus, ESG programs within firms are essential parts of strategy of the organization as a whole in the contemporary environment, and therefore ESG disclosures have moved from optional positive news flashes to disclosures of critical operational elements within the organization. In addition, as ESG operations have become more material within organizations, stakeholders want more disclosure of the objectives and performance of ESG related programs. Most recently, the Securities and Exchange Commission has moved towards ESG requiring disclosures in the annual filings for investment funds. (SEC Press Release May 25, 2022)

Some ESG type disclosures have been mandated by the global community and have a specific required format for compliance, however most ESG disclosures lack a set required format and in general the disclosures are a response to outside community and investors asking organizations to be accountable for social goals. "Sustainability performance data, combined with financial data, is important for the organization to manage and to (voluntarily) communicate its value-creation capacity and capability to global stakeholders" (Herz et al., 2017).

Identification of risk is a critical component of both the developing ESG objectives and the decisions on the timing and nature of ESG disclosures because the success of the strategy relies on an accurate risk assessment. Reporting on the ESG initiatives also has risk. The scope of the ESG disclosures vary and the approach to auditing these ESG disclosures is in the developmental stage. (AICPA Consideration of ESG 2021) Guidance as to the preparation of ESG disclosures from professional and regulatory organizations is developing rapidly in recent times and greater expectations of solid information disclosure are evolving. (FASB Staff Educational Paper 2021)

This chapter will examine how both for profit and not for profit organizations make external disclosures of Global, Criminal Justice, Social and Political Risks in the context of ESG disclosures. Disclosures of any type of risk to an organization present the danger that organizational secrets and strategies are revealed to the public and competitors. Disclosures of assessed risk may also be used in later litigation against an organization. Because of the potential downside to external disclosure of risk, organizations were reluctant to provide information on internal risk assessments unless they were required to disclose information in specific required financial and other legal compliance disclosures. The ESG disclosure requires an organization to balance the need for public transparency with the need to keep strategic risk assessments of an organization private (AICPA Roadmap 5).

Environmental, Social and Governance (ESG) disclosure is a developing area of financial and nonfinancial reporting. Section I of this chapter will discuss the recent history of ESG disclosures, including examining the reasons for the global increase in ESG disclosures, the public sector and investor demand for ESG disclosures, and the development of guidance and requirements for ESG disclosures from professional organizations. Section II will discuss the relationship between ESG disclosures, the Enterprise Risk Management (ERM) functions within an organization, and the risk appetite of an organization. Section III will identify some specific risks that are currently the focus of ESG disclosures. Section IV will conclude with some thoughts on the future of ESG disclosures.

10.2 What is ESG? What drives ESG objectives and disclosure?

Environmental, Social and Governance objectives take many forms within an organization. ESG disclosures have become material from a reporting perspective because ESG goals are tied to corporate strategy and risk management. In May 2022 comments, SEC Chair Gary Gensler noted the new SEC objectives for requiring ESG disclosures on climate issues as a part of the annual SEC reporting and the disclosure of risk management:

> The first is bringing consistency and comparability to how a management team discloses a company's strategy, governance, and risk management with respect to climate-related risks, building upon the TCFD [Taskforce of Climate-related Financial Disclosures] framework.

> The second is disclosure for companies that set targets or use internally developed target plans, transition plans, scenario analyses, or carbon pricing as part of their risk management process.

> If you, the reporting company, have a target, under the proposal you would need to disclose your plans to get to that target. If you have a transition plan, you will need to provide disclosure about that plan. If you employ scenario analysis or use internal carbon pricing as part of your risk management, then you would disclose those too. It's up to a company to determine whether to have a target, transition plan, scenario analysis, or carbon pricing. If a company chose not to make those statements or use those tools, no disclosure would be required. The decision on whether to make these statements or use these tools, though, remains entirely up to you as the company.

> To the extent that the proposed disclosures would include some forward-looking statements, such as projections of future risks or plans related to targets or transitions, the forward-looking statement safe harbors pursuant to the Private Securities Litigation Reform Act would apply, assuming certain conditions were met. (Gensler 2022)

These comments illustrate the challenges in using current ESG information to evaluate corporate performance, the issues of often incomplete and inconsistent disclosure.

10.2.1 Defining the structure and content of ESG objectives and disclosures

Unlike United States Generally Accepted Accounting Principles (GAAP) based standards created for the format of traditional financial statements (Balance Sheet, Income Statement, etc.), ESG disclosures have differing formats and are not regulated by a central accounting authority. ESG information is usually more similar to management accounting information in that the information is tied to specific operational aspects and strategic goals of an organization. The differences in format are also based on the fact that the information is objective based, and the sustainability objectives are determined by the individual organization, rather than a regulatory authority.

> Sustainability performance (or related nonfinancial data) has unique characteristics. It is less tangible and more qualitative than financial performance data – although sustainability data is often quantifiable, as reported by companies in sustainability and corporate social responsibility (CSR) reports. It is also more forward-looking, covering multiple time periods, and often more manually sourced. To improve confidence in sustainability performance data, a different "lens" on assurance and materiality may need to be taken relative to financial data, with professional judgment at the forefront (Herz, 2017, 7).

This "lens" is sometimes referred to as the sustainability lens because the data used is derived from feedback from operational objectives but focused on nonfinancial sustainability goals.

Concern with using forward-looking ESG information is valid, as forecast models must be built on reasonable assumptions.

> Many organizations and investors already use scenario analysis for anticipating future states for other risks, including climate-related risk assessments as part of their risk management and strategic planning processes. [There are] references to entity examples and climate-related scenario analyses from the Intergovernmental Panel on Climate Change (IPCC) and International Energy Agency (IEA). These examples and those in the TCFD's [Taskforce of Climate-related Financial Disclosures'] Technical Supplement: The use of scenario analysis in disclosure of climate-related risks and opportunities provide detailed information on applying scenario analysis to climate-related risks. This tool can also be applied to other ESG-related risks (e.g., regional water availability, outsourcing labor cost models), which could emerge in distinct ways over time. (COSO Compliance Risk Management 2020)

Some professional organizations have provided guidance on best practices for the scope and format of ESG Disclosures. One major accounting authority providing guidance in the ESG disclosure space is the *Committee of Sponsoring Organizations of the Treadway Commission* (COSO). COSO is a professional organization comprised of 5 major accounting reporting standard setting bodies, the *American Accounting Association* (AAA), the *American Institute of Certified Public Accountants* (AICPA), the *Institute of Management Accountants* (IMA), the *Institute of Internal Auditors* (IIA) and the *Financial Executives Institute* (FEI). COSO has been instrumental with post-Sarbanes-Oxley (SOX) guidance on risk assessment and has taken an active role in the developing the current ESG framework. After the passage of SOX in 2002, COSO produced a series of white papers by authors who were active in the profession on the implementation of Enterprise Risk Management (ERM) strategies. ERM contemplates an organization-wide approach to risk, a proactive and continuous attention to evaluation potential risk. COSO continued this mission of providing guidance by producing papers concerning risk and cybersecurity and other emerging issues. As the demand for ESG disclosures has grown, COSO has developed practical implementation guidance and an analysis of the risk attached to ESG disclosures, using the ERM comprehensive framework. Viewing ESG disclosures as a part of the entire organizational risk structure helps to define the underlying objectives for sustainability disclosures and the scope and format of the information necessary to provide meaningful disclosures.

In a 2018 publication, *Applying enterprise risk management to environmental, social, and governance-related risks*, COSO examines and attempts to define ESG-related risk and related disclosures, noting the vast differences in scope of ESG disclosures in different organizations:

> ESG-related risks are the environmental, social, and governance-related risks and/or opportunities that may impact an entity. There is no universal or agreed-upon definition of ESG related risks, which may also be referred to as sustainability, non-financial or extra-financial risks. Each entity will have its own definition based on its unique business model; internal and external environment; product or services mix; mission, vision, and core values and more. The resulting definition may be broad (for example, may include all aspects of the International Integration Reporting Council's (IIRC) six capitals, []) or narrow (for example, may include only a selection of priority environmental and social issues) and may evolve over time. (COSO and WBCSD 2018)

Since ESG disclosures are so closely tied to the strategic plan of an organization, some organizations may choose not to provide all ESG risk related information to the public. One challenge on ESG reporting is that if the ESG reporting is not compelled for compliance reasons, there is no set format for consistent review of progress on social goals in comparison with other organizations. Indeed, even within the same organization there is no requirement that the disclosures remain in the same format, with the same scope each year. There is no requirement that organizations provide ESG reporting at all. So, organizations may choose a very selective approach on the ESG items that they choose to report on in any given year.

10.2.2 Global ESG disclosure guidance

There is no one consistent authority for ESG reporting, and this has opened up a wide variety of best practices consulting. Some existing guidance from global accounting organizations to support external ESG-related risk disclosures include the Sustainability Accounting Standards Board, the United Nations Sustainable Development Goals. There are also Climate Change advocates, the Climate Disclosure Standards Board (CDSB) and the Taskforce of Climate-related Financial Disclosures (TCFD). Finally, the Global Reporting Initiative (GRI) and The International Integrated Reporting Council (IIRC) encourage a comprehensive reporting model that puts ESG information within the larger context of financial reporting.

The Sustainability Accounting Standards board (SASB) provides an Implementation Guide and Reporting Guidelines Financial filings, the most widely used framework. The SASB provides a framework for management to assess financial materiality of sustainability issues, considering risk, for inclusion in financial reports and recommends minimum disclosure requirements by sustainability issue, covering many industries.(SASB.org)

As we face global problems and critical issues with politics, criminal justice issues and climate change, governments, and groups of interested individuals have put pressure on organizations to provide transparency for their operations. One example is the United Nations Sustainable Development Goals that offers 17 ESG-specific reports encouraging objective setting through these specific goals. (UN SDG)

An example of a specific sustainability issue motivating disclosure is climate change, where interested groups have sought accountability for repair of past harm done by organizations and some outside groups have pushed organizations to set higher social goals in the context of their strategic planning. In a profound way, global demand for ESG disclosures has centered around the interrelated nature of risk and ESG goals as assessed by a broad societal view. There are many groups that assess the global impact of the actions of organizations and attempt to create a priority of action on some social goals. The Climate Disclosure Standards Board (CDSB) provides a Framework Financial filings and annual reports. In CDSB guidance recommends reporting requirements for disclosing environmental information in mainstream reports where that information is material to an understanding of companies' financial risks and opportunities, as well as the resilience of their business models. The Taskforce of Climate-related Financial Disclosures (TCFD) recommends voluntary disclosures for companies to report on governance, risk management and impacts of climate change on the organization and provides industry-specific guidance.

Some organizations embrace a more comprehensive reporting model. Global Reporting Initiative (GRI) ESG-specific reports provide a widely adopted framework for reporting material economic, environmental, social and governance issues and advises reporting on topics that present risks to a company's business model or reputation. The International Integrated Reporting Council IIRC advocates <IR> Framework Annual reports that provide a framework for integrated reporting on all six capitals (i.e., financial, manufactured, intellectual, human, social and relationship, and natural). With regard to ESG and Risk, the IIRC advises entities to disclose the specific risks that affect the ability to create value over the short, medium, and long term and how the organization manages them.

One example of this effort to create social goals and prioritize efforts of organizations to add strategic responses to their business plans is the World Economic Forum:

> Each year, the World Economic Forum's Global Risks Report surveys business, government, civil society and thought leaders to understand the highest rated risks in terms of impact and likelihood. Over the last decade, these risks have shifted significantly. In 2008, only one societal risk, pandemics, was reported in the top five risks in terms of impact. In 2018, four of the top five risks were environmental or societal, including extreme weather events, water crises, natural disasters, and failure of climate change mitigation and adaptation. The World Economic Forum also highlights the increasing interconnectedness among ESG risks themselves, as well as with risks in other categories – particularly the complex relationship between environmental risks or water crises and social issues such as involuntary migration. (COSO and WCBSD 2018, 2)

10.2.3 The investor demand for ESG objectives and disclosure

Investor interest in ESG issues has also motivated most companies to respond with more comprehensive disclosures in a serious way.

> There is also growing interest from investors seeking to understand how organizations are identifying and responding to ESG-related risks. In recent years, environmental and social proposals in the US have accounted for around half of all shareholder proposals submitted – representing the largest category of proposals (the other categories include board, anti-takeover/strategic, compensation or routine/other). (COSO and WBCSD 2018, 4)

Recognizing the increased demand for ESG reporting, in 2016 the Securities and Exchange Commission (SEC) polled investors and issuers to determine stakeholder feelings about whether the SEC should mandate ESG disclosures.(Ho 115) The SEC has not yet revised regulations to increase ESG reporting requirements:

> One reason may be the sharp divergence between investors and issuers on whether the problem ESG reform must solve is a question of underreporting or disclosure overload. Eighty-three percent of all respondents in this study support expanding ESG disclosure in some form, with 13% opposed. As Figure 2 shows, 96% of investor comments and 78% of "other" respondents on this issue supported expanded ESG disclosure, compared with only 15% of issuers. Surveys of institutional investors and corporate boards since 2016 indicate that recognition of ESG materiality has grown stronger among both groups since then, suggesting that support for ESG disclosure would be stronger if the SEC were to pose the same questions today. Interestingly, of the 17 law firm comments included in this study, only 7 (41%) supported ESG disclosure reform. (Ho 115)

Fulfilling the expectations of investors can be challenging to an organizations. Unlike the established framework for reporting financial statement information under US GAAP, there was traditionally little guidance on the content of these ESG disclosures which are supplemental information to the financial statements and include financial and nonfinancial information. As a result of this lack of standard format for ESG disclosures, there is a challenge of creating a consistent method of providing assurance and auditing of the ESG disclosures.

Auditors want to have verifiable information in ESG disclosures that are meant to show organizational progress on social goals and objectives. This is why certain parts of the financial reporting are not reviewed by auditors, such as forecasts and soft information. Because ESG disclosures have this type of soft information and forecasting it provides a challenge to assurance. (AICPA Roadmap 2021, 15)

Reporting on social goals follows less of a US GAAP based format but is more similar to managerial accounting disclosures. Because of this the scope and nature of disclosures are not mandated. Existing risk must be evaluated as a part of the analysis of the current situation. Also, the evaluation of potential risk involves an element of forecasting. Forward-looking information must be based on reasonable assumptions to be effective.

10.2.4 ESG disclosure trends

Either on a voluntary basis or compelled by regulation or investor groups, most large organizations have responded to the trend to providing ESG disclosures. It was noted by COSO that over 85% of fortune 500 companies provided some type of ESG disclosure in 2017. (COSO and WBCSD 2018, 91)

COSO noted the increase of mandatory ESG disclosures across the globe: "There has also been growth in ESG-related regulation and disclosure requirements – totaling 1,052 requirements (80% of which are mandatory) in 63 countries." (COSO and WBCSD 2018, 91)

The European Union and Singapore have instituted mandatory ESG Disclosures:

> From 2017, the European Union Directive on Non-Financial Reporting requires that companies that operate in EU member states and meet certain criteria prepare a statement containing information relating to environmental protection, social responsibility and treatment of employees, respect for human rights, anti-corruption and bribery, and diversity on boards. Regulatory bodies and stock exchanges are also responding to growing investor demands for uniform ESG information linked to financial performance.

> In 2017, Singapore introduced a listing rule for listed issuers to prepare an annual sustainability report, identifying material ESG factors, policies, practices, performance, targets, and a board statement. (COSO and WBCSD 2018, 91)

10.3 COSO view: ESG objectives and disclosures and enterprise risk management

Organizations with solid internal control procedures gather a lot of information on current and emerging risks. The risks of any strategy including ESG strategies are evaluated in the context of Enterprise Risk Management (ERM). Organizations develop risk tolerances as a part of the ERM process and continuing and emerging risks are evaluated using the 5-part ERM analysis. Once ESG related strategies are in place, an organization considers the content of ESG disclosures, potential opportunities, and disadvantages, along with challenges to auditing risk related information. Finally, we will discuss trends in future disclosure and potential impact.

10.3.1 Internal controls: Enterprise risk management and risk assessment

Risk Management is a process used by for profit and nonprofit organizations in their strategic planning, internal control, and assessment, and it an exercise of professional judgment for the board of an organization. (Glover 3) Professional judgments are best made through a consistent process, for example the KPMG Professional Judgment Framework takes a 5-step approach. The five steps in this Professional Judgment process are 1) defining the problem, 2) considering alternatives, 3) gathering information, 4) reaching a conclusion and 5) communicating the conclusion to all levels of the organization. (Glover 3)

After the Sarbanes-Oxley Act (SOX) of 2002 was passed in response to the accounting scandals of the 1990s, the *Committee of Sponsoring Organizations of the Treadway Commission* (COSO) developed guidance on *Enterprise Risk Management* (ERM) as a part of the commitment to internal control. ERM is a comprehensive process where the leadership of organizations (the Board of directors) determine risk appetites and assess Key Risk Indicators (KRI) including social and political risk factors as a part of an overall ongoing evaluation of performance and strategic decision-making. (Anderson 2020)

In the post SOX years, the added commitment that organizations made to accountability through strong internal control, corporations also sought to demonstrate to investors their action towards implementing policies concerning sustainability and social goals. In addition to the demand for stronger internal controls, investors have demanded accountability from organizational leadership as to sustainability and social goals. Recently Environmental Social and Governance-related Risks (ESG) reporting has met the demand for additional required disclosures of ESG impact in addition to other financial disclosures (COSO and WBCSD 2018).

ESG disclosures are investor-facing presentations of financial and nonfinancial information, measure and present Criminal Justice, Social and Political risks. It is interesting to note how the structure of ESG disclosures are shaped by the work that COSO has done on ERM, which is usually done for use solely within the organization, and how a study of interaction between organizational risk appetites and KRI identification will shape the external reporting of social and political risk in the context of organizational strategic goals.

The ERM process: The ERM process as created by COSO contemplates applying strategy challenges to the complexity of structure in an organization. (Anderson 2020) The COSO cube illustrates the interactivity of the internal control function within an organization.

The starting point of internal control is that the board of directors should establish risk tolerances and communicate these risk tolerances to the management levels of the organization. Internal auditors then evaluate the actual performance of the organization against these risk tolerances (Patchin 2012)

Key Risk indicators: In addition, the internal control function within a company must identify KRI Key risk indicators that will identify where potential future risk lies for the organization KRIs. (Beasley 2010) These KRIs are separate from Key Performance Indicators (KPIs), which measure whether actual real-time performance of an organization meets expectations. KRIs are rather an examination of trigger events that might cause significant change due to risk in the organization. (Patchin 2012)

10.3.2 Before ESG objectives and related disclosures: Risk appetite should be well communicated and understood within the organization and incorporated into strategy

Simply put, an organization needs to have a well-developed and clearly communicated set of risk appetites, and to apply these to strategic decision-making on a consistent basis. While this is a process that requires systematic periodic evaluation, it is also important to note that some organizations have a professional culture that embraces this process and for others the internal processes of communication are not as well developed (Patchin 2012)

Transparency of risk appetites within an organization must begin with the top management communication of risk appetites to everyone in the organization that is working to achieve strategic goals of the organization. In the COSO White Paper *"Risk Appetite-Critical to Success Using Risk Appetite to Thrive in a Changing World,"* COSO defines risk appetite as "The types and amount of risk, on a broad level, an organization is willing to accept in pursuit of value"(Rittenberg 2012) In order to be an effective tool for an organization, risk appetites must be tied to the strategy of the organization, but the authors of the white paper urge companies to go beyond just measuring actual risk as a metric, and work towards having the workers at every level of an organization understand the philosophy of the risk appetite as set by the top management of the corporation, in order to come up with strategic innovations at all levels of the organization.

> *Risk appetite is much more than a metric*. Often, it is treated as part of an approach where each metric is assigned a target appetite. Although such an approach is important, a better application of risk appetite can lead an organization to proactive, forward-looking opportunities that tie appetite and strategy together for future action. (Rittenberg 2012)

Discussions on risk appetites established by the board and top management are an important part of communicating organizational strategy throughout an organization. These discussions can include ESG issues such as climate related objectives.

> *Risk Appetite helps increase transparency*. A well-formed and communicated risk appetite provides awareness of the risks the organization wishes to assume as well as those it wishes to limit. (Rittenberg 2012)

It is a challenge for management to apply the abstract concept of risk appetites and risk management to decision-making and implementation of strategy unless there is clarity and guidance from the board. Institutional policies can also be created to reflect the risk appetites. (Rittenberg 2012).

To be effective, appetite must be:
- Operationalized through appropriate tolerances, and where necessary, codified through policy
- Stated in a way that assists management in decision-making
- Precise enough to be useful in making decisions and in monitoring by management and others responsible for managing risk
- Applied by those with decision-making authority from the board through senior and middle management on down into the entity (Rittenberg 2012)

10.3.3 Implementing risk appetites in organizational operation through the 5-part COSO ERM framework

Once a risk appetite is established by the board, in order to be effective, the risk appetite must become a living part of the day-to-day strategic operation of the organization.(Galligan 2015) The goal of integrating the risk appetites within the organization is accomplished through the final step in the five-part COSO ERM framework, a continuous review of risks in the organization. The five principles associated with the management of compliance risks within organizational operation are 1) to identify risk 2) to assess severity of risk 3) to prioritize risk 4) to implement risk responses 5) to develop a portfolio view. (DeLoach 2014)

Step 1 is risk identification. In order to convey a clear understanding of risk tolerances the board must describe the compliance risk identification and assessment process in documented policies and procedures. In addition, documentation within the organization must identify compliance risks associated with planned strategy and business objectives . This assessment of strategy includes scanning internal and external environments to identify risks and creating a process for identifying new and emerging risks. (DeLoach 2014)

Step 2 is assessment of risk severity, again the process should be systematic:
- Adopt a uniform scale/scoring system for measuring severity of compliance risks
- Consider qualitative and quantitative measures
- Establish criteria to assess impact and likelihood of compliance risk event occurrence
- Assess severity of risk at different levels (organizational, regional, affiliate, etc.)
- Consider design and operation of internal controls intended to prevent or detect compliance risk events
- Minimize bias and inadequate knowledge in assessing severity (e.g., minimize self-assessments, use multidisciplinary teams) (DeLoach 2014)

Step 3 is prioritizing risk responses:
- Prioritize compliance risks based on assessed level of risk relative to meeting of business objectives

- Use objective scoring based on assessment
- Consider use of other assessment criteria (trend, velocity, etc.) in prioritizing compliance risks
- Consider possible effects of planned changes in strategy and operations
- Develop risk-based action plans for mitigation (risk responses, implemented in next step)(DeLoach 2014)

Step 4 is implementing risk responses:
- Design compliance risk responses that consider the impact on other (non-compliance) risks and risk responses
- Assign accountability for each compliance risk response (including timeline, etc.)
- Follow up to determine whether compliance risk responses have been properly implemented as designed
- Consider compliance risk responses when developing monitoring and auditing plans (DeLoach 2014)

Step 5 is developing a portfolio view or an overall organizational view of risk. At the broader level, the board considers risk interactions (i.e., how mitigating a compliance risk can affect other risks). Having regular meetings/communications between compliance and business units assists this process. (DeLoach 2014)

10.4 ESG risk: Objectives risk and disclosure risk

10.4.1 ESG objectives risk: Integrating ESG and sustainability into strategy

The history of ESG stems from a movement for greater sustainability disclosures. The triple bottom line philosophy encouraged organizations to engage in a separate process of sustainable disclosures. The COSO white paper released in 2013 closes with a reiteration of the practical benefits of using the triple bottom line and social auditing practices as a part of corporate strategy. "Organizations that choose to embed sustainability into a COSO-based risk management program can achieve the following competitive advantages:"(Faris, et al. 2013, 11)

First, the white paper shows a holistic view of the corporation reveals a strong connection between sustainability and strategy.

> **Alignment of sustainability risk appetite to the organization's corporate strategy and the new world view of company value.** Having a holistic view of sustainability risk that looks across the entire enterprise enables organizations to do a better job of anticipating and responding to issues as they arise. (Faris, et al. 2013, 11)

Sustainability Objectives and related ESG disclosures should be prepared in a way that allow corporations a better understanding of the global environment in which they operate. This added level of review that an ESG objective provides improves operational performance because it allows familiar issues to be viewed in a new way.

> **Expanded visibility and insights relative to the complexity of today's business environment.** Embedding sustainability into an organization's ERM framework enables the sustainability function to gain valuable insights regarding the sustainability risks the organization faces and the materiality of those risks. These are insights the sustainability function can then share with management and the board so that they have a clear understanding of the sustainability risks relative to the complexity of the business environment. (Faris, et al. 2013, 11)

When corporations embrace sustainability, the corporation demonstrates that they find value in intangible and nonfinancial goals; and that the decision makers within the corporation understand the connection between sustainability goals and strategic success.

> Stronger linkage of company values and non-financial impacts to the organization's risk management program. Identifying sustainability risks and opportunities can be challenging. However, organizations that understand how to link them to their value drivers are better able to understand the impacts on the business in non-financial ways. (Faris, et al. 2013, 11)

Using a *"sustainability lens,"* considering sustainable goals as a part of overall operational strategy, is an additional level of review, and this additional level of review can provide definite benefits. The additional level of review that a sustainability lens provides helps make strategy and operations more effective, comprehensive, and innovative. Management must also incorporate a long-term approach for sustainability goals, and this long-term consideration can benefit other comprehensive program goals. (Faris, et al. 2013, 11)

The implementation of this *"sustainability lens"* can also be a benefit as an aspect of reputation management, as stakeholders perceive a more aware and effective management team, a management that is in tune with social and sustainability needs. (Faris, et al. 2013, 11)

> **Better ability to manage strategic and operational performance.** Organizations can create competitive advantage by managing sustainability risk to improve business performance, spur innovation and boost bottom- line results. Companies that conceive their products or services through a sustainability lens will attract funding from external investors and boost stakeholder confidence. Sustainability as part of the value proposition is also becoming as relevant to market capitalization as innovation or R&D. (Faris, et al. 2013, 11)

Finally, the Social Audit practices connected with sustainability help corporations to deploy capital in the most efficient way to achieve sustainability and systematic goals. The corporation can examine the benefits and multiple efficiencies achieved with effective capital deployment.

Improved deployment of capital. Organizations that have used the COSO ERM Framework to embed sustainability risk management practices have better opportunities to allocate capital more effectively – in ways that maximize capital efficiency or that send the right messages to stakeholders based on the organization's corporate values and strategy, but in all ways enable the organization to reach its sustainability and, more importantly, its corporate objectives. (Faris, et al. 2013, 11)

10.4.2 ESG disclosure risk: Would mandatory SEC reporting on ESG cause disclosure overload?

On May 25, 2022, the Securities and Exchange Commission (SEC) proposed amendments to rules and reporting forms to promote consistent, comparable, and reliable information for investors concerning funds and advisers' incorporation of environmental, social, and governance (ESG) factors. The process of incorporating ESG disclosures into annual SEC reporting indicates a shift in the attitudes of the SEC towards ESG and its materiality to the comprehensive view of the corporate management strategy. (SEC Press Release 2022) In March 2021, the SEC created a Task Force on ESG reporting. (SEC Press Release 2021) (Posner 2022), and the result of the work of this group is a series of proposed amendments. SEC Chair Gary Gensler noted. "ESG encompasses a wide variety of investments and strategies. I think investors should be able to drill down to see what's under the hood of these strategies. This gets to the heart of the SEC's mission to protect investors, allowing them to allocate their capital efficiently and meet their needs."(Katz 2021) Industry professionals called the announcement of the proposed amendments regarding ESG disclosures a "watershed " moment in the development of ESG disclosure requirements(McKee, et al. 2022).

The Proposed amendments refer to investment funds with an ESG focus, with a goal of preventing false or misleading disclosures:

> While the Commission has not generally prescribed specific disclosures for particular investment strategies, ESG strategies differ in certain respects that we believe necessitate specific requirements and mandatory content to assist investors in understanding the fundamental characteristics of an ESG fund or an adviser's ESG strategy in order to make a more informed investment decision. First, the variation discussed above concerning ESG investing, combined with the lack of a more specific disclosure framework, increases the risk of funds and advisers marketing or labelling themselves as "ESG," "green," or "sustainable" in an effort to attract investors or clients, when the ESG-related features of their investment strategies may be limited. (SEC Proposed Amendment 2022)

The Securities and Exchange Commission (SEC) first considered expansion of required ESG disclosures within the S-K regulations, in 2016 questions to stakeholders. (Ho 115) How do we determine the proper scope of SEC required disclosures? Are existing voluntary ESG disclosures enough in the minds of investors? The polled investors did not feel that voluntary ESG disclosures provided adequate information:

> Although 46% of all comments by companies and business organizations argued that voluntary sustainability reporting outside the federal disclosure regime adequately meets investor needs, less than 1% of investors thought so. In fact, 96% of investors asserted, often strongly, that ESG information contained in these reports is inadequate for investment purposes and costly to analyze. They stress that in the absence of a standardized ESG reporting framework, investors must glean material in-formation from among immaterial information in voluntary sustainability reports that is directed at other stakeholders and often available only from individual company websites that investors must scour at their own cost. (Ho 120)

The SEC considered this feedback:

> For these reasons, the SEC's own Investor Advisory Commission was among those urging the SEC to consider the need to develop a framework for ESG risk disclosure. The majority of investors cited two primary reasons why voluntary sustainability reporting is inadequate. The first is that the broader stake- holder-orientation of most voluntary reports means they are not subject to the same investor-oriented materiality standards that apply to public filings. The second is that the plethora of reporting frameworks and standards reduce the comparability of any resulting data. Comments from the American Institute of Certified Public Accountants also noted that the majority of public companies do not connect the personnel and processes associated with sustainability reporting to those responsible for financial reporting. (Ho 121)

On the issue of whether disclosure overload would overwhelm investors, the SEC 2016 inquiry found the following:

> In short, companies and business groups were more likely to express concerns about investors' information overload than investors themselves. Many investors noted that advances in technology permitting machine reading and automated analytics enable efficient analysis of more extensive disclosures, provided that the information is presented in a comparable format, and that over disclosure concerns are therefore outdated. These comments emphasize the importance of consistency and comparability, which is difficult to achieve solely through principles-based disclosure. (Ho 121)

One important concept is whether disclosure is material for investor understanding of potential investment. In 2016, the SEC noted that it had changed its position on the materiality of ESG information from its stated viewpoint in 1975:

> noted in the Concept Release, the SEC determined in 1975 that "disclosure relating to environmental and other matters of social concern should not be required of all registrants unless appropriate to further a specific congressional mandate or unless, under the particular facts and circumstances, such matters are material." In the Concept Release[2016], the SEC for the first-time sought comment on precisely this issue – the extent to which "public policy and sustainability matters" are now considered to be material in terms of their "importance . . . to informed investment and voting decisions, "and to identify such issues specifically. (Ho 116)

The comments obtained by the SEC in 2016 indicated that investors felt that materiality of ESG disclosures should be industry driven, and reflective of market risk issues.

Thirty-three percent of all comments on section IV.F agreed that ESG materiality is sector specific. In addition, nearly 20% of the 219 investors who responded to questions in this part of the
Concept Release identified ESG factors as material to systemic, market, or portfolio-wide risk,
while no issuer responses did so. Comments identified a wide range of material ESG issues;
those raised most frequently included climate risk and environmental matters, political contributions, human rights, and international tax strategies. The potentially broad scope of circumstances that may render specific ESG information material is a concern of some companies and
counsel with respect to potential ESG disclosure. Several investors, however, emphasized that
under the SEC's materiality standard, information is material based on its importance to the
"total mix" of information rather than because of its significance in isolation. (Ho 116)

10.5 Conclusions: The future of ESG objectives and disclosures

Discussing organizational assessment of social and political risks is at the heart of
ESG disclosures. Making progress towards ESG goals is only possible if the related
risks are accurately assessed and these risk assessments are appropriately applied
in the creation of strategic plans and operation, as well as in the disclosure process.
ESG programs are best served when there is a continuous ERM process of assessment of risk, implementation of these risk assessments into ESG programs, and
measurement of progress toward social goals. ESG disclosures provide transparency
in the measurement of these social goals to the public stakeholders.

Thinking about the future of ESG here are some essential factors:

– ESG disclosures have already become an essential part of external reporting,
through transparency of financial and nonfinancial information to stakeholders
such as investors and global regulators.
– ESG disclosures express the approach the organization has to meeting social
goals and provide an opportunity to discuss the timeline and success or failure
of social goals. Because ESG disclosures are issue specific reporting can be tai-
lored to cover ongoing progress to a goal, not just focused to a specific year.
– ESG disclosures should express the risk appetites that are developed through
ERM and applied internally in an organization. The internal attitudes and assessment of risk within an organization are fundamental to creating successful
programs to meet social goals.
– The scope and accuracy of ESG disclosures also depends on an understanding
of the needs of investors. The investors have started a push for standardization
through required disclosure. In contrast to reporting organizations, concerns
about disclosure overload are dismissed by investors. Because investors desire
a standardized format to analyze ESG performance, SEC mandated ESG disclosures will be a future step in ESG regulatory compliance.

The process of ESG disclosures is drawn from the internal control processes of an organization. Understanding ERM policy of a company and its risk appetites helps to see how the organization develops strategies to meet social goals.

As more transparency is demanded there will be development of more consistent forms of ESG disclosures that are verifiable through audit and assurance standard procedures.

References

AICPA Attestation Engagements on Sustainability Information Guide (2021).

AICPA Consideration of ESG-related matters in an Audit of Financial Statements (2021).

Anderson, R.J. & Frigo, M.L. (2020). Creating and Protecting Value: Understanding and Implementing Enterprise Risk Management, COSO 2020. URL: https://www.coso.org/Shared%20Documents/COSO-ERM-Creating-and-Protecting-Value.pdf

Association for International Certified Professional Accountants and Center for Audit Quality, ESG reporting and attestation: A roadmap for audit practitioners, February 2021.

Beasley, M.S., Branson, B.C. & Hancock, B.V. (2010). Thought Leadership in ERM, Developing Key Risk Indicators to Strengthen Enterprise Risk Management, COSO 2010. URL: https://www.coso.org/Shared%20Documents/COSO-Key-Risk-Indicators.pdf

COSO, World Business Council for Sustainable Development (WBCSD), Applying enterprise risk management to environmental, social and governance-related risks COSO 2018 https://www.coso.org/Shared%20Documents/COSO-WBCSD-ESGERM-Guidance-Full.pdf

DeLoach, J.,& Thomson, J. (2014). Governance and Operational Performance | Improving Organizational Performance and Governance, COSO 2014. URL: https://www.coso.org/Shared%20Documents/Improving-Organizational-Performance-and-Governance.pdf

Patchin, C, & Carey C. (2012). Thought Leadership in ERM | Risk Assessment in Practice COSO (2012) URL: https://www.coso.org/Shared%20Documents/COSO-ERM-Risk-Assessment-in-Practice-Thought-Paper-October-2012.pdf

Galligan, M. and Rau, K. (2015) Deloitte: COSO in the Cyber Age, COSO 2015. URL: https://www.coso.org/Shared%20Documents/COSO-in-the-Cyber-Age.pdf.

Gensler, G. (April 2022). Building Upon a Long Tradition" – Remarks before the Ceres Investor Briefing. US Securities Exchange Commission.URL: SEC.gov | "Building Upon a Long Tradition" – Remarks before the Ceres Investor Briefing.

Faris, C., Gilbert, B., & LeBlanc, B. (2013). Miami University Brian Ballou, Dan L. Heitger, Demystifying Sustainability Risk: Integrating the triple bottom line into an enterprise risk management program, 2013 COSO. URL: https://www.coso.org/Shared%20Documents/COSO-ERM-Demystifying-Sustainability-Risk.pdf

Financial Accounting Standards Board, FASB Staff Educational Paper: Intersection of Environmental Social and Governance Matters with Financial Accounting Standards, March 2021. URL: https://www.fasb.org/page/ShowPdf?path=FASB_Staff_ESG_Educational_Paper_FINAL.pdf&title=FASB%20Staff%20Educational%20Paper-Intersection%20of%20Environmental, . . .

Herz, R., Monterio, B.J, & Thomson, J.C. (2017). Leveraging the COSO Internal Control – Integrated Framework to Improve Confidence in Sustainability Performance Data. URL: https://www.imanet.org/-/media/73ec8a64f1b64b7f9460c1e24958cf7d.ashx

Ho, V. (2020). Disclosure Overload? Lessons For Risk Disclosure & ESG Reporting Reform From The Regulation S-K Concept Release, 65, Vol. L. Rev. 67.

IFRS Foundation, Effects of climate-related matters on financial statements, November 2020.

Glover, S.M. & Prawitt, D.F. (2013). Enhancing Board Oversight: Avoiding Judgment

Katz, D.A. (May 2021). SEC regulation of ESG's disclosures. Harvard Law School Forum on Corporate Governance. URL: SEC Regulation of ESG Disclosures (harvard.edu).

McKee, S., Giordano, M., Godin, L, & Hodge, M. (May 2022). Four quick reactions from KPMG on SEC's proposed rules for investment companies. URL: Investor Protections: SEC proposed Names Rule and ESG Investment Practices Disclosure (kpmg.us).

Posner, C.P. (May 2022). ESG disclosure rules and the SEC's mission. Harvard Law School Forum on Corporate Governance. URL: ESG Disclosure Rules and the SEC's Mission (harvard.edu).

Traps and Biases (COSO 2012-3) https://www.coso.org/Shared%20Documents/COSO-Enhancing-Board-Oversight.pdf

Rittenberg, L. & Martens, F. (2012). Thought Leadership in ERM, Enterprise Risk Management – Understanding and Communicating Risk Appetite COSO. URL: https://www.coso.org/Shared%20Documents/ERM-Understanding-and-Communicating-Risk-Appetite.pdf

Sustainable Accounting Standards Board (SASB) (2022). URL: https://www.sasb.org

Society of Corporate Compliance and Ethics (SCCE), Health Care Compliance Association (HCCA), Enterprise Risk Management, Compliance Risk Management: Applying the COSO ERM Framework |COSO (2020-2). URL: https://www.coso.org/Shared%20Documents/Compliance-Risk-Management-Applying-the-COSO-ERM-Framework.pdf

United Nations Sustainable Development Goals. (2022). URL: https://sdgs.un.org/goals.

United States Securities and Exchange Commission. (May 2022). Enhanced disclosures by certain investment advisors and investment companies about environmental, social and governance investment practices. URL: Proposing Release: Enhanced Disclosures by Certain Investment Advisers and Investment Companies about Environmental, Social, and Governance Investment Practices (sec.gov)

United States Securities and Exchange Commission (March 2021). *SEC Announces enforcement task force focused on climate and ESG issues*. URL: SEC.gov | SEC Announces Enforcement Task Force Focused on Climate and ESG Issues.

Stephen A. Morreale

11 Socio-political risks and their impact on criminal justice organizations

11.1 Introduction

In recent times, political upheaval, social outrage, attacks on the federal and state political system, and blatant social and political differences have wreaked havoc in criminal justice agencies. Police departments, corrections agencies, courts, and other related components of the criminal justice system in America and across the globe face social and political risk. The rise and accessibility to social media can drive negative and unconfirmed stories across the globe in an instant. Live streaming of events, the ability to video record from Smartphones, and Body-worn cameras has led to an expectation of video evidence in most criminal justice proceedings.

From the United States to Canada, the United Kingdom to Ireland and beyond, the criminal justice system is under intense scrutiny by human rights and civil rights activists, and under attack from radical and extremist groups. (Langton et. al., 2021; Nieuwenhuis, 2015)

There is ambiguity and misunderstanding of socio-political risk in criminal justice agencies. The training police officer receive fails to properly address factors or its impact on criminal justice issues. Certain societal issues are often incorporated in certain training modules that address relevant topics including domestic violence, mental health or intellectual or developmental learning disabilities. However, other critical societal issues such as poverty, racial disparities or homelessness are left on the periphery of basic police training.

Many in positions of criminal justice leadership do not have the political savviness to recognize the potential impact of citizen advocacy and the reaction of politicians to those constituents. With the rise in availability, use and influence of social media, agencies can be caught off-guard and unprepared, if they avoid anticipating, planning, and conducting risk mitigation strategies based on the outcries and potential resultant pressures and changes in practice or laws.

As we look at the issues that confront the Criminal Justice system; there are a variety of political and societal differences of opinions, outcries and pressures on patterns, practices, and organizational approaches. Calls for police reform has led to the "defund the police" movement and includes accusations of systemic racism, police bias and abuse of force. The policing discipline has reacted to these accusations by retracting services and unions telling members to seriously consider if they want to put themselves in "harm's way" for an ungrateful or appreciative public. The rise in convictions and incarceration of minority members, caused opposition to mass incarceration. Mandatory sentencing was found to institutionalize men of color, at high rates, disproportionately in our society (Larkin and Bernick, 2014)

New progressive District Attorneys have resisted prosecuting minor cases and even more serious criminal behavior. Bail reform has tied the hands of judges so that even violent offenders are released without any bail conditions. Correction facilities have discharged inmates to reduce overcrowding. Courts have released convicted parties to serve home confinement or community service. Police agencies have been decimated with the resignations and retirements of countless officers frustrated by the scrutiny and criticism. Each of these actions have a direct impact on crime, community safety, and policing.

Leaders of criminal justice agencies have been confronted with a number of issues over the years, which include immigration, racial injustice, racial equality, and fairness. These issues have focused on the behavior of police and use of force or official action against citizens at the hands of police. There have been calls for improved trust, procedural justice, and fair and impartial policing. De-escalation and in some cases, a call for the revision or modification of deadly force statutes and police practices have occurred (Todak and James, 2018).

11.2 Politics and the influence on criminal justice

Prior efforts to focusing on police reform attempted and created some change, but never to the extent expected. At the federal level, the Kerner Commission of 1968 was convened in response to the 1967 riots in Detroit and Newark. (DOJ Kerner Commission Report 1968) The report focused on recommendations for the criminal justice system, including policing. Very few of the recommendations were adopted. After the establishment of Law Enforcement Assistance Administration (LEAA), police education was enhanced, law enforcement academic programs at community colleges were created and later, criminal justice education programs were established at colleges and universities. Most of these classes were taught by sociologists. Doctoral programs were created to provide scholars and academics with specializations in criminal justice.

The Mollen Commission and Knapp Commissions in New York City were created to ferret out corruption in the ranks. These commissions were created by the political apparatus in reaction to the behavior of police agencies. (Knapp Commission Report, 1973, Mollen Commission Report, 1994)

The attention and political influence from these Commissions had wide-ranging effects on the practice of criminal justice. Since laws are promulgated by legislators, politicians hold a powerful oversight and impact on the criminal justice system. There are political influences in criminal justice at the federal, state, county, and local levels.

11.3 Police and criminal justice reform

Cries for police reform in the criminal justice system have caused unprecedented changes in public safety. In many states, this is actively being considered by politicians on all levels of government. However, the discussion for reform has not engaged practitioners in the process. There have been decisions to decriminalize certain crimes, or reduce sanctions for minor theft, or drug possession cases.

In California, New York, and Massachusetts, and a dozen other states, significant legislation has been passed to create reform for police. This requires police, corrections, and courts to adopt new polices, practices and guidelines to meet the requirements of new legislation. In many cases, it is the outcry of society and community members that can often lead to "knee jerk" reactions by politicians. In some circumstances, laws were created that were unnecessary or conflict and contradict other legislation (Buchholz, 2021)

Reports indicate that many states have implemented laws to implement police reform. Changes have been made to Use of Force, Duty to Intervene, Ability to Decertify Officers, and Centralized Police Misconduct Repository. (Brennan Center, 2021)

As individuals rise through the ranks of criminal justice organizations and assume positions of power and influence, they become aware of the input and influence of society and political organizations on their agencies.

Policing and other law enforcement institutions have a natural reluctance and resistance for change. However, agencies can "turn on a dime" when new laws or directives are issued. Recently, we saw the immediate reaction for public safety agencies toward the issues of Covid-19. Most police agencies were tasked with mask enforcement and social-distancing complaints. The rise of public health sector involvement in the pandemic became pronounced. In short order, police agencies were required to make rapid changes, create policy, and implement strategies to meet the new challenges. (Herman, 2020)

There is significant impact on policing from the political apparatus. In Ireland and the United Kingdom, changes have been initiated to meet the demands of those societies. In the Republic of Ireland, a reform commission was formed and many of the recommendations were seen as aspirational, because there was no funding provided. (Commission on the Future of Policing in Ireland Report, 2018)

In New York State, the Governor notified all police agencies that they must create plans for reform and reinvention within 10 months. (Police Reform, 2021) As a result, the City of Ithaca plans to reconfigure their police department, reducing the number of armed officers and creating a Department of Community Solutions and Public Safety. The complaints from police officials were that legislators failed to include the perspectives and concerns of police agencies into the law-making decisions.

In Massachusetts, the move for reform established the Massachusetts Police Officers Standards and Training Commission (POST). This is the first time that a POST agency has had oversight over police officers training and behavior.

Based on a number of high-profile use-of-force incidents nationwide involving the police and African Americans, there was a national outcry for police reform. Led by several advocacy groups including Black Lives Matter, the American Civil Liberties Union, the National Urban League, and other local, state, and federal political leaders, dozens of states have created laws to address police reform.

The frustration with implementing meaningful police reform is that it has been called for since the 1960's following the race riots in many urban centers in the United States. Unfortunately, many of the recommendations from the President's Commission on Criminal Justice were ignored because of the costs associated with these platforms. Clearly, funding is a major impediment for current and previous reform efforts.

Lack of national standards for police training in America and the differentiation of officer readiness creates a chasm in consistent and congruent policies. Without a standard for training, we find wide and varied differences for recruit training from state to state. There has been a discussion for consideration of a National Police College in the United States. Police leaders continue to call for a new commission to explore policing and the criminal justice system. The last significant report by the U.S. government was in 1968. (United States, National Advisory Commission, 1968)

In New York and California, actions by the state legislature eliminated the need for cash bail, which has created a "revolving door" for offenders. This has frustrated police and has led to reoffending, often with serious or fatal consequences for citizens.

11.4 Societal issues – social advocacy

When considering the great number of societal issues and social causes, criminal justice components are affected in a number of ways.

When ~~one~~ reflecting on the many societal issues confronting communities, the list is long and ever-changing. The list below includes only a fraction of the issues, representing the sometime divisive nature of our society, which is constantly evolving. While not all-inclusive, the below list represents the varied issues that the criminal justice system contends with.

> Unemployment, mandatory sentencing, inequitable enforcement of laws, domestic violence, homelessness, terrorism, bullying, abortion, income inequity, religious discrimination, Islamophobia, Semitism, hate crimes, cyberbullying, school discipline, vaccination, and mask enforcement, gun control, alcohol and drug abuse, strikes, curfew enforcement, gender inequity, voter ID laws, gambling, identity theft, organized crime, environmental crime, racial discrimination and systemic racism, global warming, climate and energy, transportation, mental health, domestic terror groups, advocacy groups focused on social justice, environmental justice, anti-vaccination, and human rights. (Millie, 2013 and Armenta, 2017)

Those for and against these issues become vocal advocates or detractors for their cause and often march in support or protest. The police and other components have to respond to these events, sometime leading to arrests, court proceedings and jail visits.

On campuses, police have to deal with providing security to ensure safety of contentious guest speakers. Students with differing perspectives argued against inviting speakers with certain viewpoints that do not reflect their own.

Before new laws are considered by legislators to address rises in crimes related to social issues, police all over the globe are called upon to respond to complaints regarding these and other societal issues.

11.5 Immigration

Police agencies have found themselves in a "tug of war" between the federal government and state and local officials. For many years, it was customary for police agencies to assist federal agents in searches and arrests. Recently, based on the political divide in America, many state government and local governments have prohibited police agencies to assist Immigration and Customs Enforcement agents in enforcing violation of federal immigration laws. This creates a dilemma and conflict for sworn officers. However, many feel that involving local officers in immigration enforcement is contrary to their efforts for improving community policing relations. The police work with their community partners to improve relationships and encourage active participation and involvement with those in live in these areas. Some agency heads feel that engaging individual in "citizenship status inquiries" will push undocumented members away from police. (Russo, 2019)

On our southern border, border towns and states are dissatisfied with the staffing and resources the federal government has provided in regard to illegal border crossing. Texas and Arizona have detailed state and local officers to stop illegal aliens from illegally entering the U.S. Some use state trespassing laws to arrest those who have entered the country without proper documentation or who fail to enter legally. This creates conflict between the states and the federal Government.

11.6 Social – political issues in corrections

Over the years, police and prison scandals have negatively affected the corrections field. In New York, significant security and humanitarian issues have been reported at Rikers Island. Broken cell doors, lack of supervision and inmate-on-inmate violence have drawn the attention of advocacy groups and public officials. Overcrowding, early release, and a lack of funding for rehabilitative programs exacerbates the release of prisoners into the community.

Correctional facilities have had to grapple with social and political issues. As laws were adopted, mandatory sentencing caused a spike in incarceration rates. Correctional facilities have had to adapt to address substance abuse, lack of education of inmates, mental health conditions, and medical conditions of inmates.

In California, several actions by voters and legislators caused the release of thousands of inmates back to the communities. In 2019, Proposition 57 led to the release of thousands of inmates back to the communities. This action caught many communities and police department's off guard as they had to wrestle with releasees, some of whom had been incarcerated for violent crime. (CDCR.gov, 2019)

During COVID, more than 75,000 prisoners were released from incarceration to reduce the spread of COVID in the facilities. The disconnect between legislative actions and lack of consideration for communities and public safety agencies created safety issues for those communities.

11.7 Drug and alcohol enforcement

Over the years, a rise in substance abuse in America and across the globe has led to enhancing penalties related to drug possession and distribution. Neighborhood needs, wants, and demands forced state political apparatus to respond with enhanced penalties. Enhanced penalties for possession near schools and for possession of "crack" cocaine filled jails and prisons. In subsequent reviews of these laws, it was determined that the enhanced penalties for crack cocaine, compared to powdered cocaine had a disproportionate effect on enforcement in poor, minority neighborhoods.

There has been criticism about Zero Tolerance policies and criminalizing drug abuse, with an attempt to dampen the enforcement actions for possession. Some would prefer to adjust policies towards harm reduction and allow for those substance abusers to seek treatment or drug substitution therapy. These societal concerns and reactions from political leader's place police, courts, and corrections leaders in a predicament. With laws on the books, and outcries from neighborhood and business leaders to clamp down on open-air drug markets and public use, police have the responsibility to enforce existing laws. Over the past several years, many courts tacitly legalized marijuana by dismissing many cases brought before the bench.

Much like the reversal on the legality of alcohol, society overtime softened its stance on the consumption of alcohol in society, and based on social pressure, Congress reversed the prohibition with the Harrison Act in 1933. As we look back in history to the prohibition era, and the efforts of the federal government to seek out those manufacturing, transporting, and distributing alcoholic beverages, enforcement operations and entities were forced to stand-down following the passage of the 18th Amendment to the U.S. Constitution, which allowed the consumption of alcohol in American society (Rorabaugh, 2018)

During the prohibition years, U.S. Treasury Agents risked their lives to investigate and prosecute bootleggers. Many lost their lives in this pursuit of justice. Similarly, there has been a relaxation of marijuana laws. Some states have decriminalized marijuana and others have legalized it including allowing for medicinal use. Many segments of the criminal justice system had to adjust to accommodate these new laws now allowing for the use of marijuana under restrictions and stipulations. As with prohibition, many agents and officers risked and lost their lives in the fight against marijuana trafficking and distribution. Over time, as society changes and laws change to meet the will of the people, police agencies will have to adapt and modify their actions and behavior to reflect these changes.

As events unfold, agencies often choose to remain silent rather than providing detail and perspective. This "willful ignorance" may not be the best approach. In the current climate, remaining silent may now be prudent for leaders of criminal justice organizations to avoid backlash, but it offers no support or explanation of the process that agencies go through to move forward to improve or avoid serious incidents from occurring. Review of existing policies, consideration of updating or creating policy and training to modify agency approaches could mitigate future risk.

Communicating these changes can help to provide transparency and reduce mistrust or misunderstandings.

11.8 A pivot with the covid pandemic

What is important is communication of the thinking and actions of criminal justice leaders. The Covid pandemic has caused public safety personnel to take immediate actions to change policies and procedures, and limit public contact in facilities. These changes may be continued after gaining control of the pandemic. However, this is an illustration of the capability of criminal justice organizations to be adaptive and resilient during a worldwide pandemic.

Police and corrections officials had to deftly maneuver while serving as uniformed representatives of government at the of local, county, state and federal levels for policy and authority. The increase in political decisions, the involvement of public health officials and local board of health focused on public health, created rules for each community about what entities could open, capacity limits, mask, and social distance policies.

Job losses, unemployment, masks mandates, non-contact and isolation created agitation, loneliness, and depression. In some areas crime increased. Police had to modify work policies and procedures but could not stop responding to calls. There was a lull in ancillary police actions including vehicle stops and arrests, again to limit unnecessary contact. Suicides were on the rise, serious illness and Covid-related deaths rose to unprecedented numbers.

In the past few years, the public safety hazards ~~of~~ related to the Covid-19 pandemic have significantly influenced emergency service policies and shifted to meet mandates from political leaders and public health officials.

Police response was expected for complaints about mask enforcement, on planes, in stores and restaurants, and social distancing at large events and family gatherings.

In countless cites, states and countries, vaccine mandates for public safety officers in policing and corrections have created a crisis. Many police and corrections officers in the field resisted the mandate, unions challenged the orders and police and corrections officers who refused to be vaccinated were placed on either placed unpaid leave or terminated. These actions led to a reduction in safety and services, and in some cases, the National Guard had been ordered to supplement the missing personnel. (Marcum 2020)

11.9 Establishing risk management units in agencies

Since 2010, some major city police agencies established risk management sections. The NYPD established the Risk Management Bureau, with a Deputy Commissioner responsible for "measuring the performance of police officers and identifies officers who might need enhanced training or supervision. Employing a data-driven approach with information taken from lawsuits, misconduct complaints, and internal probes, the NYPD can quickly monitor patterns of potential misbehavior and take necessary corrective action as part of an early intervention system. The bureau also assesses whether the department's training and policies are effective or need revision." (NYC.gov)

In corrections, the Michigan Department of Corrections established a Risk Identification, Risk Assessment, and Risk Mitigation unit. Audits are conducted throughout the state to respond to risks or to help identify risks in facilities. (Michigan.gov/corrections)

Wicks asserts (Police Chief Magazine, 2017) that in order to build a culture of risk management, "the concept must be taught, reinforced, and consistently branded throughout the systems of the agency (e.g., training, policies, procedures, communications, incentives and rewards, role modeling, discipline)."

A report by the U.S. Department of Justice's Community Oriented Policing Services Office, (COPS) *Risk Management in Law Enforcement* (US Department of Justice, 2018) focuses on fundamental components at the core of risk management: The first

step is to recognize the risks of a particular job. Next, prioritize those risks according to "potential frequency, severity, and available time to think prior to acting."
Last, take action to manage or mitigate the recognized and prioritized risks. The
COPS Office report offered several specific strategies to improve risk management
in law enforcement organizations. These include leadership and culture, accredita-
tion, recruiting and hiring the right people, enhanced training, developing appropriate systems of supervision and review, sentinel event reviews and early warning
systems, police-community relations, use of force, and officer safety and wellness.

Archbold (2005) found few law enforcement agencies adopted risk management
units. Risk Management has been found to is an effective tool in business and
health care industries. Risk Management Units can add social and political risk mitigation to the cyclical review process. Adding these elements to the review process
can help agencies prepare and react to potential issues they could face based on
social or political concerns which might impact the police, courts, or corrections.

11.10 Citizen disagreement with government

Criminal justice agencies have had to deal with countless disagreements with political decisions. From matters relating to immigration and border control, voting
rights, protests, enforcing mask mandates and other Covid regulations, police and
courts have been drawn into "hot-bed" issues arising from government laws and
policies. State, and local police interaction have been thwarted by politicians. In
countless states and municipalities, politicians have forbidden local and state police to assist federal immigration authorities. This places police in a quandary,
as they are sworn to uphold the laws and constitutions of the U.S. and their state.
(Yesufu, 2013)

On January 6, 2020, a large group came to Washington, D.C. to attend a rally to
protest the 2020 presidential election results. Following the rally, a mob marched to
the U.S. Capitol and stormed the building, eventually breaching the U.S. Capitol,
breaking windows, and overpowering security forces. Congress was in session at
the time, looking to certify the election. Many officers were injured, and a trespasser
was killed as they attempted to enter the legislative chambers. One officer was
killed and several committed suicide following the event.

In Portland, Oregon and Seattle, Washington, protesters seized control of areas
of the city, claiming them to be "autonomous zones", with the intent to keep police
outside the boundaries. In an unprecedented step, police facilities were evacuated
and abandoned under threat of attack from protesters. In 2020, the police in the
cities of Seattle and Minneapolis abandoned local precincts under the threat of violent mobs. (Malone, 2020)

11.11 Dealing with mental health issues

There has been a precipitous rise in calls for service for those in mental health crises during the pandemic. Police agencies are ill-equipped or improperly trained to assess and handle these cases. However, the police are often the first to be called when a person is "acting out" or decompensating due to mental health episodes, and drug or alcohol abuse incidents, leading to anti-social behaviors. Many police agencies have started collaborating with clinicians to help in the response to these types of calls. Mental health is a social problem across the globe and requiring police to provide appropriate service/aid to these individuals puts both parties at risk.

In Ireland, An Garda Siochana, (Garda) Ireland's National Police, a new pilot program will pair a certain number of police patrols with psychiatric nurses from Health, Safety and Environment (HSE). Modeled after the jail diversion program, also known as the co-response program, the Garda plans for a pilot program in Limerick City commencing in April of 2022. Six psychiatric nurses from the National Health Program (HSE) will be seconded to the Garda. (Eden, 2021)

An Garda Siochana is working with practitioners from other agencies to create a pilot in Limerick, Ireland, where Garda patrol units will be paired with psychiatric nurses to respond to calls relating to potential mental health crises, coined Community Access Support Teams. (CAST). (Eden, 2021)

In preparation for this new program, the Garda has collaborated with agencies from the Framingham, Massachusetts, Police Department USA, Worcester, Massachusetts Police USA, Toronto Police Department, Public Safety of Northern Ireland, Police Scotland, William James College in Newton, Massachusetts, USA, and Worcester State University.

11.12 Protests

The United States as a country was born out of protest. In recent times, protests have become common-place cities around the U.S. and abroad. Many of these protests were against police brutality, racism, and election concerns. White supremacists marched in Virginia. Weston Baptist Church zealots marched on military burials and traveled nationally to picket the funerals of gay victims of murder or gay bashing, as well as people who have died from AIDS. Police agencies need to provide security for these events allowing the events to continue uninterrupted and keep others from interfering with the rights for civil protest and free speech. This places police officers in the middle of groups with opposing views and can lead to violence conflict.

The U.S. Capital was attacked by insurgents looking to overturn the presidential election in 2021. Countless officers were injured, police suicides followed, and one person was killed trying to break into the building. (Kydd, 2021)

As the unrest continues, certain events have been protracted. Protests focused on officer-involved shootings caused by police officers, especially among people of color, have given rise to worldwide protests. In Seattle, Washington, and Portland, Oregon, continued protests, civil unrest, and the creation of autonomous zones have seen a reduction in police presence. Government facilities have been attacked and a cry for "black equity" continues to be sounded.

The rise in dissatisfaction, and emboldened threats against law enforcement have led to attacks on police officers, and police-related facilities.

Police, corrections, and courts can find themselves drawn into these public protests. Protests often start as peaceful but are joined by radicals and extremist groups determined to cause havoc and destruction. Police are there to preserve the peace, and to allow individuals to exercise their constitutional right of free speech. In some cases, radical groups are drawn to protests and taunt and cite the protesters, since they hold a different point of view. Police are often placed in the middle of these violent confrontations, between protesters and agitators. This happened in several cities across the U.S. including Charlottesville, Virginia, Washington DC, New York City, Seattle, WA, and Portland, OR. (Jenkins, 2020 and Kilgo, 2021)

In some situations, political leaders have ordered police not to respond to at protests in protective military gear, such as helmets, batons, or shields. Failure to prepare for potential violent confrontations places officers in harm's way. Another dilemma is that these protests are protected by our Constitution and Bill of Rights for Freedom of Speech. In the European Union (EU) and United Kingdom, human rights play a significant role in the allowance for protesting. Police are hesitant to tread on these sacred rights, as are prosecutors who balk at bringing charges against protesters stemming from the right to assemble and speak out.

11.13 Public policy

Police are rarely asked for their input on societal issues, which impact the communities they serve. However, affinity groups, such as regional supervisors, state police commanders, chief associations, and corrections leadership, may serve as strong proponents to relay concerns of law enforcement, provide details, and provide recommendations for legislative and policy change considerations. While police and corrections leaders should generally be removed from politics and political interference, lawmakers need to have details and suggestions from criminal justice practitioners rather than operating in a "bubble." Better decisions based on more comprehensive information led to better laws, with less unintended consequences can benefit society.

11.14 From defunding to refunding policing

The criminal justice system has internal and external forces to contend with. This includes police, corrections, courts, juvenile justice, and other social services. In response to several high-profile police use-of-force incidents, a number of activist groups have called for defunding police. Almost immediately following the death of George Floyd, the New York City Council reduced the budget of the New York Police Department by $1 billion dollars. (Elliott, 2022)

In Boston, the City Council cut the overtime budget of the Boston Police Department for 2020. According to the Guardian (March 2021) nearly 40 major cites saw the defunding of their police agencies. Portland, OR, Austin, TX, Minneapolis, New York, Los Angeles, Chicago, Seattle, Milwaukee, Philadelphia, Baltimore, and San Francisco saw significant reductions of their budgets. In Austin, TX, a cut of 33% totaling $153 million caused the Austin Police to announce that they would no longer responds to non-emergency calls. In many American cities, police officers acting in the capacity of school resource officers were summarily removed from academic institutions.

Police reform has been implemented in many U.S. states, focusing on limiting use of force, a duty for other officers to intervene, and qualified immunity.

In Massachusetts, the reform efforts have created a Police Officer Standards and Training (POST) Commission. The composition of the group charged with creating these new training standards was limited to only one police representative, a police chief. The investigative entities created to review police complaints purposely excluded former law enforcement officers.

In Ireland, a Commission entitled The Future of Policing in Ireland (Independent Commission, 2018) was convened with an American police leader, Kathleen O'Toole, serving as the chair of the commission. Similar to the report from 2017 following the work of the U.S. President's Commission on the Future of Policing in the 21st Century, commissioned by President Obama, The Future of Policing report recommended 6 pillars for attention and improvement. (Independent Commission, 2018)

While there have been calls for defunding police from protesters and advocates, a seemingly knee-jerk reaction from many state legislators and city officials was to cut the police budgets. The intention of this "reallocation of funds" appeared to be that the money from police expenditures could be shifted to social service organizations to meet the needs of individuals and situations now handled by police. Vermeer, et al, 2020)

However, in a short period of time, it became obvious that reducing the number of police in American cities was leading to an increase in violent crime. Also, it appears that creating new response to policing or police calls for service will take a great deal of planning and preparation. Many of the calls for service can be unknown in nature, from the mundane to those that lead to people in crisis. Unarmed social workers may not be prepared or equipped to deal with angry, despondent individuals in a time of crisis.

This lapse in staffing can create safety issues across the country especially in urban centers.

11.15 Socio-political issues beyond the USA

The Patten Commission (Independent Commission on Policing in Northern Ireland, 1999) was convened to review and make recommendation to foster peace and change the culture of the policing entity. The report made several recommendations, which included renaming the Royal Ulster Constabulary as Public Service of Northern Ireland, (PSNI) a new governmental Policing Board and Ombudsman, a move to 50/50 recruitment to allow for Protestant and Catholic members of PSNI, and other process improvements. (Gormley-Heenan, and Aughey, 2017)

In Northern Ireland, Brexit caused significant changes in policing approaches and the ability to interact with its island neighbor, the Republic of Ireland. Political issues continue with hard border consideration, which would reduce travel and commerce between the UK and EU, having an impact on Ireland - Northern Ireland cooperation and interaction. (Gormley-Heenan, and Aughey, 2017)

11.16 Learning from sentinel incidents worldwide

Each time a serious, questionable incident occurs, it would be of great value for agencies to create focus groups, conduct tabletop exercises, and practical exercises for staff to prepare and adapt for any eventuality. This approach can mitigate the potential impact if a similar event were to occur in that jurisdiction. Being proactive, considering how the agency might respond to such an event, or change in law or policy can help the agency be better prepared to react. After Action Reviews (AAR) can be valuable to help the agency learn for prior practices and prepare for future incidents.

11.17 Expectations of criminal justice agencies

With the exception of fire and medical services, police agencies are generally the only agency expected to provide a 24/7/365 response. This means that when everything else is closed, police are called on to respond. Police agencies, who work in collaboration with the courts and corrections, are called when there is no one else to call. The move to include social service agencies can be valuable if the services are available during the evening and on weekends. In order for this process to be effective, this will be required.

With the rise in mental health calls, homelessness, domestic disturbances, or neglected children, the police may be the only available outlet for those in need, after normal business hours, in evenings and on weekends. Police agencies have to deal with political and societal issues, and they have not been properly trained in these areas. Every time an incident occurs, the response is to train the police on similar incidents. These situations might include citizens on the "autism spectrum", hearing deficiencies and other intellectual or developmental difficulties. This places an additional burden on already overstretched police officers.

Many of societies social ills and issues have fallen on the police. Society and government institutions have failed to provide appropriate funding for the appropriate social service response. Most child welfare, mental health professionals, and social service providers work a traditional Monday through Friday, 9am to 5pm schedule. Lack of access for those in need have contributed to this crisis. Police are the safety net during these calls for help. (Auerbach and Miller, 2020)

In order to deal with the repeated calls, many police agencies are collaborating with mental health organizations to assist in the de-escalation and diffusion of volatile mental health cases. Some agencies have contracted with mental health clinicians to form co-response teams. Pairing police and clinicians to respond to mental health calls has led to positive outcomes and clinical referrals as opposed to custodial outcomes.

In some jurisdictions, smaller law enforcement agencies have opted to pool resources in a regional manner. This allows agencies to share a group of clinicians, which provides response coverage and the opportunity for cost-sharing measures.

11.18 Transnational crime

Crime knows no boundaries. Police agencies at the state, local and federal levels in the United States and abroad must deal with crime and criminal elements outside their borders. (Albanese, J., 2012). Terror threats, cybercrime, cyber-attacks, attacks on infrastructure, and human trafficking have infiltrated other jurisdictions. These crimes can be hard to investigate, given that the perpetrators may operate in other jurisdictions thousands of miles away, often in unfriendly and uncooperative countries. Most local agencies do not have the capacity to investigate these crimes and lack the legal venue or authority to address criminal behavior when it is committed outside their jurisdictional boundaries. With anonymizers to hide internet locations, it can be difficult to track the location of the attack or criminal. In these circumstances, high-level cases may be referred to a federal investigative agency. Some of these cases can have political ramifications.

11.19 Leading criminal justice organizations through the socio-political morass

Amongst the many organizational issues that police leaders must contend with, the added layer of socio-political issues must be considered. Leaders need to be attuned to ongoing social dialogue and political discussions. They need to maintain vigilance to anticipate potential issues and problems that may rise in their communities.

Criminal Justice leaders should make themselves available to elected officials at all levels of government and be prepared to make honest and critical assessments of their agencies with a focus on improving outcomes as the centerpiece of these reviews. Their input and insight should not be dismissed but rather solicited and acted upon in good faith by political leaders. (Bass 2000)

11.20 Conclusion

The push and pull and cycle of different political views of crime and criminal justice are stark. From liberal, progressive, and conservative views, the criminal justice discipline can be at odds with varied views and opinions of the stakeholders. In most western countries, police and other components are expected to follow the Rule of Law.

Offering two models of Criminal Justice, Packer (1968) explained, the Crime Control Model is more conservative, where the Due Process Model is more liberal. These tend to see the conservatives as the party that is autocratic and the liberals as the party of that protects the rights of the accused. These seem to be at opposite ends of the spectrum although there are some overlaps.

The varying differences in the political sphere may fluctuate based upon the current climate within any given municipality, state, or country. When crime rates increase, the conservatives who support the crime control model would more likely be elected. Whereas when there are instances of alleged or actual misuse of power or brutality, the public view may elect the liberal political parry to affect changes to the law enforcement apparatus of the affected jurisdiction.

The importance of communication and involving criminal justice agencies in the decision-making process could be vital to future legislative efforts. While it may not be prudent for police leaders to voice their individual concerns on legislative drafts, the collective voice of police, probation, courts, and corrections officials through their regional and state representative organizations could be a valuable in the legislative process. The consequences, and in many cases the unintended consequences of legislation, can be detrimental in communities when decisions are made that hamper the effectiveness of public safety.

We have witnessed the knee-jerk reactions of political decisions that cause significant backlash. The defunding of police has demoralized officers, driven many to retirement or alternative careers and has caused spikes in violent crime in major cities. Removal of School Resource Officers has led to public outcry to replace these police officers in the schools. (Reilly, 2020)

Recognizing the many layers and ever-changing social and political challenges and issues is important for leaders to consider when deliberating responses and planning for the delivery of services.

While there is no doubt that there is room for improvement in law enforcement, a continuing dialogue with community and political leaders can help to assuage parties with different social and political agendas and help establish a better rapport so that opinions from all sides are considered before implementing new policies and guidelines.

This chapter was intended to raise awareness and create deeper a thought process about the complicated nature of policing, corrections, and the courts in negotiating the ever-changing social and political realities. Social media has played a significant role in offering a narrative on the inequities and inefficiencies of the criminal justice system. There is clearly room to improve in multiple areas of the criminal justice system. The discussion, while no exhaustive or all-inclusive, can assist criminal justice leaders as they grapple with the many different factors, changing demands and changing social and political views that drive the system.

The criminal justice system continues to improvise and adapt based on the ~~calls~~ demands for significant change. Discussions about reducing use of force, de-escalation tactics, using less than lethal force, improving training and tactics, enhancing recruiting techniques and officer retention help focus on improvements in these critical areas and help identify best practices moving forward. Institutions including the Police Executive Research Forum, the National Police Foundation and the International Association of Chiefs of Police have been focusing on these and other important issues to further explore and offer recommendations for member agencies.

Each of these organizations can provide guidance and leadership in order to shape the preparedness of criminal justice organizations in the future. Being proactive, anticipatory, formulating departmental responses to critical incidents, and creating contingency plans can help law enforcement agencies deal with the ever-changing landscape of social and political concerns in the communities that they serve.

References

Albanese, J. S. (2012). Deciphering the linkages between organized crime and transnational crime. *Journal of International Affairs*, 1-16.

Archbold, C. A. (2005). Managing the bottom line: risk management in policing. *Policing: An International Journal of Police Strategies & Management*.

Armenta, A., & Alvarez, I. (2017). Policing immigrants or policing immigration? Understanding local law enforcement participation in immigration control. *Sociology Compass*, *11*(2), e12453.

Auerbach, J., & Miller, B. F. (2020). COVID-19 exposes the cracks in our already fragile mental health system. *American Journal of Public Health*, *110*(7), 969-970.

Bass, S. (2000). Negotiating change: Community organizations and the politics of policing. *Urban Affairs Review*, *36*(2), 148-177.

Brennan Center for Justice, Subramanian, R. and Arzy, L., *State Policing Reforms Since George Floyd's Murder*, May 21, 2021, https://www.brennancenter.org/our-work/research-reports/state-policing-reforms-george-floyds-murder

Buchholz, K., Police Reform: Which States Have Acted on Police Reform? May 25, 2021, Statista.

California Department of Corrections and Rehabilitation (CDCR) https://www.cdcr.ca.gov/covid19/expedited-releases/

Commission on the Future of Policing in Ireland Report, September 2018, www.policereform.ie.

Kilgo. D.K. & Mourão, R.R., (2021) Protest Coverage Matters: How Media Framing and Visual Communication Affects Support for Black Civil Rights Protests, *Mass Communication and Society*, 24:4, 576-596.

Dirikx, A., Van den Bulck, J. and Parmentier, S. (2012) *The Police as Societal Moral Agents: "Procedural Justice" and the Analysis of Police Fiction, Journal of Broadcasting & Electronic Media*, 56:1, 38-54, DOI: 10.1080/08838151.2011.651187

Eden, L., November 19, 2021, Framingham Police Co-Response Program Heads to Ireland as Pilot in 2022, *MetroWest Daily News*.

Elliot, C. NYPD, defunded by $1 billion, reports shoplifting levels highest they've seen in 30 years, February 2, 2022, *Law Enforcement Today*.

Ellison, K. (2021). The Death of George Floyd, the Trial of Derek Chauvin, and Deadly-Force Encounters with Police: Have We Finally Reached an Inflection Point? Or Will the Cycle of Inaction Continue? *Ann. Rev. Crim. Proc.*, *50*, i.

Figueroa, M. (2020). Toward an Independent Administration of Justice: Proposals to Insulate the Department of Justice from Improper Political Interference. *Fordham Law Legal Studies Research Paper Forthcoming*.

Goldstein, H., Problem-Oriented Policing (1990 and 2015) Create Space Publishing.

Gormley-Heenan, C., & Aughey, A. (2017). Northern Ireland and Brexit: Three effects on 'the border in the mind'. *The British Journal of Politics and International Relations*, *19*(3), 497-511.

Herman, M., Police: Mask Mandates Difficult to Enforce, July 09, 2020, Newsmax, Accessed at https://www.newsmax.com/us/mask-mandates-enforcement-police/2020/07/09/id/976455/

Independent Commission on Policing for Northern Ireland, & Patten, C. (1999). *A new beginning: Policing in Northern Ireland*. Stationery Office.

Jenkins, B. M., & Butterworth, B. R. (2020). *Metal Against Marchers: An Analysis of Recent Incidents Involving Vehicle Assaults at US Political Protests and Rallies*.

Knapp Commission Report. (1973)

Kydd, A. H. (2021). Decline, radicalization and the attack on the US Capitol. *Violence: An International Journal*, *2*(1), 3-23.

Larkin, P., & Bernick, E. (2014). Reconsidering mandatory minimum sentences: The arguments for and against potential reforms. *The Heritage Foundation*.

Langton, S., Bannister, J., Ellison, M., Haleem, M. S., & Krzemieniewska-Nandwani, K. (2021). Policing and Mental ill-health: Using Big Data to Assess the Scale and Severity of, and the Frontline Resources Committed to, mental ill-health-related calls-for-service. Policing: A Journal of Policy and Practice, 15(3), 1963–1976.

Malone, S., June 12, 2020, Seattle Mayor Praises Extremist Takeover Of 'Autonomous Zone' As 'Patriotism,' *The Police Tribune*.

Marcum, C.D., 2020, American Corrections System Response to COVID-19: an Examination of the Procedures and Policies Used in Spring 2020. *American Journal of Criminal Justice*, 45, 759–768.

McDevitt, J., Farrell, A., Andresen, W. C. (2005) *Enhancing Citizen Participation in the Review of Complaints and Use of Force in the Boston Police Department*.

Michigan.gov, https://www.michigan.gov/corrections/0,4551,7-119-1378-162416–,00.html https://www.theguardian.com/us-news/2021/mar/07/us-cities-defund-police-transferring-money-community

Millie, A. (2013) 'What are the police for? Re-thinking policing post-austerity', in J.M. Brown (ed.) *The Future of Policing*, Abingdon: Routledge.

Mollen Commission Report, 1994. Oliver, W. M., & Marion, N. E. (2008). Political party platforms: Symbolic politics and criminal justice policy. *Criminal Justice Policy Review*, 19(4), 397-413.

Nieuwenhuis, M. (2015). The Netherlands' disgrace: racism and police brutality'.

Packer, Herbert L. (1968). *Two Models of The Criminal Justice Process*. Stanford University Press.

Pham, H. (2005). The constitutional right not to cooperate-local sovereignty and the federal immigration power. *University of Cincinnati Law Review*, 74, 1373.

Pickett, J. T. (2019). Public opinion and criminal justice policy: Theory and research. *Annual Review of Criminology*, 2, 405-428.

Police Reform and Reinvention Collaborative, (2021) New York State, https://policereform.ny.gov/

Reilly, K. (2020). Police do not belong in our schools. *Students are demanding an end to campus cops after the death of George Floyd. Time Magazine*. https://time.com/5848959/school-contracts-police.

Rorabaugh, W. J. (2018). *Prohibition: A Concise History*. Oxford University Press. ISBN 978-0190689957.

Russo, C. H., Cities Nationwide Refuse to Cooperate with ICE's Mass Deportation Raids, Jun. 21, 2019, Huffington Post.

Saunders, J., Kotzias, V., & Ramchand, R. (2019). Contemporary police stress: The impact of the evolving socio-political context. *Actual Probs. Econ. & L.*, 1430.

Todak, N., & James, L. (2018). A systematic social observation study of police de-escalation tactics. *Police Quarterly*, 21(4), 509-543.

U.S. Department of Justice, COPS Office (2018) Risk Management in Law Enforcement.

United States of America. National Advisory Commission on Civil Disorders, & United States. Kerner Commission. (1968). *Report of the national advisory commission on civil disorders*. US Government Printing Office.

Vermeer, M. J., Woods, D., & Jackson, B. A. (2020). *Would Law Enforcement Leaders Support Defunding the Police? Probably-if Communities Ask Police to Solve Fewer Problems*. RAND.

Wicks, M. (2017). Risk Management: A key component in public safety. *Police Chief Online*. Retrieved December 2, 2021, from https://www.policechiefmagazine.org/risk-management-key-component-public-safety/?ref=c318be9b30448d5d9c2e2a0fe701dbf0.

Yesufu, S. (2013). The Development of Policing in Britain in the Next Five Years. The Police Journal, 86 (1), 66–82. https://doi.org/10.1350/pojo.2013.86.1.556

David T. Mulcahy
12 The use of task forces internationally: Mitigating socio-political risks for law enforcement agencies

12.1 Introduction

The ability that leaders have to collaborate, innovate, and adapt their responses to events (active shooters, hostile and violent acts and perpetrators) will be critical in a world where surprise and uncertainty are becoming all too common characteristics of public safety. (Straub et al., 2017).

Task force participation increased significantly after the September 11th, 2001, attacks (DOJ, 2011). Collaborative efforts in a post 9/11 era have formed between federal, state, and local law enforcement agencies have been created in order to coalesce practitioners and specialists in sub areas of the criminal justice system. These initiatives are designed to target specific criminal activity, usually in correlation with a particular geographical area. By combining communal resources, intelligence sharing mechanisms, and varied skill sets of multiple law enforcement agencies to focus on targeted crimes/criminal patterns, task forces create a formidable crime control paradigm and effective way to combat crime. Fusion Centers have been constructed to promote ongoing information sharing primarily coordinated at the federal level. For example, the Federal Bureau of Investigation and the U.S. Department of Justice will partner with state, local and tribal police agencies to further specific criminal control activities (Goldstein, 2020). These centers may be affiliated with emergency management agencies in case of a natural disaster and assist with relief efforts. Since 2018, the United States Department of Homeland Security has documented 79 fusion centers, resulting in The National Network of Fusion Centers (DHS, 2019; Lambert, 2010). Fusion Centers are decentralized, self-organizing and respond with their respective partners to address specific areas of criminal and/or terrorist activities (Lambert, 2010). They rely on intelligence gathering and through diversifying information sharing protocols, they provide specific attention to problematic areas and obtain accurate information regarding criminal activity and organizations.

12.2 Advantages to task forces and impact on criminal investigations

In the United States, there has been tremendous collaboration and growth within the task force community since 9/11 (DOJ, 2011). The focus of task forces ranges from drug trafficking organizations (DTO), human trafficking, domestic (United States) and transnational organized crime syndicates as well as specific offense targets like anti-terrorism, crimes against children, opioid abuse, fugitive task forces, etc. (O'Brien, 2011). By combining resources, Task Forces create collaborative relationships expanding the traditional boundaries of law enforcement agencies and can include community-based corrections, victim assistance providers, reentry organizations and other significant stakeholders. Effective task forces can leverage their resources whereby developing more effective and efficient responses for criminal justice related agencies (McGivern, 2021).

Task Forces can provide a unified front over specific offense targets and supplement those involved with joint training opportunities and hone skill sets which are applicable to other areas. "The task force concept increases the effectiveness and productivity of limited personnel and logistical resources, avoids duplication of investigations and consequent wasteful expenditure of resources in matters of concurrent jurisdiction, and expands the cooperation and communication among federal, state and local law enforcement agencies" (Ashley, 2003, 2). Goals for Task Forces participants include lowering crime rates and suppressing recidivism, tuning in, and adopting "best practices" techniques from information sharing and collaborative efforts. This is achieved by coordinating community outreach and partnerships, fostering support to deter crime and strengthening relations between the community and law enforcement agencies (Ashley, 2003).

12.3 Steps to creating a successful task force and assessing risk

When constructing a task force, there are several important issues to keep in mind. First and more importantly, what is the "buy-in" from participating leadership and their respective agencies? Successful task force initiatives need ongoing support from Chiefs and Commissioners of participating units. There needs to be unanimous agreement that efforts will be targeted to specific goals and that the groups involved are at a strong level of readiness for information sharing and can measure and assess data collection (Walker, 1996). Senior leadership must be able to accurately assess the individual team members abilities to collaborate and help develop team strategies. Law enforcement members must have the ability to continuously learn, adapt and work cooperatively in a team management style.

Task forces need to have the encouragement and motivation of all participants. This will engage team members to identify the applicable criminogenic factors that need to be addressed in targeted populations. Good examples of successful task force participation include *The Safe Streets Initiative* (1992) and *Operation Ceasefire* (1996). *The Safe Streets Initiative* spearheaded by the Federal Bureau of Investigation was designed so that the Special Agents in Charge (SAC) of each FBI field division could initiate efforts to partner with local and state law enforcement partners to launch long-term, proactive investigations focused specifically on gangs, violent crime, and aide in the apprehension of fugitives of violent crimes (Rachlin, 1993). This collaborative effort also incorporated state and federal prosecutors together with law enforcement to execute in a comprehensive crime control strategy to reduce violent crime (Rachlin, 1993). *Operation Ceasefire* (also referred to the *Boston Gun Project*) is a problem-oriented policing initiative first implemented in 1996 in Boston, Massachusetts, USA. The program was specifically aimed at youth gun violence as a large-scale problem. The project assembled an interagency group of criminal justice practitioners and law enforcement. Research included assessment that applied various techniques to create an understanding of what was driving youth and gun violence. Once factors were determined, intervention strategies were applied and managed. Ongoing evaluations of the project were conducted to assess success (Kennedy, Braga & Piehl, 2001).

Task force integration begins with a policy that identifies strict procedures related to chain of command. There needs to be direct and continuous interagency communication with a designated point of contact. Regardless of the origin of the task force, a memorandum or memorialized agreement needs to be officiated and agreed upon by all participating agencies. This contract will assist in mitigating specific risks that can develop and arise from multi-agency/jurisdictional investigations and operations. A *Memorandum of Understanding* (MOU) helps manage the accountability of all participants and establishes points of responsibility and tracking procedures (SAFECOM, 2004). The MOU is a document that designates the broad guidelines of the agreement between all participating agencies. Its primary purpose is to communicate the expectations and what has been negotiated and agreed upon on prior to the partnership. Examples include, "How investigations are handled?" "Is there a lead agency?" "What protections exist for officers involved if something goes wrong?" "What is the official chain of command?" "Who does the task force report to?" These procedures need to be mutually agreed upon and accepted by the leadership of all involved as well as those directly responsible for oversight of the task force and their operations (SAFECOM, 2004).

Risk management is necessary when conducting all law enforcement operations. Most organizational functions include some type of risk – personal, integrated within individual roles, hazard of the position, or not anticipated. All agencies are at risk for potential lawsuits and officers can face civil and criminal prosecutions which impact their reputations, positions, and assets. Examining risks at all levels is critical for any agency. Strategies needed to mitigate these risks should be designed at both the organizational as well as personal level. However, when dealing with multi-agency action plans, it is crucial that social and political risks are recognized and moderated during the organization and execution of all operations. (Scism, 2017) "While some risk management programs focus largely on internal personnel liability concerns, such as

early warning systems, other programs appear to encompass not only personnel liability, but organizational liability from a more global perspective." (Scism, 2017).

When assembling a task force, organizers must consider all conditions of risk
that threaten the viability and potential success of the group. One important factor
that should be closely examined is the political environment in play, not just inter-
agency, but intra-agency. Another factor is the current climate of the community
which will be affected and its relationship with law enforcement agencies at the
local, state, and federal levels. Stakeholders must investigate and analyze crime
rates and specific criminogenic incidents within the targeted community that the
task force will be operating in. (Copple & Copple, 2018) By developing a comprehensive risk management program, it is easier to identify the sociopolitical risks and
establish policies and procedures that are necessary for better collaboration to
reach established goals. It is critical that all participating law enforcement agencies
be on the same page. Law enforcement is by nature and design process-oriented
and bureaucratically structured. Thus, when constructing a task force, even when
respective officials agree on the constructs, there needs to be a positive buy-in that
must be encouraged and secured by leadership. This leadership cadre must have a
unified philosophical approach that is comprehensive, goal oriented and supported
on all levels. (Copple & Copple, 2018).

Social and political risks must be prioritized and managed during the length of
time the task force is in existence. Solid leadership and continual, open lines of
communication with all members is imperative. Risks must be assessed at the
macro and micro levels. Sociopolitical risks impact the agencies involved and effect
the organizational structure and management of the task force on a (macro-level)
and microlevel. Examples include negative media press on one of the participating
agencies, a team member violating ethics or the code of conduct, an officer involved
shooting, (OIS) etc. (Copple & Copple, 2018). Once risks are identified and the potential consequences calculated, mitigation procedures can be enacted to minimize
the damage. This enables on-going monitoring and critical assessment by agency
leadership to potential evolving risks.

There has been minimal research conducted in the United States as well as
globally focusing on partnerships and collaboration in the law enforcement community. In particular, integrating traditional policing agencies with other groups including corrections and/or probation/parole agencies (Jannetta & Lachman, 2011).
With a critical eye on law enforcement agencies around the world and the criminal
justice system as a whole, innovative "modus operandi" systems within the community setting creates an intersection where knowledge, resources, and dialogue
foster essential changes within the field.

Partnerships within task forces normally result in an expansion of roles and ongoing rotating responsibilities for participating officers. This movement is known in
organizational and military studies as *mission creep* (Murphy & Worrall, 2007;
Corbett, 1998). *Mission creep* (1993) is when there is a spreading out, an expansion

of a particular project or undertaking which demonstrates a positive growth effect (Corbett, 1998). Each success will build to a more ambitious initiative and will continue until a failure results and will inevitably discontinue the project. Mission creep was first identified in 1993 in a *New York Times* article discussing the Somali Civil War and UN Peacekeeping intervention. It has also been detected with Fusion Centers. Earlier goals to relay intelligence gathering have been targeted for doing more than that and violating civil rights of United States' citizens (Monahan & Palmer, 2009).

For task force operations to be successful, leadership becomes a key component (Northouse, 2003). In order to maintain accountability of all participants and confirm that interagency boundaries are maintained, effective and strategic leadership must exist. The most common definition of leadership is, *"a process whereby an individual influences a group of individuals to achieve a common goal"* (Northouse, 2003). Leadership is not seen as an individual personality trait, but a continuous interaction between people. This continual interactional flow fosters a process to achieve the primary goals of the mission statement. There are basic ethical problems inherent in cultivating a strong leadership style with task forces. The managerial position(s) within the task force can be an issue. However, since policing is inherently paramilitary in structure, academy and field training programs teach and train law enforcement officers to respect the chain-of-command (Copple & Copple, 2018). Another ethical dilemma is how leadership responds to bad or misguided behavior that results in problems or scandals for their agencies. The American Society for Public Administration believes that responsibility and responsiveness are more important than accountability of leaders (Gawthrop, 2005).

There are several leadership modalities and how it fits within the task force is dependent on the person and style they utilize. Examples of applicable leadership styles include the *Trait Theory*, which highlights that leaders are born not made; *Situational Theory* in which the leader in charge analyzes the work environment to decide the most effective form of leading based on assessing the commitment of workers, competencies, and maturity; and *Transformative Theory* of leadership which is done when an organization is posing for change and examines psychodynamics and leadership, team leadership initiatives and servant leadership (Lewis, 2003). It is extremely important to determine how leadership roles are delegated within the task force. This leadership issue continues to be an ongoing problem in criminal justice agencies. According to Kuykendall and Usinger (1982) there is not enough delegation that occurs, specifically in criminal justice agencies. Effective leadership delegation has been replaced by "micromanaging," which is a significant political risk for any criminal justice agency but specifically, the task force community. Those who hold leadership positions *"like to have their hands in the pot"* but are not necessarily *"watching it cook."* Strong leadership encourages morale growth and creates a pathway for effective communication. Poor delegation creates an environment where task force members begin to question their competency or commitment to the cause. For organizational success, positive growth and achievement of established task force goals, leadership must facilitate the encouragement of employees, professional development, and strong morale (Scism, 2017).

12.4 Leadership, understanding existing biases and effects on increasing risks

There are potential biases that can impact a task force success. Selection of team members, establishing the hierarchal/command and control protocols, and setting targets/goals of the task force can have a detrimental effect on the short and long success of the task force. Herbert Simon introduces the concept of heuristic biases defined as mental short cuts that permits individuals to make judgements and solve problems efficiently and swiftly (Cherry, 2019). In the world of law enforcement, practitioners are normally limited with time and decision-making choices that are based on the intelligence gathering mechanisms and the accuracy of that information. Tversky & Kahneman (1974), presented their research on using heuristics and the connection with cognitive biases. Because law enforcement often involves fluid, quickly evolving situations requiring split-second decision-making processes, the ability to develop short cuts in judgement, can lead to biases that can have a negative impact on the group and obstruct the team from making positive decisions and reach their goals. One example is *anchoring bias* (Marewski & Gigerenzer, 2012). This occurs when a person (or team) is influenced by the initial notification of information, which in the world of investigations, can originate from confidential informants, law enforcement observations and information provided by the public. If the group relies too heavily on the initial information, this could potentially hinder how they process that information and can make it more difficult to consider other factors which may be just as important before planning the actions needed.

The *Dunning-Kruger* effect (1999) is another type of cognitive bias (Cherry, 2019). Essentially this is when people believe themselves to be more intelligent and skilled than they really are. It is a combination of low self-awareness and not having the capacity to understand where they overcompensate their abilities. Dunning and Kruger (1999) believe this occurrence leads to individuals failing to comprehend their shortcomings, overestimate their skill levels and are unable to see their own mistakes. Having a little knowledge leads to overconfidence and potentially disastrous mistakes (Cherry, 2019). This is detrimental to those who hold leadership positions, especially in law enforcement. Strong leaders, who oversee task forces and other complicated operations, recognize their shortcomings, are open to and listen to constructive criticism and are not insulted by recommendations to improve results.

In a task force environment, the issue of *Groupthink* can play heavily into the decision-making processes. Groupthink happens when a group of individuals' wish to maintain group loyalty and cohesiveness, and this becomes more important than making the best choices to fulfill the mission and goals of the group. There is a lack of critical thinking and acting independently from the group when considering the outcome of a situation. According to Janis (1982), groupthink is "a deterioration of mental efficiency, reality testing, and moral judgment that results from in-group pressures" (Janis, 1982, 9).

It is crucial for strong leaders to use methods to mitigate groupthink in order to reduce risk not only to the task force but to the respective agencies involved. Examples include having the group leader be open to individual/group objections, refrain from giving their personal opinions so that the group won't automatically defer to their viewpoints and opinions and establishing subgroups to examine the goals or objectives to determine multiple solutions to the same issues (Janis, 1982). According to Inspector General Mark Spencer of Prince George's County Sheriff' Department, "the law enforcement leader – his or her vision for constitutional policing, the standards are set, the political support for that vision, and the way they infuse that vision and philosophy – is the foundation" (Scism, 2017). Positive police culture begins with "visionary humane police leadership." It is understood that negative cultural factors for task forces include, use of force protocols, officer involved shootings and community complaints. However, a strong task force leader can mitigate these issues by encouraging problem solving, collaboration, communication, and awareness of officer wellness (Copple & Copple, 2018).

12.5 Criminal justice reform on a national level

Over the past four decades, the incarceration rate has more than quadrupled and is now unprecedented in world history. Approximately 2.2 million people are incarcerated in the United States and has the world's largest prison population. There are approximately 7 million people under the supervision of the corrections system, either locked up or probation or parole. Historical analysis demonstrates that crime control strategies such as the "Broken Windows Theory" that perpetuated programs such as *Stop, Question and Frisk, Tactical Narcotic Teams* (TNT)/*Street Narcotics Units* (SNU) and the FBI's *Safe Streets Gang Unit* were created to identify and mitigate violent crime (FBI, 2011). However, despite the significant reduction across most major crime indexes (including the Bureau of Justice Statistics), these aggressive and proactive strategies had the adverse effect of driving incarceration rates up to unprecedented levels. In response to the government's crackdown on crime and subsequent punitive sanctions, communities, advocate groups and politicians identified the aforementioned crime control strategies as driving forces behind custodial sentences. Criminal justice reform started to gain traction over the last several years.

The Fair Sentencing Act of 2010 (FSA), enacted August 3, 2010, reduced the statutory penalties for crack cocaine offenses. The FSA eliminated the mandatory minimum sentence for simple possession of crack cocaine and increased statutory fines. It also directed the United States Sentencing Commission to amend the U.S. Sentencing Guidelines to account for specified aggravating and mitigating circumstances in drug trafficking offenses involving any drug type. (USSC, 2015). *The Anti-Drug Abuse Act of 1986* implemented the initial disparity, reflecting Congress's view that crack cocaine was a more dangerous and harmful drug than powder cocaine. This was subsequently identified as untrue and rooted in racial disparity that unfairly targeted minorities. Over the next decade, high profile cases including the Freddie Gray, Michael Brown and Eric Garner further eroded the relationship between minority communities and law enforcement. This came to a head in May 2020 when George Floyd died while in the custody of the Minneapolis Police (Balsamo, 2020). This event further fueled the fire of the Defund the Police movement, bail reform and decriminalization of many low-level quality of life crimes (Balsamo, 2020). Despite the well-intended goal of reducing mass incarceration and creating a more equitable criminal justice system, crime rates have spiked across the country. According to *The Guardian* (2021), the U.S. has experienced its largest-ever recorded annual increase in murders, according to new statistics from the FBI, with the national murder rate rising nearly 30% in 2020 – the biggest jump in six decades. Murder increased in every geographic region, including small towns, suburban areas, and large cities. At least 77% of the murders were committed with firearms" (Beckett, 2021). The Task Forces and fusion centers previously referenced were created to target crimes and groups engaged in the violence and related activities. However, the geographical areas that are targeted for enforcement operations are often low income, high minority-based that create a strategic paradox. Programs such as the NYPD's COMPSTAT have been the "backbone" of crime control strategies in New York City since the early 1980's and is credited with reducing crime in the city to historic lows. This is done by using computational or computerized statistics (COMPSTAT) to identify criminal patterns and "hotspots" as well as holding precinct commanders accountable for the crime reduction strategies in each geographical area of responsibility (Bass, 2012). However, the program is not without critics. In June of 2020, the NYPD Captain's Endowment Association petitioned the Mayor and Police Commissioner to end the COMPSTAT program saying [it] "pressures precinct commanders for crime reduction by artificially forcing bosses to harass communities of color." (Brown & Tracey, 2020) Critics point out that the NYPD weaponized COMPSTAT by wielding it as a tool of punishment, embarrassment, and coercion (O'Neill & Shea, 2017).

Law enforcement Task Forces serve additional purposes other than just collaborating on crime control interdiction strategies. Law enforcement task forces are created to help work with community partners to improve relationships between the police and citizens. In Chicago, the City recognized the disconnect and frayed relationship between the police department and the communities they serve. In order to bridge this gap, Chicago created the *Police Accountability Task Force* with the primary mission of "laying the foundation to rejuvenate the trust between the police and the communities they serve by facing hard truths and creating a roadmap for real last transparency, respectful engagement accountability and change" (Aune, 2016). In July 2020, the city of Los Angeles, California, announced the establishment of the Community Safety Partnership Bureau within the LAPD "placing a nationally recognized model for community policing at the heart of the City's public safety efforts." (LA Mayors Office, 2020.) Police enforcement actions inevitably put law enforcement at odds and create friction in police-community relations. However, based on many of the criminal justice reform programs and structures being redesigned to fit the current societal processes, the collaborative efforts of all parties with the emphasis of training and education can only advance the relationship in the right direction.

12.6 Body worn cameras: Their use and impact on collaborative task forces

According to the *National Institute of Justice* (2018) the use of body worn cameras (BCW) have several positive applications for law enforcement personnel. The potential benefits of BCW's may also assist task forces, although there are risks posed to agencies that need to be considered before full implementation. Benefits include assisting task forces with transparency of investigations, executing arrest and search warrants and providing legal protections to all parties. BWC footage can be used to support corroborating evidence in existing cases. There is also evidence to support that BWC's can enhance what's known as the "civility effect" whereby citizens are more compliant with law enforcement officers and officers conduct themselves in a supportive format to enhance community relationships (Chapman, 2018). The expectation is that the use of BWC's "level the playing field" and protect law enforcement personnel as well as civilians.

12.7 Project of Government Oversight (2016)

However, there are concerns and risks with implementing BWC policies and guidelines. Privacy and constitutional issues, oversight mechanisms, and judicial methodologies involving the use of BWC evidence in court proceedings create potential problems. According to *The* Project of Government Oversight in 2016:

Body-worn cameras are not a panacea. Implementation without proper policies in place can result in significant detriments to law enforcement agencies and the communities they serve. Among these concerns is the potential impact on a broad range of constitutional rights and values. Accordingly, agencies must weigh the benefits and detriments of body cameras when deciding whether and how to implement them (POGO, 2016).

Because collaboration between agencies is necessary for successful task force applications, these and other factors need to be assessed for risks for officers and the communities they serve. Consideration should include but not limited to implementation and recording procedures, "tagging" technologies, data mining, management and maintenance, rules in conjunction with state and federal funding, on-going policy changes and alerts, and public access to the data (POGO, 2016). These issues need to be addressed with the understanding that this is developing technology and additional focus is needed to examine the policies as they directly relate to task forces and accountability of officers.

12.8 International task force participation

Task Forces are created to combine resources, facilitate information gathering and sharing protocols and work toward a stated mission goal. However, the concept of task forces can permeate almost any level of private or public sector work. Task forces can also have a global outreach that brings together not just multiple agencies from different levels of government but ones that cross international borders. Whether it's joint military operations, allocating law enforcement resources to investigate the exploitation/human trafficking of children or the common mission of creating equality in the teaching/education profession around the world, the task force paradigm can provide the blueprint for successes on every level.

The Combined Task Force 150 (CTF-150) is a multinational task group composed of warships from numerous Coalition nations with the primary mission of patrolling the Indian Ocean as part of the global war on terrorism. The ships of CTF-150 operate throughout this area to prevent terrorism and the illegal trade of drugs and weapons which funds and supports international terrorist organizations. CTF-150 was established near the beginning of Operation Enduring Freedom and is made up of warships from the UK, France, Canada, Germany, Pakistan, Australia, Denmark and the United States (Channon, 2019).

The Violent Crimes Against Children International Task Force (VCACITF) created in 2004 and is considered the largest task forces in the world and includes members from 40 different countries. Working side-by-side with the FBI, Task Force members are a "select cadre of international law enforcement experts working together to formulate and deliver a dynamic global response to crimes against children through the establishment and furtherance of strategic partnership, the aggressive engagement of relevant law enforcement, and the extensive use of liaison, operational support and coordination." (Lambert, 2010)

The International Task Force on Teachers for Education 2030, also known as the Teacher Task Force (TTF) is a partnership that was created in 2008 to advocate for teachers and for the teaching profession around the world. This group advocates for the profession, raising awareness, expanding knowledge, and supporting countries toward achieving targeted goals." There are over 150 members including national governments, international organizations, NGO's and CSO's. (TeacherTaskForce.org, 2021).

Many of the challenges of international task forces mirror those of the local groups. Among the primary issues are limited resources (staff and time); conflict or general difficulty with other members; fear of unfavorable reputation; competing priorities (leadership may prioritize addressing other crimes); prioritization of one case/crime over another; concern that participation on a task force may conflict with their primary mission. Additional difficulties may include language barriers, social distance, and political/social discourse (OVC, 2021). Open lines of communication, establishment of guideline and protocols and strict adherence to same as well holding everyone [equally] accountable can minimize these challenges and establish a solid blueprint for success (Lunenberg, 2010).

12.9 The pandemic and gun violence and rising violent crime rates in the U.S

In March 2020, the world faced a global pandemic due to COVID-19. The onset of the pandemic had a massive impact on crime in the U.S. Not surprising, with national lockdowns and mandated curfews implemented by states to reduce the spread of COVID-19, crime rates plummeted 23% in the first months of the pandemic. However, two crimes that have not dropped are shootings and homicides. (Klein, 2021). The FBI released the 2020 Uniformed Crime Report (UCR) indicated a 6% drop in overall crime in the U.S. ***but a 5% increase in violent crime and 30% increase in homicides***. The overall drop in crime corresponds with a decrease in population mobility during the pandemic. Stay-at-home orders and business closures prevented people from driving, shopping, and walking around in general.

According to the NYPD crime statistics, gun arrests have increased 37% in the first 8 months of 2021. (NYPD, 2021). In response to the uptick in gun violence in the city, the NYPD created a working task force called the Gun Violence Strategies Partnership (GVSP) through the Office of Crime Control Strategies, Joint Criminal Investigations Section. The mantra for this unit states, "timely and accurate intel, rapid deployment, effective tactics and relentless follow-up" (BJS, 2013, 2). To this end, GVSP implemented a 90-day initiative partnering with the Bureau of Alcohol Tobacco Firearms and Explosives that brought together an unprecedented group of law enforcement agencies that meets 5 days a week to breakdown all daily gun arrests, daily shooting arrests, individuals involved (indirectly) in shootings, daily arrests with open gun arrests, and daily shots fired arrests. Along with multiple NYPD units, the initiative brings together members from New York State Parole, New York City/State Department of Corrections, New York Sherriff's Office, United States Probation Offices in the Southern and Eastern District Districts of New York, Federal Bureau of Investigation, Drug Enforcement Administration, Home Security Investigations, New York State Police, and investigative analysts for High Intensity Drug Trafficking Area (HIDTA). The key component to this Task Force is the presence and active participation of the five New York City District Attorney Offices. With the challenges of bail reform and the difficulty of obtaining reasonable bail for violent offenders, the information sharing and collaborative efforts on the part of the participating law enforcement partners allows Assistant District Attorneys to obtain real-time data/information that help them to prepare and submit strong bail packages increasing the likelihood of detention.

These collaborative efforts between the prosecutors and law enforcement also helps to build solid cases allowing for more robust plea-bargaining and when necessary, trial preparation. This initiative is a dynamic partnership, and the administrators are constantly asking questions including, "how can we do better" and "what other resource can we provide our partners to assist the process." To this end, it was determined that because of the volume of data and information that is collected on daily basis and shared during the daily briefings, additional resources in the form of investigative analysts were added to the collective efforts to process, collate and refine the data points from the law enforcement sources and provide assessment portfolios that assist in the investigation and prosecution of the identified targets. As of the writing of this chapter, the 90-day initiative is coming to end. However, all participants appear to be in agreement that there have been tremendous strides made toward closing the information and intelligence gaps that have existed for a long time. The successes that have been identified since the inception of the program should allow the initiative to be extended to allow additional time to continue the positive gains and results from these collaborative efforts.

12.10 Community corrections and task forces

"The ability that leaders have to collaborate, innovate, and adapt their responses to events (active shooters, hostile and violent acts, and perpetrators) will be critical in a world where surprise and uncertainty is becoming all-too-common characteristics of public safety" (Straub, Cowell, et. al, 2017). The correctional field has long been a passive participant in the task force community. Whether it's philosophical differences among agencies, judicial preferences, or lack of adequate training of officers, probation and parole agencies have remained on the sidelines when he came to active Task Force participation. This started to change after 9/11 and there has been a slow migration by community correctional agencies toward becoming equal partners by providing vital intelligence required by law enforcement to conduct comprehensive investigations and be proactive in developing crime control strategies. A large body of research suggests that "criminogenic risk factors" (i.e., major changeable risk factors for criminal behavior that do not include symptoms of mental illnesses) (Monahan & Skeem, 2014) robustly predict various measures of recidivism and are useful targets for intervention to reduce rearrest among people under correctional supervision (Monahan & Skeem, 2014; Andrews, Bonta, & Wormith, 2011).

A major factor that is predictive of future recidivism is the [offenders] prior criminal history and the types of crime that he/she previously engaged in at some point in their lives. According to the FBI, there are approximately 33,000 violent street gangs criminally active in the U.S. These groups are sophisticated, well organized and they use violence and intimidation to control neighborhoods and boost illegal money-making activities. (FBI.gov, 2011) The majority of these gang members are under some type of community supervision. Although probation and parole agencies are focused on rehabilitative efforts and reintegration back into the community, one of the primary functions of community corrections is the protection of the community. To this end, probation and parole officers must employ a variety of techniques and mechanisms to achieve the goal of community protection. Effective supervision of violent gang members and organized crimes figures entail collaborative efforts with law enforcement. In the natural progression of fulfilling the mantra of community protection, community correctional officers embedded in law enforcement Task Forces brings the totality of job responsibilities full circle. The intelligence sharing allows law enforcement to receive actionable intelligence on the individuals and groups that are most likely to engage in the criminal activity most investigated by Task Forces. The U.S. Probation Office in the Southern District of New York are active Task Force participants with Joint Firearms Task Force (ATF/NYPD), the Safe Street Task Force (FBI/NYPD) and are currently onboarding officers with El Dorado Task Force (Homeland Security Investigations/NYPD.) These collaborations should continue to create strong working relationships among the partners and identify the individuals who perpetrate the majority of violent crimes in the New York City.

12.11 Conclusions and projections

The collaboration between local, state and federal law enforcement partners has seen tremendous success over the last several years. In order for Task Forces to operate at an optimal level, participating partners must work to manage the political and social risks associated with each agencies participation. This can be done by creating an environment where all involved agencies learn the roles and capacities of other agencies, create strategic, coordinated, and collaborative relationships, extend outreach to community-based corrections, identify victim service providers, expand and support access to resources that creates a more effective & efficient response, generate a greater buy-in and support from all partners that promotes a unified front and provide joint training opportunities for all involved.

An important and integral component of any task force is the ability and willingness of senior management to make a fair and honest assessment of the group identifying the strengths and weaknesses and providing constructive criticisms where required. This assessment should be based on the proper engagement & identification of applicable issues facing the group, utilizing Probation & Parole assets who have the information, motivation, and means to help design aneffective intervention strategies, adhering to strong chain of command directives and encouraging inter-agency communication by assigning a point of contact, trusting the command and control authority of the Task Force, memorializing the agreements (MOUs) to avoid conflict of interests and finally, be open to new ideas, advocate for learning, trusting the process, and working together to achieve the mission statement.

References

Andrews, D. A., Bonta, J., & Wormith, S. J. (2010). The Level of Service (LS) assessment of adults and older adolescents. In R. K. Otto & K. Douglas (Eds.), Handbook of violence risk assessment (pp. 199–225). New York, NY: Routledge.

Ashley, G. (September 17, 2003). Testimony of Senate Judiciary Committee. URL retrieved: Untitled (senate.gov).

Aune, S. (April 2016). Police and racism: It's still a systemic problem. Daily Cougar. URL retrieved: Police and racism: it's still a systematic problem (thedailycougar.com).

Balsamo, M. (June 2020). When protesters cry "defund the police": What does that mean exactly? Associated Press. URL Retrieved: https://apnews.com/article/american-protests-police-don ald-trump-ap-top-news-crime-157539e98d2b6a546ca5ecdf4f88f098

Bass, Paul (2012). CompStat Ramps Up. *New Haven Independent.*

Beckett, L. (September 2021). US records largest annual increase in murders in six decades. The Guardian. URL retrieved: US records largest annual increase in murders in six decades | US news | The Guardian

Brown, S. R. & Tracey, T. (June 2020) NYPD captain's union president banned from crime data meetings after questioning top brass rant. The Daily News. URL retrieved: NYPD union chief banned from police crime data meetings – New York Daily News (nydailynews.com)

Bureau of Justice Statistics (BJS) (2013). Compstat: Its origins, evolution, and future in police agencies. Washington, DC: Police Research Forum. URL retrieved: PERF-Compstat.pdf (ojp.gov).

Channon, M. (2019). Royal navy patrols tankers attack area as Iran tension grows. Devon Love: UK & World News. URL retrieved: Royal Navy patrols tanker attack area as Iran tension grows – Devon Live.

Chapman, B. (November 2018), Body-Worn Cameras: What the Evidence Tells Us. National Institute of Justice, Office of Justice Programs. URL retrieved: https://nij.ojp.gov/topics/articles/body-worn-cameras-what-evidence-tells-us.

Cherry, K. (2019). How cognitive biases influence how you think and act. *Very Well Mind*. URL retrieved: https://www.verywellmind.com/what-is-a-cognitive-bias-2794963.

Copple, C. K., and Copple, J. E. (2018). *Risk management in law enforcement: Discussions on identifying and mitigating risk for officers, departments, and the public*. Washington, DC: Office of Community Oriented Policing Services.

Corbett, R.P. (1998). Probation blue? The promise (and perils) of probation-police partnerships. *Corrections Management Quarterly*. 2. 31–39.

Department of Homeland Security (DHS). (September 2019). Fusion centers. URL retrieved: Fusion Centers | Homeland Security (dhs.gov).

Department of Justice. (September 2011). Fact sheet: The department of justice ten years after 9/11. Office of Public Affairs, 11-1136. URL retrieved: Fact Sheet: the Department of Justice Ten Years After 9/11 | OPA | Department of Justice.

Federal Bureau of Investigation (FBI) (2011). 2011 National gang threat assessment: Emerging trends. URL retrieved: 2011 National Gang Threat Assessment – FBI.

Gawthrop, L. C. (2005). Public administration in a global mode: With sympathy and compassion. *Public Integrity*, 7, 3, 241–259.

Goldstein, P. (December 2020). What are fusion centers and what kind of technology do they use? State Tech. URL retrieved: What Is a Fusion Center? | StateTech Magazine.

Jannetta, J. & Lachman, P. (2011). *Promoting partnerships between police and community supervision agencies: How coordination can reduce crime and improve public safety*. Community Oriented Policing Services/United States Department of Justice.

Janis, I. L. (1982). Groupthink: Psychological studies of policy decisions and fiascos. Boston: Houghton Mifflin.

Kennedy, D. M., Braga, A. & Piehl, A.M. (2001). Reducing gun violence: The boston gun project's operation ceasefire: A research report. United States Department of Justice, Office of Justice Program. NIJ #188714, 1–77. URL retrieved: Reducing Gun Violence: The Boston Gun Project's Operation Ceasefire (ojp.gov).

Klein, M. (May 2021). EconoFact Chats: Crime in the time of covid. *EconoFact chats*. URL retrieved: EFChats-Transcript-CrimeintheTimeofCOVID.pdf (econofact.org)

Kruger, J., & Dunning, D. (1999). Unskilled and unaware of it: How difficulties in recognizing one's own incompetence lead to inflated self-assessments. *Journal of Personality and Social Psychology*, *77*(6), 1121–1134. https://doi.org/10.1037/0022-3514.77.6.1121.

Kuykendall, J. & Roberg, R.R. (1982). Mapping police organizational change: From a mechanistic toward an organic model. *Criminology*, 20, 2, 241–256.

Lambert, D. (December 1, 2010). Intelligence-led policing in a fusion center. *FBI: Law Enforcement Bulletin*. URL retrieved: Intelligence-Led Policing in a Fusion Center – LEB (fbi.gov).

Lewis, J.P. (2003). Project Leadership. New York: McGraw-Hill.

Los Angeles Mayor's Office (July 2020). Mayor Garcetti announces creation of LAPD community safety partnership bureau. URL retrieved: Mayor Garcetti announces creation of LAPD Community Safety Partnership Bureau | Office of Los Angeles Mayor Eric Garcetti (lamayor.org).

Lunenberg, F.C. (2010). Communication: The process, the barriers and improving effectiveness. *Schooling*, 1, 1, 1–11.

McGivern, K. (September 10, 2010). If we fail, people die': Joint Terrorism Task Force reflects on changes since 9/11. *ABC Action News*. URL retrieved: 'If we fail, people die': Terrorism Task Force reflects on growth (abcactionnews.com).

Monahan T. & Palmer, N.A. (2009). The emerging politics of DHS fusion centers. *Security Dialogue*, 40, 6, 617–636.

Monahan, J., & Skeem, J. L. (2014). The evolution of violence risk assessment. *CNS spectrums*, *19*(5), 419–424. https://doi.org/10.1017/S1092852914000145.

Marewski, J. & Gigerenzer, G. (2012). Heuristic decision making in medicine. *Dialogues in Clinical Neuroscience*. 14. 77–89.

Murphy, D. & Worrall, J. (2007). The threat of mission distortion in police-probation partnerships. *Policing: An International Journal of Police Strategies & Management*, 30. 132–149. 10.1108/13639510710725668.

New York Police Department (NYPD) (2021). NYPD announces city-wide crime statistics for august 2021. URL retrieved: NYPD Announces Citywide Crime Statistics for August 2021 | City of New York (nyc.gov).

Northouse, P. G. (2003). Leadership: theory and practice. New Delhi: Sage.

O'Brien, L. (September 2011). The evolution of terrorism since 9/11. *FBI: Law Enforcement Bulletin*. URL retrieved: The Evolution of Terrorism Since 9/11 – LEB (fbi.gov).

O'Neill, J. & Shea, D. (February, 2017). Crime data helps police thrive: NYPD commissioner. *USA Today*. URL retrieved: Crime data helps police thrive: NYPD commissioner (usatoday.com).

Office of Victims of Crime (OVC) (2021). Human trafficking. URL retrieved: Human Trafficking | Help & Resources | Office for Victims of Crime (ojp.gov).

The Project on Government Oversight (POGO) (2016). Guidelines for the use of body-worn cameras for law enforcement. URL: Guidelines for the Use of Body-Worn Cameras by Law Enforcement (pogo.org).

Rachlin, H. (1993). Making the streets safer. *Journal of Law and Order*, 41, 4, 59–62.

SAFECOM. (2004). Writing guide for a memorandum of understanding. Homeland Security/SAFECOM. URL retrieved: DHS-MemorandumOfUnderstanding.pdf (fcc.gov).

Scism, R. M. (August 7, 2017). Risk management for law enforcement. *Police Magazine*. URL retrieved: Risk Management for Law Enforcement – Patrol – POLICE Magazine.

Straub, F., Cowell, B., Zeunick, J., and Gorban, B (2017). Managing the response to a mobile mass shooting: A critical incident review of the February 20, 2016 Kalamazoo mass shooting. Washington D.C.: Police Foundation.

Teachers Task Force (TTF) (2021). International task force on teachers for education 2030. URL retrieved: https://teacherstaskforce.org.

Tversky, A., & Kahneman, D. (1974). Judgment under uncertainty: Heuristics and biases. *Science*, 185, 1124–1130. *DOI*:10.1126/science.185.4157.1124.

United States Sentencing Commission (USSC). (2015). 2015 report to the congress: Impact of the fair sentencing act of 2010. URL retrieved: 2015 Report to the Congress: Impact of the Fair Sentencing Act of 2010 | United States Sentencing Commission (ussc.gov).

Walker, D. (1996). The organization and training of joint task forces. Maxwell Airforce Base, AL: Air University Press. URL retrieved: Organization and Training of Joint Task Forces (defense.gov).

Wray, C. (December 7, 2017). Oversight of the federal bureau of investigation. Statement Before the House Judiciary Committee. *Federal Bureau of Investigation News*. URL retrieved: Oversight of the Federal Bureau of Investigation – FBI.

Michael Sheehy and Cathryn F. Lavery

13 Freedom to express, professionalism, and public safety: Socio-political risks with social media for law enforcement agencies and practitioners

13.1 Introduction

Social media platforms have had a significant impact on our culture and created new forms of communication and relaying of information. Throughout the past few decades social media has expanded its definition. . "Social media refers to websites and applications that are designed to allow people to share content quickly, efficiently, and in real-time" (Hudson, 2020). What once began as *Facebook, Instagram* has morphed into microblogging, *Snap Chat* and *Group Me*. The evolution and use of social media has extended into the criminal justice system. Public agencies post notices, messages, policies, etc. As well, many law enforcement practitioners have on their own accord, established personal social media sites to maintain relationships with family, friends, and colleagues.

There have been consequences on the use of social media with law enforcement, both positive and negative. The initial purpose by police agencies has been to utilize (to help or assist) by creating a bridge for improving communications and community/police relationships via social media. Law enforcement agencies' pages, Instagram accounts and Twitter "handles" have been used routinely to notify the community on routine issues, including traffic, to emergency messages due to weather, natural disasters, etc. (Bullock, 2018). Law enforcement has used social media tools to identify missing persons, provide alerts to communities on local criminal activity, tracking neighborhood crimes patterns, burglaries, thefts, and cybercrime. The public has used social media platforms (i.e., cell phone cameras/videos) to document interactions with police – both positive and negative. The George Floyd case (2020) is an example of how social media can indirectly and directly influence perceptions and belief systems of large swaths of society. In Minneapolis, Minnesota, George Floyd had been accused by a store clerk of using a counterfeit twenty-dollar bill. The ensuing police intervention resulted with Officer Derek Chauvin kneeling on Mr. Floyd's neck for over nine minutes. This was all documented on cell phones and resulted in a wrongful death suit by the family who was awarded $27 million. Derek Chauvin convicted in June 2021 of two counts of murder and one of manslaughter and was sentenced to 25 years in prison. The remaining officers at the scene will be facing trial in March of 2022 (Gile, 2021).

13.2 Risk management in law enforcement

Risk management is not a foreign subject to policing. According to Chief Matthias Wicks of Tulsa, Oklahoma, Public Schools stated, "Risk management protocol is one of the most important components in law enforcement and public safety, both in the daily administrative mayhem and operational duties" (Fritzvold, 2019). Risk-based modalities which need to be incorporated into educational training for police include, personal safety risks, external risks (gangs, pandemics, natural disasters), internal organizational risks, potential litigation (human rights violations, violations of due process, procedures, etc.) and technology risks (ransomware, drones, etc.) (Fritzvold, 2019). According to Rice & Zegart (2018), when examining political risks for law enforcement agencies, questions that should be asked include:

"How can we get good information about the political risks we face? How did we ensure rigorous analysis? How can we integrate political risks in business decisions?" (Rice and Zegart, 2018, 158). Senior management of agencies and organizations in the private, public, or nonprofit sectors must understand that organizational, social, or political risks must be specifically identified, and mitigation processes implemented to minimize potential negative outcomes and consequences. Concrete information and awareness of these risks include insights which originate from human behavior, emotions, knowledge, and perceptions of issues. Integrating these foundational sources is critical to the information gathering process. Reliable information and critical feedback can result by asking appropriate questions based on research, a thorough examination of possible problems and scenarios and strategizing resulting outcomes from the challenges agencies' face (Rice & Zegart, 2018).

The risks associated with social media issues are not independent and the impact of social and political risks posed, can have a detrimental effects on police agencies. Before examining the link between social media and social and political risks, one must consider, why does political and social risk matter for law enforcement? These risks are regularly applied to private organizations, the corporate sector, and public agencies like hospitals and convalescent homes. Why and how does it impact law enforcement? Many law enforcement agencies do not have the necessary understanding of the impact of social media. In fact, law enforcement practitioners are encouraged not to use social media, especially through the hiring and vetting stages of employment. However, in recent years police agencies have come to better understand the influence of social media. There is an acknowledgement that social media is no longer a passive outlet rooted in observation and simply an alternative to gather information. It is an active outlet of personal opinions, passionate outcries, and a podium of expression of the First Amendment. The power and extensive growth of the internet and social media has contributed to the decline of traditional news outlets, like newspapers and its influence has skyrocketed (Bullock, 2018).

The concept and training of policing stems from a militaristic style and rank in file chain of command (Skolnick, 2010). There is a presumption that police respond and behave in a particular way in order to preserve the reputation and principles of the field. Early research has suggested that law enforcement officers have a specific working personality (Skolnick, 2010). Meaning that their training in the academy and cross over to the streets cultivates and encourages a personality based on suspicion, danger, social isolationism, and authority. In his research, Skolnick (2010) suggested that officers are trained in a way that they believe they are different from the general public. The police uniform, the inherent dangers of their work and constant public scrutiny, create a belief system that requires that police officers rely on each other and separate themselves from the general population. This is one reason why there is so much criticism and speculation on the *"blue wall of silence"*. The blue wall of silence is this unwritten code that prohibits law enforcement officers from providing negative information against other officers. The standard message given is that "cops don't tell on cops "(Skolnick, 2010; Huq & McAdams, 2016). It is understood that this philosophy has led to damaging consequences for policing. Examples such as the Serpico case, that focused on corruption in the NYPD in the mid to late 1960's, which led to the *Knapp Commission* investigation of 1970; The Rodney King case in 1991 with the Los Angeles Police Department in California; the Michael Dowd case in the 75 Precinct in Brooklyn, New York, which led to the *Mollen Commission* in 1993 and the Abner Louima incident in 1997, which resulted in criminal convictions of police officers and human rights violations (Rosenberg, 2021). The Mollen Commission "found disturbing patterns of police corruption and brutality, including stealing from drug dealers, engaging in unlawful searches, seizures, and car stops, dealing and using drugs, lying in order to justify unlawful searches and arrests and to forestall complaints of abuse, and indiscriminate beating of innocent and guilty alike."(Cole, 1999). The "blue wall" philosophical context subtly has encouraged police to turn a blind eye to corruption, criminality, human violations, and violence among other officers (Serwer, 2021).

In recent years, senior law enforcement officials have crafted policies addressing the use of social media. However, while major concerns regarding the balance and expression surrounding free speech in connection to public safety have been addressed, not all current policies extend their focus past an agencies immediate response to protect their officers and staff. A limited number of agencies have introduced on-going education on social media issues to members of their organizations, specifically with regard to accountability and ethics (Kaplan & Haelein, 2010; IACP, 2021).

Instant access to unvetted or edited information via social media outlets present numerous points of risk for police. The public nature and qualities that are necessary for law enforcement to execute their jobs appropriately, leads to speculations and scrutiny. Increased exposure and combative and controversial occurrences involving law enforcement, has led to persistent analysis, and opened, unregulated discussions (PERF & COPS, 2013). The true nature and developing traits of officers that have been shaped by their education and training, as well as by public perceptions has contributed to a confusing and unclear portrait of the role and responsibilities of police, not only in the United States, but globally (Bullock, 2018).

13.3 The sociopolitical risks for police with social media

The inherent nature of social media and the perception of police can make the link between the two entities unpredictable and explosive. Professional and personal credibility of police officers is paramount to carrying out the duties and responsibilities of the position. If an officer or an agency's reputation are at risk or dissected negatively, it can compromise existing investigations. Commentaries through social media can taint jury pools and damage individual reputations. "*Cop baiting* is when individuals intentionally create confrontational situations with officers to exploit them for personal or political motives" (Waters, 2012). Examples can range from efforts to antagonize police, actively interfering in a formal police action, or setting off false alarms to distract officers. An example occurred in Australia, when a motorcyclist went to the Springwood Police station near Brisbane, stopped in front of the stationhouse and revved his engine, resulting in a huge blast of exhaust clouding up the immediate area of the station, causing police confusion in and around the station (Coe, 2018). These types of actions by citizens are done to antagonize officers, and expend unnecessary time and resources with the goal of provoking the police and trying to have them react unprofessionally. *Cop Baiting* presents a serious predicament for law enforcement. Any resulting videos recorded and posted to Facebook, Twitter or YouTube can be damning for officers and may lead to a financial costs resulting from litigious action against the officer and agency (The Police Foundation, 2014). This phenomenon can severely impact an officer's credibility, as well as their agencies reputation in the community (Waters, 2012).

13.4 Positive instances of social media and law enforcement in both the United States and internationally

Before evaluating the sociopolitical risks for police, it is important to discuss how and when social media platforms have benefited law enforcement and when it has significantly increased risk levels that could negatively impact individual officers as well as the agency.

Toronto Police Services (TPS) has been one of the leading police agencies in managing social media platforms. Over two hundred officers have been trained on utilizing social media outlets for their departments to create positive steps with police community relationships (Waters, 2012; PERF & COPS, 2013). TPS enacted policies and training sessions to ensure quality control to mitigate risks for the agency. For example, a guide was circulated that included tips and advice for officers on social media. TPS acknowledged that officers' personal social media accounts should allow for a certain level of privacy, but as an employee and a member of Toronto Police, they ultimately represented the department. A reminder that "the Internet is forever" (Waters, 2012; IACP, 2021). Once an officer conducts an internet "search" or posts comments to a message board, it cannot be undone. With regard to any information sharing on social media on community or political issues, or expressing personal opinions, officers must be aware of general and legal privacy issues, not only for themselves and their families, but for the department. Finally, officers need to "treat others as they want to be treated" (IACP, 2021).

In a 2013 study, over 92% of law enforcement agencies utilized social media platforms to connect with their communities (Siner, 2013). The stated goals of agencies include connecting with their communities, assisting victims of crime and information sharing of pertinent community issues (i.e., weather announcements, incidents of crime, missing persons).

Social media has created some positive impact for the public in regard to certain situations involving law enforcement. Having instant access to information is helpful to convey important information to the public in regard to natural disasters, traffic accidents, or crime updates. Police departments are obligated to be the bearer of bad news and must report on tragic events and respond to public concerns. However, police departments are also using social media platforms to convey messages that help build community trust and improve relations as well as humanize officers and the department as a whole.

Police departments have developed social media pages for self-promotion purposes as well as to encourage public engagement. Departments have chosen to create optimistic posts pertaining to community events and positive police interactions with the public to further this goal. Public relations officers have begun to create posts and updates that consist of police appointments, promotions, and acts of kindness by members of their departments to engage the community (Ruddell & Jones, 2013). Many departments use social media platforms to create posts asking for the community's help to locate the owners of a lost pet or property. The community as a whole is now engaged and feels a sense of pride helping a fellow neighbor. Departments also take advantage of the platforms to advertise police sponsored functions that allow community members to meet and interact with officers helping to build relationships.

Westchester County, New York, located about 20 miles north of New York City, tends to have smaller police departments, with less members that varies based on location and population. The Village of Pelham, a small one square mile hamlet, has capitalized on the use of social media to engage the community and involve citizens not only with law enforcement oriented joint events, but community-wide events (Facebook.com/PelhamPDNY, 2021). The department's social media account has been used to create constructive social media posts which have helped improve public relations. One of the goals of their administration is to strengthen bonds with events such as "Coffee with a Cop" or *National Night Out*, which is held across the United States every year that brings together police, emergency personnel (including fire and emergency management services) with their communities to educate about local crime, personal and public safety, crime prevention, and forming neighborhood watch groups. This is done specifically in an enjoyable venue (IACP, 2021). These national initiatives are aimed at bridging gaps between law enforcement and the community with open conversations in a relaxed environment amongst police officers. Events such as this along with inspirational online posts illustrating the department's dedication to serving the community and reinforce their general concern for their citizens. Local departments, like the Village of Pelham, where resources are limited and they are faced with intense public scrutiny, tries to ensure the police are involved in as many public positive events possible, including parades, public gatherings, and youth organizations. Social media not only to advertise and promotes pro-social events but allow community feedback on posts. The goal is to highlight this partnership and reassure the dedication that the members of law enforcement have to the community.

Many administrations have assigned officers to monitor social media sites and posts created by the public. This has become a significant investigative tool leading to the apprehension of suspects and solving crimes. In 2013, the Palm Beach Sherriff's Office used social media to monitor the posts of an individual suspected of several robberies and burglaries in the Palm Beach County area. Officers were able to uncover numerous photos of suspect Dupress Johnson, a 19-year-old male, with guns, drugs, and large quantities of cash on his social media account (Moye, 2017). The continuing investigation led officers to his Lake Worth home where they discovered guns and proceeds from previous crimes. This individual was believed to be the ringleader of a burglary ring responsible for stealing over $250,000 worth of valuables throughout the county (Moye, 2017).

The Wilkes-Barre Township Police Department of Pennsylvania have developed a new social media program that has created a positive reactions not just for the department, but for the township. The police have taken a humorous approach by using comical memes, gifs, and pictures to supplement notifications. By creating a more relaxed and humorous image themselves, it has drastically reduced the potential of social and political risk not only for the department, but for individual officers. The goal to have the public give feedback, comments and possibly identify with issues and situations posted. The initial hope was to use humor to reflect on non-dangerous situations in the community. During the early experimental phase, the comments and memes received a mixed response by citizens. However, the re-action to these notifications have become more positive. According to one officer, "If anyone anywhere does anything, somewhere, someone is going to be offended. As long as our supporters outnumber our naysayers, I don't see any reason for us to change" (Scinto, 2017).

Since the start of this experiment with humor on their Facebook page this pro-gram has started to gain more solid traction. Although Wilkes-Barre township has only 2,000 residents, the police department's page has over 55,000 "likes". It has generated comments from individuals who are interesting in visiting the areas to reconnecting with former community members. One example of a post targeted seeking the owner of a bag of contraband. The department posted a humorous tag with the police trying to "reunite" the owner over with their $1,600 worth of crack cocaine. These posts have led to more serious posts, emails, and phone calls regard-ing criminal activity in the area. The Wilkes-Barre police department also created "*The Law of the Day*", which was done in a proactive effort to educate the commu-nity on current and new laws and legislation. This initiative has been positively re-ceived (Scinto, 2017). By presenting information in a positive and lighthearted manner, the department has developed a model program allowing officers to utilize social media platforms to further the goals of bridging the gap between the police and the community.

13.5 Negative instances of social media and law enforcement in the United States and internationally

With new avenues of communications for police and new advanced technologies, comes new challenges, and problems. Social media is an outlet here to stay and must be viewed as an additional tool for law enforcement, not only in establishing community relationships, but for investigations and solving crimes. In June of 2019, seventy-two Philadelphia officers were removed from their current assignment and remanded to desk duty pending investigations. *Plainview Project*, a social media da-tabase monitoring organization created by Emily Baker-White, discovered over 300 sexist, racist, and prejudicial comments on posts on Facebook. They were all posted by current and retired Philadelphia police officers. According to Baker -White, "We found a very high and concerning number of posts that appear to endorse, cele-brate or glorify violent vigilantism. We included posts that we thought could effect public trust and policing" (Allen, 2019).

In July of 2019, the United States Department of Homeland Security disciplined and sanctioned members of United States Customs and Border Patrol (CBP) for posting racially offensive and sexually vulgar messages on social media accounts targeting known democratic party members and migrants from Central and South America (Parison & Owen, 2019). According to documents, Border Agents created a private Facebook group called, "I'm 10–15", in reference to a code used to broadcast that an illegal immigrant has been placed into custody. During the investigation, it was determined that Customs and Border Patrol officials had known these posts existed since early 2018 (Parison & Owen, 2019).

In July 2021, New York Police Department's Sergeant Ed Mullins, who is also president of the NYPD Seargent's Benevolent Association, was remanded for trial after he posted on social media comments using offensive and profane language. Seargeant Mullins post on twitter referred to a New York City Council member as a "first class whore" and referred to the NYC Health Commissioner as a "b**ch" on twitter responding to a negative comment she made about police officers. Mullins is facing three internal charges and disciplinary hearings for use of offensive language and abuse of authority. Mullins sued to prevent the internal disciplinary process arguing his tweets were protected by the First Amendment. The judge disagreed (Rosenberg, 2021).

Six officers in Northern Ireland were disciplined for "unprofessional" comments posted on their social media pages. One posted homophobic comments and one revealed the details of a security threat briefing. In another incident, after police assisted a mentally ill person found naked and, in a ditch, an officer posted multiple hashtags, including, #hideandstreak. The individual's mother accused the Police Service of Northern Ireland (PSNI) of "cyberbullying" an emotionally disturbed person. In a formal statement, the PSNI said that officers' ability to post on social media platforms can be revoked if "they bring the service into disrepute" (Bell, 2019).

In the United Kingdon, over 800 cases of police officers were investigated for violating social media guidelines including, "friending" victims and posting racist comments. This research was found through the Freedom of Information requests between 2009–2014 in England and Wales (College of Policing, 2014a). The College of Policing stated that there was "no place for officers who abuse trust placed in us by the public", and penalties included written warnings, disciplinary hearings, and resignations (9% of cases) (College of Policing, 2014a).

The world was shocked after the January 6th Capitol riot in Washington, DC. The events at the Capitol, which the Federal Bureau of Investigation classified as an act of domestic terrorism, resulted in four civilians and one United States Capitol Police officer dead and over 140 other officers injured (Ziegler, 2021). An additional four officers died by suicide (Breuninger & Mangan, 2021). After a thorough investigation, it was found that many participants had served in the United States military (active or retired), police or been employed by the government (Rubin, 2021). A distressing example is from former New York Police Department officer Thomas Webster. Although in his prior career he protected government officials and other officers, during the January 6th riot, he allegedly assaulted a Capitol police officer with a metal flagpole (Rubin, 2021). Two other current officers from Virginia's Rocky Mountain

Police Department posted a "selfie" on social media with their middle fingers extended in front of the statue of an American Revolutionary hero. The two were fired (Rubin, 2021). *Tik Tok, Facebook,* and other social media outlets were used to recruit and organize participants for the capitol riot on January 6th, ignoring the policies on these sites that disallow use of their platforms to threaten or invite violent activity (Rubin, 2021). The ongoing debate in the Unites States around the events of January 6th, 2021, have been exacerbated and complicated by the confusing partisan interpretations of the event by government officials and the media. In particular, how did communication on social media contribute to the recruitment of participants and the influence of the Far Right's message using messages and posts focused on anti-liberal, pro-QAnon verbiage and negative comments about the 2020 election results. One example is of the Sheriff's office Lieutenant Roxanne Mathai, of Bexar County, Texas. Mathai posted a video of herself saying, "We're going in, tear gas and all". The FBI was alerted to this post that resulted in an investigation and she was immediately terminated. Arrested individuals have claimed that their posts are protected by the First Amendment (free speech) rights (So, Januta, & Berens, 2021). However, many participants were confronted with criticism, anger and even arrests due to their own social media posts (So, Januta, & Berens, 2021). Lauren Boebert, a Republican representative from Colorado tweeted on the January 6th, "Today is 1776". She was called to resign. Her response was to tweet, "WE'RE NOT GOING TO SHUT UP" (So, Januta, & Berens, 2021).

Although the First Amendment offers broad safeguards for American citizens, it does not apply to criminal actions and activity. According to attorney David Snyder, Executive Director of the First Amendment Coalition, "You don't get to throw a trash can through a store window because the store window was along a demonstration path" (So, Januta, & Berens, 2021).

13.6 Law enforcement's impression about social media and its impact on their public perception

The expansion of social media platforms has opened extensive lines of communication between law enforcement agencies and their communities. It has provided a pathway for creating a new for departments and officers. Posting and information sharing to their community for day-to-day events with additional uses of videos, pictures, memes, etc., provides a way for police departments projecting, monitoring, and maintaining a positive image (Bullock, 2018; Lipshultz, 2018; Slater, 2013). Social media provides positive reinforcement for agencies and has been a valuable resource for officers identifying specific issues that need addressing in their community (Bullock, 2018; Lipshultz, 2018).

The effective use of social media has not been an easy transition for law enforcement. Even though police officers often have regular exposure to news crews and television cameras, the increased, ongoing exposure has created apprehension and concern. According to the Pew Center for Research (2017), 29% of senior law enforcement officials and high-ranking administrators believe the media, as a whole, treats officers unfairly. This is in contrast to 42% of rank in file officers who strongly agree that the media treats them unfairly. According to Gramlich and Parker (2017), this has resulted in a disconnect between officers and their communities. High-level managers who believe that the media treats police unfairly, base this opinion on the public's misunderstanding of the day-to-day tasks and stress of policing (Gramlich & Parker, 2017). This highlights a disengagement of senior officials understanding of the perceptions and needs of their officers. This can lead to significant risk factors, regarding social public perception, and way officers perceive their administrators and the public. This can contribute to officers experiencing low morale, job dissatisfaction and compassion fatigue (Grant, Lavery & DeCarlo).

According to McNamara & Zefass (2012), there is a conflict for police and senior management between balancing the organizational needs, understanding the risks posed for using social media and how significant a role social media platforms play within law enforcement communications. (Bullock, 2018). Social media, for better or worse, has permanently altered the human form of communication. For an occupation fueled by social isolationism due to their position and public accessibility as well as being deeply rooted in human services and focusing on public safety – entrenching social media as a normal part of policing is a challenge, not only for organizational change but as a transformative toll for reforming police-community relations (Loader, Vromen & Xenos, 2014).

13.7 Recommendations for law enforcement agencies to mitiagte sociopolitical risks and utilize responsible social media platforms

"It takes twenty years to build a reputation and five minutes to ruin it. If you think about that, you'll do things differently" Warren Buffet (Rice & Zegart, 2018, 137). That quote resonates throughout most professions but should be taken under serious advisement for law enforcement when it comes to using social media platforms. In order to mitigate social and political risks for officers and agencies, senior leadership needs to consider three points when constructing and monitoring their own sites or when training their officers to meet the challenges and risks associated with social media (The Police Foundation, 2014). The first requires getting the tone of the messages right. Information sharing via social media is standard in our global society.

However, the tone in the statements, tweets, and comments presented to the public directly influences how the information will be read, processed, and interpreted. Senior management needs to gauge the tone of the messages and take accountability for any negative feedback. Agencies need to experiment with social media platforms using a formal versus an informal approach and measure responses of the community (Police Foundation, 2014). Besides convening messages in the proper way, police agencies must use tools to engage the public and build positive relationships with their community. The patterning throughout Europe is to relay information to the public in a professional manner, which some interpret as impersonal and very formal (Denef, et al., 2013). Finally, using twitter, Facebook, etc. has been shown to be a good method for intelligence gathering, conducting investigations, and involving community members to increase trust levels (Ruddell & Jones, 2013).

Leadership must understand the social risks that have a significant impact on how the public and any available information is perceived and interpreted. Some community policing initiatives via social media may have good intentions and negative outcomes. For example, in 2014, the New York Police Department asked the public to tweet pictures of themselves with officers. However, some of these pictures and videos showing interactions between officers and the public were negative (Police Foundation, 2014). Some risks law enforcement agencies face includes posting information with mistakes (spelling, verbiage, or poor grammar) and not vetting information properly so that inappropriate details are posted (victim's name, details of crime scenes which should not be for public consumption, etc.).

It is recommended that agencies create a strong policy and set specific procedures and protocols on how information is posted and the possible interpretations of the posts by their community members. In the United States, research has shown using Twitter can lead to a slight reduction of crime rates and an increase of tips for current investigations (PERF & COPS, 2013). It has been documented that law enforcement monitoring of social media accounts and applying investigative analyses has been a successful tool with regard to particular crimes, including child sex trafficking, human trafficking, and illegal narcotics distribution (Police Foundation, 2014).

Taking steps to mitigate social and political risks for police officers and their agencies can prevent many challenges that can negatively impact the perception and reputation of the agency. On-going training and monitoring of social media outlets used by the agency and linking accounts with officers, will help ensure some activities and commentaries will not be posted. Training for officers on monitoring should extend not only to how posts are perceived by the public, how to elicit tips on criminal activity in the area, and also assist officers by promoting department sponsored events, awards given to officers and highlight activities and affirmative interactions with the community. Better for a member of the department to intercept online posts containing possible extremist opinions, negative commentary, or prejudicial language of an officer before identified by a member of the public. It will also support officers by educating them on best practices with online postings and social media platforms. This can eliminate future behavior, rather than punishing officers after the damage is done. It is important for leadership to confirm that any social media platforms used by officers and the agency does not use offensive language and profanity. Officers in particular should never make public comments on police protocols, open investigations, or victims. Officers should never make openly negative comments about their work, their community, or express extreme political or social views for the public to see. Although some law enforcement practitioners are divided relating to the concept of free speech, free press, and expression, it must be emphasized that such views may violate other individuals' or officers' rights and may increase the sociopolitical risks potentially hurting the agency and putting lives in danger. Although discussed and encouraged in academies and in their specific agencies, law enforcement needs to understand that they are held to a higher standard. When assessing law enforcement in the United States, it is crucial to understand the job stressors experienced each day by officers, and the inherent disconnect between police and communities. If stronger policies are in place and senior management and officers are given ongoing training in areas like social media and balancing freedom of expression, the reduction of social and political risks will be evident.

The generations of millennials and Generation Z have been raised with social media, "apps," and a dependency on smart phones. Many rely on social media as their continuous flow and acceptable form of communication and news. In contrast, the members of law enforcement range from remaining Baby Boomers and Gen Xers, all of whom have been present since the introduction of community policing (1984), the use of videos to film police actions, and through periods of social, political, and economic reforms of policing (Hansen, 2011). Their personal knowledge base and understanding of social media has resulted with sporadic use, parental control, and a level of discomfort using social media outlets like Snap Chat, Instagram, Facebook, and Twitter (Hansen, 2011). Another recommendation would be to bring in outside trainers rather than conducting in-service training within the department. This can result in many positive outcomes for police officers. This will not only make officers feel more comfortable with the use of social media platforms but help them understand their own level of responsibility regarding personal use of social media. This can be accomplished without having the judgement of their superiors or feeling compelled to change their personal protocols, which could result with some resentment.

According to Stuart (2013), *The Institute for Criminal Justice Education* found in a 2011 survey that less than 40 percent of responding agencies had policies regarding social media use, and less than 15 percent provided training on what is appropriate to post (ICJE, 2011). This points to the critical importance of developing a comprehensive policy for all law enforcement agencies on social media. There should be an understanding given to protect the free speech rights and of any off-duty officers who use personal computers, but there needs to be an integrated and systemic awareness of the consequences. Senior administrators must establish appropriate and fair controls over the use of social media. This could not only increase its benefits while reducing incidents of misuse by officers. On-going training can be established and accomplished. By taking certain necessary steps not only mitigates any social or political risks but can "create a presence on social media sites which opens a new door of communication with the general public." (Stuart, 2013).

The nature of policing around the world have been under scrutiny for years. Recently, in the United States, the 2021 Derek Chauvin trial, the 2020 death of Kentucky's Breonna Taylor, and the 2015 case of Freddie Gray, Jr of Baltimore, Maryland sparked outrage and protests seen internationally. These incidents have forced policing agencies to reexamine their tactics and use of force. Unfortunately, many instances of their current practices have been caught on video and posted globally sparking anger and negative attention. Social media can be an effective tool to recreate trust and bridging initiatives with their communities. Steven White (2013), chairman of the *Police Federation of England and Wales*, stated, "(Police) Forces must ensure officers are effectively trained and aware of the latest social media protocols. It is important to acknowledge that the majority of police officers perform their duties with the utmost integrity, discretion and in accordance with the high standards of behavior rightly expected of them by the public" (Siner, 2013). It is imperative that policing agencies establish protocols and policies for all employees on using social media for both the agency and private use. With the amount of information sharing, misinformation and the reliance on social media platforms for communicating, this is an issue that must be a priority of concern for police agencies.

References

Bell, J. (February 2019). PSNI's six frisky years on Facebook and Twitter. *Belfast Telegraph*. Retrieve from: http://www.belfasttelegraph.co.uk/news/northern-ireland/revealed-psnis-six-risky-years-on-facebook-and-twitter-37844830.html.

Breuninger, K. & Mangan, D. (August 2021). Two more police officers die by suicide after defending capitol during riot by pro-Trump mob, tally now 4. *CNBC.com*. Retrieved from: Trump Capitol riot: Police officer suicides rise to 4 deaths (cnbc.com).

Bullock, K. (2018). The police use of social media: Transformation or normalization? *Social Policy & Society*. 17, 2, 245–258. Cambridge University Press, UK: doi:10.1017/S1474746417000112.

Coe, C. (2018). The bikie performs brazen burnout in front of a police station before falling off his motorcycle while trying to flee. *Daily Mail*. Retrieved from: http://www.dailymail.co.uk/news/article-6170327.

Cole, D. (1999). No equal justice: Race and class in the American criminal justice system. New York, NY: New York Press, 23–24.

College of Policing (January, 2014a). College of Policing encourages use of social media. Retrieved from: https//college.pressofficeadmin.com/component/content/article/45-pressreleases/681.

Crump, J. (2012). What are the police doing on Twitter? Social media, the police, and the public. Policy & the Internet. Retrieved from: What Are the Police Doing on Twitter? Social Media, the Police and the Public – Crump – 2011 – Policy & amp; Internet – Wiley Online Library.

Denef, S., Bayerl, P. and Kaptein, N. (2013) Social media and the police – tweeting practices of British police forces during the August 2011 riots. *Paris: CHI 2013, Proceedings of the SIGCHI Conference on Human Factors in Computing Systems.*

Fritsvold, E., (2019). Introduction to crime data & crime statistics. *Media Politics & the Science of Criminal Justice.* San Diego University of San Diego.

Gerber, M. (2014) Predicting Crime using Twitter and Kernel Density Estimation, *Decision Support Systems* 61, pp.115–125.

Gile, M. (2021). 3 ex-Minneapolis cops asks for trials separate from Derek Chauvin to avoid prejudice. *Newsweek.* Retrieved from: https://www.newsweek.com/3-ex-minneapolis-cops-ask-trial-separate-derek-chauvin-avoid-prejudice-1615850.

Gramlich, J & Parker, K. (2017). Most officers say media treats police unfairly. Pew Research Center. Retrieved from: Most officers say the media treat police unfairly | Pew Research Center.

Grant, H. B., Lavery, C. F., & Decarlo, J. (2019). An Exploratory Study of Police Officers: Low Compassion Satisfaction and Compassion Fatigue. *Frontiers in psychology, 9,* 2793. https://doi.org/10.3389/fpsyg.2018.02793.

Hansen, W. (2011). How social media is changing law enforcement: Social media raises positive and negative issues for police. *Government Technology.* Retrieved from http://govtech.com/public-safety/How-Social-Media-Is-Changing-Law-Enforcement.html.

Hudson, M. (June 2020). What is social media? Definitions and examples. *Small Business.* URL retrieved: Social Media: What Is It? (thebalancesmb.com).

Huq, Aziz Z. and McAdams, Richard H., Litigating the Blue Wall of Silence: How to Challenge the Police Privilege to Delay Investigation (January 8, 2016). University of Chicago Legal Forum, Forthcoming, U of Chicago, Public Law Working Paper No. 555, Available at SSRN: https://ssrn.com/abstract=2712967

IACP (2021). *International Association for Chiefs of Police Center for Social Media,* International Association of Chiefs of Police. Retrieved from: http://www.iacpsocialmedia.org.

Institute for Criminal Justice Education (ICJE). (2011). Social Networking Survey. Retrieved from: http://www.icje.org/articles/SocialMediaSurvey.pdf.

Kaplan, A. M., & Haenlein, M. (2010). Users of the world, unite! The challenges and opportunities of social media. Business Horizons, 53(1), 59–68.

Lipschultz, J. (2018). Social media communication: Concepts, practices, data, law and ethics (2nd Ed.). New York, NY: Routledge.

Loader, B., Vromen, A. & Xenos, M. (2014). The networked young citizen: Social media, political participation and civic engagement. *Information, Communication and Society,* 17, 2, 143–150.

Macnamara, J.R., & Zerfass, A. (2012). Social Media Communication in Organizations: The Challenges of Balancing Openness, Strategy, and Management. International Journal of Strategic Communication, 6, 287–308.

Moye, D. (December 2017). Dupree Johnson charged with 142 felony counts after copy sees his Instagram page. *Huffington Post.* Retrieved from: Dupree Johnson Charged With 142 Felony Counts After Cop Sees His Instagram Page | HuffPost.

Parison, J. & Owen, Q. (July 2019). CBP launches investigation into private Facebook group mocking law makers as they blast immigrant treatment. *ABC News.* Retrieved from: http://www.abc news.go.com/politics/CBP-launches-investigations-private-facebook-group/.

Police Executive Research Forum (PERF) & Community Oriented Policing Services (COPS) (May 2013) Social Media and Tactical Considerations for Law Enforcement, Washington: US Department of

Justice, http://www.policeforum.org/assets/docs/Free_Online_Documents/Technology/social%20media%20and%20tactical%20considerations%20for%20law%20enforcement%202013.pdf.

Police Foundation (2014). The briefing: Police and use of social media. Retrieved from: Police Foundation Social Media Briefing.qxd (police-foundation.org.uk).

Rice, C. & Zegart, A. (2018). Political risk: Facing the threat of global insecurity in the twenty-first century. London, UK: Weidenfeld & Nicolson.

Rosenberg, R. (February 2021). Ex-NYPD cop locked up for 'heinous' for 1997 sexual assault should stay in prison: Feds. New York Post. Retrieved from: Ex-NYPD cop who sodomized Abner Louima should stay in prison: feds (nypost.com).

Rubin, O. (April, 2021). Number of capitol riot arrests of military, law enforcement and government personnel rises to 52. *ABC News*. Retrieved from: Number of Capitol riot arrests of military, law enforcement and government personnel rises to 52 – ABC News.

Ruddell, R. and Jones, N. (2013) Social media and policing: matching the message to the audience. *Safer Communities* 12(2) pp.64–70.

Scinto, S. (June 2017). Police force turns to internet memes, social media for better police engagement. *Government Technology*. Retrieved from: Police Force Turns to Internet Memes, Social Media for Better Public Engagement (govtech.com).

Serwer, A. (2021). The capitol rioters attacked police: Why isn't the FOP outraged? *The Atlantic*. Retrieved from: http://theatlantic.com/ideas/archive/2021/08/blue-wall-silence/619612.

Siner, E. (September 2013). The promises and pitfalls of social media for police. *All Tech Considered: NPR*. Retrieved from: The Promises And Pitfalls Of Social Media – For Police: All Tech Considered: NPR.

Skolnick, Jerome. (2010). A Sketch of the Policeman's Working Personality. *Race, Ethnicity, and Policing: New and Essential Readings* (Rice S. & White M., Eds.). NYU Press. Retrieved August 16, 2021, from http://www.jstor.org/stable/j.ctt9qg380, 15–31. DOI: 10.18574/nyu/9780814776155.003.0001.

Slater, J. (2018). Positive impact on policing through social media. Strategic Social Media Lab. Retrieved from: http://strategicsocialmedialab.com/postive-impact-on-policing-though-social-media/.

So, L., Januta, A. & Berens, M. (January 2021). Off-duty cops, other officials face reckoning after rallying for Trump in D.C. *Reuters*. Retrieved from: Off-duty cops, other officials face reckoning after rallying for Trump in D.C (yahoo.com).

Stuart, R. (2013). Social media: Establishing criteria for social media. Law Enforcement Bulletin. Retrieved from: Social Media: Establishing Criteria for Law Enforcement Use – LEB (fbi.gov).

Tran. M. (2014). #myNYPD Twitter callout backfires for New York police department. The Guardian. Retrieved from: #myNYPD Twitter callout backfires for New York police department | New York | The Guardian.

Village of Pelham Police Department. (2021). Retrieved from: Village of Pelham Police Department-NY – Home | Facebook.

Waters, G. (November 2012). Social media and law enforcement: Potential risks. *Law Enforcement Bulletin*. Retrieved from: Social Media and Law Enforcement – LEB (fbi.gov).

Ziegler, S. (January 2021). Police union: Over 140 officers injured in capitol siege. Police 1. Retrieved from: Police union: Over 140 officers injured in Capitol siege (police1.com)

Heath Grant

14 Social risk while doing social good – risk management considerations in the not-for-profit world

14.1 Introduction

Reflecting on a career that has involved working with many non-governmental organizations (NGO) over the years, experience now offers many planning considerations that would have been helpful to know beforehand; most of these experiences would fit under the umbrella of risk management and mitigation strategies. This chapter will highlight advantages of having a solid risk management program from the onset in which the identification and open discussion of potential risks is a critical and essential part of an NGO's culture. It is well known that there are many general risks faced by NGOs which need to be carefully addressed and attended to on a regular basis (ANM, 2008). This includes fund raising, tax liabilities, monitoring misuse of funds, possible incidents of fraud, etc. However, examining the social and political risks for non-profit agencies can be more taxing and cumbersome as risks can change, escalate and decrease. What is important is that the NGO be aware of risks which can impact their agency in many ways.

Having a great vision of positively impacting the world in some way does not shield NGOs from many of the same threats found in private organizations. In fact, NGOs are exposed to these same threats, and many others uniquely pertaining to their role as non for profits working towards positive change. Therefore, it is even more critical in this environment to adequately assess the social and political risks that might be potential threats towards successful and sustainable outcomes and which correlates directly to why the organization was founded on in the first place.

Social risks refer to the potential for losses due to any type of threat (both internal or external to the organization). In addition to the organization's ledger, social risks "affect the normal operation of the business" (Talbot, 2017) and can include a significant variety of concerns for an NG), ranging from a misuse of funds to incorrect representation of the organization in the media. For the private corporate organization, such risk is most easily understood as affecting the bottom line of the company in terms of profit or productivity. For an NGO executive, social risks can potentially impact possible revenue streams through fundraising and alternative strategies. For example, an incorrect portrayal of the organization's mission or programs in the media could drive significant volunteer resources and/or potential funders away from the organization. Social risks can also drive down the quality of services provided, thereby impairing the organization's capacity to achieve the desired social impacts upon which it was originally founded. For example, negative perceptions of the organization (true or false) might block its access to needed services (such as job placement or housing services) for its target population.

14.2 Critical risks to the NGO

14.2.1 Lack of strategic focus

NGOs are possibly more vulnerable to risks if there is an unclear strategic direction and the poor communication across the organization by leadership. This can possibly stem from initial good intentions of their founders. Staff and volunteers are drawn towards an NGOs mission and thus the strategic plan either becomes lost within the positive initial actions due to the emotional and psychological investment in the agency and its goals and purpose. Monitoring of social and political risks may assist agency leadership in developing and modifying a mission that can incorporate, guide and protect the agency as well as the employees and volunteers. In addition to running NGOs, the author has decades of experience providing technical assistance to NGOs as a collaborative evaluator facilitating needs assessments, strategic planning, and overseeing impact evaluations for example. This lack of strategic consensus and /or understanding is one of the most common social risks to surface in even some very good organizations.

This threat of a lack of a clear consensus or vision has the highest probability of harming an NGO because it impacts all aspects of the organization's operations. When strategic plans (or lack thereof) are unclear, or where there is not uniform "buy-ins" across staff, funders, and other key stakeholder, the effects can have tremendous significance. A sound strategic plan should be what is communicated to funders, whether private investors, government grants, or other potential revenue sources. All decisions related to staffing, program scaling, assessment, and innovation can only be soundly based if guided by a clear strategic vision. If the strategic plan is not well-defined and clear-cut, an NGO executive will not be able to know the best places to commit available organizational funding and resources.

14.2.2 Increasing service delivery to scale – quantity with quality

Even greater threats can emerge from a poor strategic vision when the lack of clarity leaves ample room for conflict to get into the organization. This author unfortunately witnessed this on several occasions as consultant to multiple NGOs internationally. In one case example, an innovative crime prevention program was successfully piloted in two major cities in the United States. Although a formal evaluation had yet to be done, it was clear from both major participants and stakeholders in both cities that the program was impactful in improving relationships with peers and teachers, as well as notable academic and behavioral outcome, such as improved grades, decreased anxiety and disciplinary challenges, etc. As a result, there was significant demand for program growth in both cities and amongst funders.

However, underneath the surface of this project was a tension among major stakeholders regarding whether the program should continue to expand by hiring, training, and deploying its own teachers, or investing in what is known as "*a train the trainer*" strategy (TOT). This would allow for regular public-school teachers to be able to offer the program within curriculum time at their own schools. Most NGO executives have to consider how to expand their programs and services to reach more people in their target populations, and without sacrificing quality (this expanding services to greater scale is widely known as 'scaling').

When scaling a program, both options are sound, depending upon the circumstances. Choosing to use only teachers that are an organization's own employees is an example of direct activities, whereas training other teachers outside the scope of the project or by outreach, are considered indirect activities (Uvin et al, 2000). There are positives and negatives to both forms of scaling. Each carries with it its own set of social and political risks to manage and carefully consider.

The direct service model allows the organization to control the quality of delivery, and thus the reputational risks if the delivery deviates unsatisfactorily from the program model and does not produce the same outcomes (Uvin et al, 2000). On the other, indirect activities (such as TOT strategies) can undermine the program brand should the delivery quality be undermined as teachers and students report dissatisfaction with what was delivered in classrooms as part of the program expansion into other areas. The strategic risk emerges if trained external teachers or program providers no longer implement the program dosage or model as originally intended. For example, poorly trained external teachers may decide to stop including essential modules from a curriculum over time, or no longer implement services according to the full model that has demonstrated success.

The author has worked with both models of delivery. For example, as lead trainer for the *Culture of Lawfulness* program from 1999 to 2013, a global *train the trainer* model was created to accredit and train public school teachers in Mexico, and then Colombia, Peru, El Salvador, the former Soviet Republic of Georgia, and Lebanon. These teachers were trained to train other teachers to directly deliver this social and emotional crime prevention program in their own classrooms. Social risk was mitigated in this case because the senior administrators of the NGO wereclear from the outset about its vision to build and transfer the capacity for all future program delivery to various countries (usually through the appropriate Secretaries of Education). This meant that by following the delivery of a train the trainer program model, and some evaluation of program outcomes along the way, most of the expansion costs were no longer born by the NGO itself.

Maintaining the integrity of the program model in such a delivery model evolves into a series of negotiations with partnering organizations (in this case the *Secretaries of Education* in each respective country). These negotiations can cover a wide range of issues important to the program model, from the number of lessons implemented to the use of specific films and other lesson media. Prior to engaging in scaling using the indirect model across cultures and languages there must be significant pre-planning to avoid the threat of program model dilution. Here, an organization's education team must work with local experts to be sure that the meaning of key concepts translates well across languages and cultural contexts. If not, there is the risk that program material can be taken by target populations in completely unintended ways.

In the case of the youth crime prevention program mentioned above, the NGO's original vision was not defined with how an expansion should occur, if needed. This led to a lack of clarity in the strategic direction which resulted in a slow break-down which resulted over time. There, the quality of the program was verified in an external evaluation study that only led to an even greater interest by outside juris-dictions to bring the program to them as well. In addition to several cities through-out the United States, it grew to several countries on five continents in a very short period which put tremendous pressure on the organization. Although the direct ser-vice model remained at the heart of its expansion, indirect train the trainer models were successfully piloted with public school teachers throughout the United States and other parts of the world.

Once again, the direct service model allows for the NGO to control the quality of its scaling programs and thus minimize social risk, but this comes at significant financial cost generally. In the case of the above NGO example, they benefited from a very significant active funder base that offered the agency significant flexibility in deciding between the two options that is not usually common for relatively new NGOs. However, this led to an environment of indecisiveness which ultimately cre-ated conflict as adherents to one vision seriously clashed with the other side. Over time, relationships declined along with program delivery in some global sites.

14.2.3 Maintaining strategic direction despite major donor interests

It is understood that in life sometimes too much of a good thing can become some-thing bad. The same is true in the realm of social risk factors for NGOs. One of the organizations the author (no 1st person) worked with had a highly dedicated, high worth A-list celebrities as benefactors. However, celebrities and other funders can also pose a political threat too, as their reputations very often becomes intertwined with that of the organization itself.

In one such organization, a significant celebrity figure visited a country where program services were offered internationally. Within three days, this public figure managed to raise the equivalent of $15 million in the local currency. Of course, the CEO of any NGO would be thrilled to have such success handed to them especially since this has introduced the organization to possibly more influential investors and government officials in that country. However, this sudden infusion of attention and funding can pose a very significant threat to the organization that does not have a firm grip and understanding on its strategic plan and direction.

In this case, the celebrity was interested in having the program delivered to all public schools in a different city than the original one where the organization was in that country. The result was the global headquarters of the organization had to swiftly switch gears and dedicate the majority of time and resources towards building another infrastructure in efforts to deliver the program in another location outside of where it was defined in its strategic plan. This onerous and complex responsibility of doing this ultimately meant the CEO of the global headquarters had to become based in that newly assigned city for over a year and a half. In the end, this program expansion was successfully launched there, but at an expense of splitting the global leadership from other key strategic areas for a significant amount of time. With a solid understanding of risks and a focused strategic plan in place, sometimes social risks can be mitigated better by turning down funding or other forms of investment that might detract from the established direction and vision. Or possibly putting in place contingency guidelines in case a sudden change is directed or needed.

One of the greatest threats to the success of any organization, private or NGO, is the risk of being pulled in too many directions rather than focusing on a specific outcome or product, building it without unnecessary distractions, and then evaluating its outcomes. The author has seen many unfocused NGO executives with significant innovative missions gradually driven into the ground due a lack of strategic focus.

Knowing the organization's funders and investors is an essential part of risk mitigation in areas beyond how they might unduly influence the sound and consistent execution of the NGO's strategic plan. It is not just celebrities or other public figures that can pose a grave political risk to an organization. The political risk of not considering or evaluating the potential reputational threats of a particular funder or charity spokesperson can be overwhelming and kill a project or vision.

Funders can be a source of other risks even as the NGO so significantly relies upon their good will. As part of the NGO's risk management plan, efforts must be made to reduce or even eliminate reliance on any single source of investment for either a single program/project or its general smooth operations human, technical, or fiscal resources) (Durbin, 2021)

Without diverse revenue streams to draw upon, an NGO will become dominated by the agenda of a particular funder in ways that can dilute or divert from its strategic vision. Far worse, some NGO executives might become desperate for funding to the extent that they become less concerned with performing due diligence adequately on the funding source. In worst case scenarios, the funds may be derived from criminal sources somewhere down the supply chain. In addition to the obvious reputational risks that could come from such funding, there could also be potential criminal risks should the funds involve money laundering or serious tax evasion.

14.2.4 Be aware of founder's syndrome and other risks of embedded organizations

While an executive cannot necessarily control who are the organization's founders, risk management strategies should consider fully the possible threats that affiliation with its founders might bring to the table. Unquestionably, one of the most important risk mitigation strategies here is for the executive(s) to take the steps to fully separate the NGO from its founding entity where necessary if possible. Sometimes the inspiration for a new non-profit can spin out of the work of another, and both its experiences and lessons learned. While of course there is nothing wrong with this, once the new organization is born and has its own revenues and expenses, full financial and administrative separation is necessary. Donors need to know their funds are going to the intended project and mission. Without full separation, even he unintentional possibility of drawing funds from one to assist the needs of the other can be a serious risk.

Ensuring that there are no significant overlaps in resources and other assets (especially avoiding any form of financial co-mingling) between the organizations is a critical place to start.

Even if such independence is fully achieved, additional planning may be required to avoid potential political risks involved with the founding entity (and/or any other funders). For example, should the founding organization of an NGO come under its own criminal investigation by the Internal Revenue Service (USA), its subsidiaries (including the organizations it supports) will likely also be considered under the same microscope of detrimental social risks, ranging from legal liabilities to reputational harms which will have lasting impact on the agency.

Even consultants and key expert affiliates may soon begin to question their own connections even though they may have served in a strictly advisory function. The damage to the organization in such cases may be even greater with respect to fundraising activities. It will become very challenging to onboard new investors over time. Successful risk management may not be able to fully eliminate such circumstances, but they can identify strategies in advance to be better prepared operationally and from a public relations perspective should such events occur knowing what you know about the organization's full array of funders, spokespeople, and employees.

Of course, the founders as the original source of inspiration for the organization should not simply be seen from a perspective of social risk; legal, reputational or otherwise. Most involved in the non-profit world have some familiarity with what has become widely known as *"founder's syndrome"*. Contrary to popular belief, it is not just the person with the original vision for the organization that is susceptible to founder's syndrome (Funding for Good, 2018). *Founder's syndrome* exists when any individual (an executive, Board member, or investor) becomes seen as inseparable from the direction and success of the organization (Funding for Good, 2018).

In an organization's early stages of development, there is often truth to this perception. For it is the dogged commitment of this individual towards manifesting the organization's vision at all costs that ultimately makes the dream become a reality. The author witnessed what some founders have been able to achieve when they have literally put everything on the line for the birth of their organization, including their own personal and financial health. Such passion and drive are, of course, something to be celebrated. *Founder's syndrome* emerges as a problem when this individual is no longer able to evolve with the times and the needs of the organization. When this happens, the syndrome fully metastases into a major social risk that can bring down even the most incredible organizations.

The social risk posed by *founder' syndrome* is highly correlated with the risk of unclear or inconsistent vision strategic vision. This is possible as it often involves the founder micro-managing the executives and other staff members, despite their being hired for their own considerable expertise. The founder may not have this expertise him or herself but is unable to see this. As a result, he or she may be unable to see the need to modify or change a particular strategy even though the organizational staff or others with a greater knowledge and skills recommend such changes based on evidence. This sets the organization on a collision course with becoming dated or ineffective, dulling momentum or political capitol gained from its early successes. This occurs as the founder stirs up political or managerial conflicts amongst the staff and board members while blocking the executive's access to the resources and assets needed to keep evolving in the right direction for the desired impacts to be sustained.

Risk mitigation for founder's syndrome will include previously mentioned the separation of finances and assets. This wards off the legal and reputational risks associated with the founder but cannot alone insulate a solid non-profit executive from the other risks wrought by the syndrome. Non-profit executives must establish a diverse Board that views their role as ensuring that the organization maintains a policy of continuous improvement – ensuring that its programs are regularly evaluated and examined in the context of evidence-based best practices; the loyalty of individual members to the founder must not drive decision-making, nor should the founder's vote or voice on the board hold greater influence than the others. The author has witnessed the crippling power of founder stacked boards on multiple occasions. It is important to point out that in none of these cases did this happen due to bad intentions. Members genuinely felt that serving as a rubber stamp to the founder was operating in the best interests of the organization.

Similarly clear lines must be drawn between the Board of Directors and direct communication into the day-to-day affairs of the staff. In well-functioning organizations, the key program staff has been hired because of their skills and expertise. Micro-management of any sort from the founder or Board only raises the specters of social and political risks stemming from resultant conflicts between staff, blurring of the vision, and/or undermining the authority of the executives. Boards must limit their authority to questions of overall strategic and policy direction, as well as the needed oversight of fiduciary responsibilities. In non-profits where there are weaker boundaries between board members and staff, the author has observed situations where members are even intervening in the personal relationships and office disputes on an ongoing basis. Such an organizational structure can never work successfully or harmoniously. Inevitably there is a snowball effect to the conflicts that is exacerbated, or even sparked by the role of the Board members involved. However, Board members can and should be given opportunities to participate in the organization's planning and implementation as relates to their expertise and interest if the boundaries are made clear (such as the order of authority of the organization's executives and supervisors in managing staff activity) in advance by the CEO or other executive (Ibid).

The above is not to suggest that Boards should not be all concerned with the happiness and satisfaction of the organization's staff, as this is a leading risk in non-profit management (Hernman, 2011). Instead, the warning is advised to ward against members creating greater confusion and political conflict by stepping on the proper authority and communication lines of the organization's established management. Where staff problems are noticed by Board members, only should follow established internal complaint procedures to address them rather than becoming the "go to" alternative of the staff.

Herman (2011) highlights an important legal risk that might fly under the radar of many non-profit leaders. Abusive work environments with workplace bullying and other toxic elements is now illegal in many jurisdictions, ensuring that employee satisfaction with the workplace environment rises to a high level of scrutiny in non-profits as well as more traditional corporate business environments. What many non-profit organizations may not know, however, is that they may face legal risks from the conduct of their vendors, or even volunteers with their staff. Third party sexual harassment claims can be made against an organization if its vendors or contractors engaged in such behavior against the staff (Herman, 2011). Similarly, vendors and volunteers can also be the victims of such behavior directed towards them by the staff. Of course, reputational risks multiply the legal ones in such cases as it seriously affects the organization's bottom line in terms of both human (potential volunteer pool) and fiscal (fund-raising capacity) resources.

14.2.5 Disgruntled employees

Unhappy or disgruntled employees can pose other unique risks to the unsuspecting non-profit. If a particular staff member was chosen in country to represent the global interests of the organization in foreign countries as relates to fund-raising, board relationships and fundraising, he or she may be able to wield significant power over the main executives. The author has advised organizations faced with the backlash from emotionally unstable employees that subsequently sought to destroy the organization in their respective countries by creating falsehoods to share with funders and other key governmental and external stakeholders. Risk management mitigation should identify in advance where the organization is exposing itself to such risks of defamation and other such harms by the very nature of relationships its trust in key employees ultimately leaves them.

Such legal liabilities presenting as social risks for the non-profit organization only serve to further illustrate the idea that, at least on the surface, the social and political risks faced are often very much the same as their corporate counterparts. Many incorrectly feel that their positive mission for "social good" itself can serve as a shield against many forms of legal liability. For example, most non-profits should take significant care to protect their intellectual property just as any business would make sure that their intellectual property (IP)assets had met all the requirements for copyright protection. A non-profit's acclaimed curriculum in a direct service model may be viewed as a possible target for copying and/or unfair adaptations by other non-profits with similar missions and private individuals alike. These waters can get increasingly complex as the organization scales internationally, particularly using the indirect service delivery model where trainers are trained to multiply the reach of the program outside of the direct reach of an organization's own staff.

The legal risks associated with intellectual property goes both ways though. For example, the author had an alarming experience while preparing an organization for a re-branding and launching of its central program to find that two key lessons of the organization's original successful platform were adapted from a book without permission from the author. Such a misappropriation of copyrighted material may have at first seemed innocuous when it was used in house to reach at-risk youths in a troubled neighborhood; however, as it became packaged into an evolving rapidly expanding brand and evidenced-based program such harmless beginnings are longer acceptable or can be tolerated. Therefore, risk mitigation strategies must identify all such opportunities for both needed copyright protection and assurance of the originality of all an organization' assets. Part of this must also include training all staff on copyright infringement possibilities in the production of all organizational materials.

14.2.6 Mitigating corrupt practices in international NGOs

Once again, social risks take on a whole other scale when a non-profit's scope takes it across borders, particularly when it finds itself in foreign countries with questionable levels of integrity With a research focus in the areas of crime, corruption mitigation and violence prevention, the author has regularly worked, advised and evaluated programs and agencies. In addition to significant legal liabilities, there are considerable reputational risks should a non-profit working to combat corruption itself cut corners to "facilitate" the smooth operation of its programs in country the smooth operation of its programs in country for example. And yet, in some country's corruption is so embedded that it has become an accepted means of getting work done by locals. Thus the NGO may have even greater challenges overcoming these hurdles in a timely manner while maintaining the needed integrity to the rule of law no matter where it is operating.

These obstacles must be considered in advance with any meaningful risk management program. For example, in one non-profit organization, the author proudly presided over efforts to consolidate the costs and logistics of international program scaling, by contracting with a distributor with hubs across the United States and abroad to compile all the materials required for curriculum delivery, and then distribute them to the program sites accordingly. Prior to this, each site needed to have its own full time *Materials Coordinator* to purchase and assemble all the materials by lesson with the help of numerous volunteers.

In the main, this new consolidated supply chain saved on both costs and time even in far flung program locations such as Malawi, Africa. However, the model ultimately proved to be naïve in not considering the challenges of dealing with notoriously corrupt ports such as Brazil. There the customs system had a long reputation for challenging and fining organizations for their import and export processes even when they are done correctly (Winter, 2014). As a result, the materials ended up held in customs until it was that the local program offices were to pay these unfair and exorbitant fees. If they were to litigate the government in protest, it would not bode well for their future interactions with local authorities. It is also well known that there can be "ways around" the payment of such fines to get items held at customs released. Said ways usually involve paying bribes or some other illegal means.

The ways that non-profit organizations handle such moral dilemmas will ultimately influence their reputation in very significant ways. For this reason, some form of legal advisory process must be a part of any good risk management plan. In the case of the Brazil customs hold just mentioned, the non-profit involved was fortunate enough to have had the fiscal resources to be able to pay the fines required to release the materials after an extended hold at customs, and I time for the launch of the school year when they were needed.

Of course, non-profits must always be aware of the risks of serious harm to their employees and contractors, both within the United States and abroad. Risk managers must consider the possible threats involved in carrying out the daily tasks of the organization. Like the social risk of third-party harassment noted above, an organization can be liable for the physical harms experienced by its staff and contractors. Although it is impossible to predict all possible threats, some basic procedural changes and training could help to minimize such risks.

For example, the author was sent to Mexico City to train teachers from across the country crime prevention. The non-profit had arranged to pay all participating teachers a stipend, but only left their staff member (with the author) with American dollars to be converted upon arrival in Mexico. For some reason, she decided to do this in the Mexico City airport. Compounding the issue, the organization did not arrange for a car service to pick the author and staff member up and drive them to the hotel and training site.

As logical as it likely sounds, these are mistakes that non-profit organizations regularly make and could easily prevent. This story ended with the author and colleague's taxi being forced off the road on the way to the hotel, the author being pistol whipped, and all money and passports etc. seized at the scene.

Working in transitional and developing countries does not just bring the social risks associated with crime and corruption. The NGO can face a lot of mistrust and suspicion when it is there ostensibly to serve disadvantaged communities and its staff are seen staying in high end luxury hotels and services (Stowe, 2017). Although a planned and reference checked car service was suggested in the previous scenario, it does not have to be a luxury BMW SUV to make the staff safe from harm.

As many non-profits in the global space are advocacy organizations (e.g. human rights, rule of law promotion, democracy etc.), they are also more likely to be targets of internet vigilantism. In such cases organized are targeted online because a person or group does not agree with them philosophically or politically. (NRMC, 2020). Preventing such threats requires a sometimes-costly investment in cyber security that may be well beyond the capacity of many non-profit organizations whose main struggle is to be able to sustainably offer their core menu of programs and service. In this case, risk management related to cyber threats like *internet vigilantism* may involve being prepared with how to use social media and other public relations techniques to counter any disinformation or harmful online activities should they happen to surface. However, some level of investment in cyber-security to prevent breaches of organizational data (particularly any sensitive client or proprietary information) is essential.

No discussion of the political and social risks associated with non-profit organizations would be complete without discussing the importance of the federal tax-exempt status, or 501 c (3), which is required in the United States. These organizations are divided into two categories: public charities and private foundations, with the former being far more common. This tax-exempt status not only means the organization is itself exempt from taxes, but all donations from donors will also be tax exemptible; this of course provides an important incentive to the donors to make the donation in the first place. Additionally, income made from business associated with the organization's tax-exempt status is also tax exempt. Income made from the proceeds of ticket sales to a theatre performance produced by at-risk youth participants in the organization's curricula is exempt, but the running of a for profit theatre space on the side is not. Above all, today the tax exempt status today serves as a calling card or credibility test to the outside worlds of funding, volunteers, and key stakeholders in the professional world.

All these benefits also come with important responsibilities and risk for the non-profit organization. Tax exempt status comes with numerous restrictions related to lobbying, publications, political activities, certification, educational program standards, and other items that must be understood and managed by executives. Having one's tax-exempt status revoked is a damage to the credibility of an organization that few can ever come back from. Any non-profits should make sure to clarify any tax issues or exemption statuses or classifications that may be available to them.

14.3 Recommendations

With any organization, non-profit or otherwise, a risk management program is not necessarily about avoiding the risks altogether (Talbot, 2017). Many of the social and political risks discussed throughout this chapter may be very difficult to anticipate in all circumstances. A risk management plan helps to identify possible risks and educate them about how to choose the appropriate action should they surface. A common thread across many of the risks discussed here involve many legal liabilities that non-profits can face on the world stage, and the associated reputational risks that can surface from this. Including a sound legal advisory element to the development of a risk management plan should be an essential component.

References

Durbin, H (2021). *Five Reasons You Need to Diversify Your Nonprofit Streams*. Blog downloaded on 51822.
Funding for Good (2018). *Ten Steps to Overcome Nonprofit Founder's Syndrome*.
Herman, M (2011). *THe Top Ten Legak Risks Facing Nonprofit Boards*.
NCRMC, 2000. *200 Risk Forecast: Risk Trends Facing NonProfits*. https://nonprofitrisk.org/resources/e-news/2020-risk-forecast-risk-trends-facing-nonprofits/
Risk, H (2019). *International NGO Political Risk Management*.

Roberts, D., G. Morris, J. Macintosh, and D. Milenson. *Risk Management for Nonprofits*.
Stowe, E (2017). "Managing Risk to Scale Impact." *Navigating Risk in Impact Focused* Philanthropy, *summer 2017*.
Talbot, J (2017). *Understanding Organizational Risk* https://www.juliantalbot.com/post/2017/09/14/understanding-organizational-risk
Uvin, P, P. Jain, and L. Brown (2000). "Think: Largeand Act Smal." *World Development* Vol 28 (8), pp 1409–1419
Winter, E (2014). *On Port Fees and Bribes – Ask the Ethicist – Brazil Edition*.

Contributors

Giampiero E.G. Beroggi
University of Zurich, Switzerland

Markus Biehl
Schulich University, Canada

Kurt Engemann
Iona University, USA

Hugh Gash
Dublin City University, Ireland

Heath Grant
John Jay College of Criminal Justice, USA

Saquib Hyat-Khan
Applied Techonomics, USA

Katherine Kinkela
Iona University, USA

Nisha Kulangara
Concordia University, Canada

Cathryn F. Lavery
Pace University, USA

Cesar Marolla
Harvard University, USA

Steven Michels
Sacred Heart University, USA

Stephen Morreale
Worcester State University, USA

David T. Mulcahy
United States Probation, Southern District
of New York, USA

Jeanne M. Sheehan
Iona University, USA

Michael Sheehy
Pelham Police Department, USA

Kimberly Spanjol
Pace University, USA

Paolo Zucca
Bio Crime Center, Italy

Index

Developments in managing and exploiting risk

The objective of this multi-volume set is to offer a balanced view to enable the reader to better appreciate risk as a counterpart to reward, and to understand how to holistically manage both elements of this duality. Crises can challenge any organization, and with a seemingly endless stream of disruptive and even catastrophic events taking place, there is an increasing emphasis on preparing for the worst. However, being focused on the negative aspects of risk, without considering the positive attributes, may be shortsighted. Playing it safe may not always be the best policy, because great benefits may be missed.

Analyzing risk is difficult, in part because it often entails events that have never occurred. Organizations, being mindful of undesirable potential events, are often keenly averse to risk to the detriment of capitalizing on its potential opportunities. Risk is usually perceived as a negative or downside, however, a commensurate weight should also be given to the potential rewards or upside, when evaluating new ventures. Even so, too much of a good thing may create unintended consequences of risk, which is also an undesirable situation. *Developments in Managing and Exploiting Risk* provides a professional and scholarly venue in the critical field of risk in business with emphasis on decision-making using a comprehensive and inclusive approach.

Vol. 1: Safety Risk Management: Integrating Economic and Safety Perspectives. Edited by Kurt J. Engemann and Eirik B. Abrahamsen

Vol. 2: Project Risk Management: Software Development and Risk. Edited by Kurt J. Engemann and Rory V. O'Connor

Vol. 3: Organizational Risk Management: Managing for Uncertainty and Ambiguity. Edited by Krista N. Engemann, Kurt J. Engemann and Cliff Scott

Vol. 4: Socio-Political Risk Management: Assessing and Managing Global Insecurity. Edited by Kurt J. Engemann, Cathryn F. Lavery and Jeanne Sheehan.

www.ingramcontent.com/pod-product-compliance
Lightning Source LLC
Chambersburg PA
CBHW051334200326

41519CB00026B/7417